ISBN 978-0-282-40222-8
PIBN 10847445

1 MONTH OF
FREE
READING

at

www.ForgottenBooks.com

By purchasing this book you are eligible for one month membership to ForgottenBooks.com, giving you unlimited access to our entire collection of over 1,000,000 titles via our web site and mobile apps.

To claim your free month visit:

www.forgottenbooks.com/free847445

English
Français
Deutsche
Italiano
Español
Português

www.forgottenbooks.com

Mythology Photography **Fiction**
Fishing Christianity **Art** Cooking
Essays Buddhism Freemasonry
Medicine **Biology** Music **Ancient**
Egypt Evolution Carpentry Physics
Dance Geology **Mathematics** Fitness
Shakespeare **Folklore** Yoga Marketing
Confidence Immortality Biographies
Poetry **Psychology** Witchcraft
Electronics Chemistry History **Law**
Accounting **Philosophy** Anthropology
Alchemy Drama Quantum Mechanics
Atheism Sexual Health **Ancient History**
Entrepreneurship Languages Sport
Paleontology Needlework Islam
Metaphysics Investment Archaeology
Parenting Statistics Criminology
Motivational

A
NEW
HISTORICAL AND DESCRIPTIVE
VIEW
OF
DERBYSHIRE.

A
NEW
HISTORICAL AND DESCRIPTIVE
VIEW
OF
DERBYSHIRE,
FROM THE
REMOTEST PERIOD TO THE PRESENT TIME.

BY THE REV. D. P. DAVIES.

EMBELLISHED WITH A MAP AND PLATES.

Antiquam exquirite Matrem.—Virg.

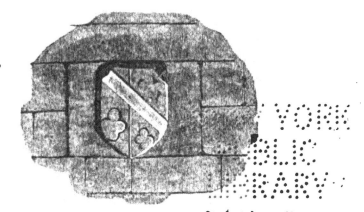

See (note) page 345.

Belper:

PRINTED AND PUBLISHED BY AND FOR S. MASON:

Id also, by Drury, Wilkins, Pritchard, and Stenson, Derby; Bradley,
and Ford, Chesterfield; Parkes, Ashbourn; Cotes, Wirksworth;
Dunn, Nottingham; Gales, Sheffield; Longman, Hurst, Rees,
Orme, and Brown, Paternoster-Row, and B. Crosby and Co.
Stationers-Court, London.

1811.

THE REVEREND

DAVID PETER,

TUTOR OF THE DISSENTING COLLEGE,

CARMARTHEN;

THIS

VOLUME

IS INSCRIBED,

AS A TOKEN OF THE GRATEFUL

REMEMBRANCE OF THE BENEFACTOR

AND INSTRUCTOR OF-HIS

EARLY YEARS,

BY HIS

SINCERE FRIEND,

AND

AFFECTIONATE NEPHEW,

DAVID PETER DAVIES.

Makeney,
April 10*th,* 1811.}

PREFACE.

THE plan of the following work has been already amply detailed in the proposals for its publication: but as these may not have been seen, by every one, into whose hands it may fall, a recapitulation of the mode of conducting it, may be necessary.

' Mr. Pilkington's valuable History, has been used, as a text-book; and so copious was the new matter which presented itself, that, with a very few exceptions, that work forms the basis only of the present. The other publications that have been consulted, are;—Hutton's History of Derby—Aikin's History of the Country round Manchester—Warner's Northern Tour—Lipscomb's Matlock—Mawe's Mineralogy of Derbyshire—Third Volume of the Beauties of England and Wales—together with numerous other works, to which referen-

ees are made at the bottom of the page. Most
of the places described, the author has himself visited: The northern, and most interesting part of the county, has engaged a great
portion of his attention; and its remains of antiquity, and objects of curiosity, were personally inspected during the course of the last
summer.

When the descriptions of the Tourists, who
had previously visited them, are correct and
concise, they are given in their own words, distinguished by inverted commas; but when incorrect, or diffuse, the paragraphs have been
re-written. In a publication of this nature,—
giving a description of a county, whose beauties, and objects of attention, have been so often delineated and pointed out by others, it is
impossible to be entirely original:—the features of nature remain the same, as when first
described; and the improvements brought about
by art, are slow, though progressive. The object of the present work, is not novelty, but
conciseness; and it has been the author's aim
to bring together, in a small compass, and to

PREFACE.

to concentrate in a cheap work, every thing interesting concerning the county of Derby.

The original matter, however, which it contains, is considerable; as will be soon perceived by any one acquainted with the former Histories of the County. And, here, the author feels it his duty, to return his thanks to those Gentlemen, who have contributed, by their communications, towards this part of the work. He would feel a pleasure in mentioning their names; but their consciousness of being the persons to whom this acknowledgement is due, will, he doubts not, be more agreeable to them, than a more public and personal avowal of their kindness.

It cannot be expected, that a work abounding in local descriptions, and interspersed with names of places, that are often differently spelt, should be entirely free from errors and mistakes: the author flatters not himself with so delusive a hope; and he would remind the captious reader of the couplet of our elegant critic :—

" Whoever thinks a faultless piece to see,
" Thinks what ne'er was, nor is, nor e'er will be."

Pope's Essay on Crit.

The ancient names of places, are printed in Italics, and are, chiefly, taken from the Translation of the Domesday Record, lately published by the Rev. Mr. Bawdwen.

For the liberal support, which the New History of Derbyshire, has met with, from a numerous and respectable list of Subscribers, the author has to express his thanks: and while he sends the work into the world, he entertains a hope, that it will answer their expectations, and obtain the approbation of the Public at large.

ERRATA.

Page	line	
157	14	for Corporation, read County.
168	16	for machanism, read mechanism.
189	1	for assylum, read asylum.
256	13	for Premonstatentian, read Premonstratensian.
326	4 bot.	for Hugh Bateman, Esq. read Mr Hugh Bateman.
339	7 bot.	for western, read eastern.
488	7	for benefactor, read benefactors.
491	3 bot.	for powers, read efforts.
521	11	for writen, read written.
567	8 bot. (note)	for religionists, read christians.
570	1 bot.	for cemetry, read cemetery.
617	1 bot.	after rate, insert, of.

CONTENTS.

AN

HISTORICAL & DESCRIPTIVE

VIEW,

&c. &c.

CHAP. I.

Introduction—Britain peopled by—the Celtæ—
Coranied—Gwiddilian Fichti—Romans—
Saxons—Danes—Normans, &c.

To the naturally inquisitive mind of man, nothing more gratifying can present itself than the historical and descriptive page. The deeds of former times, the manners of those who have preceded us on the stage of human life, afford ample and pleasing employment to the man, whose views are not confined within the narrow boundary of his own life or generation.

B

But while the presentation of the scene of the world at large, yields so much gratification to our curiosity; the more contracted view of the portion we inhabit of it, affords more satisfaction and true delight to our understanding. The country which has given us birth, the soil whose nutrition has supported us, the fields among which our childhood has been spent, and the spot on which those that are most dear to us in life reside;—these, and many like them are the ties, which rivet the heart of man to his native country, and lead him to prefer it to all others, though they may be attended with many superior advantages of climate or soil. To be informed of the state of our country some centuries ago; and how those acted, who then trod the same ground as we now do; gives us an opportunity of forming a contrast, which if duly attended to, cannot less than afford us instruction, as well as shew our attainments and improvements. Indeed a cursory view of the different nations, who first inhabited this island is necessary, before we can be qualified, to ascertain the origin of the different monuments of antiquity, which are to be met with in every part of it; and more particularly in that portion of it, which is to be the subject of our description in the following pages.

JEFFERY of MONMOUTH,* a writer of the twelfth century, says, that Great Britain was originally peopled by a party of *Trojans;* who headed by BRUTE, a great-grandson of ÆNEAS, the hero of VIRGIL, escaped from Greece, where they had been held in captivity, since their expulsion from Italy. But flattering as this account may be to that pride of ancestry, which is so natural to the *Cambro Briton;* and supported as it is, by many men of learning of the the last and preceding centuries; it must be pronounced fabulous and romantic, by every one who has paid any attention to the Greek and Latin authors; and cannot for a moment be suffered to rank among true histories.

It will be found, a very difficult, if not an impracticable task, to ascertain with certainty who were the first inhabitants of this island.— But the researches of the antiquary, and the illustrations of the critic, have of late years thrown much light on the subject. It seems very probable, that Britain was first peopled by a colony of *Celtæ;* a people who dwelt in the north-west of Germany.† This nation is represented by Greek authors,‡ who appropriate to them the name of

---

* In primis xvi. lIbris.
† Davies's Celtic Researches p. 122.
‡ Strabo L. i. Ptolomy, Quad. L. ii.

Cimmerii as well as *Celtæ*, as a very extensive and powerful race of Europe; and as constituting some of its first inhabitants. The emigration of the Celtæ, from the northern banks of the Danube, to the shores of Britain, was an event which took place in very early times; many centuries before the commencement of the christian æra. From the faint light which history throws on the customs and manners of this nation, they appear to be a people, fonder of the tranquillity of a life of peace, than of the turbulence of a warlike one. Literature and science, (if in this infant state they deserve the terms) were neither unknown nor neglected by them. Their Druids, an order of men, chosen from the first families among them; were at once their priests and legislators:*—and had their readiness in communicating, been as great, as their progress in acquiring knowledge, the nation at large would have made a more respectable appearance on the page of history than it does at present.— This, however, was not the case; the knowledge which they possessed, was imparted to the initiated only; while the vulgar, deprived by their plebeian descent of an admission into the sacred order, were suffered to remain in

* Cæs. Bell. Gall. v. xiii.

their ignorance, and to revere and admire what the impenetrable veil of mystery prevented them from understanding.

The lapse of so many centuries, has left us but few monuments of this primitive race: But their temples, those rude fabrics, displayed at *Stonehenge*, and the many other *Cromlechs* and *Logans*, to be found in different parts of the kingdom, can be ascribed to the original settlers only—our Celtic ancestors.

But the *Celtæ* were not long left in quiet possession of the island. In one of the ancient British triades,* we find mention made of " the " three usurping tribes that came into the " island of Britain, and never departed out of " it."† The first of these is the *Coranied*; who the original document alleges, came (" o " wlad y Pwyl") *from the land of pools or wa-ter.* No country on the continent answers this description but *Holland:* and for this and other reasons, it is thought that this hostile nation came from that country. On their arrival, they took possession of the country about the river Humber; and of the coast on the shore of *(mor Tawch)* the German ocean. The existence of this nation is confirmed by Cæsar,‡

---

* Welsh Arch. li. p. 80.   † Gel. Res. 156.   ‡ Cæs. Bell. Gall. iv. xil.

who upon his landing in Britain, found, that the Aborigines did not dwell on the coast where he made a descent; but on the western one, and in the interior parts. And what proves, that the people he mentions were no other than the descendants of the *Coranied*, the districts which they inhabited are called, by old geographers, *Coritani, Corii*, and *Cortani;* terms synonymous with the name of the people.

The hostile tribe which next invaded, and made a settlement in, Britain, is called in the triades, the " *Gwiddilian Fichti*, who came " over the sea of Llychlyn;" that is, from the coast of Denmark, and most probably were inhabitants of that country. They settled in the northern parts. But as these as well as the Coranied, appear to have sprung from the original Celtic stock, their language and manners could have differed but little, from those of their less warlike brethren, who had first peopled the island.

But leaving these traditional accounts, we come to a period, when the history of our island assumes a more authentic and accurate appearance. In the fifty-fifth year before the christian æra, Rome already mistress of almost every part of the known world, extended her conquests to Britain. Her armies, under the direction of Cæsar, had over-run all Gaul; and flushed with victory, that ambitious leader, took advantage of a short interval of peace, in making a conquest of this island. After having met with some resistance from the inhabitants, he landed, as is generally supposed, at Deal in Kent; and his superior mode of warfare, soon compelled the rude and unskilful Britons to give up the unequal contest.—They gave hostages for their future obedience; and Cæsar withdrew, to spend the winter in Gaul.

His departure was the signal for revolt: but the ensuing summer, the general returned with a greater force, and chastised them for their disobedience.* However, during the reign of Cæsar, and those of the succeeding emperors, the turbulent spirit of this nation often shewed itself; and it was not until more than a century after the first invasion, that the Roman arms had made any great progress in the subjugation of the island. In the reign of Claudius, Ostorius Scapula, gained a victory over Caractacus, one of the most distinguished British generals, and brought into subjection a great part of the country.† But notwithstanding these misfortunes, the Britons were not subdued: and Rome

---

* Cæs. Bell. Gall. L. vi.   † Tacit. Ann. L. xii.

had not completely established her dominion in the island, until Julius Agricola was sent over in the reign of Vespasian. This able general, by his promptitude and valour, brought the greatest part of the island into subjection, and laid the foundation for that ascendency, which the Romans held over it, for nearly four hundred years after.[*]

It was the practice of the Romans, to introduce the arts of peace, with those of conquest, into the countries which they subdued; and for that reason, their subjugation of this island cannot but be considered, as a very important æra, in its history. The introduction of laws and civilization, of arts and sciences, must have had a very great influence in polishing the manners, and in dispelling the ignorance of the Britons; and the long intercourse which subsisted between them, and that highly cultivated nation, must not only have reconciled them to the Roman language and manners; but instilled into their minds, a similar taste for the conveniencies and ornaments of life. The British youth were sent over into Gaul, to be educated in the academies, established by the conquerors in that country.[†]

---

[*] Tacit. Agr.

[†] " Gallia causidicos docuit facunda Brittanos."—Juven.

The dwellings of the original inhabitants, were nothing more than huts, built of clay; but the Romans introduced the Grecian style of architecture among them, as may be seen in the ruins of the amphitheatres, and other remains of Roman edifices, which are to be met with in many parts of the island. The military roads also, which traversed the country in different directions, must have facilitated the means of communication between the different provinces; and thus have occasioned a more speedy and extensive diffusion of knowledge. In short, the advantages which the Britons enjoyed, from their becoming a Roman province are so many; and the influence of the union with their conquerors so great, that their national character seems to have undergone a total change, and lead us to consider them in a more respectable light than that of rude barbarians.

In the beginning of the fifth century, the Roman empire, which had flourished for so many ages, began to feel the declension of her power. The hardy and warlike nations of the North, to whom she had taught the use of arms, took advantage of that want of military spirit, which usually attends the introduction of luxury, and a long series of successes; and made

daily encroachments on the power and territories of their conquerors. The emperors, in
order to avert the danger which threatened
them, were under the necessity of recalling the
armies, which were distributed in the most distant provinces, to protect the seat of empire.
Among those which were called home, were
the legions which defended Britain; and though
some time after, a small body returned to
assist the Britons in the defence of their kingdom, the Romans took their final leave of that
island about the year 448, after having held
the greatest part of it in subjection, during the
course of almost four centuries.

The Romans, at their departure, informed the
Britons, that they must arm for their own defence, and no longer look up to them for protection. But they were not in a condition to put
in practice this salutary advice. The Scots and
Picts, preferring the fertile plains of the South,
to the mountains of the North, had for some
time cast their eyes on that part of the island,
as a desirable acquisition: and when they
found, that the Romans had left the Britons to
their own defence, they thought it a favourable
opportunity for executing their project. They
attacked the northern wall, which the Romans
had built at their departure, for the security of

the Britons, and passed in large bodies to the South. Impelled by their native ferocity, heightened by the hope of plunder, they carried devastation and ruin wherever they went; and the Britons fled before them in every direction. Reduced to the greatest distress, they supplicated the Romans for assistance; but they were not in a situation to render them any. Fortunately, however, the invaders soon found the effect of their own imprudent conduct, and began to feel the pressures of famine, in a country which they themselves had ravaged.— They retreated with their spoils into their own parts; and the Britons were once more left in the peaceable possession of their country.

The Britons, knowing, that they were no longer to expect any assistance from Rome, and menaced with another invasion from their northern neighbours, were induced to take a step the most fatal to themselves, and unfortunate for their posterity.

The SAXONS, were a people who inhabited that part of Germany, which extends along the sea-coast, from the Rhine as far as Jutland. Like other Germans of that age, they were distinguished for their valour, and their love of liberty. The pursuits of agriculture were despised and neglected by them; and all the re-

fined arts of life wholly unknown. They seem
to have subsisted, principally, on the fruits of
the chase, and the plunder which they acquired
in their military expeditions. They had long
infested the eastern and southern coasts of Britain by their piracies; and their daring enter-
prises had instilled into the minds of the inhabitants, a very high idea of their courage, and
warlike accomplishments. The Britons, therefore, thought that they could do no better than
apply to such a distinguished a nation, for that
succour which had been refused them by the
Romans. A deputation was sent into Germany, inviting the Saxons to their protection: and
in 449 or 450, an army of one thousand six
hundred men, was embarked, and soon after
landed in the isle of Thanet. This body of
Saxons was headed by Hengist and Horsa, two
brothers, and distinguished leaders of that nation; and in conjunction with the native Britons, they soon compelled the Scots and Picts
to retire to their northern territories.

After the defeat of the northern invaders,
the Saxons had leisure to examine the country,
into which they had been invited as auxiliaries;
and finding that it possessed many advantages
above their own, they came to a determination
to make a settlement in it. This, from the un-

warlike appearance of the inhabitants, and the
ease with which they had subdued the Scots
and Picts, they considered as no very difficult
undertaking. Hengist and Horsa, therefore,
sent intelligence into Saxony, of the riches and
fertility of Britain; represented the inhabitants, as a race unused to arms; and the whole
island as an easy conquest. An invitation, the
compliance with which seemed to promise so
many advantages, and so little danger, was
embraced with ardour, by their enterprizing
countrymen; a large reinforcement was sent
over; and they thought themselves sufficiently
powerful to effect their purpose. They immediately threw off the mask, deserted those by
whom they had been invited, and whom they
were bound to protect; formed an alliance
with those who they came to fight against; and
proceeded to open hostilities against the Britons.

So treacherous a conduct roused the indignation of the unsuspecting natives; and brought
to action that inherent courage, which had hitherto lain dormant in their breasts. A most
bloody war ensued; but after a contest of many years, the Saxons, continually reinforced
by fresh numbers from Germany, overpowered
the Britons, and forced them to retire into
Wales and Cornwal; and in these remote situ-

ations, they were for many years left, in the
undisturbed possession of their laws and liberties. The Saxons, being thus left masters of
the greatest part of the island, in 488 established, under their successful leader Hengist;
the kingdom of Kent; the first regular Saxon
government known in Great Britain:—and in
the course of one hundred and fifty years, after
their first introduction, the kingdom was divided into seven petty sovreignties, known by
the name of *Saxon Heptarchy*. These in the
course of time, were united by conquest and
intermarriages; and in 827 Egbert was proclaimed king of England.

Thus did the Saxons, originally, lay the
foundation for that greatness as a nation, which
in future ages they have arrived at. This, however, was done by the sacrifice of every honorable principle, and at the expence of the arts
and civilization. The Britons, during their
connection with the Romans, had made such
advances in the arts and civil manners, that no
less than twenty-eight considerable cities* were
built in their provinces; besides numerous villages and country-seats, which were interspersed every where. But no sooner did the Saxons

* Gildas, Bede, L. 1.

begin to exercise their power, than every thing
was thrown back into its ancient barbarity :—
" the private and public edifices of the Britons
" were reduced to ashes; the priests were
" slaughtered on the altars of those idolatrous
" ravagers; the bishops and nobility shared
" the fate of the vulgar;"* and carnage and
ruin spread desolation over the land :—and we
find, that it was not until some centuries after
that they began to emerge from that gloom of
ignorance which they themselves had caused.

Though the internal divisions of the Saxons
seemed settled by the union of the kingdoms
of the Heptarchy under one head; their peace
was disturbed by a formidable external enemy.
The DANES, driven to extremities by the inhu-
man bigotry of Charlemagne, entertained a
rooted antipathy against the neighbouring
christian states; and possessing, what in those
times was thought, a formidable naval force,
they made frequent invasions on their enemies'
territories. Their first appearance in England
was in the year 787, when a small force landed,
with a view of learning the state of the country :† but in the course of time, they came in
very large bodies; made very extensive settle-

* Hume I. 21.   † Chron. Sax. p. 64.

ments in many parts of the kingdom; and in a few years, formed no inconsiderable portion of the inhabitants of the country.

- The last settlement of any consequence, made by foreigners, in this island, was that of the NORMANS, in the year 1066. William the Conqueror, was followed by a great number of his countrymen, who came over under his protection; and particularly by the nobility, on whom he bestowed very extensive grants in landed property, as rewards of the services which they rendered him.

Such is the sketch of the different tribes, who have peopled the island of Great Britain; which it was thought necessary to give, before the description of any particular county in it, could be well entered upon. We now see these various nations united together into one people; the distinctions of language and manners, lost in the lapse of ages; and as they are subjected to one head, so also they are known by one name.

CHAP II.

Derbyshire—its situation and boundaries—ancient divisions—Roman roads—figure—extent—population—general appearance—rivers—atmosphere and climate—soil—agriculture—produce, &c.

THE county of Derby, is situated in the middle of England; being at an equal distance from the German ocean on the East, as from St. George's channel on the West: and on the North and South, the extremities of Northumberland and Hants, are nearly alike remote.—On the North it is bounded by Yorkshire and a part of Cheshire, which is separated from it by the river Etherow; on the South by a part of Leicestershire; on the East by the county of Nottingham, and another part of that of Leicester; and on the West, it is divided from Staffordshire and Cheshire, by the Trent, the Dove, and the Goyt.

In the time of the Britons, Derbyshire is found included, in the number of the counties that made up the kingdom of the Coritani; who likewise inhabited, the counties of Not-

D

tingham, Leicester, Northampton, Lincoln, and
Rutland. But the Romans, when they had
gained possession of the island, made a new
division of it, into *Britannia prima*, *Britannia
secunda*, *Maxima Cæsariensis*, *Valentia*, and
Flavia Cæsariensis.* Under the division of
Flavia Cæsariensis, which reached from the
Thames to the Humber, was included the
county of Derby. The Romans have left indu-
bitable proofs of their having inhabited this
county; this will be more clearly shewn, when
we come to describe the places, where any remains of them have been discovered. One very
strong evidence is, the military roads, which
may be traced, traversing the county in different directions. That learned antiquarian Mr.
Pegge, about forty years ago, investigated and
described two of the principal ones, which have
been discovered in this county.† The road
which has claimed most of his attention, is
that which passes, in a north-east direction,
through Derbyshire.

This *Ilkenild-street*, he has discovered, came
out of Staffordshire, and entered this county
at Monk's Bridge, about two miles to the
north-east of Burton; and passing over Eg-

ginton heath, to Little Over, ran in a north-
east direction to the west side of the town of
Derby: then crossing Nun's Green, it reached
Little Chester, by a bridge thrown over the
Derwent at that place. From thence it proceeded to Breadsall Priory; and after running
across Morley moor, it is very visible about one
hundred yards to the East of Brackley gate. It
is then lost, till we come to Horsley park; after that it crosses the road leading from Nottingham to Wirksworth, near Horsley Woodhouse; and may be traced to a house called
Cumbersome, which is built upon it. After
crossing Bottle-brook, it goes by the Smithy
houses; it may be seen in the Street-lane, and
crossing the fields between Heage and Ripley,
it appears opposite Harthay-house. Then directing its course to Cony-green house, and
passing on the east-side of the camp on Pentrich common, it extends towards Okerthorpe;
from hence it runs to the Peacock inn, and
crossing the road goes into the fields on the
right hand, and appears again on the side of
the hill, on the other side of the road. From
this place, it extends in a direct line for Higham, through the demesne land of Shirland Hall;
then following the turnpike road to Clay-cross,
it reaches a farm called Egston; and crossing

some inclosures, the Quaker's burying ground,
and a part of Tupton moor, near the Blacksmith's shop it is lost; and beyond the middle
of Sir Windsor Hunloke's avenue, no traces of
it are discoverable; but it is thought to have
extended as far as Chesterfield.

The other road which Mr. Pegge has investigated, is that supposed to have extended from
Buxton to Brough near Hope, called the Bath-
way, or Bathing-gate. This is not so discernible as the other; but this gentleman has ascertained its existence: and beginning at its
north-east extremity, has traced its course with
clearness and certainty. It is said, that there
is another Roman road, in the neighbourhood
of Buxton, extending from Hurdlow House to
Pike Hall, in a parallel line with the turnpike
road which leads to Ashbourne.

When the Romans had quitted Britain, and
the Saxons had made a conquest of it; the *Pen-
tarchy* of the former, was succeeded by the
Heptarchy which the latter established. Derbyshire, with seventeen other counties, was
included in the kingdom of *Mercia;** and its
inhabitants, in conjunction with those of Nottingham, from their being situated North of

---

* Camden clxvi.

the Trent, were distinguished by the name of
(*Mercii aquilonares*) the northern Mercians.—
These two counties, appear to have been connected, in the administration of their civil po-
licy; and to have been governed by the same
civil officers, until the reign of Henry the
Third: (about the year 1240) when the burgesses of Derby, purchased the privilege of
having their assizes held alternately at their
own town: but from the year 1566, when an
act was passed for allowing a sheriff to each
county, they have been held, with a few exceptions, at Derby.

   The figure of Derbyshire is so irregular, and
its outlines so variable, that it can hardly be
said to bear a resemblance to any determinate
figure:—it approaches nearer to that of a tri-
angle than any other; but its numerous curves
and projections, make the resemblance more
imaginary than real. From the best survey
that has been taken of it, it is ascertained, that
its greatest length, from North to South, is
nearly fifty-five miles; and its breadth at the
northern extremity, is reckoned to be about
thirty-three; but from thence it gradually diminishes, so that at its southern extremity, it
narrows almost to a point. Its circumference
is about 204 miles. It contains 720,640 acres

of land : of these above 500,000 are cultivated,
arable, and pasture ; whilst the remainder consists, chiefly, of bleak mountainous regions, and
open commons. The whole county is divided
into six hundreds, 116 parishes ; and includes
about 34,000 houses.

BEDE, a Saxon writer of the eighth century,
says, that the inhabitants of Nottinghamshire
and Derbyshire, " possessed the land of seven
thousand families." Now taking half of these
for Derbyshire, and allowing ten persons upon
an average, to constitute each family, we shall
find upon this calculation, that the population
at that time, was no more than 35,000 inhabitants. In the beginning of the reign of George
the Second, it is asserted, that they amounted
to 126,900 ; and a few years ago, it was thought,
that they were increased to 161,142 : and it
may be expected from the flourishing state of
the cotton, and other manufactories, in the
county, that their number is much augmented
since that time.

There is no other county in England, which
presents such a variety of scenery as Derbyshire :—the northern and southern parts exhibiting, such a striking difference and contrast
in geographical features. The former abounds
with hill and dale, " and the scenery, is in

many parts, romantic and sublime; but on the whole inferior in picturesque effect to that of other mountainous countries. Beauty indeed is only resident in the vallies; the high ground appearing dreary, and destitute of entertainment: and in many situations not a single house or tree, is seen, to divert the eye of the traveller, or relieve the weariness, that arises from the contemplation of sterility and nakedness. Unpleasing however, and even disgustful to the imagination, as the moors are, they serve by way of contrast, to heighten the beauty of the dales and vallies, by which they are intersected; and the sudden change which these occasion in the appearance of the country, at once surprises and interests:—admiration is excited by comparison; and the mind readily admits, that its pleasure would have been less perfect, if the preceding scenes had been more beautiful."*

The country gradually rises until we come to the neighbourhood of Wirksworth: and then it begins to assume that picturesque and mountainous appearance, which it continues to possess to its extremity: " that chain of hills arises, which stretching northwards, is continued in a greater

* Beauties of England and Wales, IIIr. 293.

or less breadth, quite to the borders of Scotland; and forms a natural boundary, between
the East and West sides of the northern part of
the kingdom. Its course in this county is inclined a little to the West. It spreads as it advances northerly, and at length fills up the
whole of the north-west angle, also overflowing
a little, as it were, towards the eastern parts.
The hills are at first of small elevation; but
being in their progress piled one upon another,
they form very elevated ground, in the tract
called the *High Peak*, though without any
eminencies, which can rank among the loftiest
mountains even of this island."[*]   The most
considerable however in height, are the mountains *Axe-edge* and *Kinder-scout*. The former
situated to the south-west of Buxton, according to Mr. Whitehurst's calculation, rises
2100 feet higher than the level of the town of
Derby, and 1000 above that of the valley in
which Buxton Hall stands. The height of
Kinder-scout has not been ascertained; but as
it overlooks all the surrounding eminences, it
is supposed to have a still greater elevation.—
From the great elevation of these mountains,
the clouds are observed to rest upon them,

[*] Aikin's Descrip. of the Country round Manchester, p. 65.

when they pass over the high land with which they are surrounded. The prospect from these eminences is very extensive; it is even alleged, that on a clear day, the vicinities of the towns of Liverpool and.Manchester, the mountains of North Wales, and the Wrekin in Shropshire, may be distinguished with the naked eye. In that part which is called the *Low Peak*, lying near the.centre of the county, there are eminences of various heights and extents. Brassington-moor, Alport near Wirksworth,and Crich-cliff, are the most conspicuous. There is also a ridge, extending from Hardwicke towards the borders of Yorkshire in a northern direction. The southern part of 'Derbyshire is, upon the whole, a pleasant and fertile country; not distinguished in its appearance from the other midland counties. The banks of the Trent is a range of low meadows subject to inundations, for the most part well cultivated, but presenting no variety of scenery.

Like all other hilly countries, Derbyshire abounds in rivers: the principal are, the Trent, the Derwent, the Dove, the Wye, the Errewash, and the Rother.

The TRENT,* which, from the length of its

* Some Antiquarians derive the name of this river from the French word TRENTE; and to support this derivation have asserted, that it is

It then enters the cultivated and extended vale which reaches the town of Derby; where suddenly turning to the East, and crossing a wide plain, it mixes its waters with those of the Trent, near Wilne on the Leicestershire border. The length of its course is estimated at about forty-six miles;—and it has been observed, that, owing to the rapidity of its current, and its reception of the many warm springs, that mix with its waters, the temperature of the Derwent, is warmer than that of rivers in general; and that in summer, it frequently raises the thermometer to 66 degrees.

The Dove* also rises in the High Peak, at a little distance to the South of Buxton, on the Staffordshire limit: and holding a course nearly parallel to the Derwent, it " winds amidst alternate angels of mountain bases, which sometimes jut out in a bold and naked rock ; and at others, in a promontory covered with trees, or a gentle sloping bank of grass."† In its progress it passes through the very romantic spot, . *Dove Dale*, a place far-famed for its wild

---

* " Dove ; if a river from a level ground, it has its name from the British Dov tame, but if a swift river, it is of the same origin with the Dovi and Trvi in Wales;" which signify a river buried between deep banks. Ibid. p. 341, 297. Others derive the name from the colour of its water, which has a greyish tinge, approaching that of the bird of the same name.

† Grant's Tour to the Lakes.

of several rills, flowing among the mountainous regions of the High Peak; and after being increased by the various torrents which flow over these dreary wastes, it becomes a considerable stream at the little town of Derwent; from which it takes its name. At Hathersage, it is augmented by another considerable branch, from the more western part of the Peak; and taking a southerly direction inclined a little to the East, flows rapidly over its uneven bed, and passes through Chatsworth park, below which it receives the Wye, coming down from Buxton and Bakewell. After passing through Rowsley, it heightens the beauty of the pleasant vale of Darley by its progress; its course as well as its appearance is then changed; it takes a more easterly direction, and its stream is ingulphed between those high and craggy rocks, which overhang it on each side, and inclose it in a narrow channel, till it is freed from its confinement, and opens with a peaceful stream into the romantic dale of Matlock.— From there it winds its course, through a narrow vale, to the town of Belper; and the different prospects, which present themselves to the eye, for the eight miles which separate these places, can hardly be equalled for picturesque beauty, or in richness and variety of scenery.

The Rother* has its source in the junction
of several small streams in the vicinity of Chesterfield; which town it passes in its course;
when taking a north-easterly direction, it enters Yorkshire between Kilmarsh and Beighton.
. These rivers are well stocked, with almost
every kind of fresh-water fish.   Formerly a
great quantity of salmon was caught in the
Derwent; but owing to the wears, that have
been erected, and the many other obstructions
these fish find in their progress up the stream,
there have been but few, if any, caught during
late years.   The Dove and the Wye are famed
for the quality and quantity of their trout; and
the grayling is a fish which is seldom met with,
except in the Trent and Dove.   Besides these,
the pike, the barbel, the carp, the chub, and
the gudgeon are found in very great plenty.

Derbyshire is not deficient of those advantages, which arise to an inland country, from
the possession of the means of water carriage.
As early as the year 1729, the Trent was rendered navigable as far as the town of Burton:
but since that period, an unspeakable benefit
has been conferred on the commerce of this

---

* Rother. From the Brittish Rhudder, or Rhud-dwr, reddish water,
or water flowing over a reddish bed of clay or stones.

county, by the communication which has been
opened between it and every part of the king,
dom, by the means of *navigable canals*. Of
these, there are no less than seven, which cross
the county in different directions.

The first that was opened in this county, was
that which was planned by Mr. Brindley, a
gentleman of Derbyshire; an account of whose
life will be given, when we come to treat of the
parish in which he was born. He made his
survey in 1758, and in 1766 the bill for making
a navigable canal from the river Trent near
Wilden-ferry in Derbyshire, to the river Mersey
near Runcorn-gap, was brought into Parliament
and passed.

" This canal which, by its planner, was ingeniously termed the *grand trunk* (in allusion
to the main artery of the body, from whence
branches are sent off, for the nourishment of
the distant parts,) and which is commonly
known by the name of the Staffordshire canal,
takes its course from the north-west to the
south-east, across the county of Chester, and
thence across Staffordshire beyond its middle;
when turning short in a north-eastern direction
parallel to the Trent, it accompanies that river
into Derbyshire, and enters it near the place
where the high road from Derby to Leicester,

crosses the Trent over a bridge, substituted to the former Wilden-ferry. In length it is ninety-three miles. Its fall of water, from its greatest elevation at Harecastle-hill, is 326 feet on the northern side, and 316 on the southern; the former effected by thirty-five locks, the latter by forty. Six of the most southern locks are fourteen feet wide, adapted to the navigation of large barges, and one of the northern is of the same width. The common dimensions of the canal are twenty-nine feet breadth at the top, sixteen at the bottom, and the depth four feet and a half. The canal is carried over the Dove in an aqueduct of twenty-three arches, the ground being raised to a considerable height for the space of a mile and two furlongs.— Over the Trent it is carried by an aqueduct of six arches of twenty-one feet span each; and over the Dane, on three arches of twenty feet span. There are besides near 160 lesser aqueducts and culverts, for the conveyance of brooks and small streams. The cart bridges erected over it are 109; the foot bridges eleven. This great work was begun on July 17th, 1766. It was carried on with great spirit by Mr. Brindley, while he lived, and was finished by his brother-in-law Mr. Henshall, who put the last hand to it in May, 1777."[*]

* Aikin's Descrip. p. 118.

CHESTERFIELD CANAL—In 1769, Mr. Brindley surveyed the course of an intended canal, from the town of Chesterfield, to the river Trent; and in 1770 an act was obtained for putting his plan into execution. The tract of the canal is from Chesterfield by Rickett's mill, near Stavely-forge, by Stavely town and coal-works, the Hague, and near Eckington and Killimarsh, to Harthill, which it penetrates by a tunnel; thence to Worksop and Retford, where it crosses the Idle and at length arrives at the Trent, which it enters at Stockwith, a little below Gainsborough. Its whole length is about forty-six miles:—its rise from Chesterfield to Norwood is forty-five feet; and its fall from thence to the Trent 325 feet, for which it has sixty-five locks. The tunnel at Norwood is 2850 yards; and that at Drakehole 153 yards. This canal was completed, so as to be navigated in 1776; but the expence of the work amounting to £160,000, was so much beyond the estimate, that shares fell to a very depreciated value; but lately they have recovered themselves considerably.

LANGLEY-BRIDGE, or ERREWASH CANAL.— In the year 1777, the owners of the extensive coal-mines, lying in the south-western part of this county, obtained an act, for making a na-

vigable ·· canal from Langley-bridge to the
Trent opposite to the entrance of the Soar.—
This canal commences in the Trent near Sawley, and runs nearly parallel to the little boundary river Errewash; and after passing the
collieries in the neighbourhood of Langley and
Heanor, it terminates in the Cromford canal at
Langley-bridge. It is joined by the Derby
canal, between Sandiacre and Long-Eaton;
and there is an iron rail-way branch to Brins-
ley coal-works. The general direction of this
canal is nearly North for eleven miles and a
quarter; its fall 108 feet eight inches, by means
of fourteen locks.

PEAK-FOREST-CANAL.—The act for cutting
this, was obtained in 1794, and it was finished
in 1800. It proceeds from the Ashton-under-
Lyne canal near Dunkinfield-bridge; and crossing the river Tame passes Denton, Chad-kirk
and Maple-Chapel to Whaley-Bridge, (to which
a branch is carried) where it enters Derbyshire;
and is carried forward to the bason and lime-
kilns at Chapel-Milton, where it terminates.
From the latter place, a rail-way passes Chapel-en-le-Frith to Loads-knowl limestone quarries in the Peak. The line of canal is fifteen
miles in length, and that of the rail-way six.
Mr. B. Outram was the engineer; and not-

withstanding its being carried through the most hilly country, there are no locks. This canal at present pays thirty per cent. Mine-waters may be used for the supply of this Canal, but only the flood-waters of rivers.

CROMFORD CANAL, begins at Cromford near Matlock, and running for some way parallel to the Derwent, passes Crich, Bull-bridge, Fritchley, Heage, Hartshay, Loscoe, Heanor, and joins the Errewash canal at Langley-bridge. It runs in general in a south-east direction for fourteen miles; of which the first eleven are level; but the latter three have a fall of about eighty feet. Besides several smaller tunnels, there is one, near Ripley, 2966 yards in length; over this, there is a reservoir of fifty acres of water when full; the head or embankment of which is 200 yards long, thirty-five feet in height in the middle of the valley, the base being there fifty-two yards wide; the top of the bank is four yards wide. This reservoir is said to have cost £1600.* There is a cut to Pinxton coal-works, of three miles in length: another to Swanwick coal-mines: and also a collateral one of near half a mile, from the Derwent aqueduct-bridge, to Lea-bridge, stone-

* Dr. Rees' Cyclopædia.

sawing-mill and wharf; but this latter cut is
private property. There is a rail-way branch-
ing to Crich lime-works, for a mile and a half;
and another to Beggarlee coal-works, an equal
distance. The principal engineer to this canal
was W. Jessop, Esq. and it was completed before the year 1794. The total cost is said to
have exceeded £80,000. Several new cuts
have been proposed to be made from this. In
1797, it was in contemplation to make one
from the summit-level to the collieries in Codnor Park. Notice was given in 1801 of an intended Belper canal, which was to join this
near Bull-bridge; and in 1802 a cut was proposed to be made from the Derwent aqueduct
on this canal, to near Dethick, and thence near
the Derwent and Wye rivers, to the town of
Bakewell.   *

ASHBY-DE-LA-ZOUCH CANAL. The act for
this canal was obtained 34th Geo. III.. It joins
the Coventry Canal at Marston-bridge, about
two miles to the South of Nuneaton; it then
passes Hinckley, Stoke Golding, Dadlington,
through Bosworth-field, and near Market-
Bosworth; then crosses the river Sence to Gos-
pal Park, goes to Snareton, and through a
tunnel to Measham, Oakthorpe, and across
Ashby-woulds, and through Blackfordby to

Ashby-de-la-Zouch. This canal, with all its branches, is fifty miles long, and 252 feet lockage.*

DERBY CANAL; the act for which, was obtained 33rd Geo. III. commences in the Trent, at Swarkestone-bridge; and crossing the Trent and Mersey Canal terminates at Little Eaton, about four miles North of Derby. The length of this branch is about eight miles and a half, with a rise of about twenty-nine feet. There is a rail-way branch of four miles and a half to the Smithy-Houses; and thence to the collieries near Denby. Another branch of this canal begins at Derby, and holds an easterly direction, nearly parallel to the road leading to Nottingham, which passes Chaddesden, Spoonden, Burrowsash, and joins the Errewash canal between Long Eaton and Sandiacre: its length is eight miles and a half, with a fall of twenty-nine feet. This canal is forty-four feet wide at top, twenty-four at bottom, and five feet deep; except the upper level at Little Eaton, which is made six feet deep, to retain the water of wet seasons like a reservoir; the locks are ninety feet long, and fifteen feet wide within side. Adjoining the town of Derby, is a

---

* Phillips' Inland Navigation, p. 329.

large wear, where the canal crosses the Derwent, which was navigable to this place for many years before this canal was undertaken; and the proprietors thinking that the tolls would necessarily fall off on the completion of this canal, agreed that the Company should purchase the whole concern for £3996. A little West of the Derwent, the canal crosses a brook in a *cast-iron* aqueduct. This canal was finished in 1794; the company were authorised to borrow £90,000, the value of shares being £100. Manures are to pass toll-free, and puncheons or clogs of wood, to be used as supporters in the adjacent coal-mines, and road materials, excepting for turnpike-roads. If the Mansfield turnpike-road tolls, are reduced below four per cent. on their debt, this company is to make them up to that sum. The profits of the concern are not to exceed eight per cent. and after £4000 is accumulated, as a stock for contingencies, the tolls are to be reduced.— Five thousand tons of coals are annually to go free of all rates, for the use of the poor of the town of Derby; and three members of the corporation, and the same number of proprietors, to be chosen annually to distribute them. Horses pay one penny, and cattle a halfpenny each, for the liberty of passing along the railway branch.

The ATMOSPHERE and CLIMATE of Derbyshire vary very much in its different parts. From its northern situation, even the southern part of the county is colder, and more frequently visited by rains, than many of the more central counties of England. In summer, cold and thick fogs are frequently seen hanging over the rivers, and surrounding the basis of the hills; and hoar-frosts are not unfrequent in the month of June. Old people seem to think, that the seasons have undergone a change within the last forty or fifty years: and though it is natural for age to magnify the advantages of its youth, yet many observers, endowed with philosophical skill, and candid judgment, have agreed that some change has taken place, in the temperature of the year. Thus, it is said, that the winters in this county, are found in general to be more moist and mild, and the summers more humid and cold than they formerly were; and that consequently, the seasons are later and more backward.

Owing to the great elevation of the northern part of the county, it is found much colder than the southern. Some kind of grain will not grow at all in the Peak; and even that

which is sown in the most sheltered vallies, is
seldom ready to be cut till late in the year.—
The winters are, in general, very severe; and
the frost continues so long in the ground, that
it cannot be broken up until the season is far
advanced : the consequence is, that the corn
has seldom sufficient time to ripen, and is cut
down, and left to wither in the sun, and to be
dried by the air.

The mountains are so high in the Peak of
Derbyshire, that they attract and intercept the
clouds in their progress over them : this region
is therefore distinguished from all others by the
greater quantity of rain which falls upon it.—
Sometimes it descends in torrents, accompanied with violent storms; carrying every thing
before it, and causing great ravages on the
side of the hills, and in the cultivated dales :
but they are seldom of long duration, and often disappear as suddenly as they come on.
" We arrived," says a late tourist,* who witnessed one of these storms, " just in time to
take shelter amongst those massy rocks, from
the most tremendous storm of thunder and
lightning I had ever witnessed.—Fixed, as it
were, not only on the summit of a mountain,

---

* Hutchinson's Tour through the High Peak of Derbyshire, p. 91.

but on the highest land in the country, for perhaps one hundred miles round; and in a thunder storm when the hills echoed the loud peals
again and again, with almost as loud responses;
while the vivid lightening was playing from the
clouds beneath; were altogether such a sublime
assemblage, that I could not but think myself
fortunate in having arrived at this momentous
period.

"I clearly observed the clouds pass with the
most amazing rapidity, on the sides and summits of the mountains; in one moment veiling
the whole country in impenetrable mist, and
then as instantaneously passing from the sight.
Another flash of lightening, and another awful
burst of thunder; and in a single moment, the
scene was again cleared up, by the impetuous
passing clouds. I had never before experienced
such a singular sublimity; I could scarce think
it natural; it had more the appearance of magic or enchantment!"

These sudden and violent storms, however,
clear the air of every thing noxious: the atmosphere is found to be pure and healthful;
and, like most high situations, free from epi-
demic diseases, though it is found, that in the
deep vallies and narrow dales, agues and fevers
are not uncommon.

One disease, however, is endemick in these parts, and extends as far South as Derby: it is the *Bronchocele* or *Derbyshire neck*. It is a swelling seated on the fore-part of the throat, occasioned by the enlargement of the *thyroid gland;* but not unfrequently the gland becomes subdivided into several fleshy portions, connected closely to each other by cellural membranes. The form and contents of this tumour are very various: during the first years of its existence, it is reddish, and moderately compressible; endowed with little sensibility, highly vascular in its texture, not readily going into suppuration, and leaving the external skin of its natural colour. It is generally believed that the swelling, in the greater number of cases, is truly sarcomatous or fleshy; while some have said, that the bronchocele consists of a honey-like matter; others, that it contains little portions of bone and hair; others, that it is inflated by air; and some, that it is distended by a watery, or puriform fluid: all these opinions may be occasionally true. Females, children, and persons of relaxed and delicate constitutions, are more subject to this affection, than males, adults, and persons whose habits are rigid and vigorous: but sometimes persons of apparently good constitutions, of either sex, are affected by it.

No satisfactory causes have been assigned for this disease. Some have attributed it to the drinking of hard, cold or snow water; the use of food not sufficiently nourishing; the repulsion of some cutaneous disorder; the abuse of vinous or spirituous liquors: but the bronchocele will be found to prevail where none of these causes exist. It is found in many countries besides Derbyshire, and particularly in Swisserland :* indeed it predominates in most coun-

---

* The inhabitants in one part of this country, particularly in the republic of Vallais, are very much subject to *goîtres*, or large excrescences of flesh that grow from the throat, and often increase to a most enormous size. The causes which produce a frequency of this phænomenon in this country form a very curious question.

The springs that supply drink to the natives are impregnated with a calcareous matter called in Switzerland *tuf*, nearly similar to the incrustations of Matlock in Derbyshire, so minutely dissolved as not in the least to affect the transparency of the water. It is not improbable that the impalpable particles of this substance, thus dissolved, should introduce themselves into the glands of the throat, and produce goîtres, for the following reasons : because *tuf*, or this calcareous deposition, abounds in all those districts where goîtres are common. There are goîtrous persons and much *tuf* in Derbyshire, in various parts of the Vallais, in the Valteline, at Lucerne. Freyborg, and Berne, near Aigle and Bex, in several places of the Pays-de-Vaud, near Dresden, in the valleys of Savoy and Piedmont, near Turin and Milan. But the strongest proof in favour of

tries, affected by great humidity of the atmosphere, joined with excessive heat: it augments in the spring time, and diminishes in the autumn; it is less prevalent in a cold and dry winter, than during a season of dampness and moderate warmth. It is purely a local complaint of the neck, unattended with the least danger, unless it extend to a size to affect the breathing, which is seldom the case. The remedy is simple; and if the patient be of a moderately good constitution and under twenty-five years of age, the cure is almost certain: but at a more advanced period in life, it is improbable, and seldom if ever succeeds.*

The soil of Derbyshire, is almost as various as its appearance. In the northern parts of the

---

'this opinion, says the author, is derived from the following facts. " A surgeon whom I met with at the baths of Leuk informed me, that he had not unfrequently extracted concretions of *tuf-stone* from several goîtres; and that from one in particular, which suppurated, he had taken several flat pieces, each about half an inch long. He added, that the same substance was found in the stomach of cows, and in the goîtrous tumours to which even the dogs of the country are subject.— He had diminished and cured the goîtres of many young persons by emollient liquors, and external applications; and prevented them in future, by removing his patients from the place where the springs are impregnated with *tuf;* and if that could not be contrived, by forbidding the use of water which was not purified." GUTHRIE's GEOGRAPHY, p. 526.

* Cyclopædia, v. *Bronchocele.*

county, very extensive peat-bogs exist; in
which have been found buried at a considerable
distance below the surface, large pieces of timber, very little decayed. The soil in these
parts, consists chiefly of ligneous particles, being the roots of decayed vegetables, mixed with
argillaceous earth or sand, and a coaly substance
derived from decayed vegetable matter. The
surface presents nothing but the barren black
moss, thinly clothed with heath or ling. But
in many parts of the Peak there is to be found,
what the natives call a *corn loam:* this seems to
consist of a virgin earth, impregnated with nitre. Where this corn loam is in sufficient.
quantity, and meets with a stratum of marl
or clay, it forms a desirable field for cultivation; but these spots are over-balanced by
vast tracts of barren hills and mountains,
whose sides present very little soil, being chiefly composed of rocks. When the limestone
forms the mountain, the soil though scanty, is
productive of the finer grasses, which form
good pasturage for sheep.* On that part which
is called the *East Moor,* there is scarcely any
vegetation; not a dale or a glade which seems
to have received the cultivating hand of man,
or the fostering smile of nature.

---

* Vide Reports to the Board of Agriculture.

The most common soil in the southern parts, is, a reddish clay or marl. This' soil, which in this district has little or no stone beneath the surface, is also found to prevail, through the middle part of the extensive tract of limestone, which lies on the north-west side of the county; and consists of much calcareous earth, which readily effervesces with acids. It is thought that the colouring principle of this soil, is the calx of iron; as the water which passes through it, has been found to be slightly chalybeate. Some parts of the southern district is interspersed with small beds of sand or gravel; which are in general siliceous, and therefore insoluble in acids. The large tract of country which produces coal, is covered with a clay of different colours; black, grey, brown, and especially yellow. This kind of soil is also found in some parts where the grit-stone is met with; but there, it is frequently of a black colour, and bituminous quality. That on the north-east side of the county, where limestone prevails, is of a brown colour and loose texture. The soil on the banks of the rivers, and in the vallies, is different from that of the adjacent parts, and evidently has been altered by the depositions from the frequent inundations.

Owing to the barreness of the soil, and the

coldness of the climate, there is but little corn grown in the northern parts; and the attention of the farmers, is chiefly turned to grazing and breeding cattle. Of these, large herds are brought from Cheshire and Yorkshire in the spring, and fetched back in the autumn; for their pasturage during the summer, the owners pay a shilling a head per week; which but ill remunerates the poor tenant, who, in general, pays from ten to fourteen shillings an acre in rent, for this naked and unyielding ground. At Chelmorton and Stoney Middleton, a considerable number of cattle are yearly fattened, and disposed of, at the Manchester and Sheffield markets. The land in, and about the parish of Glossop, is chiefly used for pasture: and very little corn, except black oats, is grown in this, or in any other part of the High Peak.

But as we approach the southern extremity, tillage becomes more frequent; and on the eastern side of the county it chiefly prevails.—The midland tracts, have a mixture of pasture and arrable land, according to the soil and situation: but the banks of the Dove are chiefly occupied with dairy farms. About the town of Derby all kinds of grain are cultivated: and the produce is in general very abundant. In

the extensive fields in the neighbourhood of
Chaddesden and Chellaston, a great quantity
of wheat, and that of a particularly fine sort, is
raised: the course of tillage invariably pursued
there, is—fallow, wheat, barley, beans, or
peas. The ground here is mostly prepared by
a wheel-plough, drawn by two horses going
a-breast: though the double furrowed plough
also has been introduced into the southern
parts of the county. Barley is much cultivated in many parts of the county: but more
particularly at Gresley and Repton. These
parishes lying near the extensive breweries of
Barton, the farmers have been induced to grow
this grain, because of the ready sale they find
for it there: the whole produce has been estimated at 5000 quarters annually. The produce
of wheat in the county is scarcely equal to the
consumption: that of beans and oats nearly
answers the home demand. Extensive crops of
cabbage and turnips are raised: and the cultivation of artificial grasses, seems more attended to now, than it has been for some years: indeed the whole agricultural system of the county, is in a state of progressive improvement.

But an uncommon species of culture, in
which about 200 acres of this county are employed, is that of *camomile*. " A loamy soil

is chosen for its cultivation, and, after
the ground is well prepared by thorough clean-
ings, about the end of March, the roots of an
old plantation are taken up, and divided into
small slips, which are planted in rows about
eighteen inches asunder, and about the same
distance in the rows. The plants are kept clean
by frequent hoeing and weeding with the hand.
In September the flowers are fit to gather: their
perfection depends on their being fully blown,
without having stood so long as to lose their
whiteness; the flowering continues till stopped
by the frosts. The gatherings are repeated as
often as successions of flowers appear; but
this depends very much on the season, dry
open weather furnishing more successions than
wet or dull weather. When the flowers are
gathered they are carefully dried, either in
kilns very moderately heated, or on the floors
of boarded rooms, heated by slow fires: the
object is, to keep the flowers white and whole,
and this is best effected by drying them as
slowly as possible. The produce varies from
two hundred weight, and even less, to four,
five, and, in some few instances, six hundred
weight per acre. The price has also varied
from 40s. to £7. per cwt. The plants usually
stand three years, of which the first affords the

H

smallest produce; and the second the greatest
and the best. When the plants are continued
beyond three years, the ground becomes foul,
and the flowers weak. When dried, the flowers
are packed in bags; and afterwards sold to
persons in the neighbourhood, who transmit
them to the druggists in London."

But upon the whole, Derbyshire is more of a
grazing and dairying, than a corn county.—
Great attention has, of late years, been paid to
the breed of *Cows;* and the country gentlemen
have spared no expence in improving it. The
cows are in general horned, large, and handsome; yield upon an average about ten quarts
of milk a day, and in good grass fatten very
soon. They are most commonly speckled, with
large and well-turned horns; though of late
the short-horned Lancashire breed has been introduced, and seems to be preferred. As butter making is not the primary object of the
farmer, the quantity and not the quality of
the milk is chiefly attended to. The Derbyshire cheese is of a good quality, generally
mild, and in taste though not in richness, resembling the Gloucestershire. The process of
making it varies considerably; the most common is the following: " When the milk is sufficiently cold, (the colder it is, when put to-

gether for making cheese, is here considered the better) a sufficient quantity of rennet is put to it to make it come in an hour. It is then stir-red, or broke with the hand very small, and left to settle about thirty minutes; then the whey is got from the curd as much as possible, and the latter gathered in a firm state into the cheese-pan. A vat is then placed over the pan, and the curd broken *slightly* into it, and afterwards pressed by the hand in the vat, whilst any *crushings* will run from it: a small quantity of curd is then cut off round the edge of the vat, and broken small in the middle of the cheese, which, after a little more pressing, is turned in the vat, and the same method of cutting the edge off is again observed: after-wards a clean dry cloth is put over and under the cheese in the vat, and it is consigned to the press for one hour: It is then again turned in the vat, and pressed ten hours, when it is ta-ken out, and salted on both sides. If the cheese is of the weight of twelve pounds, a large handful of salt is used for each side. After-wards it is again put in the vat, wrapped in another clean dry cloth, and carried back to the press, where it is kept two or three days, but turned every twelve hours: the last time it is turned, it is put into a dry vat without a cloth, to take away any impressions. This kind of cheese is in perfection, at a year and a half, or two years old. To keep it clean and make it look well, it is rubbed while soft, twice a week with a linen cloth, and afterwards once in every week or fortnight with a hair-cloth."* It is expected that the produce of each cow for the season, on a good dairy farm, should be about 300 weight of cheese; of which it is calculated that nearly 2000 tons are sent annually to London, and for exportation to the ports on the eastern coast. It is all made of new milk, and the whey which it produces is gathered into large earthen cream pots, every twenty-four hours, and there left to cream: this is skimmed off, and boiled twice or thrice a week, and in some dairies removed to clean vessels every three days, in order to keep it sweet: to this is added a small quantity of milk-cream, and they are churned together. If the butter thus produced be eaten while it is fresh, it will be found very little inferior to milk butter; but a few days' keeping makes it rancid and strong.

Nature seems to have adapted the *Horses* in Derbyshire, to the different regions in which she designed them to labour. In the northern

---

* Brown's View of the Agriculture of the Country.

districts, the breed is small, of a light and
slender make; and shew great agility in ascending and descending the steep mountains, over
which they are employed in carrying limestone
on their backs. Accustomed to a scanty fare,
they are very hard, and able to undergo very
great fatigue. In the southern parts, the horses
are, in general, of a strong and heavy kind;
but well adapted for the pursuits of agriculture.
However, this beautiful animal, may be found
in the perfection of its symmetry in the stables
of many gentlemen in the county.

The *Sheep* also, in Derbyshire, vary in their
size: those that are bred in that part which
borders upon Leicestershire, differ but little in
weight from that county breed; weighing from
twenty to thirty pounds per quarter. But they
gradually diminish in size as we proceed northwards; so that in the High Peak they weigh
no more than from fourteen to seventeen pounds
the quarter: those on the grit-stone land being
three pounds lighter, than those on the limestone land. But the difference in their fleeces,
is still more remarkable; those of the grit-stone
sheep being much lighter and thinner than that
of the other.

Goats, in former times, appear to have been
much attended to in the county; but it is a

species of animal, which we seldom or never
meet with now. Swine, in all their different
breeds, may be met with every where: and
rearing and fattening them answer very well
to the labouring class.

Of the Deer kind, the fallow is the only
species now to be found in Derbyshire;—very
large herds of these may be seen in the parks
at Chatsworth and Kedleston. Other animals,
tame and wild, common to other counties, may
be found in this; none of which, however, offer any thing remarkable.

The natural history of the birds of Derbyshire, will differ but little from that of other
English counties. The black, or ring tailed
eagle, seems in former times, to have been an
inhabitant of the northern parts: but it is now
more than fifty years since the last has been
seen. The osprey, another species of eagle,
has also been seen of late years. The following, according to Mr. Pilkington, is a list of
the birds that are common to the county, and
of those less so, which have been seen at various
times, in different parts of it:

Common:—The white, the brown, and the
tawney or screech owl; the cuckow, wry neck,
king's fisher, red grouse, partridge, the common
pigeon or stockdove; the starling, misseltoe,

thrush, field fare, throstle, and the water ouzel; the bullfinch, brown bunting, yellow-
hammer, reed, house, and hedge sparrow; the
chaffinch, goldfinch, the brown and red headed linnet, and the sky the wood and the tit
lark; the grey wagtail, the redbreast and red-
start; the yellow or willow and common wren,
white ear, whin chat, and stone chatter; the
white throat, the swift, the house swallow, martin, and the great blue, the cole, and the long
tailed titmouse.

Less common:—The merlin, honey buzzard,
moor buzzard, ring tail, and spotted falcon;
the long and short eared owl, the greater and
smaller butcher bird, and the greater and
smaller spotted wood pecker; the nuthatch,
creeper, the black cock, quail, and the rock
pigeon; the ring ouzel and rose-coloured ouzel, the Bohemian chatterer, haw grosbeak,
crossbill, and brambling; the fly catcher, nightingale, petty chaps, golden crested wren, and
the goat sucker.

Water fowls. *Common:*—The heron, wood-
cock, corncrake or landrail, moorhen, and the
coot. *Less common:*—The curlew, godwit, red-
shank, lapwing, grey sand piper, ruff and reeve,
spotted sand piper, oyster catcher or sea pie,
grey scollop toed sand piper; the tippet, the

dusky and the lesser grebe, puffin or fire eyed
grebe, the great grey gull, black headed gull,
greater and lesser tern, the goosander, red
headed smew; wild swans, white fronted geese,
the barnacle, the pochard or dun bird; the
brent goose, the long tailed, the velvet, the
golden eyed, the white throated, and the Gar-
ganey duck; the shiel drake, and the cormo-
rant.*

The produce of the manufactories in the
county, are various and extensive. The manufactories, of cotton, into thread, stockings,
and calico, at Cromford, Belper, Derby, and
other parts; of wool into hose, and cloth, on
the borders of Nottinghamshire, and in the
neighbourhood of Tideswell; of iron on the
north-east side, adjacent to Yorkshire; of silk,
and also of ornaments made of spar, at Derby;
are the principal, and will be taken notice of
when we come to treat of these places.

* Pilkington, I. p. 480.

CHAP. III.

Subterraneous Geography—Mines—and Minerals, &c.

THE SUBTERRANEOUS GEOGRAPHY of Derbyshire may be considered, under the three divisions, of limestone, coal, and grit, land: and in the following pages, the tracts of land, where these are found; some general circumstances relating to the dispositions, properties, and probable formation, of the various kinds of strata which compose them, will be stated.

Limestone.—The most extensive tract of this land, is in the north-west part of the county; and may be considered, included within a boundary line, commencing at Hope, and proceeding in a south-westerly direction, on the west side of the Peak Forest, by Buxton to the head of the Dove; and following the boundary of the county on that side, for twelve miles, extends into Staffordshire. In the South, this line commences again, at Thorpe, and proceeding to Ashbourne, Wirksworth, Matlock, Winster, Bakewell, by the East of Stoney Middleton to the North of Hope, where it terminates.

I

There is also a smaller tract of limestone land, on the East side of the county, forming the ridge from near Hardwicke by Bolsover and Barlborough to the borders of Yorkshire, through which it passes with little interruption, as far as Tinmouth Castle in Northumberland. It spreads also in an easterly direction into the county of Nottingham. There are several detached beds of limestone, situated at Ashover, Crich, Turnditch, in the parish of Duffield, Muggington, Ticknall and Osmaston; none of which, however, exceed two miles, in length or breadth.

Coal: the tract of country where this is found may be included under a line, commencing in the South, at Stanton, on the borders of Nottinghamshire; and proceeding in a north-westerly direction, through Morley to the neighbourhood of Belper, and thence in a zig-zag northerly course, by the West of Pentrich, the East of Dethick; through the parishes of Ashover and Dronfield, to the Yorkshire border.— The eastern line enters Derbyshire, from Nottinghamshire, a little to the South of Hardwicke-Hall, and proceeds northwards by Bolsover and Killimarsh; and is bounded by the ridge of limestone, which has been already described as lying in that part. It is said that

this tract of coal, which has received the name
of the *great northern rake*, extends even to the
borders of Scotland; with the exception of a
limestone bed, of three miles in breadth, which
interrupts it near Ferry-bridge in Yorkshire.—
Coal has also been found at Chinley-hill, near
Chapel-en-le-Frith; at Newhall, in the parish
of Stapenhill; in Hartington near Buxton;
and at Church Gresley, Calke, and Measham,
in the southern extremity of the county. But
the ground where it is found in these places, is
not extensive; as it appears to be no more than
three miles in length and two in breadth.

Grit-stone: though this does not comprehend
all the county, which does not fall under the
two former divisions, it occupies a much greater
extent of land than either of them. In the
North and north-west extremity of the county;
and through the tracts which lie between the
principal beds of coal and limestone, it uniformly prevails: but the most extensive tract
of grit-stone is found in the East-moor, which
extends, in various breadths, as far South as
the town of Derby: small beds appear at Allestry, Mackworth, Langley, and many other
places in the county.

To these three subterranean districts may be
added a fourth; in which no beds of stone of

any kind are to be met with, near the surface.
That part of the county lying to the South of
a line, drawn through Derby from Ashbourne
to Nottinghamshire, (with the exception of
those small spots already pointed out) will
comprehend this tract.

Strata.—" The book of nature," said that ingenious philosopher, Mr. Whitehurst, " is open
to all men, written in characters equally intelligible to all nations : but, perhaps, in no part
of the world more than in Derbyshire : for
amidst all the apparent confusion and disorder
of the *strata* in that mountainous country,
there is, nevertheless, one constant invariable
order in their arrangement, and of their various productions, or impressions, of animal,
vegetable, and mineral substances."*

" The uppermost stratum, which, for the
sake of perspicuity, we shall denominate No.
1, is ARGILLACEOUS GRIT, and its accompanying beds *clay, coal, iron-stone,* &c. its thickness is various, according as the surface is more
or less uneven. It is an assemblage of sand, and
adventitious matter, in a base of argil: fracture, granular: of a dull colour : smell, earthy,
when breathed on: does not effervesce with

acids: does not take a polish: may be easily
scraped with a knife: has often brownish red
veins: and is often ferruginous: by exposure
to the atmosphere, it decomposes. This stratum generally indicates iron ore, which is frequently found under it in laminæ and nodules.
The iron-stone is both sulphureous and argillaceous, but the latter is the most common:
it lies in irregular beds; is of a brown colour,
and compact nature; smell, earthy; and yields
about thirty per cent. The strata of argillaceous grit and iron are generally incumbent on
coal, which lies in laminæ, of various quality
and thickness, and frequently abounds with
pyrites, and argillaceous iron ore in nodules:
fracture, generally splintery, laminated, sometimes regular, with a bright gloss, and very
brittle: contains much sulphur and petroleum.
Between the layers of coal, and frequently incumbent on that substance, are various strata
of a schistose clay, called by the different names
of *under-soil, bind, clunch, hard-stone, metal,
plate,* &c. according as it is more or less indurated.   All these are of unequal thickness;
being sometimes only a few inches; at others,
several feet.   Nodules of iron ore are frequently found, which easily divide, and shew very
fine impressions of plants, flowers, coralloids,

and shells. All the strata, indeed, incumbent
on coal, whether argillaceous stone, or clay,
contain a great variety of impressions of vegetables; and particularly the bamboo of India,
striated, and jointed at different distances: the
euphorbia of the East Indies; the American
ferns, corn, grass, and many other species of
the vegetable kingdom, not known to exist in
any part of the world in a living state. These
vegetable forms, and the strata containing
them, are said to be a certain indication of
coal, not only in Derbyshire, but in every
quarter of the kingdom. The stratum of argillaceous grit may be observed in the vicinity
of Smalley, Heanor, Derby, Heage, Alfreton,
Carnfield, Chesterfield, and many other places. The surface of the country where it appears, is in general uniform; the hills are nearly
regular, and rise by an easy inclination, forming vales of considerable extent. '

   " No. 2, Coarse SILICIOUS GRIT; composed of
granulated quartz, and quartz pebbles, of various sizes, but seldom exceeding a quarter of an
inch in diameter: some retain the sharpness of
fragments newly broken; others appear to have
been rounded by attrition. This stratum is
about 120 yards in thickness, and variable both
in appearance and texture: near the surface it

is very friable, and not unfrequently contains adventitious matter. It gives fire with steel, resists acids, and is often coloured by iron: fracture, irregular; does not take a polish. It is not stratified, but contains varieties of grit-stone in laminæ: some are called free-stone, and employed for buildings: others are termed mill-stone grit, and used for mill-stones. A particular variety is laminated with mica, and is somewhat elastic: it easily divides with a knife, and being an excellent substitute for slate, has become an article of commerce: this stratum is not productive of minerals; but there are some instances of lead ore having been found in it; frequently it contains chrys-tallized fluor, and barytes, and is incumbent on shale or schistus, from which it is separated by a thin seam of clay. This substance forms long and narrow mountains, rather than hills; it is uppermost at Wirksworth Moor; Crom-ford Moor, near Winster; the East Moor; Birchover; Matlock Town; the Edge-side Hills; from Eyam to Castleton, and various other places. No impressions either of animal or ve-getable figures have been discovered in it. .

" No. 3, SHALE, or SCHISTUS; of a dark brown, or blackish colour, bituminous, and appearing like indurated clay. Its thickness,

according to the respective measurements of
Mr. Whitehurst and Mr. Ferber, varies from
120 to 150 yards. This stratum is not considered as generally productive of minerals;
though iron-stone in nodules, and thin beds,
has sometimes been found in it : and also veins
of lead ore : the latter arise from the limestone,
on which the shale is incumbent, but become
less and less mineralized as they ascend. In its
sparry veins,are frequent cavities, called *lochs*
by the miners, which are incrusted with a great
variety of fine and rare crystallizations of calcareous spar. It contains no impressions either of
animal or vegetable bodies : but impressions of
marine substances are sometimes discovered in
it, much impregnated with pyrites. By exposure to the atmosphere, this shale decomposes
in laminae: its fracture is dull : it absorbs
moisture: contains sulphur, burning with a
blue flame, and becoming of a reddish-brown
colour: frequently resists acids: but sometimes effervesces slowly, and more quickly as
it approaches the limestone, from which it is
separated by a thin bed of clay: in some cases
it even contains a large portion of calcareous
earth : the limestone, in return, partaking of
its dark colour, to the depth of several feet to
where they are in contact. The waters passing

through it are chalybeate, and frequently
warm. Shale most commonly appears uppermost in vallies formed by limestone mountains
on one side, and gritstone on the other, where
it is generally covered with *ratchel*, a name
given to a confused mass of loose, irregular
stony substances, that has probably been composed of shattered pieces, fallen from the adjoining eminences.

" No. 4.—LIMESTONE regularly stratified,
but varying considerably in thickness, being
in some places not more than four fathoms, yet
in others upwards of 200. This stratum seems
wholly composed of *marine exuviæ*, and abounds
with a variety of shells, entrochi, coralloids,
madrepores, and many other species of crusta-
ceous animals. In it are found the principal
veins or fissures which contain galena, sulphuret, and native oxyde of zinc, a variety of
ochres, fluors, barytes, calcareous crystallizations, pyrites, &c. It lies in laminæ, more or
less thick, and is frequently separated, at irregular distances, by a marl, containing adventitious substances; in some places only a few
inches thick; but in others two or three feet.
This limestone forms a variety of beautiful
marbles; some black; others of a brown red,
much used for chimney-pieces, and different

ornaments; some mottled grey, and some of a
light stone colour. All the varieties have a
fœtid smell, when rubbed with a harder substance: when calcined, they become white,
and compose a strong cement. The limestone
in the Peak Forest is regarded as the best: it is
compact, and sonorous when struck; its fracture, scaly bright. It is much used for the
purposes of agriculture, and burns to a fine
white lime, losing nearly thirty per cent. of the
carbonic gas during the operation, which occupies about thirty hours in a strong fire. On
the surface of this stratum, rotten-stone is
sometimes found, particularly near Wardlow
Mire and Ashford: it is generally accompanied
with a silicious substance, in nodules, called
chert, which is likewise found in large detached masses, and thin strata, within the limestone. This substance is full of marine figures,
and animal remains: its origin has been commonly attributed to a partial dissolution of the
limestone stratum. The forms and general appearance of the limestone mountains are greatly diversified; they exhibit evident marks of interior convulsions of the earth, which have
dislocated and thrown the strata near the surface into every variety of confusion. In many
parts they are perpendicular, and overhanging;

presenting bare and rugged forms, and pursuing the wildest directions. Various openings
or caverns, locally termed *shakes*, or *swallows*,
exist in the limestone: these are large fissures,
the depths and communications of which cannot be ascertained; yet they have been rendered of great service in several mines, through
being made receptacles for the *deads*, or rubbish; and have also been appropriated as aqueducts to carry off the water.   This stratum is
uppermost at Winster, Ashford, Eyam, Buxton Hills, Moneyash, the southern vicinity of
Castleton, and various other places.

  " No. 5.—Toadstone; a substance exceed-
' ingly irregular in appearance, thickness, and
disposition; not laminated, but consisting of
one entire mass, and breaking alike in all directions.   It is sometimes of a dark brown colour, with a greenish tinge, and superficially
full of holes; but at a greater depth more compact: the holes are sometimes filled with calcareous spar, and sometimes with green globules:
—this variety is apparently in a state of decomposition: the fracture irregular.   Other
varieties have the appearance of basalt,   or
whin-stone, and are of equal hardness; they
contain hornblende, with patches or streakes
of red jasper: some specimens, found near

Buxton, contain zeolite, and calcedony. These
varieties assume so many different characters,
according to their various states of decomposition, that their primitive qualities are difficult
to be traced. The exterior, or what has been
exposed to the atmosphere, resembles a scoria,
or vitrified mass: the fracture of a dull colour;
earthy smell when breathed on. 'Toadstone,'
observes Mr. Whitehurst, ' contains bladder
holes, like the *scoria* of metals, or Iceland lava,
and has the same chemical property of resisting
acids. It does not produce any minerals, nor
figured stones, representing any part of the
animal or vegetable creation ; nor are any adventitious bodies enveloped in it : neither does
it universally prevail, as the limestone strata ;
nor is it like them, equally thick ; but in some
instances varies in thickness, from six feet to
600. It is likewise attended with other circumstances, which leave no doubt of its being
as much a lava as that which flows from Hecla,
Vesuvius, or Etna.' This substance forms the
surface in many parts of the county, beginning in the neighbourhood of Matlock, and
dividing the limestone for a considerable distance: near Buxton, and particularly at Wormhill in that neighbourhood, it is of considerable extent, uneven and rocky : but far less so

than the preceding stratum. The miners in different parts of Derbyshire distinguish it by the various names of *black-stone, channel, cat-dirt,* and *black-clay;* but the same appellations are very frequently given to substances which scarcely resemble toadstone in any respect but colour; hence, mistakes have arisen, and properties have been attributed to it which it does not possess. .

" No. 6.—LIMESTONE of the same qualities as No. 4, and productive of similar minerals and figured stones: below this, no miners in Derbyshire have yet penetrated. It should be remarked, that *vegetable forms* have never yet been discovered in any of the limestone strata."[*]

Though the above be, the general disposition of the strata, yet in particular instances, this order is diversified, and the numbers multiplied. The inferior measures are not always arranged with equal regularity; sometimes they separate each stratum, the thickness differing from three inches to three feet, and appearing of various colours, from the ochre yellow to the brown and ash green; small pieces of pyrites are generally found in them.

Of the *toudstone,* of which no more than three

---

beds have been discovered in any part of the
county, there are some peculiar circumstances
worthy notice. The mineral veins, or fissures,
in the limestone strata are always cut off and
intersected by this substance, when it alter-
nates with the limestone. For when a vein is
exhausted in the first bed, that is, in the first
black limestone; the ore disappears on reaching the toadstone, and no vestige of it is found,
until the bed of toadstone is entirely dug
through. The toadstone also, so ‘completely
separates the different strata of limestone, that,
though the gallery over the miners’ heads be
inundated, yet they can carry on their work
undisturbed by the water, so close is the texture, and so free from fissures, is this substance.
Another peculiarity of the toadstone, is, that
it is found to fill up the fissures in the limestone strata, immediately under it, in proportion to their width.

These peculiar circumstances attending the
toadstone have led Mr. Whitehurst to believe,
that it was formed by a different law from
others; and that the origin of its formation,
was greatly posterior to them. He supposed
that the substances that go under the names of
toadstone, *channel*, *cat-dirt*, and *black-clay*, is
actual *lava*. He imagined that a central fire

must at some former time have existed, which
by its expansive force, elevated and burst the
incumbent strata, and threw them into their
present state of disorder and confusion. " Fissures being thus opened over the melted matter, the violent pressure might cause it to
ascend, till it met an obstruction superior to
the impelling force; and the lava being thus
circumstanced, would consequently have a
proportionable lateral pressure, and might
therefore penetrate between the strata, and
force its way till it lost its fluidity by the cool-
ness of the adjacent beds. Being thus extended to some distance, and passing over
other fissures, it might fill them up more or
less, as they happened to be more or less wide,
and the lava more or less fluid."* This seems
to be confirmed, by the discovery, that the
stratum of clay lying under the toadstone, is
burnt to the colour of a brick for near a foot
in thickness. This hypothesis, however, has
been controverted by M. B. Faujas St. Fond,
a member of the National Institute at Paris;
who says, that this substance is no other than
that known on the continent by the name of
trapp. But Mr. Mawe has re-examined the

* Whitehursts' Enquiry.

mine visited by M. St. Fond, and seems to
think, that, that respectable geologist was de-
ceived by the ignorance or imposition of the
miners; and that the toadstone is as much a
lava, as that which flows from Hecla, Vesuvius,
or Etna.

It has been observed, that the position of the
strata is governed by a uniform law; their de-
clination always tending towards those parts
of the country, where the grit-stone has appeared on the surface; but the degree of their
dipping is various and irregular. In some
places they dip at the rate of six inches in a
yard; in others twelve, and even eighteen in a
similar space. In particular places, this dipping seems to be much influenced by the vallies; the strata on one side being nearly horizontal; while on the opposite they have an oblique, and sometimes perpendicular direction.
At Chesterfield and Heanor, the strata have a
peculiar position. They dip for a considerable
space towards one common centre, and by this
means form a kind of bason, or deep circular
figure.

-The strata of clay-stone land, yielding coal,
are found to be exceedingly various in their order, thickness, and quality. They are in general composed of different sorts of clay, smut

or soft coal, bind, black shale, clunch, and hard coal. The position of these strata is very seldom found horizontal, but dip in almost every direction.

Having thus taken a cursory view of the subterraneous geography of the county, and briefly described the different strata; we come to treat of its minerals and mines. These are provinces which afford ample room for investigation: at all times the mineral kingdom is worthy inspection; and as its productions are not only to be met with, in great variety in Derbyshire, but as they constitute a very great part of its natural riches, it will deserve particular attention.

Lead.—The lead mines in Derbyshire appear to have been worked in very early times: Camden is of opinion, that Pliny alludes to this county, when he says, " in Britain, on the surface of the ground, lead is dug up in such plenty, that a law was made on purpose to stint them to a set quantity."* But whether this be the case or not, it is certain that lead mines were known and worked in the time of the Romans; as several pigs have been found, at different times, with Roman inscriptions on them.

L

* Camden, p. 494.

The first of these was accidentally discovered
by a labouring man in 1777 on Cromford moor,
lying in an oblique direction, about a foot beneath the surface of the ground. It was purchased by a gentleman in the neighbourhood,
for a trifling sum of money, and is now lodged
in the British Museum. It bears this inscription:—IMP. CAES. HADRIANI. AUG. MEI. LVI;
which has been interpreted:* *The sixth legion
inscribes this in memory of the Emperor Hadri-
an.* It is therefore supposed, that this pig was
cast about A. D. 130.   In 1783 a second block
of lead was met with in Matlock; the letters
on this are in sharp relief, and very perfect:
but as the words are very much abreviated, and
likewise consist of compounded letters, it is very
difficult to ascertain the meaning of the inscription.   But the learned antiquarian to
whom we have just alluded, thinks that it may
admit the following construction:—LUCIUS,
ARUCONIUS VERECUNDUS MERCATOR LUNDINEN-
SIS: *The property of Lucius Aruconius Verecundus, lead merchant of London.* This block
on the upper surface, is nineteen inches in
length, and three and a half in breadth; on
the lower, it is twenty-two inches long, and
four and three-quarters in breadth; and weighs

* By Mr. Pegge in Archaelog. Vol. IV.

eighty-four pounds. Since the above, another
block has been found at Matlock, bearing the
following inscription :—TI. CL. TR. LVT. 'BR:
EXARG: which the Rev. Mr. Gifford supposed
stood for the words; *Tiberii, Claudiani, Trium_*
viri, Lutudari, Britannorum ex argentaria. This
pig weighs twelve stones and five pounds.

These different inscriptions afford undoubt-
ed evidence, that the lead mines in the neighbourhood of these places, were worked by the
Romans: and it is very probable, that from that
time to the present, none of the different nations who inhabited Britain were ignorant or
negligent of this treasure. We have reason to
believe, that the Saxons and Danes, who, immediately succeeded the Romans, availed themselves of this source of national wealth ; as one
of the mines in the neighbourhood of Castleton, is called *Odin*, the name of one of their
northern deities: and this name, also proves
that this mine was opened before the prevalence
of the Christian Religion.

Dugdale says,* that Eadburga, abbess of
Repton, in 714 sent a leaden coffin to St. Guth-
lac, patron-saint of Croyland abbey, who died
that year: and in the year 835 Kenewara, ano-

* Mon. Angl. V. I. p. 88.

ther abbess of Repton, granted her estate at
Wircesworth, to Humbert, the Alderman, on
condition, that he gave lead to the value of 300
shillings, to archbishop Ceolnoth, for the use
of Christ Church at Canterbury; so that lead
must have been in common use and well known
before those times. The Castle of the Peak,
built as early as the time of William the Conqueror, appears from a survey taken of it in
queen Elizabeth's time, to have been covered
with lead. In Doomesday-book mention is
made of three lead mines at Wirksworth, one
at Crich, one at Ashford, one at Bakewell, and
another at Metesford, a manor which is described as situated in the neighbourhood of
Matlock.

In the sixteenth year of Edward I. Reginald
de Leye and William de Meynell, were appointed by the crown, to make enquiry " concerning the liberties which the miners of the
High Peak, claim to have in those parts, and
which they have hitherto used; and how, and
what manner, and from what time and by
what warrant."   At the proper time and place,
the privileges of the miners were enquired into, and confirmed to them. These are contained in sixty-four articles for the High Peak
Hundred; and fifty-three for the Wapentake of
Wirksworth.

The regulations respecting the rights of the miners are numerous and various. Two great courts are to be held every year; at Easter and Michaelmas: and if required may be called every six weeks.* Those of the High Peak are held at Money-Ash; and those of the Wapentake at Wirksworth. At these courts a Barmaster presides;† who with twenty-four jurymen determines all disputes that may arise among the miners. The Bar-masters are chosen by his Majesty's farmers of the mineral duties:‡ these have from time immemorial, been let on lease. The present farmer of those in the High Peak, is, the Duke of Devonshire; and of those in the Wapentake of Wirksworth, is, Mrs. Rolles. They have a steward each, and Bar-masters in the districts which they hold of the crown.

The duties of a Bar-master, are various and perplexing; his principal office is to put the miners in possession of the veins they have discovered; and collecting the portion of ore due to the lessee. When a miner has discovered a vein of ore, in any part of the king's field, he may obtain exclusive title to it, if it be not in an orchard, garden, high road, or dwelling-

* Article XVI.   † Art. agreed to at the Great Court Bar-mote 1665.
‡ Note to Art. I.

house.* Possession is to be given by the Bar-
master, in the presence of two jurymen, marking
out in a pipe or rake work two *meares* of ground,
each containing twenty-nine yards; and in a
flat work, fourteen yards square. But should
a miner neglect to avail himself of his discovery, beyond a given time; then, the Bar-
master may take possession of the vein, and
dispose of it to another. The Bar-master is
also to superintend the admeasurement of the
the ore, and to receive the dues of the lessee of
the crown: this part of his office is attended
with some difficulty, from the variety of claims,
which differ greatly in different places. By
the articles, a thirteenth of the ore is due to the
king; but there is seldom more than a twenty-
fifth taken. There is also a due for tythe; and
another called *cope*, which is paid by the buyer.
In mines which are private property, such tolls
are paid as the parties agree upon.

The ore is measured out in a dish, containing
in the High Peak sixteen pints; but only fourteen in the Low Peak. The brazen dish, by
which the measures in the Low Peak are regulated, appears from the inscription upon it, to
have been cast in the reign of Henry VIII.—
" This dishe was made the iiij day of Octobr

the iiij yere of the Reigne of Kyng Henry the
viij before George Erle of Shrowesbury Steward
of the Kyng most Honourable houeshold and all-
so Steward of all the honour of Tutbery by the
assent and consent as wele of all the Mynours
as of all the Brenners within and adioynyng the
Lordshyp of Wyrkysworth Percell of the said
honour This Dishe to Remayne In the Moote
hall at Wyrkysworth hanging by a Cheyne so
as the Mchanntes or Mynours may have resorte
to the same att all tymes to make the trw Me-
sure at the same."

The articles before alluded to, contain many
privileges which the miners strenuously contend
for. By article XIV. the Bar-master or his deputy, is to lay out a road for the miners to go
and come from their work; and also for carrying to and from their work the running water to wash their ore. This is done in the following manner:—The Bar-master takes with
him two of the twenty-four jurymen, and walking between them, with his and their arms extended, they walk from the mine, to the most
convenient place, they can soonest come to the
king's high road, pricking down peggs or stakes
on each side as they go along; and within those
stakes, the miner may carry to, and from, the
mines, whatever and whenever he pleases; even

if it was standing corn.* By article XLIV. it
is provided, " that if any miner be killed or
slain, or 'damped upon the mine, within any
groove; neither Escheator, Coroner, nor other
officer, ought to meddle therewith, but the Bar-
master or his Deputy." By article XIII. it is
enacted, " that no person ought to, sue any
miner for debt, that doth belong unto the
mines, in any court but the mineral court; and
if any person do the contrary, he shall lose his
debt, and pay the charges in the law." By
article XXXII. it is provided, that " no officer
ought for trespass or debt, to execute or serve
any writ, warrant, or precept, upon any miner being at his work in the mine; nor when
the miners come or go to the Barmote Court,
but the Bar-master, or his deputy only." By
article XLVIII. it is also enacted, " that if any
person or persons, feloniously take away any
ore, or other materials from any groove, shaft,
or meare of ground, houses, coves, or smelting-
houses, or elsewhere; if it be under the value
of thirteen-pence halfpenny, the Bar-master
shall punish the offender in the stocks, or otherwise, as it is fit for such offenders to be pu-
nished. But if the ore or other materials, be

---

* Miner's Guide, p. 34.

above thirteen-pence halfpenny in value, then we say it is felony."

The method of discovering veins of *lead ore* is various; but the practical miner is led to believe, where a vein is likely to be found, by the nature and quality of the ground and stone: and as most veins that are situated in the bowels of the earth, have some branch that proceeds from the main vein, nearly to the surface of the earth, he need only turn up a little of the earth to be satisfied. Veins of lead ore, are commonly distinguished by the names of *Pipe*, *Rake*, and *Flat* works.

A *pipe work* lies between two strata of lime-stone regularly extending above and below. The whole body of the pipe, generally consists of several ranges or branches, that run parallel to each other, and tend to one level at last.— Sometimes the rock is pierced through by these branches; and, in that case, it is best to follow its course, as they often lead to a fresh range. Should no ore be discovered on such a pursuit, the breadth of the work is ascertained: its length is indeterminate, depending much on the dipping of the measure. A pipe work has commonly two levels, which are called the *upper* and *nether* levels; and sometimes more.

A *rake work* is known by its being bounded,

M

by two solid sides of rock or stone; running in
a direct line from its foundation for several
meares, and sometimes miles; and penetrating
many fathoms into the earth. It seldom varies
from the first range in which it was discovered;
unless, (as is the case sometimes) it lead to a *pipe
work*; and then it is called both *rake* and *pipe*.

A *flat work* is not confined between any two
sides, or bounded to any particular by-skirt compass; but spreads itself every way, and keeps
one level. It does not lie very deep in the
earth; but resembles the pipe work by being
confined between a roof and sole; but it spreads
wider, and seldom extends above a hundred
yards. It is sometimes found near the surface
in the solid rock, and is very weak and poor,
being seldom thicker than a man's finger. •

The veins of lead ore, are generally enclosed
in a yellow, red, or black soil; and are found
connected with cauk, spar, or some other mineral. The pipes seldom penetrate the strata,
but follow the dip of the country in which they
are found. The rakes, are still more irregular
in their direction: in the High Peak they, generally, point East and West; and in the Wapentake, North and South. It is not uncommon, for two veins, to cut each other at right
angles; and sometimes, the pipe and rake unite,

and run together for a considerable way, thus forming a rich and strong vein.

The lead ore in Derbyshire, like that found in most other places, contains silver; but not a sufficient quantity, to repay the expences attendant on the separation. This was found, by the attempts that were made, some years ago, to extract it; but the event not answering the expectations of those who were engaged in it, the object was given up, and no such works now exist in the county.

The lead ore, most commonly found here, is that known by the name of *galena:* it lies generally in larger and smaller veins and masses; frequently in nodules with *cauk*—another name for barytes. One sort of galena is found crystallized in cubes, with the angles truncated; this is of a bright lustre and flaky fracture.— There is another variety, which, when broken, is remarkably bright and foliated; and by exposure to the atmosphere becomes tarnished, and decomposes. Another kind of galena, from its being very hard, is called, the steel-grained lead ore: this when broken, has a granulated appearance, resembling the fracture of steel. Small holes, with their surfaces black, as if corroded, are frequently observed, in the masses of galena. Carbonate of lead is some-

times seen on it, in various forms and states ;—
some of the crystals appearing semi-metallic,
others a dirty white, and some transparent.
The prism and the double hexagonal pyramids,
joined at the base, are the most general shapes.
" *Slikenside*, is a singular variety of galena, of
a bright metallic lustre, with a reflection approaching that of a mirror. It appears thinly
plated on one side of a substance called *kevel*
or *keble*, and usually forms the side of a vein,
or cavity; but sometimes composes a kind of double vein, the smooth surface on each side being
closely in contact, though without the least degree of cohesion. When pierced by the miner's
tool, or divided by a sharp iron wedge, it first
begins to crackle, and in a few minutes, rends
with considerable violence, exploding with a
noise as if blasted with gun-powder. The miners are sometimes wounded by the fragments,
when, regardles of the danger, they neglect
to retreat sufficiently early ; in these cases,
they are often cut violently, as if they had been
stabbed in various places with a chissel. This
extraordinary phenomenon, has never been satisfactorily explained : its occurrence is chiefly
confined to the *Haycliff* and *Lady-Wash* mines
at Eyam, and the *Odin* mine at Castleton. In
the former a prodigious explosion happened in

the year 1738; at which time Mr. Whitehurst affirms, the quantity of 200 barrels of minerals were blown out at one blast; each barrel being supposed to contain, three and four hundred weight. During the explosion, the surface of the ground was observed to shake, as if by an earthquake."*

A variety of carbonate lead sometimes occurs, not adhering to the galena. Masses of a horn colour, semi-transparent, and crystallized on the surface, have been found; and other carbonated nodules, easily reduced to a sandy powder, are often found in a loose ferruginous earth. There is an argillaceous variety, called wheat-stone found in a large vein: this, in general, contains arsenic; is of a light stone colour, heavy, with black spots. It is not transparent; the fracture earthy, with a few metallic scales: this is extremely easy of fusion, and during the operation it emits a strong smell of sulphur and arsenic. Phosphate of lead, of a leek green colour, in hexagonal prisms, is sometimes discovered on barytes attached to a sand stone. Molybeate of lead, of a fine yellow colour, sometimes appears in the cavities of gale-

---

* Beauties of England, p. 324.

na, and of carbonated lead : but this variety is not often met with.*

The miners have four terms by which they denominate their ore, according to its quality: the largest and best is called *Bing;* the next which is almost equal in quality and size, is termed *Pesey;* the third, which passes through the sieve in washing, is named *Smitham;* and the fourth, which is caught by a very slow stream of water, is stiled *Belland;* this is inferior to the rest, owing to the admixture of foreign qualities. All the ore that comes from the mine, is beaten and knocked into small pieces, and afterwards washed and sifted before it is sold: this part of the business is performed by women and children, who are employed by the miners for a very trifling remuneration.

The ore being thus prepared, is taken to the smelting furnaces. In former times, the business of smelting the ore into lead, was accomplished by the means of wood fires; and on the western side of the highest hills in the neighbourhood of Wirksworth and Crich, the work was carried on from time immemorial. But this imperfect method was laid aside, and followed

* Mawe's Mineralogy.

by a mode of smelting, which though rude
and defective, was an improvement upon it.—
The *hearth furnace*, consists of large rough
stones, placed so as to form an oblong cavity,
about two feet wide, fourteen long, and two
deep; into which fuel and ore are put in alternate layers: the heat is raised by a large pair
of bellows. The fuel is wood and coal; and
when the heat becomes sufficient to smelt the
ore, the lead runs out at an opening in the
the front of the furnace, into a trough placed
before the hearth; from whence it is conveyed
into moulds, and cast into blocks, called half-
pigs. This lead is very soft, pure, and duc-
tile; but owing to the imperfection of this manner of smelting, a considerable quantity of metal remains mingled with the slags: these are
therefore thrown again into the furnace, and
the metal disengaged from them, by a powerful fire of cokes: but the lead produced by this
second process, is inferior in quality to the
former.

At present, however, there is but a small portion of ore smelted in this way; and the *hearth*
has almost entirely given place to the introduction of the *copula furnace*. The copula
furnace, invented by a physician of the name
of Wright, is of an oblong form, resembling a

long, but not very deep chest; the top and
bottom being a little concave. The fire being
placed upon iron bars, at the height of three
or four feet, at one end, and a chimney being
built at the other extremity; the flame is drawn
over the ore placed in the body of the furnace,
and by its reverberation, smelts it, without
coming into contact with the fuel. One of
these furnaces will hold a ton of ore; but the
usual charge is, about eighteen hundred weight.
The time required for fusing this quantity, is
indeterminate; as some kinds of ore will be
ready in six hours, while others require seven,
eight, or nine, according to the nature of the
substances attached to them. That which is
united to spar, is the most easy of fusion; and
it is customary, sometimes, to throw a small
quantity of this mineral into the furnace, to
accelerate the progress; but in general, the minerals which are combined with the ore, assisted by a little coal slack, are sufficient to smelt
it. The lead, after it is smelted, is poured into
moulds of various sizes; for the blocks are of
different weights, according to the markets
for which they are intended: either Hull,
Bawtry, or London. Two of these blocks make
a pig, and eight pigs make a *fodder*.

But all the lead in Derbyshire, is not dis-

posed of in this state or form. A portion of
it is rolled, in works erected for the purpose, in
the neighbourhood of the furnaces, into sheets
for various uses. A considerable quantity is,
also, converted into *Red Lead*, by the mer-
chants and smelters, who reside in different
parts of the county. This process is accomplished in a kind of oven, having its floor divided into three apartments: the middle one
contains the metal, and the two others the fire.
The heat is reverberated from the roof on the
metal, and converts it to a calx or powder.—
Great care is requisite for the due regulation
of the heat: but with the nicest adjustment, it
seldom happens that the metallic principle, is
entirely destroyed by the operation: it therefore becomes necessary, to separate the calcined part from it; for this purpose, it is ground
very small in a mill, and then washed. After
that, the calcined part is again exposed to the
heat of the furnace, and being continually
stirred, acquires a red colour, and is fit for use.
The annual produce of lead from the Derbyshire mines, is not exactly ascertained; but
may be estimated at an average, between five
and six hundred tons. It is generally thought
to be on the decline; some of the richest mines
being either exhausted, or become more diffi-

cult to work; but on the other hand, from the improvements in the art of smelting, and the more effectual methods employed to clear the mines of water, by new levels and improved fire engines; advantages have been gained, that may perhaps supply the deficiency.*

The greatest impediments, that the miners find in working the mines, are foul air and water. To relieve them from the first, a pipe or tube is generally introduced down the shaft, and extended along the roof of the gallery, to the place where the miners are at work; and thus a free circulation of air is obtained. Many adits, or as they are here called, soughs, have been opened from the bottom of some neighbouring valley, and made to communicate with the works by different channels or galleries, for the purpose of carrying off the water. The most considerable adit in Derbyshire is at Youlegrave, running from the Derwent to Alport; and called the Hilcar Sough. It is two miles in length, and was driven at the expence of £30,000. The miners pay a certain proportion of lead ore to the proprietors as a duty; but as they have now penetrated below the level of the adit, their works are but ineffectu-

ally drained by it, But the relieving of the
mines at Wirksworth, is only a secondary object of this adit at present; as the water delivered by it at Cromford, has proved of very
great value :—The stream is employed in working the extensive cotton works, that are carried
forward at that place ; and as it is not liable to
any considerable increase or diminution, it has
proved to be of very great advantage.

There is another *sough* driven from the level
of the Derwent, and is called Wirksworth-
Moor sough :—it is situated to the East of that
town, and nearly three miles in length. It has
been observed, that a low level, in the limestone, drains a large tract of country ; all the
waters falling into it for a considerable distance.*

Iron:—the ore of this metal is found in very
great abundance, in all those tracts of country
where coal has been discovered ; the Chinley-
hills in the vicinity of Chapel-en-le-Frith excepted. It lies at different depths in the bowels of the earth: and, frequently, from the
great dipping of the strata, appears on the surface of the ground. When this happens to be
the case, a hole like the the shaft of a coal pit,

---

* Beauties of England, III. p. 302.

is made : which being gradually enlarged every
way, in the search after the ore, assumes the
shape of a bell. After penetrating in this way,
for about eighteen yards, the pursuit there, is
given up, and a new pit sunk, of a similar
depth and form. Owing to this practice of mixing the lower beds, with the soil near the surface ; the land receives greater injury by working of iron mines, than those of coal ; whence
it is not thought worth while, to dig for iron
ore, unless the beds are thought to be very valuable.

The beds of iron ore, are various in their
thickness; but generally from two to twelve
inches. The most valuable that have hitherto
been found, are those in Morley Park near
Heage, at Wingerworth, Chesterfield, and Stavely. The ores found at these places are various
in texture and colour :—Those of the argillaceous kind, are the most common, and most frequently used in the iron works :—" They form
a thin stratum in the coal countries, and sometimes enclose shells and coralloids. Calcareous,
or sparry iron ores, of a fine brownish red colour, sometimes bright yellow, scaly, and dirty
brown, are found in amorphous masses, near
the surface, and filling insulated places. The
calcareous matter seems predominant: the crys-

tallization is frequently preserved, or appears
in different stages of decomposition. This
kind is very useful to mix with other iron ores,
and is said to make a good iron for converting
into steel."*

The ore, after it is taken out of the mine, is
burned in the open air, in beds, first with coke
and then with slack; and afterwards broken into pieces and screened. It is then taken to the
furnaces: these are of a circular or conical form;
having a fire with the blast at bottom. After
the furnace is built, some time is requisite to
prepare it for use. A small fire is first made
under the timp, and fuel is continually added,
until it is raised as high as the mouth of the
newly erected furnace; when it is filled to about
half its height, the blast is employed; so that
the walls are not liable to be injured by a too
sudden and strong heat. When the furnace is
thus duly prepared and seasoned, the process
of smelting the ore begins. Fuel, ore, and
flux, in alternate layers, are continually put in
day and night; and the fire is not suffered to
go out, till the furnace wants repairing; which
is sometimes a period of many years. The fuel
is generally coke, though charcoal is sometimes

used; and the flux is, universally, limestone.
The process of smelting, occupies different
times, according to the size of the furnace, and
other circumstances. Different sorts of iron
are produced by varying the proportions of ore,
flux, and fuel. The smelting of the ore is accelerated by the application of a blast, produced by a pair of cylinders, which are worked by a fire engine or water wheel. When the
fusion of the ore commences, the smelted metal passes through the layers of coke and limestone; and collecting at the bottom of the furnace, is let out into beds of sand, moulded to
the forms required: these are called pigs, about
three feet and a half in length, and weighing
about 100 pounds. The metal first obtained,
is brittle and void of due malleability; but to
give it this property, and to adapt it to the various uses for which it is employed, it is carried
to the forge, where it is wrought into bars.—
The quantity of iron produced annually in this
county, amounts to between fifteen and sixteen
thousand tons. The principal founderies and for-
ges, are those at Butterley near Ripley, Morley
Park, Wingerworth, Chesterfield, and Stavely.

Calamine: or native oxid of zinc, is found
at Castleton, Cromford, Bonsall, and Wirksworth. It occurs of various colours, and dif-

ferent qualities. It is found in nodules, after
enveloping calcareous spar, which it soon decomposes. It has sometimes been found in the
figure of the rhombic and dog-tooth spar;
and frequently occurs in the form of grapes.—
It is sometimes in an ochreous state, combined
with ferruginous matter; but the compact kind
is the best, and is most esteemed when of a
waxy colour. It generally contains about sixty pounds per cwt. of zinc, and some iron. It is
found at various depths, but generally near a
vein of lead ore. Sometimes the two minerals
are mixed, and run by the side of each other
for a considerable way: but generally the vein
of one mineral ceases, where the other begins;
and a good vein of both is never found in the
same place. Calamine generally lies in a bed
of yellow, or reddish brown clay. The beds
resemble pipe works, and their direction is the
same with the dip of the measures.

The calamine, when got out of the mine, is
first washed in a current, and then again in
sieves in a vessel of water; and all the foreign
particles, as cauk, spar, and lead ore, are
picked out from it. It is next calcined in a re-
verberatory furnace; nearly of the same form
and construction with the copula, but having
a flat roof and bottom; after which it is again

picked, ground into a fine powder, and washed: it is then fit far use. The quantity of calamine at present annually produced in Derbyshire, is about 500 tons. Its value in its crude state, is from three to four pounds per ton; but in its prepared state, it is sold at nine or ten.*

A century and a half ago the miners were entirely ignorant of the properties, and value, of calamine; and it is not fifty years since its use in the composition of brass, and bell metal, was made a secret of in this county. After being calcined and powdered, it is mixed with charcoal and copper, in thin plates, or in grains, and exposed to a heat, at first not sufficient to melt the copper, but afterwards increased; so that the mass, which is a compound of the two metals, is fused, and is now called brass.†— Zinc, which is the name of the metal produced from the ore of calamine, has of late years been rolled, by a gentleman of Derby, into sheets; and recommended as a substitute for sheet-lead. But a more valuable purpose for which Zinc is used, is for exhibiting the phænomena produced by Galvanism; a science as yet in its infancy, but promising very great discoveries in the material world.

---

* Aikin's Description.   † Shrimshire's Chymical Essays, Vol. II. p. 61.

Blende, or *Black-jack*, also got in Derbyshire, is another ore of zinc, less valuable than
calamine. It occurs in various colours and
qualities, frequently crystallized, and generally accompanying fluor and barytes. The colour of this ore is a blackish brown, inclining
to a metallic lustre, and partially transparent.
There is a variety of this ore, called *ruby blende*,
which is crystallized on calcareous spar, and of
a beautiful transparent red. Another variety,
is called *pigeon-necked blende*, from its iride-
scent hues.

Copper :—This metal, has hitherto been
found only in a small quantity in the county.
Pieces considerable in size, detached from any
vein, have been frequently met with, at Matlock and Bonsall. A slender vein of this ore
has been discovered some years since at Great-
rock Dale, between Tideswell and Buxton;
and another has been met with at Russop-Edge,
near Chapel-en-le-Frith: but at present neither
is worked.

Pyrites ;—a combination of sulphur, with
iron, arsenic, and vitriol; are found in very
great variety, in almost every part of the county. Some are found in a bright coloured vein,
running through transparent fluor, and very
beautiful, at Ashover: and also other varieties

4   o

of a golden colour, sprinkled over the surface
of the fluor. The pyrites generally found, are
exceedingly hard, and strike fire with steel.

   Black-wad, an ore of manganese and iron
has been found in different parts of the county,
in masses, of a dark brown, or blackish colour: when broken, capillary veins, of a metallic lustre, appear. When mixed with lin-
seed oil, it becomes ignited in the space of forty or fifty minutes. It is esteemed by painters
for its drying quality; and is very much used
for ship painting. Manganese is one of the
principal ingredients consumed for producing
gas for the process of bleaching: but that
which is met with in Derbyshire, has been
found of too weak a quality for that purpose.
In an analysis of this mineral, by Mr. Wedgewood, twenty-two parts, were found to contain
nearly two of indissoluble earth, chiefly micace-
ous, one of lead, about nine and a half of iron,
and the same quantity of manganese.

   Martial ochres, are extremely abundant.—
They are supposed to result from the decomposition of iron ores; which is accomplished by
water and fixed air. The best, of a rich yellow colour, is found in a cavern, called the
Water-hull, near Castleton. Dark brown ochre
is met with in the lead mine, under the High

Tor, at Matlock; a pale yellow ochre is to be found in a mine near Winster; and balls of a darker yellow are found in the shale at Hassop. The colours of these ochres are said to be the most durable pigments in nature.

Coal.—Whether this mineral had been discovered in Derbyshire, in the time of the Romans, is uncertain; but as it seems probable, that it was dug up in a neighbouring county,†

* The most probable supposition with respect to the *origin of coals* is:—that at some former time, (perhaps at the time of the deluge, according to Moses's account) the earth was covered with water; and that the trees and other vegetables, collecting in strata at the bottom; and mixing with an immense quantity of sea weeds and sea animals; and being afterwards covered with clay or sand, and undergoing a gradual decomposition; have formed so many strata of coal. That coal is of vegetable origin, is evident from the variety of vegetable remains and impressions, that are found both in the strata of coal, and in the earthy strata above and below them. That it is of submarine origin, also appears from the presence of shells, petrified fish, and other productions of the ocean. The erroneous popular opinion, that coals grow like vegetables; so that mines that have been once worked out, may be opened and worked again in a series of years; is, like many other ridiculous opinions, given up, from its inconsistency with reason and experience.

† In the West-Riding of Yorkshire, are many beds of cinders, heaped up in the fields; in one of which, a number of Roman coins, was found a few years ago. From Horsley, it appears, that there was a colliery at Benwell, about four miles West of Newcastle-upon-Tyne, supposed to have been actually worked by the Romans.

coal is but little sulpbureous, and yields a large quantity of ashes. That which is found at Newhall and Measbam, is very nearly of the same kind.

The coal near Buxton is sbattery and exceedingly sulphureous."*

Coals are always found under strata of grit, which is a mixture of sand and clay; or under schistus, which is clay hardened, and splitting into layers, forming either slates, or a substance called shivers, according to its fracture. When a stratum of coal is come to, that is considered worth the working, it is dug out from the superior and inferior strata, which are generally grit, or schistus, and which are then termed the roof and floor. In doing this, care is always taken, to leave columns of the coal standing here and there, sufficient to support the roof. When a roof is shivery, it is frequently necessary to support it with a roof of timber. These means being taken to support the superior stratum, the miners proceed to very considerable distances from the original pits; and occasionally new shafts or pits are sunk, to facilitate the removal of the coals, and to afford a proper ventilation in the mines.

* Pilkington, Vol. I. p. 179.

The first operation after sinking the engine-pit of a coal mine, is the working or driving in the coal, and sinking the first coal pit. After the pit is sunk to the coal, the miner begins his work: he first digs or undermines with his pick-axe, at the bottom and one side, into the seam or stratum as far as he can; he then forces down the great pieces of coal, by a wedge and mallet. The coals thus procured are brought to the bottom of the pit in corves or baskets, which are hooked upon a chain, and drawn or wound up by a rope to the surface. This is often effected by a machine called a gin, wrought by horses. But of these winding ma-chines, there are various kinds; some worked by water, and others by fire engines.

There are two very great evils, to which coal mines are subject; the hydrogen gas, called by the workmen, *fire damp;* by the explosion of which many lives are lost: and carbonic acid gas, commonly called *choak damp,* which is not so fatal as the former. Hydrogen gas is principally generated by the contact of pyrites with water, in some of the old workings of the collieries, which have been neglected, and not sufficiently ventilated: it there accumulates until discovered by the occasional visit of some of the overmen, whose office it is to examine

the old workings, called *wastes*. Sometimes
for want of due caution it causes the death of
many of the miners, being set on fire by their
lights. On these occasions the men throw
themselves on their faces, on the ground, to
avoid the return of the blast, as there is more
danger to be apprehended, from the vacuum
formed by the total consumption of the infla-
mable gas, than from the effect which the fire
has upon them. It seldom happens after the
explosion, that the men are much burnt; they
suffer more from the violent concussion of atmospheric air, rushing into the workings to
fill up the vacuum, than from any other cause.
After an accident of this kind, it is considered
dangerous to enter the pit for some days, on
which account it is to be feared, many lives are
lost, which might have been saved by immediate assistance.

But the only effectual method of preventing
accidents of this nature, is to pay a due atten- ·
tion to the state of the old works, and to cause
a thorough ventilation by the methods usually
adopted, which are the following:—The air is
put in motion, by means of a furnace placed
near the edge of one of the shafts, inclosed in
a covered building, from which is a tube descending into the pit. The heated air thus as-

cending through the chimney, is succeeded by
the cold from the shaft, which in its turn is
replaced from the lowest part of the mine.—
The whole is thus successively removed, and
its place is supplied by air which finds its way
from above, through another communication-
shaft open to the day.

Choak damp is rarely attended with any ill
effects, and is easily discovered, by its ex-
tinguishing a candle. The safest method of
exploring collieries subject to this evil, is to
walk as erect as the place will allow; for
choak damp being heavier than atmospheric
air, occupies, of course, the lower part of the
mine. It is more difficult to exhaust this gas
by ventilation, than fire damp; as the latter
ascends, from its being lighter than atmospheric air; whilst the other, by its gravity, is forced
upwards with great difficulty. It is not exactly determined, by what means choak damp is
generated; but it is generally supposed to proceed from the putrefaction of vegetable substances.*

Pieces of coal of a very large size, sometimes
weighing upwards of three and four hundred
pounds, are found in the Derbyshire mines:
but what quantity is got every year, it is im-

* Cyclopædia, v. Coal.

4   D

possible to ascertain exactly; it is certainly
very large: for besides the home consumption,
which is very great, a considerable portion is
conveyed by the Errewash canal into Leicestershire, and by the Chesterfield into Nottinghamshire; besides the large quantities, that are sent
to Sheffield and London.

Sulphur; has been met with, in the cellular
parts of baroselenite, and also in galena. It
has been found in a layer four inches thick in
the mines at Haslebage near Bradwell; and in
a layer of one inch thick in the toadstone at
Tideswell-moor. It was in so pure a state in
these places, that it would flame with a candle. Sulphur has also been discovered in the
Odin mine at Castleton; and sometimes in the
shale, in different parts of the county.

But of all the " inflammable substances discovered in this county, the most peculiar and
remarkable is the *elastic* bitumen, or mineral
cahqutchouc. This has been found in various
states; and has apparently the same properties,
as the common vegetable India rubber. It is
generally found between the stratum of the
schistus and the limestone; *rarely* in small cavities, adhering to the *gangert,** and sometimes

---

* *Gangert,* a term derived from the German, is synonymous
with the *matrix.*

containing lead ore, fluor, and other bodies.—
When first detached, the taste is very styptic, as
if blended with decomposed pyrites. It varies
in colour, from the blackish or greenish brown,
to the light and red brown, and is easily compressed; but sometimes the same piece is less
elastic in one part than another: on burning it
the smell is rather pleasant. One variety, but
very rare, contains nodules of indurated shining
black bitumen, resembling jet. Another variety has been seen in a *marine shell*, in a piece
of limestone. A third variety, but extremely
scarce, has been found of a dull red colour,
and transparent, in crystallized fluor. A variety yet more rare, but less elastic, appears to
be composed of filaments, and has a singular
acid taste. ' The characteristics are very different from any other sort, and might probably,
if investigated, account for the origin of this
substance: on cutting, and in other circumstances, it resembles soft cork, or old bark from
a tan-yard.' Indurated bitumen, appearing
like jet, has been found in amorphous masses,
and in globules of a shining black, but sometimes liver-coloured: this kind is electric,
when rubbed, and is sometimes found in barytes. A specimen has been met with in the
centre of an anomia at Castleton. Petroleum,

or rock-oil, is found in veins of the black marble, at Ashford; when the sun shines upon the
stone, it gently exudes. Stones containing a
considerable quantity of rock-oil were formerly met with near Stoney-Middleton; and were
so common, that the miners used to burn the
oil they produced in lamps."

Limestone; which is found in the places before noticed,* is of various qualities. At Buxton, Peak-forest, and Stoney-Middleton, it is
of a light grey colour: at Ticknal and Kniveton, it is very dark: at Hopton it is of a light
colour, hard, and abounding with small fragments of etrochi. When burned into lime, it
is much used for the purposes of agriculture in
the county; but particularly in the northern
part. A great quantity is sent into Cheshire
and Lancashire. The Crich lime is remarkably white, and much valued for ceilings and
other ornamental purposes. The Kniveton
lime, is thought nearly equal to that of Barrow
in Leicestershire.

Marble.—The marbles formed from the limestone, are extremely varigated and beautiful.
That which is called the Hopton stone, is found
at Hopton near Wirksworth; it is of a light

* Page 57.

colour, hard, but incapable of much polish:. it abounds with fragments of etrochi, and is much used for hearths, floors, and staircases. The mottled grey marble is found in many places, but particularly near Moneyash: and though there is a great diversity of shade in its ground, it may be divided into two kinds; the one with a slight tint of blue, the other a lightish grey, rendered exceeding beautiful by the number of purple veins, which over-spreads its surface in elegant and irregular branches. But that which renders the mottled grey marble so beautiful, is, the abundance of etrochi; which being intersperced through every part of it, the transverse and longitudinal sections produce an infinite variety of forms. It has been observed, that the more superficial the beds of marble, the lighter its colour, and the more abundant the etrochi. A variety is found near Wetton, of a darker colour, pre-senting very small figures, whence it has ob-tained the name of *bird's-eye* marble. The black marble is found chiefly at Ashford, where it may be obtained in very large blocks: but the strata in which it is found differ in quality. In general it is of a close solid texture, and will bear such a high polish, as to reflect like a mirror. It bears a strong resemblance to that

brought from Namur in the Netherlands. Coralloid marbles, exhibiting a variety of madrepores, are found in laminæ in various parts
of the limestone strata.

The black and grey marbles, are calcareous,
effervesce with the mineral, and are corroded
by the vegetable acids of the fermented and un-
fermented kind. The specific gravity of the
black kind, when compared with the grey, is
as twelve to thirteen.

Plater-stone, *Gypsum*, or *Alabaster*, has been
found at Elvaston and Chellaston, in large
masses, filling up cavities, in the argillaceous
grit. It never forms a stratum, but is attended
with gravel, strong red clay, and an earthy
covering, which often contains innumerable
shells. Some kinds are very hard, and of a
close texture; but it is in general so soft, that
it may be scraped with the nail. This substance derives its names, from the different
uses to which it is applied. A considerable
quantity is used for laying floors in buildings,
and it is thence called plaster-stone. To prepare it for this purpose, it is first burnt about
eight hours in the open air: when this is done,
the fire is put out, and when properly cooled,
it is beaten fine with flails, and made into
mortar. It is then spread, about two inches

in thickness upon reeds or laths covered with straw; and being afterwards left to dry, in a few days, a floor, almost as solid and durable as stone, will be formed. The expence of these floors is but trifling; but to a stranger they have a curious and uncomfortable appearance; as in many houses, not only are the floors of the ground story composed of this substance, but those also of the upper ones; thus appearing like one large cold flag, cut out to fit the the dimensions of the room. In its calcined state, when mixed with water, it forms the substance called *Plaster of Paris*. It is also extremely useful, when calcined, for moulds of figures, and even for the figures themselves: and for this purpose, it is an article of great demand at the potteries in Staffordshire. In this state it is also mixed with quick lime, to make the mortar set more strongly; and is therefore found very useful in the formation of cornices, and mouldings, and other ornamental purposes in architecture. In its native state it is called *Alabaster* and *Gypsum*; and as it takes a very high polish, it is manufactured into large columns, chimney pieces, vases, small obelisks, and an infinite variety of ornaments. Gypsum forms an article of commerce, and considerable quantities are conveyed to London and other places.

mer: pellucid quartz in fragments, colourless:
some enclosing bitumen; these varieties are
loose in the limestone: thin laminated beds of
chert, horn-stone, or petrosilex, are found near
Bradwell, Buxton, Middleton, and other places. In the Peak-forest, are numerous chert
beds of various thicknesses; some are in contact with the granulated limestone, though limestone full of shells is both above and below it;
its colour is dove blue. Large quantities of
this substance are annually used in the manufacture of earthen ware in Yorkshire and Staffordshire. Dark green chert, bearing a close
resemblance to jasper, has been found near the
high Tor at Matlock."*

"Of the *Barytic* order, the most general is
the substance called *cauk* or *cawk*, from its resembling chalk, which is not found in the North.
It occurs in great quantities, being commonly
attendant on lead ore; the colour is often white,
but more frequently a greyish white, inclining
to the cream tinge, which sometimes rises to
the ochre yellow. It is soft, but ponderous;
fracture earthy, sometimes scaly: it often contains small veins of lead ore, as thin as threads;
and sometimes small veins of fluor and blende.
Barytes occasionally occurs crystallized in ta-

---

bulated rhombs, or grit-stone; but more generally in delicate tabulated crystals, which, by combination, form spherical balls. One variety is stalactitic, sometimes with transparent crystals and native sulphur. The arborescent barytes, is composed of ligaments of various colours, intervening each other, appearing somewhat like branches with foliage: one variety exhibits dark brown and lilac figures, beautifully interspersed with blue in a geographic form, or like a coloured map, and affording beautiful contrasts. Barytes has lately been found, confusedly crystallized, of a sky blue colour; the fracture foliated. Other specimens occur in tabulated crystals, opake, white, half an inch in diameter, but as thin as leaf gold, on a cellural gypseous matrix, with native sulphur. Another variety has a plumose appearance, being covered with transparent crystals of fluor.*"

Porcelain Clay of a delicate white colour, and fine texture, has been got from a lead mine near Brassington. Some of this has been used at the porcelain works in Derby; but the greatest part of what is now dug up, is sent to the Staffordshire potteries.

Pipe Clay, of a pretty good quality, is got
at Newhaven and Bolsover. At the latter and
some other places, pipes are manufactured from
it, in its native and unmixed state.

Potter's Clay, of a yellowish or grey colour,
is found at Brampton, Stanwich near Chesterfield, Morley-moor, Heage, Smalley, and Horsley. Some of a red and grey colour is found
at Ticknall; but this is never used for the glazed ware, because it corrodes the lead. That
which is called *indurated clay* or *bind*, and
used for the improvement of land of a light
and sandy soil, is found in most coal pits.—
Clay-stone, is found in a great extent of country on the eastern side of Derbyshire.

Terra tripolitana; or as it is generally called,
rotten-stone, is found in the neighbourhood of
Bakewell; and is much used by the lapidaries,
in different parts of the county, for polishing.

Marl, a compound of clay and calcareous
earth, is found in great plenty in almost every
part of Morleston hundred. It is generally of
a red colour; but sometimes it is met with, of
a grey, and light flesh colour. One sort
of red marl, which has the appearance of a
thin shattery stone, contains but little calcareous earth, and is found very beneficial to
light or boggy land. But there is another kind

of red marl, which is more valuable; as it is found to be a very efficacious and durable manure: especially when mixed with a proportion of dung.

Slate, or *schistus tegularis*, is dug up at Hayfield, and in Chinley-hills, near Chapel-en-le-Frith. What is found is of a grey colour, and lamellar texture, shines with mica, and does not strike fire with steel. Though thick, and consequently very heavy, it is much used in covering houses, in the neighbourhood of the places where it is got.

Flint is found in small pieces, in the gravel pits in the neighbourhood of Derby; and in large lumps, in those at Stenson in the parish of Barrow. They are pure, and almost transparent.

Chert, a substance less hard and more opake than flint, is found in strata; and may be discovered running through the rocks in the Peak. A large quantity of it, is carried from the neighbourhood of Bakewell, into Staffordshire and Yorkshire; where it is used in the manufacture of earthen ware. Some kinds of chert are made into mill-stones.

Moor-stone is found in the north-west part of the county, and the East-moor. Mill-stones are made of this substance, on Kinder-scout

in the parish of Glossop; and at Grindleford
Bridge in the parish of Eyam.

Free stone is found in many places in the
the county; and in some quarries it is of a
very fine texture. The most magnificent and
beautiful houses in Derbyshire, are built of this
stone.

Peat, either white or red, according to the
quantity of ochre or pyrites which it contains,
is found throughout the north-west extremity
of the Peak, and most parts of the East-moor.
When the peat is dug up, it is soft, smooth, and
oily; but being cut into oblong pieces, and
exposed to the influence of the sun and air, during the warm summer months, it becomes brittle and inflammable, and is in many places
used for fuel. *Turf* is a substance that generally covers the peat; but in some places it is
found alone. It is a yellowish or brownish bituminous earth, interwoven with the roots of
moss, heath, and other shrubs.

The *extraneous fossils* found in Derbyshire,
are worthy of notice, on account of their amazing number and variety. They occur in almost every part of the county; but some classes are more numerous than others. The etrochi, a species of star fish, are extremely abundant: and the number of anomiæ, is, likewise

very great : continued beds of the former may
be traced for upwards of twenty miles. Indeed,
the mountains of limestone, which extend
· through the High and Low Peak, seem to be
composed of marine productions.

Coralloids. The cone within cone coralloid,
is found in a bed ten inches deep, on the surface of the shell marble, at Tupton near Wingerworth ; the cones in this, are very distinct.
Another fine specimen of the same species, has
been found at Blackwell ; and a third at the
depth of forty-seven feet at Aldercar, in the parish of Heanor. Coralloids, with small tubes,
have been met with at Eyam, agreeing in every
particular, with the coral, lately found in the
red sea, named *tubularea purpurea: porpites*
and *madrepores,* have also been obtained at the
same place.

At Stoney-Middleton, some very perfect specimens of *pori fungitæ* have been met with ;
cornia fungitæ at Ashover, as well as the elegant screw stone. Millepores, coral, branched, with the surface and extremity punctured,
as if with the point of a needle ; and tubipo-
res, a congeries of coralline tubes, paralleled
or variously curved, have been procured at
Middleton Dale. Ammonites, cornu Ammo-
nis or nautilis, serpent stone, flat, spiral, repre-

senting a worm or small serpent coiled up, are
very abundant in the black marble of Ashford:
astroites, coral of tabular texture, with small
stars on the surface, and honey-comb work
within side, is likewise procured there.

At Castleton have been found, the *corallina
reticulata*, or sea fan: plates of *echini*, very
curiously formed, the plates pentagonal, with
a small point, rising in the middle: spines of
echini: *belemnites*, cylindrical, but conical at
one, and sometimes at both ends, about three
inches long, and three quarters of an inch
thick: anomiæ, bivalve, one valve gibbous,
and often perforated at the base, the other
plane: *retepores*, *terrebratulæ*, and *ostreopec-
tines*. *Gryphites*, bivalve, oblong, somewhat
resembling a boat, but narrow, and remarkably curved upwards at one end, the valve
plane, has been met with in the red clay over
the gypsum at Chellaston. *Rushes*, branches
of *yew*, and a substance greatly resembling a
cauliflower, have been found petrified at Matlock. A regular stratum of *muscle shells* has
been discovered, eleven yards deep, at Swanwick: and muscle shells have been found in
iron stone at Tupton, Chesterfield, and Cotmenhay: at the latter place, they were obtained at the depth of eighty-four yards.

Animals and *Insects.*—At Ashford, a small *alligator*, and groups of flies, have been found in the black marble. The tail and back of a *crocodile*, are said to have been found there also, and to be preserved in a cabinet at Brussels. A *beetle* and a *butterfly* have been found in iron-stone at Swanwick.

Vegetable Impressions.—An entire *sun-flower* with all the reeds perfectly marked, was discovered in iron-stone, over a bed of coal, at Swanwick. The following fossils were also obtained there: the resemblance of a *bamboo*, a flower of *chrysanthemum*, very perfect; a flower of *coltsfoot*; several kinds of *fern*; *equisetum* or *horse-tail*, very perfect; a plant of *maiden-hair*; the cone of a *pine tree*; a branch of a *box tree*; a small branched *moss*; these were found in iron-stone. At Holmesfield, a resemblance of the flower of a *cactus* has been found. Various other vegetable impressions, have been met with in the iron-stone, and bind, both at Newhall and Chesterfield. Indeed there are few beds of iron-stone in Derbyshire, in which they do not in some measure appear.

4　　　R

CHAP. IV.

*Civil division—Courts—Ecclesiastical division
—The town of Derby, &c.*

THE civil division of Derbyshire is into six
Hundreds:—The *High Peak Hundred*, in the
north-west; *Scarsdale Hundred*, in the north-
east; *Wirksworth Wapentake*, in the West;
Appletree Hundred, in the south-west; *Morleston Hundred*, in the south-east; and *Reppington Hundred*, in the South. At what period, this division of the county was made, is
very uncertain; but it seems to be of later date
than Doomesday book. There we meet with
the Scavedale wapentack, Hameleston wapentack, Morlestan wapentack, Walecross wapentack, and Pechelers: a division which appears
to be of Saxon origin; and bearing but little
correspondence to the present one.

At the time of the Norman survey, the land
in Derbyshire, like all others, in those feudal
times, was divided among seventeen proprietors;—King William, the Bishop of Chester,

the Abbey of Burton, Hugh the Earl, Roger of
Poictou, Henry de Ferieres, William Peverel,
Walter de Aincurt, Geoffrey Alselin, Ralph
the son of Hubert, Ralph de Burun, Huscuit
Musard, Gilbert de Gand, Nigel de Statford,
Robert the son of William, Roger de Busli, the
Thanes of the King.

Some remains, of what an elegant historian,*
calls, " the encroachments of the feudal nobles on the prerogative of their monarchs;
their usurping the administration of justice
with supreme authority, both in civil and criminal causes," are yet to be found in Derbyshire: these are the court of the duchy of Lancaster, and the Peverel court. To the duchy
of Lancaster, belong the honor of Tutbury and
the hundred of Appletree; and the courts of
pleas, (or as they are generally called the three
weeks courts) for the former, are regularly held
at Tutbury, and for the latter at Sudbury. In
these courts a steward presides: and all debts
and damages under forty shillings, due for
goods sold, servant's wages, labourer's hire,
agistment of cattle, rent, money lent, trespas-
ses, assaults, and several other things, are re-
coverable.

---

* Robertson: Charles V. vol. I. p. 66.

In the Peverel court, which is held at Lenton, near Nottingham, a steward also presides; and sometimes actions for the recovery of small debts are brought into it : as its proceedings are less expensive and more expeditious, than those in the courts of Westminster. Most of the towns and villages in the county, are comprised within the jurisdiction of these courts.

The county of Derby sends two members to parliament; a priviledge, which it is ascertained, it enjoyed as early as the twenty-third of Edward I.; but how much sooner, has not been discovered with certainty. The assizes are held at Derby, twice a year, spring and autumn : The Epiphany, the Easter and Michaelmas sessions for the county are also held at Derby; but the Midsummer at Chesterfield.— With respect to the common judicature, Derbyshire is included in the Midland circuit.

In ecclesiastical concerns, Derbyshire forms a part of the diocese of Lichfield and Coventry; and is divided into one archdeaconry and five deaneries :—which are the following: *Archdeaconry of Derby.* Deaneries of *Ashbourne, Castillar, Chesterfield, Derby* and *Reppington.*

In the following description, the ecclesiastical division will be adopted : beginning with the southern deaneries; but giving the prece-

dency to that of Derby, as the capital of the
county is situated in it.

DERBY.

THE town of Derby is situated in a valley;
extending and opening as it advances southward, into a fine and well cultivated plain. It
stands upon the western banks of the Derwent,
on ground a little elevated above the level of
the surrounding vale : its situation is, therefore,
very pleasant; and the scenery in its environs
extremely beautiful.

Antiquarians do not agree, in the derivation
of the word *Derby*. Historians inform us, that
during the Heptarchy, the Saxons called it
Northworthig; but of this appellation, not a
trace now remains. In the time of the Danes,
it was called *Deorby;* a word said to be compounded of two Saxon ones, signifying a habitation for deer. To support this derivation, it
is alleged, that the ground on which the town
now stands, was once a park, stocked with
deer. This appears to derive some probability

from the town's arms, exhibiting a buck couchant in a park; and from one of the lanes adjoining the town being called Lodge-lane.—
But when it is recollected, that a park was not
known in England until the arrival of the Normans, and a coat of armoury until a period
much later, and that Derby was a considerable
town before the introduction of either; it does
not appear very likely, that it derived its name
from *deer in a park*. The most probable conjecture is, that the name of the town, and that
of the river Derwent have the same origin;
that originally it was called *Derwentby*, or the
town by the Derwent; and that in process of
time this name was corrupted or abbreviated
into *Deorby* or *Derby*.

Derby is undoubtedly a place of great antiquity; but in what age, or by what nation, it
was founded, is impossible to determine. It
is supposed to have been a place of some consequence prior to the Roman invasion. That
people generally fixed their stations in the vicinity of some British town; and as it is ascertained that *Derventio* or *Little Chester* was one
of these: Derby therefore appears from its
small distance from it, to have existed before
the time of the Romans.

After the departure of the Romans, Derby

became a place of consequence, under their successors the Saxons. In the reign of Alfred, it was constituted the metropolis of the county: and in the beginning of the same reign, it was occupied by the forces of Haldene, a Danish chieftain, who took up his quarters there, for the winter of 874.* Alfred, after his memorable defeat of the Danish Prince Hubba, and the consequent submission of his followers, in 880, settled a colony of them at Derby; thus proposing to repeople this place; which, like many others in the kingdom of Mercia, had been laid waste and totally desolated, by the frequent inroads of those barbarians.† During the destructive conflicts, maintained between the Saxons and Danes, in subsequent reigns, Derby was alternately in the possession of both parties. In 918, the Danes being masters of it, were attacked by surprise, and completely routed, by the heroic Ethelfleda, daughter to Alfred, and Princess of the Mercians, who took possession of the town, and all that belonged to it.‡ Shortly after, the inhabitants were deprived of the protection of this masculine and ambitious heroine, by her death;§ and

* Chron. Sax. p. 82. † Hume, vol. I, p 84. ‡ Chron. Sax. p. 106.
§ W. Malmes. lib. II. chap. 5. Matth. West, p. 182.

the town once more fell into the hands of the
Danes. But in 942 king Edmund invaded
Mercia, and drove the Danes out of Derby, to-
gether with five other towns.*

Soon after the consolidation of the Heptarchy into a monarchy under Egbert, we find
that Derby was made a royal borough; or private property of the prince. The privileges
which it enjoyed by charter in these early times,
must have been very great: as, in the reign of
Edward the confessor, (1040) Derby contained
no less than 243 burgesses or freemen; possessed of property equal to many thousands in
our times. Forty-one burgesses had twelve
plough-gates of land belonging to the borough
divided among them; besides this, they held
twelve plough-gates (as much land as twelve
teams usually ploughed in the year,) of their
own. The meadow grounds were divided into
doles, and the tillage by meers. The freemen
held their land by a kind of copyhold right:
the King, the Earl, and the Church, being the
chief proprietors. The annual rent paid by the
borough to the crown, was twenty-four pounds.
At this time, there were fourteen corn-mills in
the town. Two parts of the profits arising

* Chron. Sax. p. 114.

from tax, tolls, forfeitures, and customs, belonged to the King, and the third to the Earl.

At the time of the Norman survey, Derby
was very much reduced. It could boast of no
more than a hundred burgesses, and forty who
were minors. The fourteen corn-mills were
reduced to ten; and there were a hundred and
three dwellings waste and empty. This un-
prosperous state was occasioned, no doubt, by
the change of government; and by the loss of
lives, in the endeavour to support Harold
against the Norwegian and Norman monarchs.

On the death of Edward the Confessor,
Harold ascended the throne; and when Há-
drada, king of Norway, invaded Northumberland in the year 1066, he was joined by the
ambitious and restless Earl Tostig, Harold's
brother. Edwin Earl of Mercia was much attached to Harold; and in order to assist him
against the invader, raised his vassals, which
very much thinned Derby. Edwin joined his
forces with those commanded by Morcard Earl
of Northumberland; and before Harold could
advance, gave battle to the enemy, and was
defeated. However, in a few days the Norwegian monarch was himself defeated by Harold, who had arrived from the southern coast.

By this time the Duke of Normandy had

landed at Pevensey, and Harold was under the necessity of returning to the coast of Sussex. Edwin, with his scattered forces, joined him in his march; and passing through Derby, again drained it of many of its inhabitants to recruit his ranks. They left their homes never to return! In the battle of Hastings most of them fell, and Derby for years did not recover its population.

, Harold being slain in this decisive battle, William took possession of the English throne, by a pretended destination of king Edward, and an irregular election of the people; while, in reality, he ascended it by the right of conquest. The conqueror, in order to establish himself firmly in the public interest, had promised his daughter in marriage to Edwin Earl of Mercia; but when that nobleman claimed the fulfilment of his promise, William gave him an absolute denial. This disappointment, added to many other reasons of disgust, induced Edwin to concur with several others of his incensed countrymen, to make a general effort for the recovery of their ancient liberties.* But the king, supported by many powerful leaders, advanced with celerity into the North, and

---

* Hume I. p. 245. ˙

came upon the rebels before they were in a condition to make resistance; and finding no other
means of. safety, they had recourse to the cle-
mency of the victor. The property of the Mercian Earl was confiscated; and Derby, with a
considerable rent-roll, was given to William
Peverel, a Norman captain,* and the illegiti-
mate son of the Conqueror. In order to encourage industry and to increase the population, the new possessor augmented the privileges of Derby by a new charter. But the
annual rent was raised from £24 to £30; and
twelve thraves, or about eighteen bushels of
corn; and as an equivalent for the surcharge,
the hamlet of Litchurch, was added to the
town.

Henry I. by a charter signed at the Devizes,
granted the town of Derby to Ralph Earl of
Chester. But Mr. Hutton† is of opinion, that
this grant extended not beyond the minority of
one of the Peverels. In the reign of this prince,
Derby was made a corporate town. The charter by which this was done, was altered and
improved by Henry II.; and renewed and enlarged by Richard I. and John. In the beginning of the reign of the latter, the corporation
and burgesses were sued in the Court of Ex-

chequer, for sixty-six marks* which they owed
for rent and the confirmation of their liberties:
and in the sixth of the same reign, they were
sued for sixty marks,† and two palfreys for
rent, and ten pounds for services; and having
such a charter as the burgesses of the town of
Nottingham: and again in the twelfth year of
the same reign, the burgesses of Derby were
charged forty pounds, for the fee-farm of the
town.

In the reign of Henry III. a power was granted to the burgesses of Derby and their heirs,
of not permitting a Jew to live in the town.

Edward III. in the beginning of his reign deprived the corporation of their liberties, and
summoned the burgesses to answer at the King's
Court, " By what authority they took a toll
and paid none? Why they claimed the exclusive privilege of dying cloth, and prohibiting
it in every place within thirty miles, except
Nottingham? By what right they had to be
toll-free throughout the king's dominions; to
choose a bailiff every year; and to have a fair
on Friday in Whitsun-week, another at the
festival of St. James, which continued seventeen days? What right they had to a coroner;
and not to be sued out of their own borough?

---

* About £1,980 in our time.   † About £1,300.

And by what authority they held markets on
Sunday, Monday, Wednesday, and from Thurs-
day-eve to Friday, every week?"

To shew that they were justified in their
proceedings, the burgesses produced the charters they had received from their different monarchs; and for the privilege of toll, laid before him, one which he himself had granted
them in the first year of his reign. Upon this
he was convinced of the justice of their cause;
and, on their consenting to pay a fine of forty
marks, restored to them the enjoyment of those
liberties which he had so unjustly questioned
and seized: and when they had promised to
pay a yearly rent of £46 16s. he established
them in the rights, enjoyed by their ancestors
from time immemorial.

James I. by a charter dated at Westminster,
the seventh of March, in the ninth year of his
reign, (1611) recapitulates and confirms many
of the privileges which had been granted in
former reigns; and further grants,—" that the
Bailiffs, Recorder, and Town Clerk, or any
three of them, shall have a power to keep a
Court of Record upon Tuesday in every second
week; shall be justices of peace for the year,
and the year ensuing their election to the office
of bailiffs; shall have the return of all writs,

and process, without the interference of any
foreign justice; shall have a power to keep
Quarterly Sessions, two Court Leets, and six
Fairs yearly; shall be toll-free throughout the
whole kingdom, and take toll and tillage from
all, except the Duchy of Lancaster, which shall
pay but half."

In 1638, Charles I. authorised, that the
power of the bailiffs should in future, be vested
in one person, who was to be chosen annually,
and called a Mayor.' At that time there were
two bailiffs; and it was agreed, that one of
them should enjoy the new honour for the first
year, and the other succeed him : but the successor dying before his mayoralty commenced,
the first mayor continued in office for two
years.

But this charter was surrendered to Charles
II. in the year 1680, and the present one obtained at the expence of nearly £400. The
corporation consists of a Mayor, nine Alder-
men, fourteen Brethren, fourteen Common
Council Men, a Recorder, a High Steward, a
Town Clerk, and six Constables.

The borough of Derby sends two Members
to Parliament; the right of whose election is
.vested in the freemen and sworn burgesses; and
the mayor is the returning officer. It is impos-

sible to ascertain, when the borough was first
represented in Parliament: the perfect list of
representatives commences, with the twenty-
third Parliament of Edward 1. in. the year
1294.

A Court of Requests is held every third Tuesday at the Guildhall. It was erected in the year
1766. The principal inhabitants of the town
are commissioners, three of whom constitute a
bench, under the direction of a clerk.

William, after his subjection of England,
was sensible that the want of fortified places
had greatly facilitated his conquest, and might
at any time facilitate his expulsion. He therefore made all possible haste to remedy the defect, by building magnificent. and strong castles in all the towns. " William," says Matthew Paris,* " exceeded all his predecessors, in
building castles, and greatly harassed his subjects and vassals with these works." In this
reign, or in the reign of Stephen in the subsequent century, " when every one that was able
built a castle, and the whole kingdom was covered with them,"† probably was erected the
Castle at Derby. " On the south-east corner
of the town," says Mr. Gibson,‡ " stood for-

* Hist. p. 8. col. 2.   † Chron. Sax. p. 238.
‡ In his Camden, p. 496.

merly a Castle; though there have been no remains of it within the memory of man.* But
that there was one, appears from the name of
the hill, called Cow-castle-hill; and the street
that leads West from St. Peter's church, in ancient deeds bearing the name of Castle-gate."
Mr. Hutton, however, nineteen years ago, with
the acknowledged enthusiasm of an Antiquary,
and the indefatigable zeal of " *an old castle-
hunter,*"† discovered the vestiges of this castle
in an orchard on the summit of the hill. " One
of the mounds eighty yards long, runs parallel with the houses upon Cock-pit-hill, perhaps
one hundred yards behind them; also parallel
with those in St. Peter's parish, but twice the
distance. _ This place of security, then stood
out of the town in an open field; no houses
were near it. It was guarded by the Derwent
on one side, and on the other ran the London
road. This I apprehend was the chief approach,
because the passage afterwards bore the name
of *Castle-street.* From thence also the fields
towards the East acquired the name of *Castle-
fields.*" This author is of opinion, that the
Derby Castle was destroyed during the civil

---

* This was written in the year 1695.   † Hist. p. 23.

wars between the Houses of York and Lancaster; which is not at all improbable.

We are informed by ancient authors, that there were six religious houses in the town of Derby. Several of these were in existence at the suppression of the orders by Henry VIII; but some of them had previously decayed.

The Monastery of *St. Helens*, belonging to the order of Austin Friars, was situated on the spot, where the Spar Manufactory belonging to Messrs. Brown and Son now stands, near the upper end of Bridge-gate. It was erected in the reign of king Stephen, by Robert de Ferrieres, second Earl of Derby. He placed an Abbot and Canons in it; and for their support, gave them the Churches of Crich and Uttoxeter, the tithe of his revenue in the town of Derby, the third part of a meadow lying on the side of Oddebroo, between Derby and Markeaton, land in Aldwerk and Osmaston, and as much wood as they could draw with one cart from Duffield or Chaddesden. But early in the reign of Henry II. Hugh the Dean of Derby, gave all his lands in Derby and Derley, with the patronage of St. Peters to Albin, then Abbot of St. Helens, upon condition of his building an Abbey at Derley. This proposition was accepted; and the Abbot and

5   T

Canons quitted the noise and bustle of a town,
for the more pleasant and peaceful banks of the
Derwent. St. Helens, however, continued a
religious house some time longer; for in the
twentieth of Edward I, a *Magister Domus S.*
Helenæ Derbeyæ, is mentioned, as distinct from
the Abbot of Derley.

On the north-west side of Nun's-green, in
the meadow that was called *Nun's-Close*, stood
a priory of *Benedictine Nuns*, dedicated to *St.*
Mary de Pratis. It was founded by the Abbot
of Derley in the reign of Henry II, in the year
1160. The Bishop of Coventry committed its
care to its zealous founder, and granted him a
licence to consecrate the virgins that were received into it. Henry III. ordered five pounds
to be paid every year by the bailiffs out of the
fee-farm of the town of Nottingham, to procure the prayers of the Prioress and Convent,
for the salvation of his father King John. Henry IV, by charter in the thirteenth year of his
reign, granted to this religious house several
acres of land, in Alsop-in-the-Dale, the Peak-
forest, and in Fairfield in the same forest. It
was also possessed of land in Langley and Trusley, and of several messuages and parcels in
Aston-upon-Trent. The mills anciently situated on the Markeaton-brook, and the green

on which the Nunnery stood, belonged to it.—
These, and some other valuable revenues were
estimated at the dissolution at eighteen pounds
six shillings and eight pence a year.

A Priory of *Dominican* or *Black Friars*, once
stood on the spot where the mansion and garden
of M. Henley, Esq. are now situated in the Friar-
gate. It is thought to have been founded in very
early times; and was dedicated to the blessed
Virgin. Three roods and a half of land were
granted to this house in the reign of Edward I;
and in that of Edward II, in 1296, a patent was
obtained to purchase ten acres more. Nine cottages, eight acres of land, one meadow, and
one croft situated in the parish of St. Werburgh, were also attached to it. At the dissolution, the revenue of this priory was estimated at twenty-one pounds, eighteen shillings,
and eight pence; and in the thirty-fifth of
Henry VIII, it was granted to one John Hinde;
from whom, by different purchases, the scite has
descended to the present possessor.

Near the brook on the North of St. James's-
lane stood a cell of *Cluniac Monks.* It is of
Saxon origin, and was founded by Waltheof, a
nobleman of that nation, who was beheaded
by William the Conqueror, in the year 1074.
He dedicated it to St. James, and presented it

to the Abbey of Bermondsey in Southwark.—
In the wars between Henry V, and the French,
the Priory of St. James was detached from the
Abbey of Cluny in France, to which the whole
order was subject, and afterwards depended upon one of the same order at Lenton near Nottingham. Though protected as a poor hospital by Henry III, and considered as an alien
Priory by Edward I, at the suppression, it was
taken possession of by Henry, when it was estimated at the yearly value of ten pounds.

A *Maison de Dieu*, a hospital for leprous persons, was founded in Derby as early as the
reign of Henry II. This was intended for the
reception of lepers, and superintended by a
master.

There was also in Derby an old hospital of
royal foundation, consisting of a master and
several leprous brethren, dedicated to St. Leonard. It is thought, however, by some, that
there was but one house for the reception of
lepers, and that these two are the same; but
if there were two, one must have stood at the
Newlands, and the other at St. Mary's Bridge-
gate.

St. Mary's was an old building in the Saxon
style, situated upon the verge of the Derwent,
and forming a part of the old bridge; it is

thought to have been one of the six churches, mentioned in Domesday.* During the reign of Charles II, the Presbyterians met for the celebration of divine worship within its walls; with the exception of that short period, it had not been used as a church for many ages. In the days of its prosperity, Heanor constituted a part of its appropriation.

Such were the temples in which the Deity was worshipped three centuries ago; when it was thought a crime to give full scope to the social affections of our nature, and a virtue to repress and annihilate the strongest and most pleasing emotions of the human heart. We turn, then, with pleasure, to contemplate those structures, whose walls, so far from resounding with the praises of monkish seclusion, and the efficacy of perpetual virginity; re-echo the precepts of that amiable religion, which

* The churches mentioned there are ;—" In the borough there was in the demesne, one church with seven clerks, who held two carucates of land free in *Cestre* (Little Chester). And there was also another church of the King's, in which six clerks held nine oxgans of land in *Cornun* and *Detton* likewise free." " In *Derbii* (Derby) Geoffry Alselin has one church, which Tochi had. Ralph the son of Hubert, one church, which was Leuric's, with one carucate of land. Norman de Lincoln one church, which was Brun's. Edric has one church there, which was his father Coln's." *Orig,* 280, a 2.

confirms and encourages every virtuous feeling of the breast.

Derby contains five churches, the principal of which is *All Saints*; or as it is found written in old writings *Allhallows.* The first mention made of this church, is, in the time of Henry III, when it is said that there was a church in Derby dedicated to All Saints. In the succeeding reign, it was made a free chapel of the king, and with its prebendaries, and other appurtenances was exempted from all ecclesiastical jurisdiction, excepting that of the Pope himself: this freedom it still possesses. - This church was at that time collegiate; had a rector, who was the Dean of Lincoln; and seven collegians, who it is thought resided in a house situated to the North of the church, which even to this day bears the name of *The College.* The college possessed lands, tithes, and other emoluments in the reign of Henry VIII. to the amount of £38 14s a year clear; a sum equal to twenty times as much of our money. Henry, however, took possession of it all; but Mary, in the first year of her reign, returned a part of the property, and vested it in the hands of the corporation, whose gift the curacy now is.

In the reign of Henry VIII. or Mary, the

steeple, being in a very decayed state, was taken down, and the present elegant piece of
architecture built up in its place. This beautiful Gothic tower is the object of admiration
and praise to every one that sees it. The
workmanship is of a superior kind, and reckoned excellent; it is richly ornamented with
tracery, crockets, pinnacles and battlements;
and rising to the height of 180 feet, it towers
above the other churches and houses, and forms
a beautiful and striking object from the surrounding country.

> " MAJESTIC PILE! whose towr'd summit stands
> Far eminent above all else that rise
> In DERBY's peopled vale; . . . .
> . . . . every eye, beholding Thee,
> From the far-travel'd tasteful Amateur's,
> That with impassion'd gaze contemplates long
> The Gothic grandeur of thy tow'r, to his,
> The simple peasant boy's, bright glistening
> With nature's fire, instinctively shall own,
> THOU ART INDEED A NOBLE EDIFICE."
>
> Edward's All Saints.

There is a tradition, that this tower was built
at the sole expence of the bachelors and maidens
in the town; and that it was formerly the custom, when a young woman, a native of the
place, was married, for the bachelors to ring
the bells. Upon a fillet on the North-side, is

an inscription, in old English, *Young Men and Maids*, which seems to corroborate the tale; but upon the whole, the opinion is considered to be merely conjectural.

Between this tower, and the body of the church, there exists an uncommon instance of architectural incongruity; for to this beautiful specimen of Gothic architecture is added a Grecian body, of the chastest proportions, and most classical design. It was built from a design by Gibbs in the years 1723—4—5; and was opened for public worship on the twenty-first of November, 1725. The expences of the erection were defrayed by voluntary subscriptions, which were raised and directed by Dr. Hutchinson; of whom Mr. Hutton* speaks as follows :—" The curate, Dr. Hutchinson, not only subscribed £40 ; but being a man of genteel address, charged himself with raising the whole money, and executing a masterly work, without a shilling expence to his parish. He was a complete master of the art of begging. The people to whom he applied were not able to keep their money ; it passed from their pockets to his own, as if by magic. Wherever he could recollect a person likely to contribute

* Hist. p. 153.

to this desirable work, he made no scruple to
visit him at his own expence. He took a journey to London, to solicit the benefaction of
Thomas Chambers, Esq; ancestor of the Earl
of Exeter, who gave him one hundred pounds.
If a stranger passed through Derby, the Doctor's bow and his rhetoric were employed in
the service of the church. His anxiety was
urgent; and his powers so prevailing, that he
seldom failed of success. When the Waites
fiddled at his door for a Christmas box, instead of sending them away with a solitary
shilling, he invited them in, treated them with a
tankard of ale, and persuaded them out of a
guinea. I have seen his list of subscribers,
which are 589; and the sum £3,249 11s. 6d.
But it appears, he could procure a man's *name*
by his eloquence easier than his money; for 52
of the subscribers never paid their sums, amounting to £137 16s. 6d. The remaining £3,111
15s. being defective, he procured a brief, which
added £598 5s. 6d. more. Still, though assiduity was not wanting money was; he therefore sold six burying places in the vault for six
guineas; and twelve of the principal seats in
the church, by inch of candle, for £475 13s.
which were purchased as freeholds by the first
inhabitants."

The interior of this church is large, light,
and elegant; five columns on each side support
the roof; the windows are large and handsome:
and the symmetry and harmonious proportions
of the building, have a pleasing effect. It is
divided into two unequal parts, by a rich open
screen-work of iron. The western division is
appropriated for the celebration of public worship, with a spacious organ-gallery, furnished
with a good organ. The eastern division is separated into three parts: one is used for chosing
the Mayor, and for the vestry business; the centre is an elegant chancel; and the southern side
is the dormitory, and contains the monuments,
of the Cavendish family; and many persons of
that illustrious house, are buried in the vault
beneath.

On the South side of this repository, there
is a monument erected to the memory of the
illustrious and celebrated Countess of Shrewsbury, constructed during her life time and under her own direction. The Countess is seen,
arrayed in the habit of her time, with her head
reclining on a cushion, and her hands placed in
the attitude of prayer. Underneath is the following inscription in Latin :—

" To the memory of Elizabeth, the daughter of John Hardwike of Hardwike, in the county of Derby, esq ; and at length
co-heiress to her brother John: She was married, first, to
Robert Barley of Barley, in the said county of Derby, esq ;

afterwards to William Cavendish of Chatsworth, knt. treasurer
of the chamber to the kings Henry VIII and Edward VI. and
queen Mary, to whom he was also a privy councellor. She then
became the wife of Sir William St. Low, captain of the guard
to queen Elizabeth.   Her last husband was the most noble
George, earl of Shrewsbury. By Sir William Cavendish alone
she had issue. This was three sons, viz. Henry Cavendish of Tutbury, in the county of Stafford, esq; who took to wife Grace,
the daughter of the said George, earl of Shrewsbury, but died
without legitimate issue; William, created baron Cavendish
of Hardwike, and earl of Devonshire, by his late majesty king
James; and Charles Cavendish of Welbeck, knt. father of the
most honourable William Cavendish, on account of his great
merit created knight of the bath, baron Ogle by right of his
mother, and viscount Mansfield, earl, marquis, and duke of
Newcastle upon Tine, and earl Ogle of Ogle. She had also an
equal number of daughters, namely, Frances, married to Sir
Henry Pierpoint ; Elizabeth to Charles Stuart, earl of Lenox :
and Mary to Gilbert, earl of Shrewsbury. This very celebrated Elizabeth, countess of Shrewsbury, built the houses of
Chatsworth, Hardwike, and Oldcotes, highly distinguished by
their magnificence, and finished her transitory life on the thirteenth day of February, in the year 1607, and about the eighty-
seventh year* of her age, and expecting a glorious resurrection,
lies interred underneath."

Another monument in this division of the
church, stands near the centre, and was erected to the memory of William Earl of Devon-

---

* " This statement of the age of the Countess is certainly erroneous; as it appears from Collins's Peerage, &c. that she
was fourteen when she married her first husband, Robert Barley, esq; who died on the second of February, 1532—33; consequently, if her own death did not happen till 1607, she must
have been (at least) in her ninety-first year."

Beauties of England.

shire, who died on the 20th of June 1628, and
Christiana his Countess, the only daughter of
Lord Bruce, of Kinloss, in Scotland. It is of
the height of twelve feet, having its sides open;
and in the middle under a dome, are the whole
length figures in white marble, of the Earl
and his Lady standing upright. The busts of
their four children are placed on the angles, on
the outside. Among the other monuments deserving notice, is one by Rysbrack to the memory of *Caroline* of Besborough; and another,
by Nollekins, displaying the medallion and
arms of *William Ponsonby*, Earl of Besborough,
and husband to the above lady, who died in
the year 1763.

There is also a tablet against the South wall,
to the memory of the worthy minister by whose
industry and exertions the building was carried
forward.

In Memory
Of the Rev. MICHAEL HUTCHINSON D. D.
Late Minister of this Church,
Who from a pious zeal, and unwearied application,
Obtained Subscriptions,
And afterwards collected and paid,
Three thousand, two hundred, and forty nine pounds,
And upwards, for the rebuilding of this Church :
He died the tenth day of June,
In the year of our Lord God
MDCCXXX.

Against the wall on the North-side of the church, there is a monument erected to the memory of Richard Croshaw, Esq. He is said to have been the son of a poor nailer in the town, and to have gone to London in a suit of leather to seek his fortune. There, by industry and perseverance he gained a fortune of £10,000. It appears from the inscription, that " he was Master of the Company of Goldsmiths, and Deputy of Broad-street Ward; that during the plague in 1625, he neglected his own safety, abode in the city, to provide for the relief of the poor; performed many pious and charitable acts in his life; and bequeathed above £4,000, to the Corporation of Derby and other trustees, for the maintenance of Lectures, relief of the poor and other pious uses. The donation called *Croshaw's dole*, is distributed in this church every Sunday morning to seven poor persons, selected alternately from the five different parishes, who receive a sixpenny loaf and three-pence each.

He died in 1631, and was buried in the church of St. Bartholomew by the Exchange, in which parish he lived thirty-one years. This monument, erected by his executors, represents him clothed in his leathern doublet, with a nail-hammer in his hand: by this means

shewing that poverty is not a crime, and that
industry and honesty, reflect the most valuable
and lasting honors on the memory of man.

When the church was rebuilt, a tomb-stone
was discovered bearing the date of 1400. It is
an alabaster slab, having the figure of a priest,
as large as life, holding a sacramental cup, carved on it in scroll-lines; and round the edges is
the following inscription: *Subtus me jacet Johan-
nes Lawe, Quondam Canonicus, Ecclesiæ Colle-
giatæ Omnia Sancti Derby, ac subdecanus ejus-
dem Qui Obiit Anno Dni Millimo CCCCmo. pro-
pitiatur Deus. Amen.* This stone is still preserved, and placed in the North aisle of the
church.

St. Alkmund's Church, stands at the North-
end of the town; and was erected about the
middle of the eight century. Tradition informs
us, that Alkmund, son of Alured king of Northumberland, heading a party to restore his de-
posed father to the throne, was unsuccessful, and
put to death. He was considered as a saint and a
martyr; and his canonization soon followed. He
was interred at Littleshull in Shropshire; but
on its being discovered, that miracles were
wrought at his shrine, his credulous adherents, removed his remains to a more respectable cemetery. Derby was fixed upon, and the church of

St. Alkmund was honored with his relics and
his name at the same time. The voice of fame
and superstition, ranked his shrine next to that
of the holy Becket at Canterbury, in its power
of working miracles; and his tomb was frequently honored with the presence of many
pilgrims from the northern nations.

In very early times, this church was presented to the abbey of Derley; to which it was subject till the dissolution, when it was seized by
Henry. In the following reign, Mary made it
over to the Corporation of Derby, who, ever
since, have had the presentation. In the king's
books, St. Alkmund is represented as a vicarage of the value of £11 6s. 8d.* and since the
year 1734, it has enjoyed an endowment of
sixty pounds a year; bequeathed by an old
bachelor, of the name of Goodwin, who was
descended from an ancient family in the town
of Derby.

The steeple contains six bells: and the building has a number of rude heads, and other
sculptures designed for ornaments, in different

---

* " This must have been a mistake, or some of the emoluments were lost; for in the reign of George I. the income was
only eight pounds, per Annum, and divine service, was performed but once a quarter." Hutton, p. 138.

parts. In the parish are included, Chester,
Derley, Quarndon and Little Eaton; and the
two last have chapels of ease.

The church of. *St. Peter*, is situated near the
southern extremity of the town: and is thought
to be the same as the one mentioned in the time
of king Stephen, dedicated to the same apostle.
In that early age it was given to the abbey at
Derley. In 1530, a chapel was founded in
this church, by Robert Liversage, a dyer, of
Derby; he endowed it for the continued support of a priest who was to celebrate divine
worship, and say mass every Friday; and afterwards he was to distribute thirteen *silver*
pence, to thirteen poor men or women, who
might then be present. In this church was
also a chantery founded in honour of the Virgin Mary. It was endowed with various messuages, cottages, gardens, lands, tenements,
meadows, and hereditaments, which were
granted by queen Mary to the Corporation of
Derby. The living is a vicarage; and when Derley abbey was dissolved, the advowson was granted to the Corporation. The steeple contains
six bells; and the villages of Normanton, Bolton, and Litchurch, belong to this parish.

St. *Werburgh's* is situated on the western-
side of the town, upon the Markeaton brook.

This church was, also, given in the reign of
Stephen to the abbey of Derley; but at the
dissolution it was recovered, and the vicarage
is now in the hands of the king. It is probable, that the ancient church on this spot, was
built before the conquest; but being situated
so near the Markeaton-brook, its foundation
was sapped by floods, and in 1601 the tower
fell to the ground. To prevent the recurrence
of a like accident, a new one was built on the
East-side of the body of the church, contrary
to the situation of steeples in general: but this,
like the former, fell on the fifth of November,
1698. The present steeple has fixe bells, and
the interior of the church, is light and handsome. There was a chantery to the blessed
Mary in this church also; which was endowed
with various messuages, gardens, cottages, and
lands; which in the reign of Mary, were in the
tepure and occupation of ten different persons,
and by her were granted to the Corporation of
Derby. Osmaston is part of the parish.

St. Michael's church stands in Queen-street,
at no great distance from that of St. Alkmund's.
It belonged to the abbey of Derley, and was
taken possession of by Henry at the dissolution;
but Mary gave it to the bailiffs and burgesses
of the town of Derby. The living is a vicar-

5   x

age; being united with St. Werburgh's, and
has service once a month. The village of Al-
veston belongs to this parish.

Besides the above mentioned churches, there
are several other places of public worship in the
town of Derby.

The *Unitarians* have a meeting-house in Friar-
gate. This is a very old interest:—as early as
the reign of Elizabeth, they had their private
places of assembling; and in the reign of king
Charles II. they obtained a licence, for celebrating divine worship, in the old chapel standing on St. Mary's-bridge. In the reign of
James II. they left the old chapel, and removed
to a large room near the Market-place. There
they continued to assemble till the erection of
the present meeting-house, in the reign of king
William.

The *Independents*, or *Calvinists*, have a place
of worship near the Brook-side. This chapel
was erected in the year 1785, by persons who
had seceded from the congregation in Friar-
gate, owing to a difference of opinion on religious doctrines.

The *Baptists* both *General* and *Particular;*
the *Quakers;* and the *Methodists*, have their
respective chapels.

One of the most considerable charities in

Derby, is the Devonshire *Alms-houses*, situated
near All Saints; and founded by the famous
Countess of Shrewsbury in the reign of queen
Elizabeth, for eight men and four women. To
each is granted two rooms, a sufficiency of
coal, and half-a-crown a week. They are clad
in dark cloathes, badged with E. S. *(Elizabeth*
Shrewsbury) on a silver plate. The original
building, which was of stone, was taken down
about forty years since, and the present edifice
erected from an original plan, at the expence
of the Duke of Devonshire. The design of the
front is unlike the style of architecture which
generally characterizes establishments of charity; and would lead us to suppose, that it was
the entrance to a nobleman's park, or pleasure-
ground. The rules for 'the observance of the
inmates are:—" that they are not to marry or
get drunk, without expulsion; to lie one night
out incurs a forfeiture of four-pence; if absent
one day, six-pence; to miss prayers at All-
Saints two-pence; to strike a blow one shilling;
and if three blows, a discharge."

In Bridge-gate there are eight alms-houses,
for an equal number of poor and aged of both
sexes. They are called the *Black Alms-houses*,
from the black gowns worn by the inhabitants,
who receive eighteen-pence a week each. This

foundation was laid by the family of Wilmot
of Chaddesden, near 300 years ago; who ordered £40 a year, to be paid from the tithes
of Denby, for its support.

Another alms-house for the widows of clergymen, is situated at the top of Friar-gate;
and was instituted in the year 1716, by Edward
Large of Derby, who endowed it with an
estate, which produces £17 a year each, to the
five residents.

A fourth charity of this class, called *The
Grey-coat Hospital*, from the colour of the
dress, once stood in Walker's-lane. It was supported by ample endowments; but the estate
has vanished, and the building converted to
other purposes.

For the education of the children of the poor,
there is a *Free-School* in St. Peter's church-
yard. It was originally erected by the Corporation of Derby, with a part of the donations
belonging to the abbey of Derley, which had
been presented to them by Mary. It is endowed with lands, set a-part for its use; the re-
ceipts of which now support two masters. Several Sunday Schools have, likewise, been recently established in the town.

The principal buildings in Derby, besides
the churches and meeting-houses, are a County

and Town Hall, a County Gaol, an elegant Assembly Room, and a Theatre.

The *County Hall* is situated at the bottom of St. Mary's-gate: it was erected in the year 1660; and is a large and heavy building of free-stone. The *Town Hall* is a handsome structure, built by the Corporation, about the year 1731, on the scite of a more ancient one of wood and plaister, on the South-east side of the Market-place.

The *County Gaol* is situated on the western-side of the town, near the upper-end of Friar-gate. It was erected in the year 1756, at the expence of the Corporation, aided by a dona-tion of £400, presented by the Duke of De-vonshire. It is a solid, plain, and respectable building of brick, well adapted for the pur-pose of its destination. The front, is from an excellent design, displaying solidity and strength; without that affectation of incongru-ous ornament, so frequently exhibited in mo-dern buildings of a similar character.

The *Assembly Room*, is an elegant building of stone, situated on the North-side of the Market-place. Its foundation was laid in the year 1763, and completed, by subscription, in 1774. To this, also, the Duke of Devonshire, with most of the nobility and gentry of the county, was a very liberal contributor. A variety of musical instruments are sculptured on the pediment, figurative of the design of the building.

The *Theatre*, a neat building of brick, stands in Bold-lane, and was erected in the year 1773, at the expence of Mr. James Whitley.— The interior is plain and commodious.

Concerning the *Trade* of Derby, old authors' are nearly silent. It is thought that the oldest carried on in the town was that of a *dyer:* and to corroborate this opinion, reference is made to the privilege enjoyed by the inhabitants in the reign of Edward III,[*] and to the name of *Full-street*, which is said to have been the residence of the professors of that art. It is certain, however, that *Wool* was among the articles of its most early commerce:—this was brought from the beautiful sheep-walks of the Peak, and retailed in the neighbourhood. *Malt* was another article, for which Derby was famed.— " The reputation of Derby," says Camden,[†] " at present proceeds from the assizes for the county being held there, *and from the excellent good ale brewed in it.*"

Trade was confined to these articles until the

---

* See p. 132.   † Britannia, p. 492.

commencement of the eighteenth century;
when the *stocking-frame* machine, said to have
been invented by ·a clergyman of Calverton,
near Nottingham, .in the reign of James I, was
introduced into the town. This was a considerable additon to the commercial interests of
the place; but what gave it a pre-eminence in
this respect, was the erection of the first mill
in this country for the manufacture of silk.

" The original mill, called the *Silk-mill*
to denote its pre-eminence, being the first
and largest of its kind ever erected in England,
stands upon an island in the river Derwent.
Its history is remarkable, as it denotes the power of genius, and the vast influence which even
the enterprizes of an individual has on the
commerce of a country.

" The Italians were long in the exclusive possession of the art of silk throwing, and the mer-
chants of other nations were consequently dependent on that people for their participation
in a very lucrative article of trade, and were
frequently deprived of their fair profits by ex-
orbitant prices charged for the original material. This state of things continued till the
commencement of the last century, when a person named Crotchet erected a small mill near
the present works, with an intention of intro-

ducing the silk manufacture into England; but his machinery being inadequate to the purpose, he quickly became insolvent, and the design was for some time abandoned. At length, about the year 1715, a similar idea began to expand in the mind of an excellent mechanic and draughtsman, named John Lombe, who, though young, resolved on the perilous task of travelling into Italy, to procure drawings, or models of the machines necessary for the undertaking.

" In Italy he remained some time; but, as admission to the silk-works was prohibited, he could only obtain access by corrupting two of the workmen, through whose assistance he inspected the machinery in private; and whatever parts he obtained a knowledge of, during these visits, he recorded on paper before he slept. By perserverance in this mode of conduct, he made himself acquainted with the whole; and had just completed his plan, when his intention was discovered, and his life being in extreme hazard, he flew with precipitation, and took refuge on ship-board. The two Italians who had favoured his scheme, and whose lives were in equal danger with his own, accompanied him, and they all soon landed in safety in England: this happened about the year 1717.

" Fixing on Derby as a proper place for his purpose, he agreed with the corporation for an island, or swamp, in the river, 500 feet long, and 52 wide, at a rent somewhat below eight pounds yearly. Here he established his silk-mill; but during the time employed in its construction, he erected temporary machines in the Town-Hall, and various other places; by which means he not only reduced the prices of silk far below the Italians, but was likewise enabled to proceed with his greater undertaking, though the charges amounted to nearly £30,000.

" In the year 1718 he procured a patent to enable him to secure the profits, thus arising from his address and ingenuity, for the term of fourteen years; but his days verged to a close, and before half this period had elapsed, treachery and poison had brought him to the grave. The Italians, whose trade rapidly decreased, from the success of the new establishment, were exasperated to vengeance, and vowed the destruction of the man whose ingenuity had thus turned the current of their business into another channel. An artful woman was sent from Italy in the character of a friend; she associated with the parties, and was permitted to assist in the preparation of the silk. Her influence was

privately 'exerted on the natives who had fled
with Mr. Lombe from Italy, and succeeding
with one, she prepared to execute the long-
meditated plan of death. The victim lingered
in agony two or three years, when the springs
of life being completely exhausted, he breathed
his last. Slow poison is supposed to have been
the means employed to deprive him of existence; and though suspicion was almost strength-
ened into certainty, by the circumstances that
transpired on the examination of *Madam* ——,
the evidence was not decisive, and she was discharged. Her associate had previously ran
away to his own country. The other Italian,
whose name was *Gartrevalli*, continued in Derby, and afterwards worked at a silk-mill erected at Stockport, in Cheshire; but died in poverty. The funeral of John Lombe was celebrated in a style of considerable magnificence.

" The death of this lamented artist did not,
as the Italians hoped, prove fatal to his patriotic scheme, for the machinery was in full action, and the business becoming more successful, gave employment to about 300 people.—
John Lombe was succeeded by his brother William, whose melancholy disposition led him to
commit suicide; on which the property descended to his cousin, Sir Thomas Lombe.—

Shortly afterwards, August 29th, 1724, the lease of the ground was signed by the corpora.. tion; for, though the building had been long completed, the deeds had not hitherto been exchanged.

" Previous to the expiration of the patent Sir Thomas petitioned Parliament for a renew_ al; pleading, 'That the works had taken so long a *time* in perfecting, and the people in teaching, that there had been *none* to acquire emolument from the patent.' This statement was not altogether correct, as it appears that the petitioner had already accumulated up- wards of £80,000. The application, however, was not altogether unsuccessful; for govern- ment, willing to reward the promoters of nation- al benefit, and at the same time to spread the knowledge of such a useful invention, granted him £14,00 in lieu of a new patent, and on condition that he should suffer a complete model of the works to be taken: this was ac- cordingly executed, and afterwards deposited in the Tower for public inspection.

" Sir Thomas Lombe dying on the 3d of February, 1738, the silk-mill became the pro- perty of his lady, and was twice advertised for public sale; but the trade being greatly decayed, through the erection of mills in other

places, no bidders could be found, though the
second time the works were put up at as low a
sum as £1000. On the 20th of February, 1739,
the lease was assigned from Lady Lombe to
Richard Wilson, Esq. and in July following
the agreement was completed, and the property transferred to the latter, for a sum not exceeding £4000. The premises have been occupied many years by Mr. —— Swift, who
has made various important additions to the
machinery, and employs about 240 hands,
(principally women and children).*

"The extensive fabric which contains the machinery, stands upon huge piles of oak, double
planked, and covered with stone-work, on which
are turned thirteen stone arches, that sustain

* " As the above account of the introduction of the silk-
mill into England essentially varies from almost every other
that has been published on the subject, it becomes expedient
to mention, that the chief authority on which it is related, is
the ' History of Derby,' by Mr. Hutton. This gentleman
was personally known to GARTREVALLI; and in his infancy
was well acquainted with the names both of the other Italian,
and of the female to whose arts John Lombe fell a victim;
but the lapse of threescore years, as he observes, in a letter with
which he has favored us, ' has driven them out of his mind.'
Various particulars of his statement we have substantiated by
local enquiries, and by referring to original documents; from
which some particulars are inserted in the text, that Mr. Hutton was probably unacquainted with."—Beauties of England,
vol. III. p. 368.

the walls. Its whole length is 110 feet; its breadth, thirty-nine; and its height, fifty-five feet, six inches. It contains five stories, beside the under works, and is lighted by 468 windows. In the three upper stories are the Italian winding engines, which are placed in a regular manner across the apartments, and furnished with many thousand swifts and spindles, and engines for working them. In the two lower rooms are the spinning and twist mills, which are all of a circular form, and are turned by upright shafts passing through their centres, and communicating with shafts from the water-wheel. Their diameter is between twelve and thirteen feet; and their height, nineteen feet, eight inches. The spinning mills are eight in number, and give motion to upwards of 25,000 reel bobbins, and nearly 3000 star wheels belonging to the reels. Each of the four twist mills contains four rounds of spindles, about 389 of which are connected with each mill, as well as numerous reels, bobbins, star-wheels, &c. The whole of this elaborate machine, for one only it is, though distributed, as we have mentioned, through five large apartments, is put in motion by a single water-wheel, twenty-three feet in diameter, situated on the west side of the building.

" An adequate idea of this complicated assemblage of wheels and movements cannot be
conveyed by words; to be distinctly conceived,
it must be seen: and even then considerably
more time is requisitue to obtain a knowledge
of its parts, and of their dependence on each
other, than is generally allotted by the casual
visitant.   All is whirling, and in motion, and
appears as if directed and animated by some
invisible power; yet mutually dependent as
every part is, any one of them may be stopped
and separated at pleasure.   This arises from
every movement being performed by two wheels,
one of which is turned by the other; but when
separated, the latter preserves its rotorary motion, while the other stops as the impelling
power no longer operates.   The whole number
of wheels is about 14,000.

   " All the operations are performed here, from
winding the raw-silk, to organizing or preparing it for the weavers.   The raw-silk is chiefly
brought in skains, or hanks, from China and
Piedmont; that produced in the former country is perfectly white, but the produce of the
latter is of a light yellow colour.   The skain is
first placed on an hexagonal wheel, or *swift;*
and the filaments which compose it are regularly wound off upon a small cylindrical block

of wood, or *bobbin*. To wind a single skain is the work of five or six days, though the machine is kept in motion for ten hours daily; so astonishingly fine are the filaments of which it is formed. In this part of the process many children are employed, whose nimble fingers are kept in continual exercise by tying the threads that break, and removing the burs and uneven parts, some of which are the cases that the silk-worm fabricates for its own grave, or rather for its dormitory, while Nature prepares it for a new mode of existence. The silk thus wound upon the bobbins, is afterwards *twisted* by other parts of the machinery, and is then sent to the *doublers*, who are chiefly women, stationed in a detached building, which stands on the same island, on piles like the silk-mill; though not half so broad is nearly thirty feet longer. Here four, seven, or ten, of the threads are united into one, according to the uses for which they are designed; the fine kind going to the stocking-weaver: the others to the manufacturer of waistcoat-pieces, &c.

" It has frequently been remarked, among other absurdities, that when the machine is completely in motion, ' it works 73,726 yards of organize silk-thread by every revolution of the water-wheel,' which turns once round every nineteen seconds. The mere view of the machine is sufficient to convince any person, that the quantity of yards wound every circuit of the wheel cannot be told; neither, indeed, is it open to calculation; for the threads are so continually breaking, (not to mention other difficulties that render the attempt insuperable) that the power of numbers must ever be inadequate to ascertain the amount."

Besides this mill, there are several other works of a similar nature, now established in Derby. The situation of the town on the banks of the Derwent renders it favorable for the institution and carrying on, of manufactures which require the aid of water: and the improvements in mechanism are no where more obvious, than in the various and extensive works constructed here, for a variety of purposes. The mills established by the Messrs. Strutts, for the manufacture of silk and cotton, are particularly ingenious; and the facility attained by them in working the several articles of manufacture, has contributed to the extension of these branches of business in a very eminent degree.

The *Porcelain Manufactory* was established about the year 1750, by a gentleman of the name of Duesbury. Since the decease of the

original institutor, very great improvements
have been made, in the preparation of the materials, and in the appearance of the ware. It
is thought to be equal in fineness of texture
with the French and Saxon, while it far surpasses them in workmanship, and elegance.—
The paintings are in general rich and well
executed; and the gilding and burnishing very
beautiful.

The materials from which the ware, called
porcelain, is manufactured, is procured from
Cornwall; and is a fine grey clay, mixed with
flaking matter. These materials, first undergo the operation of grinding, and then are
made into a paste; which, when it is perfected,
is taken to the workmen, who form it into a
variety of useful and ornamental articles. Vessels of a round shape, are formed by a person
called a *thrower*; who shapes them on a circular block, moving horizontally on a vertical
spindle. They are then taken to a lathe, where
they are reduced to their proper thickness, and
afterwards finished and handled. When this
process is gone through, they are conveyed to a
stove to dry, and when all the moisture is evaporated; they become fit for baking. The
ware is placed in earthen vessels, of different

6 z

shapes and dimensions, among a white sand,
to prevent their adhering to one another; and
set in a kiln or oven, piled one on another to
the top. When the kiln is full, the aper-
tures are carefully closed, and the ware baked
by the heat proceeding from the flues. After
the ware has undergone this first baking, it is
taken to another apartment, where it is dipped
in a glaze of the colour and consistence of
cream: it is then taken to the *glaze-kiln*, where
it is baked in a less intense heat than the former, and receives its glossy appearance.

After the ware has been glazed, it is taken
to the painters, who ornament it with landscapes, figures, &c. The colours used are prepared from mineral bodies; and in order to
fix, and give them a proper degree of lustre,
they are conveyed to a kiln, where every coat
of colour receives a fresh burning. Two burn-
ings are generally sufficient for the ornaments
of common porcelain; but the most elegant
ware, has the colours laid on at different periods, and therefore require the action of fire
several times, before they attain their full effect and beauty. When the ware is ornamented with gold, that metal is used in an amalga-
mated state, and laid on by a brush: in this
case, it is necessary to commit the vessel once

more to the kiln, where the gold re-assumes its
solidity, and being rubbed after it comes out,
with some polishing substance, acquires a brilliant appearance.

At this manufactory, many very elegant *bis-
cuit-figures*, or white ware, are constructed.—
The materials for the construction of these
figures, are reduced to a liquid of the consistence and appearance of thick cream, and then
poured into moulds of plaster or gypsum.—
The moisture contained in the mixture, being
very soon absorbed by the mould, the paste
which composes the figure, becomes hard and
tenacious, and easily separates. The different
parts of the figure; the head, the arms, the legs,
and numerous other appendages, which belong
to many of them, are cast in separate moulds,
and when dried, and prepared, are joined to
the principal figure, by a paste of the same
kind as the figure itself. When the figures
have their limbs, &c. complete, they are conveyed to the kiln, and by the operation of a
regulated and continued heat, are rendered
beautifully white and delicate. They then undergo the same process as the other ware in
laying on the different colours. The manufactory belongs at present to Messrs. Duesbury
and Key; who employ about 200 workmen.

The manufactory of Messrs. Brown and Son, situated at the upper-end of Bridge-gate, for sawing and polishing marble, and forming the fluor spar, or Blue John, into a great variety of ornaments, is well worthy notice. The machinery employed here, which is novel and simple, but very ingenious, is set in motion by a large steam-engine. , The machinery for sawing and polishing the marble, consists of a set of saws, made of thin plates of iron, inclosed in a sliding frame, attached to the vibrating poles to which the cranks are fixed. These saws, by the assistance of sand and water, cut the marble in a perpendicular direction. A set of saws consists of many plates, so that the block to which they are-applied, may be separated by one process into as many slabs as may be thought necessary. When the slabs are sawn, they are taken to be polished by an equally ingenious method.

" When the *Blue John* is to be made into a vase, or any other ornamental form, that renders the use of the lathe necessary, it is carved with a mallet and chissel, into a rude resemblance of the object intended, to be produced, and being afterwards strongly cemented to a plug or *chock*, is screwed upon the lathe. A slow motion is then given to the work ; and a bar of steel, about two feet long, and half an inch square, properly tempered, and pointed at each end, is applied to the fluor, on which water is continually dropping, to keep the tool cold, preserve it from friction, and enable it the more readily to reduce the substance upon which it acts. As the surface becomes smoother, the tool is applied with more freedom, and the motion of the lathe accelerated, till the fluor has assumed its destined elegance of form. When the turning is completed, pieces of grit-stone, of different degrees of fineness, are applied with water to bring the article to a proper ground for polishing with fine emery, tripoli, and putty, or calx of tin. These means are continued till the fluor is incapable of receiving a higher degree of polish; which is known, when water thrown on it will no longer increase its lustre."

The manufacture of stockings, as before noticed,* has long been introduced and pursued at Derby; and no where, since the invention of the stocking-frame, has that business received so important an improvement as in this town. About the year 1756, Messrs. Jedediah Strutt and William Woollatt obtained a patent

---

* See page 159.

bridge of three arches has also been thrown
over the Derwent, on the North-east side of
the town, to the road leading to Nottingham:
which, together with the silk-mill, the weirs,
and the broad expanse of the river, forms a
very pleasing prospect, on entering the town
from that side.

There are a variety of very pleasing walks in
the vicinity of Derby. Following the banks
of the Derwent in a northern direction, the
vale presents some very picturesque scenes;
while the summits of the hills of the Low-Peak,
form the distant boundary of the horizon.—
The walk through the grove to Darley, and
that on the eastern side of the river to Little-
Chester, independently of the objects of curiosity which may be traced in the latter, are
highly delightful and agreeable. And, indeed, in almost every direction, the inhabitants
may find scenes, where they may enjoy a
healthful exercise, as well as, gratify the
sight by a succession of prospects, distinguished by the softer features that attend cultivation.

CHAP V.

(CONTINUATION OF DERBY.)

Remarkable occurrences—Entry of the Preten-
der—Eminent men—The Infirmary—Ord-
nance Depot, &c.

THE state of Derby in early times has been
already noticed :* the want of records prevents
us from enumerating many of the interesting
events, which must have happened during the
lapse of the several succeeding centuries; but
a short sketch shall be given of those which
have been recorded,† and which have taken
place in the town since the year 1513.

"In the year 1514, Sir William Milnes, the
judge, was obliged to keep his assize and county court, at the Market-cross,.

"In 1534, two gallows were erected for

6. A a

---

* See page 126.

† " The articles distinguished by inverted commas, are
extracted from a parchment roll, in which remarkable
events, for a long series of years, are recorded by different
attornies of the town of Derby."—Pilkington.

hanging prisoners; and in 1535, the dissolution
of the abbies in the neighbourhood commenced.

"In 1545, Mr. Griffin was at St. Peter's
church, and would have taken Mr. George
Curson away, being a ward. The town bell
was rung, and resistance made."

In 1554, Sir John Marriott, vicar of St. Alkmund, hung himself by one of the bell-ropes,
in the belfry.

"In 1555, Joan Waste was burnt as a heretic,
in Windmill-pit, near the road leading to Barton." This woman, who was poor and blind,
had been in the habit of attending the service
of the church during the reign of Edward VI.
when the protestant doctrines were taught; and
when Mary came to the throne, she became
the object of persecution to the ministers of
that furious bigot, because of her disbelief of
the doctrine of transubstantiation. She was
accused of heresy before the bishop of the diocese, and commanded to renounce her opinions;
but persisting in her error, she was committed
to the custody of the bailiffs, who took care of
her till the writ arrived, when she suffered as a
martyr to the protestant faith.

.. "In the year 1586, the plague carried away
many of the inhabitants of St. Peter's parish.

"In 1587, a great flood broke down St. Mary's-bridge, and carried away the mills, situated at the bottom of St. Michael's-lane.

"In 1588, there was a great affray between Mr. Vernon and Mr. Langford's men, who were parted by the burgesses, and the inhabitants collected by the ringing of the town bell."

1595.—Sir Thomas White gave £400 for the use of the town.

1601.—A woman burnt in Windmill-pit, for poisoning her husband.

"In the year 1603, the burgesses began to break open the commons, which had been inclosed. The year ensuing they continued the practice, and the justices of peace were sent for, to decide the matter; several were indicted and suffered imprisonment." It is thought that the land, which lies between St. Alkmund's and Darley, on the banks of the Derwent, was the common in dispute.

"1608, during the reign of James I. the witches of Bakewell were executed.

"In 1610, a violent quarrel took place between the electioneering parties of Sir Philip Stanhope and Sir George Grealey; in consequence of which, the assizes for that year were held at Ashbourne." In the same year three prisoners were drowned in the gaol, by a sudden rise of the brook.

1634.—A great snow, in which four persons perished between Chaddesden and Derby.

"In 1635, king Charles I. visited Derby, on his return from Ripton in Yorkshire, and slept at the great house in the Market-place. The corporation presented the Duke of Newcastle, by whom he was attended, with a fat ox, a calf, six fat sheep, and a purse of gold, to enable the king to keep hospitality in the town. They also presented the Elector Palatine with twenty broad pieces.

"In the year 1636, the spring was uncommonly forward; and the plague again made its appearance in the town.

"In August 1643, king Charles I. marched through Derby, and erected his standard at Nottingham." On this occasion he borrowed £300 of the corporation, and all the small arms they could procure, which he promised to return at the end of the war; but this promise he was never able to fulfil. "In the November following, Sir John Gell took possession of the town, and garrisoned it for the parliament; keeping the main-guard at the Town-hall.— About the end of the summer of 1645, the town was disgarrisoned and the soldiers disbanded. The assizes were held this year in Friar's-close, owing to the plague raging in the town.

" In the year 1652, during the Common-wealth, the ceremony of marriage was performed by the justices of the peace.

" In 1659, an insurrection was raised against the government of Richard, son to Oliver Cromwell; who, a short time after, resigned the Protectorship.

" 1660.—The present mace was made; before this time the mayor had two old ones, formerly used by the bailiffs.

" In 1661 the Derwent was dried up, and in many places the water was so shallow, that people might walk over its bed dry-shod. The hall was also regulated this year; and Sir Simon Degge chosen recorder."

1662.—A terrible hurricane blew up trees, broke down the pinnacle of St. Werburgh's, untiled the Town-hall, and many houses in the Market-place, Full-street, and the *South* of All Saints; but on the North not a tile, nor scarcely a straw was moved. A woman drowned herself at St. James's-bridge: a young child in her arms, was carried down the stream to a sand-bed, where, recovering breath, it cried, was taken up, and saved.

1665.—Derby was again visited with the plague, at the same time in which London fell under that severe calamity. The town was

forsaken; the farmers declined the Market-
place; and grass grew upon the spot where the
supports of life had been sold. To prevent a
famine, the inhabitants erected at the top of
Nun's-green, a little way out of the town,
what bore the name of Headless-cross, consisting of about four quadrangular steps, covered
in the centre with one large stone; the whole
near five feet high.. Hither the market-people,
having their mouths primed with tobacco as a
preservative, brought their provisions; taking
care, at the same time, to stand at a distance
from their property, and at a greater from the
town's-people, with whom they were to traf-
fic.   The buyer was not suffered to touch any
of the articles before purchase; but when the
agreement was made, he took the goods, and
deposited the money in a vessel filled with vi-
negar, set for that purpose.   A confidence,
raised by necessity, took place between the
buyer and seller, which never existed before or
since; the first could not examine the value of
his purchase, nor the second that of his money.
It was observed, that this dreadful affliction
never entered the premises of a tobacconist, a
tanner, a soap-boiler, or a shoe-maker.

In 1673, there was a great flood upon the
Markeaton-brook, which carried away the hay,

filled the cellars of houses at the upper end of
Rotten-row, and broke down three of the then
ten bridges.

" 1674, on the 18th of February, the funeral
of Christiana, Countess of Devonshire, was so-
lemnized in great state. The Earl of Ayles-
bury with his son, and many other honourable
persons and gentlemen, and four heralds at
arms, attended at the solemnity. Dr. Framp-
ton preached a funeral sermon from Prov. xiv. 1.
In the afternoon a funeral oration was made by
Mr. Nealer from ii. Samuel chap iii. 38, in
commemoration and commendation of Colonel
Charles Cavendish, who was slain in the intes-
tine wars about Newark, in the year 1643, whose
bones were brought at the same time, and likewise laid up in the vault at All-hallows church.
One hundred pounds were given as a dole to
the poor of Derby.

1675. A quarrel between Henry Mellor, and
the corporation, occasioned about forty law-
suits, relative to an inclosure. A fire at Northampton, destroyed most of the town. The inhabitants of Derby, out of compassion, sent
the sufferers £150; and Mr. Grey, their town-
clerk, twenty.

" In the year 1680, the association of the inhabitants to preserve their rights against the

encroachments of the crown was burnt; the town charter given up, and the present one procured, at the expence of nearly four hundred pounds.

"On the twenty-first of November, 1688, the Earl of Devonshire came to Derby with a retinue of five hundred men. He invited many gentlemen to dinner, and openly declared his sentiments in favor of the Prince of Orange, who had just landed in England. After reading to the mayor, and the commonalty, the declaration of the prince, he delivered another made by himself, and the nobility and gentry in concert with him; declaring,—' that they would, to their utmost, defend the protestant religion, the laws of the kingdom, and the rights and liberties of the subject.' But through fear, the inhabitants did not immediately declare themselves the supporters of the Prince; for a detachment of his troops entering the town a little time after, the mayor durst not billet them: a spirited constable, however, of the name of Cook, sent them into quarters.

"On November 5, 1698, a great flood caused a great part of St. Werburgh's church to fall.*

* This produced a paltry rhyme from a person of the name of JOHN PEGGE:
  Fifth of November, Gunpowder plot,
  The Church is fall'n; and why not?

1705,[*] furnishes the annalist with as dreadful an instance of human depravity, and the want of parental and brotherly affection, as ever has been recorded.—About the reign of Oliver Cromwell, or the beginning of that of Charles II, a whole family of the name of *Crosland* were tried at Derby assizes, and condemned, for horse-stealing. As the offence was not capital, the Bench, after sentence, entertained the cruel whim, of extending mercy to one of the criminals; but upon this barbarous condition, that the pardoned man, should hang the other two. When power wantons in cruelty, it becomes detestable, and gives greater offence than even the culprits. The offer was made to the father being the senior. As distress is the season for reflection, he replied

6   B b

which was thought at that time, (though to us their less serious descendants, it appears as devoid of sense as of harmony) of so criminal a nature, and of so much consequence, that it raised the clamour of the Establishment against its rhyming author, and the body of Christians to which he belonged.

[*] It is necessary to observe, that the memorandums which are not inclosed in inverted commas, are related on the authority of Mr. HUTTON ; which, like the following account, are sometimes delivered in his own words ; but the peculiarity of his style, will, in general, render an acknowledgment unnecessary.

with meekness, ' was it ever known that a father hanged his children? How can I take
away those lives, which I have given, have
cherished, and which of all things, are the
most dear?' He bowed, declined the offer, and
gave up his life. Barbarous judges! I am sorry
I cannot transmit their names to posterity.—
This noble reply ought to have pleaded his
pardon. The offer was then made to the eldest
son, who trembling answered; ' Though life is
the most valuable of all possessions, yet even
that may be purchased too dear. I cannot
consent to preserve my existence by taking
away his who gave it; nor could I face the
world, or even myself, should I be left the only
branch of that family which I had destroyed.'
Love, tenderness, compassion, and all the
appendages of honor, must have associated
in returning this answer. The proposition was
then of course made to the younger, John, who
accepted it with an avidity, that seemed to tell
the court, he would hang half the creation, and
even his judges, rather than be a sufferer himself.—He performed the fatal work without remorse, upon his father and brother, and ac-
quitted himself with such dexterity, that he
was appointed to the office of hangman in
Derby, and two or three neighbouring coun-

ties, and continued it to extreme old age. So
void of feeling for distress, he rejoiced at a
murder, because it brought the prospect of a
guinea. Perhaps he was the only man in court
who could hear with pleasure a sentence of
death. The bodies of the executed were his
perquisite: signs of life have been known to
return after execution; in which case, he prevented the growing existence by violence.—
Loving none, and beloved by none, he spent a
life of enmity with man. The very children
pelted him in the streets. The mothers endeavoured to stop the infant cry with the name of
John Crosland: He died without regret about
the year 1735.

In the year 1715 frequent riots were raised
in favor of the house of Stuart: There were
several persons in the town, who wished for
the re-establishment of the Pretender on the
throne of England. Among the Jacobites
three of the established clergymen of the town
ranked themselves: Sturges of All-saints pray-
ed publickly for *king James;* but after a moment's reflection, said, " *I mean king George.*"
The congregation became tumultuous; the military gentlemen drew their swords, and ordered him out of the pulpit, into which he never
returned. He pleaded *a slip of the tongue;*

but had he been as conversant in his New Testament as in politicks, he might have pleaded as an excuse the commandment, *to pray for our enemies.*

1735.—The steeple of All-saints church was within a few minutes of being consumed by fire. This was occasioned by a plumber, who, going to close some leaks in the leaden roof, made a fire on the top of the steeple upon a hearth of loose bricks, which he carelessly left unextinguished. Some days elapsed before a smoak was observed issuing from the battlements: and it was some time before any one, would venture up on the dangerous, but necessary business of exploring it. At last, however, this was done: the aspect was dreadful; the roof was melted, the sleepers burnt, and the main beam consumed to the very edge of the wall which supported it.—Thus a masterpiece of elegant workmanship was snatched from the flames in the moment of destruction.

But the most remarkable event, that has happened in Derby within the last century, is the entry of the Pretender, in the winter of 1745.

James, son of James II, after his two unsuccessful attempts to reinstate himself on the throne of his ancestors in the years 1708 and

1715, was compelled to take an asylum at
Rome; where Pope Clement VII. granted him
an annuity of about £3000. This fugitive prince,
during his residence at Rome, publicly professed the popish religion, and was treated
with every external appearance of royalty.—
His eldest son was styled Prince of Wales, and
treated as the presumptive heir of a crown;
and the younger son retained the imaginary
title of the Duke of York.

Charles Edward, which was the name of the
elder son, and the second who bore the name
of Pretender, was now in the twenty-fifth year
of his age. His person was tall, genteel, and
graceful: his manners free, generous, affable,
and engaging: his spirit brave, active, and en-
terprising. Since his disappointment of the
intended invasion of England in 1744, the
young adventurer was wholly intent on raising
an insurrection in that country. The ambitious hopes of ascending a throne perpetually
fired his heart; this was his principal meditation, and this he was determined to attempt.

A strong party had been forming in his favor,
among the discontented and disaffected chiefs
of the northern parts of Scotland; which, together with the succours expected from the
French, raised very sanguine hopes of success

in the breast of the young Prince. Impatient
to visit Scotland, he took leave of the old Chevalier (for that was the title which the first
Pretender had assumed after his Scotch expedition in 1708,) at Rome, and went to France,
where he was furnished with some supplies.—
On the fourteenth of July 1745, he embarked
on board a frigate of eighteen guns, with seven
of his exiled adherents at port St. Lazare in
Bretany; and on the twenty-seventh of the
same month, landed at Moidart, between the
islands of Skey and Mull.

He was joyfully received, by the chiefs of
many of the clans, who resorted to their favorite prince, and paid him every external mark
of respect; and the young Pretender soon assembled upwards of two thousand men. About
the end of the month of August, the rebels,
left their encampment in the neighbourhood of
Fort William, and directed their march through
Badenoch and Inverness to Perth and Dundee,
where they proclaimed the Pretender and increased their numbers to four thousand men.
The young Chevalier marched from Perth on
the eleventh of September; he passed the
Forth on the thirteenth; on the sixteenth, at
night, he arrived in the neighbourhood of
Edinburgh; and at five the next morning, the

city was surrendered to him without any resistance. He made his public entrance in the
highland habit, at the head of one thousand of
his best looking men, who conducted him to
the royal palace of Holyrood-house.

The Pretender's army, amounting to upwards of five thousand men, advanced to the
village of Duddington, and from thence on the
twentieth of September to the neighbourhood
of Preston-Pans. There, the young Chevalier,
after a short and animating address, led his
men against the royalists, who were soon thrown
into confusion, broke, dispersed, and totally
routed. About four hundred of the royal
forces were killed in this engagement, and the
prisoners amounted to near twelve hundred
men. Among the slain was Colonel Gardiner,
who fell, covered with wounds, near the walls
of his own garden. The loss of the rebels was
very trifling. The consequences of this victory
were highly advantageous to the Pretender.—
Great numbers of eminent persons now openly
professed their attachment to him, and his army was continually increasing, till they became sufficiently formidable to think of in-
vading England.

This determination was put in execution
very shortly. On the first of November they

decamped in three divisions; the first column
led by the young Pretender, the second by the
Duke of Perth, and the third by the Earl of
Kilmarnock; who taking different routs, through
Tweedale, Lauderdale, and Tiviotdale, assembled near Carlisle on the eighth, invested it on
the ninth, and summoned it to surrender on
the tenth: which, however it did not do until
the fourteenth. The rebels had no intention of
continuing at Carlisle; but to march forwards
with all possible expedition, in hopes of arriv-
ing in London, while a general panick was scattered over the nation. They left a garrison of
two hundred men in the castle of Carlisle, and
began their march southwards on the twenty-
first of November. After entering Penrith, they
advanced to Lancaster on the twenty-fourth:
from whence they proceeded to Preston on the
twenty-seventh, and the next day took possession of Manchester. Here they continued
only one day, for they set out on the thirtieth
for Derby, in two divisions, which united at
Macclesfield on the first of December: the next
day they resumed their march in two columns,
one of which entered Congleton, and the other
passed near Gawsworth: on the third, the one
divison proceeded to Leek, and the other to

Ashbourne: from whence they marched on the fourth and united at Derby.

The inhabitants of Derby, aware of the danger which threatened them, had done all in their power, to provide for their own safety. A general subscription was made by the town and country gentlemen, which had enabled them to raise near six hundred men; which they added to the one hundred and fifty levied and maintained at the sole expence of the Duke of Devonshire. The confidence which they placed in this small corps, together with the expectation that the Duke of Cumberland would come to an engagement with the rebels the next day, put the town's people in high spirits. But when they were informed, that a division of the Pretender's army had arrived at Ashbourne, the greatest terror and confusion prevailed.—About ten o'clock the night preceding the entry of the Chevalier, the drums beat to arms, and the soldiers, on whom they had a few hours before rested their hopes, marched, by torchlight, to Nottingham, with the Duke of Devonshire at their head. Several of the principal inhabitants of the town, after having con-

7 · · c c

---

* Memoirs of the Duke of Cumberland.

veyed away or secreted their most valuable
effects, departed themselves with their families:
nothing but distraction appeared in every countenance, while inevitable destruction seemed at
their very doors.

About noon the following day, (the fourth of
December) the Pretender's vanguard entered
the town; and, after seizing a valuable horse,
belonging to a respectable inhabitant, they
proceeded to the George Inn, and demanded
billets for nine thousand men. They then enquired for the magistrates; but upon their being informed they had fled, they seemed satisfied: however, they afterwards found an alderman, whose lameness had prevented his flight,
and seizing upon him, he was obliged to proclaim the Prince. To prevent any unfavorable
impression being made on the minds of the army, the bells were rung, and several bonfires
were kindled. About two o'clock in the afternoon, Lord Balmarino arrived, accompanied
by thirty of the life-guards. These composed
the flower of the army, and being dressed in
the same uniform, which was blue, with scarlet
waistcoats trimmed with gold lace, made a fine
appearance. They were drawn up in the market-place, where they continued till three,
when Lord Elcho arrived with one hundred

and fifty men, the remainder of the guards: these, upon the whole, were fine figures, but their horses were very much jaded.

Soon after, the main body of the Pretender's army entered the town in tolerable order, marching six or eight a-breast; carrying eight white standards with red crosses. This part of the army, composed of all ages and sizes, was clad in almost every kind of dress, and marked with fatigue and dirt. Their music was chiefly the bagpipe, which it is well known has a surprising effect on the martial spirit of the hardy Highlander. Orders were immediately issued to proclaim the Prince, which was done by the common cryer. At dusk the young Chevalier arrived: he entered the town on foot, accompanied by a part of his guards. Although anxiety and fatigue had made some impressions upon him, he yet was handsome: He was dressed in a green bonnet laced with gold, a white bob wig, the fashion of the day, a highland plaid, and a broad sword. He was surrounded by a large body of men, who conducted him to Lord Exeter's, now N. Edwards's, Esq. in the Full-street, where he took up his quarters. The Dukes of Athol and Perth, Lord Balmarino, Lord George Murray, Lord Pitsligo, old Gordon of Glenbucket, Lord

Nairn, and other persons of distinction, with their chief and general officers, took possession of the best houses in the town. Many of the inhabitants had forty, and some fifty men each, quartered upon them, and some gentlemen's houses nearly a hundred.

On their arrival at Derby, the rebel chiefs held a council of war; but the only resolution they appear to have formed, was that of levying money on the inhabitants. Having obtained a list of those persons, who had subscribed for the support of the lawful government, they obliged them to pay an equal sum towards the support of the Pretender. They demanded the produce of the land-tax, excise, and post-office; the latter was refused them; but from the two former, added to the contribution, they actually procured a sum little short of £3,000. Articles of dress were every where applied for, for they were very much wanted, as many of the misguided men, were but half covered: some they procured with money, but when that was wanting, they did not hesitate to take them without payment. The conduct of the inhabitants towards their unwelcome visitors, was humble and obliging, and every care was taken to prevent insult and depredation: but all efforts to attain this end were ineffectual. On the second day, they seized on all kinds of property, and behaved in so outrageous a manner, that many of the more respectable inhabitants, thought it prudent to conceal themselves. During their stay they beat up for volunteers, at five shillings advance, and five guineas, which was to be paid on their arrival in London: but they were joined by only three unprincipled and idle fellows;—*Cook*, a travelling journeyman blacksmith; *Edward Hewit*, a butcher; and *James Sparks*, a stocking-maker: men of degraded lives and sullied characters.

On the evening of the second day, instead of marching forwards, as was expected, another council of war was privately held at the headquarters. Their situation by this time appeared critical; and many of the chiefs assumed a bold and commanding tone: so warm at last did their debates grow, that they were overheard by Alderman Eaton, who constantly attended the Duke of Perth, and was waiting for him near the Prince's lodging. It was urged by the chiefs, that—" they had followed their Prince with alacrity; that their love for his cause, was equal to the hazard they ran. That the French had not fulfilled their engagements in sending the necessary supplies, nor in mak-

ing a diversion in the West to draw the military attention.   That the English promises were
still more delusive; for they had been given to
understand, as soon as the Prince's standard
should be erected in England, the majority
would run with eagerness to join it; instead of
which, they had raised only one slender regiment in their long march, which barely supplied their travelling losses.   That the English
were extremely loyal to the House of Stuart,
when warmed by a good fire and good liquor; but
the warmth of their fire, their liquor, and their
loyalty, evaporated together.   That they were
then in the centre of an enemy's country, with
a handful of men : to retreat was dangerous;
but to proceed must be certain destruction."

The situation of the Pretender at this time
was most critical : the Duke of Cumberland
had encamped his army on Meriden-common,
near Coventry; while Marshal Wade was advancing by rapid marches from the town of
Newcastle.   These dispositions of the royal
forces, threw the rebels into the greatest per-
plexity, as they found themselves enclosed by
two considerable armies; and the nearest of
them under the command of a young, intrepid,
and well-esteemed General.   Their fear naturally bred confusion, and their danger created

distrust. Their councils were agitated with
all the disorder and passion, attendant on men
in their dangerous situation, and desperate circumstances. Some were for advancing, and
giving the Duke battle: but the majority were
for returning to Scotland, and joining the forces
under Lord John Drummond, before they were
cut off from all possibility of effecting their
retreat.

It was therefore determined upon, to re-tread
their steps towards Scotland: and early on
Friday morning the drums beat to arms, and
their bagpipes played about the town. The pass
at Swarkeston-bridge had been previously secured, and it was therefore expected, that they
would march thither, and pursue their rout
towards London. But about seven o'clock,
they left the town, and took the road to Ashbourne. In their retreat the Prince rode a black
horse, said to have been Colonel Gardiner's,
slain at Preston-Pans. Their hussars rode into
the adjacent country, and plundered the inhabitants of horses, and every other kind of valuable property. Two of the rebels went to
Clifton near Ashbourne, and demanded a horse,
which being refused, they shot the person to
whom it belonged. They likewise in the same
violent manner, took away the life of the inn-

keeper at Hanging-bridge, between Ashbourne
and Leek. , . . ! . . . . : . . ..:
. When the rebels had quitted Derby, the magistrates ordered a return of their number in
every house to be made, during the two nights
of their stay; when it appeared that there
were,

Fint night,..............7,098, . . .
Second night,..........7,148.*

: The Pretender's army, on their abandonment
of Derby, marched with such expedition through
Ashbourne, Leek, Manchester, Leigh and Wig-
gan, that they re-entered Preston on the twelfth;
and continued their march northward with the
same celerity; but they shewed a warm spirit
of resentment for their disappointment, by
plundering the country, and levying contributions wherever they could. Soon after the departure of the rebel army from Preston, the
royalists under the Duke of Cumberland came

* The following is an exact account, as they were quartered
in the several parishes :

Parishes.	First night.		Second night.
All-Saints,	2,979,	....	3,027.
St. Werburgh's,	1,590,	....	1,641.
St. Peter,	1,091,	....	1,001.
St. Michael,	724,	....	724.
St. Alkmund,	714,	....	755.
	7,098,		7,148.

up, and very much harrassed its rear: which, together with that of Marshal Wade in front, placed the rebels in a dangerous situation. But after a skirmish at the village of Clifton, the Pretender led his troops to Carlisle, from whence they proceeded unmolested; and crossing the Eden and Solway, re-entered Scotland, in two columns, and directed their march for Glasgow. From Glasgow they proceeded to Stirling, in the neighbourhood of which, they had an engagement with the royalists, and defeated them. On the twenty-ninth of January, 1746, the rebels left Stirling, and retiring over the Forth at Frew, proceeded to Perth; there they separated into three columns, with the intention of forming a junction at Inverness. Here they remained until the fifteenth of April, when the army under the Duke of Cumberland arrived in the neighbourhood of the town. The young Pretender, immediately drew out his army on Straghallan-moor, near Culloden-house, four miles to the East of Inverness, where he intended opposing the progress of the royal army.

The hour was now approaching, to determine all the expectations of the rebels, who principally depended on their personal strength, and dexterity in the management of the broad

7 D d

sword. The royal army decamped from Nairn; and after passing a morass, came in full view of the rebels, who were drawn up in line of battle, behind some huts and old walls, on the moor, near Culloden-house. About one o'clock on the sixteenth of April the engagement commenced; and the rebels, after a desperate struggle of twenty-five minutes, dispersed in a general confusion. Their flight was precipitate; and the royalists pursued them with a dreadful slaughter.

The fatal battle of Culloden dispelled every remaining hope of success, entertained by the Pretender and his adherents. Many of the principal Scottish chiefs were made prisoners by the royalists, and afterwards fell by the hand of the executioner: while the young Chevalier himself escaped with the greatest difficulty. He sustained an innumerable variety of hardships, before he could leave Scotland: but he continually eluded the most vigilant search of the royal forces, until the third of September, when a privateer from St. Malo, arrived at Lochanach, and delivered him from his melancholy situation, by carrying him to Morlaix in France; accompanied by a few of his faithful friends, who had long wandered with, or followed him from shore to shore, and from island to island; surrounded with imminent dangers, encountering incredible difficulties, and partaking of all his calamities. Soon after this unsuccessful expedition, the Pretender retired to Rome, where, this last but one,* of the imprudent Stuarts, died in the year 1788.

Thus was a rebellion, which had created a most unprecedented alarm throughout the whole

---

* Henry Benedict Marie Clement, Cardinal York, and brother to Charles Edward Stuart, the Pretender, died at Rome in the year 1807. At the close of the year 1745, he went from Rome where he constantly resided, to Dunkirk, to put himself at the head of 13,000 men, who were to have landed in England, to support his brother Charles. But these troops having not embarked before intelligence was received of the issue of the battle of Culloden, he returned to Rome; where, much against the consent of his brother and the friends of his family, he took orders; and in 1747, was made Cardinal, and afterwards Bishop of Frescati, and Chancellor of the Church of Rome. From that time Cardinal York, (the name he assumed on his promotion) devoted himself to the functions of his ministry, and seemed to have laid aside all worldly views till his brother's death ; when he had medals struck, with the following inscriptions—viz. on the obverse. Hen. IX. Mag. Brit. Fr. et. Hib. Rex. Fid. Def. Card. Ep. Tusc. and on the reverse, a city, (or Rome) with a figure of religion, a lion couchant at her feet, and Non desideriis Hominum, sed voluntate Dei. It is in large bronze. The Cardinal was the last of the Stuarts; of whom Voltaire says, "few princes have been more unfortunate; nor have we any instance in history of a family so unhappy for such a number of years."

country, happily quelled: and though it is to
be regretted, that after so complete a victory
as that of Culloden, the scaffold should have
streamed with blood; yet, every liberal mind,
must rejoice, that his country escaped the ty-
ranny of a usurper, who believed in the divine right of kings, and their absolute power,
and was a slave to the grossest superstition.

1768. The King of Denmark arrived at the
George.

The town of Derby, during the lapse of near
700 years, has given the title of *Earl* to several
potent and noble families. It is asserted by
some writers, that the honor was first conferred
on one of the Peverels, Lords of Nottingham:
however this may be, it was certainly enjoyed
by Robert de Ferrariis, a grandson of Henry
de Ferrariis, who came over with the Conquer-
or, and settled at Tutbury Castle. This nobleman, having with some other northern chiefs,
opposed and defeated David king of Scots, at
the battle of North-Allerton in Yorkshire, was
created Earl of Derby, by king Stephen. But
he enjoyed the title no more than one year;
and in 1139 was succeeded by his son Robert:
he founded the religious house of St. Helen's,*

* Page 137.

built and endowed the Abbey of Merry-vale,
near Atherston, was a liberal benefactor to the
Priory of Tutbury; and ordered at his death,
that his body should be wrapped in an ox's
hide and interred in the Abbey of Merry-vale.
He died in 1147, and was succeeded by his son
William: who married Margaret, the heiress
and representative of the Peverels; with whom
he received the vast fortunes of that house, and
became immensely rich. He held 203 lordships, 114 of which were in Derbyshire. Robert, his son, inherited his title and property;
and died in 1173, the 19th of Henry II. The
title was next enjoyed by William de Ferrariis,
son of the latter. He rebelled against Henry
II. and against his successor Richard I. who
deprived him of his honors and estates. The
castles of Nottingham, Lancaster, and Derby,
with the honor of Peverel, were given by king
Richard to his brother John Plantagenet.—
When John, however, mounted the throne, he
restored the confiscated estates of the father to
the son, William, whom he created Earl of
Derby, by a special charter at Northampton,
in the first year of his reign. The king girded
on his sword with his own hand; and restored
to him his third penny, enjoyed by the Saxon
Earls, with other property. The year follow-

ing his being created Earl, king John granted
him the service of William de Gresley, and his
heirs, for his lands at Drakelow, to hold by
the annual payment of a bow, quiver, and
twelve arrows. He died in 1247, and was
succeeded by his nephew. William, who survived him only seven years, spent his time in
improving his estate, and studying the laws of
his country, in which he was well versed. As
he was very infirm, he generally rode in a chariot; which, owing to the carelesness of the
driver, was overturned in passing the bridge of
St. Neots, in Huntingtonshire, and he killed;
he was interred in 1254, with his ancestors in
the Abbey of Merry-vale. Robert his son was
a minor at the death of his father; but when
he came to maturity, he joined the Barons in
a rebellion against Henry III. who sent his son,
afterwards Edward I. to destroy the Earl's estates in the counties of Stafford and Derby.—
By this revolt, Robert lost his title, and a large
part of his estates; which Henry bestowed on
his son Edmund. Robert made an attempt to
purchase of Henry his confiscated property;
but not being able to raise the enormous sum
agreed upon, (£50,000), he never recovered his
title or lands. Thus, in 1265, after the Ferrers had enjoyed the Earldom 127 years, and

the estate 199; by the imprudence of one, the
the wealth and honor were for ever lost to their
descendants.

This ancient family, having been deprived of
the Earldom, the title was not disposed of till
the year 1829; when Edward III. by an act of
Parliament, created Henry Plantagenet, son
of Henry, Duke of Lancaster, Earl of Derby.
This Earl had a daughter, Blanche, who married John of Gaunt, to whom, of course, the
Earldom passed. It was then inherited by
their son Henry, in right of his mother; until
he mounted the throne under the title of Henry
IV. when it was vested in the crown, and the
title of *Earl* was superseded by that of *King*.

The title, however, was not long unoccu-
pied; for Henry VII. in 1485, bestowed it on
Thomas Lord Stanley, of Knocking, in the
county of Lancaster. The ancestor of this
family, came into England, as an officer in the
army of William I. under the name of *Audley*.
Nicholas de Audley, a descendant of this officer,
was created by Edward I. in 1296, Baron
Audley of Highleigh, in the county of Stafford;
but in 1391, this title became extinct. One of
this family, being proprietor of the manor of
Stanley, in the county of Derby, took it for
his surname; a practice very common in those

times. John, the seventh in descent from the
first who assumed the name of Stanley, was
married to Isabella, heiress of the house of Latham, by which marriage he acquired a great
fortune. Richard II. made him Lord Deputy,
and Lord Lieutenant of Ireland; and Henry
IV. created him Steward of his Household.
Henry VI. conferred upon him the title of Baron
Stanley of Latham, in the year 1456: He died
in 1469, and was succeeded by his son Thomas,
the first of the family of Stanley, who bore
the title of Earl of Derby. He was renowned
for arms; and commanded the right wing of
the army which Edward sent against the Scotch,
under the Duke of Gloucester. He married for
his first wife, Eleanor, daughter of Richard Neville, Earl of Salisbury; and for his second, Margaret Countess of Richmond, who with her son,
afterwards Henry VII. were the only remaining
heirs of the House of Lancaster. He was a
firm adherent to Edward V.—and Richard III.
endeavoured to conciliate his esteem by making
him Steward of his Household, and Lord High
Constable of England for life. But at the battle of Bosworth-field, Lord Stanley deserting
Richard, espoused the cause of Richmond;
who being successful, Stanley seized the crown
of Richard, and placed it upon the brow of

Henry, at the same time exclaiming in the words of our immortal Poet:—

" Courageous Richmond, well hast thou acquit thee!
Lo here, this long-usurped royalty,
From the dead temples of this bloody wretch
Have I pluck'd off, to grace thy brows withal;
Wear it, enjoy it, and make much of it."

Shakspeare's Richard III.

Henry, in return for his step-father's service, gave him the Earldom of Derby. He died in the year 1504, and was buried in Burscough Priory. The title has ever since continued in the family of the Stanleys; and has now passed through twelve descents.

Among the eminent men, which Derby has produced, Dr. THOMAS LINACRE or LINAGER, claims the first place as to priority of time.— He was born at Derby about 1460, and received the rudiments of his education at the King's School at Canterbury. He went from there to All-souls College, Oxford, where he pursued his studies, particularly physic, with great attention; and soon became a fellow. After completing his academical studies, he travelled for his improvement, and spent a considerable part of his life in Italy; where he learned Greek, and practised physic with remarkable success. He was much noticed on the continent, for his learning and general knowledge;

7   E e

and was pronounced by the Duke of Tuscany,
who shewed him many favors, the politest
scholar of the age. On his return to England,
he took his doctor's degree, and was made professor of physic at Oxford. After that he took
up his abode in London, and became first physician to Henry VII. who appointed him preceptor to Prince Arthur:—he also was made
physician to Henry VIII, Prince Edward, and
the Princess Mary. He founded two medical
lectures at Oxford, and one at Cambridge: but
that which most effectually immortalized his
name among the faculty, is his being the founder of the College of Physicians in London.
Grieved at the wretched state of physic in
England, he applied to cardinal Wolsey, and
obtained a patent by which the physicians of
London were incorporated; and by this means
prevented illiterate and ignorant quacks, to
practise the art of healing. He erected the
edifice on the scite of his own building; in
Knight-Rider-Street, which was afterwards destroyed by the great fire in 1666. Linacre was
the first President of the College, and held the
office as long as he lived. In 1509, he entered
into orders, and obtained the Precentorship of
York, which he resigned on being made Prebendary of Westminster. He died in 1524;

aged 64, and was buried under a stately monument at St. Paul's. He was a man of great
natural sagacity, a skilful physician, a profound grammarian, one of the best Greek and
Latin scholars of his time, and intimate with
Collet, Erasmus, and most of the eminent literary characters of the age. He published ;
1. A Latin translation of Proclus's Sphere,
1449 ; 2. The Rudiments of Grammar, for the
use of the Princess Mary ; 3. De emandata
Structura Latini Sermonis ; 4. A Translation of
some of the Works of Galen. He was not forgetful of his native town, for he left an annual
benefaction to Derby, which even to this day,
is called *Linager's charity.* Some of his descendants, or those of a part of his family, are
still residents in the town, and go by the name
of Linney.

JOHN FLAMSTEAD, the great Astronomer, it is
generally supposed, was born in Derby ; though
some affirm, that the village of Denby, had the
honor of giving him birth. At present it seems
impossible to ascertain which was the place of
his nativity ; as the registers of the parishes of
Derby, and that of Denby, have been examined, without affording any satisfactory evidence. He was born on the 19th of August,
1646 ; at which period, or very shortly after,

his father resided in the town. He received the
first part of his education at the Free-School in
St. Peter's church-yard; but was prevented by
ill health from prosecuting his studies, and
duly preparing himself for the University.—
During his confinement, he accidentally meet
with an astronomical book, the perusal of which
pleased him, and determined the complexion
of his future life. When very young he discovered a taste for mathematical learning, and
pursued it with unabated ardor to the end of
his days. His first attempts in astronomy,
which were, calculations of the places of the
planets, and of an eclipse of the sun by the
Caroline tables, procured him the patronage
of Mr. Emanuel Halton, a mathematician of
some eminence, who resided at Wingfield manor. This gentleman very liberally supplied
the young astronomer with the means of prosecuting his favorite studies, and presented
him with the best books then extant, on the
science. From this time, he made a very rapid
progress in his attainments; and in 1680, at
the age of twenty-three, he calculated some remarkable eclipses of the fixed stars, which
were to happen the following year, and sent it
to the Royal Society. For this paper, he received the thanks of that learned body, and

continued a correspondence with several of
its most respectable members. Soon after this
he visited London, and was introduced to the
most learned mathematicians of the age: and
in order to increase his knowledge, and preserve the reputation he had already acquired,
he entered himself a student of Jesus College,
Cambridge. In the year 1674, passing through
London, in his way to the University, he was
informed by Sir Jonas Moore, that a true account of the tides would be acceptable to the
king, (Charles II.) and advised him to compose
a small Ephemeris for his majesty's use, as a
very proper recommendation of himself to the
royal favor. By this means, he was introduced
to the king; and through the friendly offices of
Sir Jonas, who, on every occasion, extended
the fame of his industry and acquirements, he
was, in the following year appointed astronomer to the king, with a salary of £100 a year.
This appointment did not lessen his inclination
to go into the church; for in a few months afterwards, he was ordained by the Bishop of
Ely; and in the year 1684, was presented by
the crown, with the living of Burstow in Surry,
the only church preferment he ever received.
On the 10th of August, 1675, during his residence at Greenwich, he laid the first stone of

the *Royal Observatory*, built by king Charles
II. at the solicitation of Sir Jonas Moore, then
surveyor-general of the ordnance. He took
possession of the observatory in 1676, as first
astronomer royal, and directed his whole attention to the advancement of that science,
which had been the means of raising him to
the honorable station he then held, and on
which his future discoveries threw so much
light.   Most of the instruments which this indefatigable man used, were made by himself,
and his ingenious assistant Mr. Abraham Sharp;
the principal of which, were the great sextant
and mural quadrant, which after his death were
delivered to his heirs.   After having made many important discoveries in astronomy, he died
on the last day of December, 1719, aged 73,
and lies buried in his own church-yard at Burstow, where, at present no remains of any tomb
or monument to his memory can be found ; nor
does any one in the place know in what part of
the church-yard he was buried.   He was married, but left no issue.   In 1725 appeared his
great work, *Historia Cælestis Britannica*, in
3 vols. folio :—it had been prepared, and in
part printed, before his death.   In the Philosophical Transactions are many of his papers,
and in Sir Jonas Moore's System of Mathema-

tics, is a tract by him on the Doctrine of the Sphere. Mr. Flamstead was intimately acquainted with Sir Isaac Newton, and most of the learned men of the age in which he lived; many of whom have spoken of him in terms of the highest admiration.

·· THOMAS PARKER, *Earl of Macclesfield*, though not born in the town of Derby, yet claims our notice, as having spent the active part of his life in the place; and having there laid the foundation of those riches and honors, which, in more mature life, he acquired. He was born somewhere·in Staffordshire in the year 1667; and· early in life came to live at Derby, and resided many years in Bridge-gate, practising as a common· attorney. ·Possessing good abilities and industry, he soon came into great practice; which, raising him to wealth and consequence among his fellow-citizens, he was chosen to fill the office of Recorder. This opened a wider field for his talents. The man who is conscious of his abilities, and assisted by activity, seldom stops in his progress towards excellency, or is disappointed in his expectations. Mr. Parker, soon after his being made Recorder, became a pleader· at the bar, and was esteemed an eminent counsellor on the Midland circuit. His reputation was so great as a

speaker, that he was denominated the silver-
tongued counsel, and in a short time acquired
a very large fortune. So great was his interest
in the town, that in 1705, he was chosen one
of its representatives in Parliament, with Lord
James Cavendish, son of the first Duke of Devonshire: and at the election of 1707, a similar honor was conferred upon him. Thus introduced on the great theatre of the political
world, his abilities became conspicuous. The
House of Commons, sensible of his powers, appointed him one of the managers, of the trial
of Dr. Sacheverell, in 1709, which he conducted with credit to himself, and satisfaction to
the House. From this period, he advanced
towards preferment with rapid strides: for
before the election of 1710, he was made Lord
Chief Justice of the King's Bench. On this
appointment he quitted Derby, and resided in
the Metropolis. An offer was soon after made
him, of the Chancellor's Seals: but he declined the acceptance, because his sentiments
did not coincide with those of the existing ministry. But George I. entertaining the highest
opinion of his merit, in 1716, created him
Baron Parker, and Viscount Parker of Ewelme,
1718; upon which he accepted the office of
Chancellor. He was created Earl of Maccles-

field in 1721; and continued Lord Chancellor
for six years; when being accused of selling
places in Chancery, he was brought to trial,
found guilty, and condemned to pay a fine of
£30,000, and to be deprived of the Chancel-
lorship. The king, in erasing his name out of
the council-book, is said to have dropped a tear,
for the loss of his beloved minister. The last
eight years of his life, were spent in retirement;
and after struggling with political broils, for
the greatest part of his days, he died in the
arms of philosophy and friendship, on the 28th
of April, 1732, at the age of sixty-five. In
the heighth of his prosperity, Lord Macclesfield was not forgetful of the place where the
scene of his future greatness had opened. In
1722, twelve years after he had left Derby, he
contributed one hundred guineas, and his son
Lord Parker, twenty more, for the erection of
the church of All-saints.

MR. JOHN WHITEHURST, an ingenious mechanic and philosopher, like the above-mentioned
nobleman, was not a native of Derby; but
having spent forty years of the prime of his
life in the place, and having acquired his popu-
larity during that residence, he deserves our
notice, as one of its eminent men. This wor-

thy man, was born, in the year 1713, at Congleton in Cheshire; where, his ancestors are
said to have resided upon a small estate, during
the lapse of 700 years. He was brought up to
his father's business, which was that of a clock
and watch-maker. This gave him a taste for
mechanics; which increased to such a degree,
that even while yet a young man, he went over
to Ireland, for the sole purpose of inspecting a
curious clock to be found in that country.—
About the year 1735, he opened a shop at Derby as a clock and watch-maker; but that being a corporate town, and he not a freeman,
some objections were made, as to the legality
of his practising his trade. But in 1737, he
set up a clock of his own workmanship in front
of the Guildhall, at his own expence; in return for which, the corporation presented him
with the freedom of the town. Sometime after,
he made a clock, and constructed a set of chimes,
for the tower of All-saints' church. In 1775,
he was appointed stamper of the money-weights,
for regulating the gold coin, at the mint, on
which he left Derby and his occupation, and
removed to London. While he lived in Derbyshire, the Peak could not less than attract his
attention, and furnish an ample field for his
philosophic mind. The book of nature lay

open before him; and he has perused its pages,
and examined its natural phenomena, with a
patience and assiduity seldom equalled. "These
appearances," he says,* " engaged his attention
very early in life, to search and inquire into
the various causes of them:" the fruit of this
research was, an "Enquiry into the Original
State and Formation of the Earth," in one Vol.
quarto; a work by which he is advantageously
known in the world of letters. It is the labor
of years, bearing evident marks of reflection
and minute examination; he treads upon new
ground, advances positions unknown to former
philosophy, and, to use his own language, en-
deavours " to *derive* the *nature of things*, from
causes truly existent, and to *inquire* after those
laws by which the *creator chose to form the
world*; and not *those* on which *he might* have
formed it, had *he* so pleased." This work was
first published in 1778, and again, with improvements, in 1786. He also wrote Ther-
mometrical Observations; an Account of a
Machine for raising Water; Experiments upon
Ignited Substances; an Attempt towards ob-
taining invariable Measures of Length, Capacity, and Weight, from the Mensuration of

* Preface to Enquiry.

Time; a Treatise on Ventilation, particularly on Smoaky Chimneys; and some Papers in the Philosophical Transactions. He also examined the nature of garden stoves, the properties of air, and the laws of fluids. Mr. Whitehurst died on the 18th of February, 1788, at the age of seventy-five, in Bolt-Court, London, in the very house, as Mr. Hutton remarks, where a few years before, died that great self-taught philosopher, James Ferguson. He was near six feet in height, straight, and well made; but as it appears, from an excellent likeness of him by Wright, (now in the possession of his nephew, Mr. Whitehurst of Derby), thin, and wore his own dark-grey bushy hair: he was plain in his dress, and appears to have had a contemplative countenance. Mr. Whitehurst was a Fellow of the Royal Society, before which he laid some very curious papers: he was also a member of several other Philosophical Societies; and his house was the resort of ingenious and scientific men, of whatever nation or rank.

Mr. Joseph Wright, the late celebrated Painter, was a native of Derby: he was born on the 3d of September, 1734, and was the son of a respectable attorney in the place. A taste for mechanical employments discovered

itself in his boyish years; and those hours,
which were generally consumed by boys of a
similar age. in juvenile sports and amusements,
were passed by him in the company of mechanics, whose performances he frequently imitated. But very early in life, his mind seemed to
have been principally occupied in the acquire-
ment of the art of drawing; and the compa-
rative correctness of his likenesses at this time,
was a promising indication of that genius,
which, in after life, was to immortalize his
name. The discovery of the bent of his mind,
was not lost upon his parents: he was sent to
London, and placed under the tuition of a
portrait-painter of the name of Hudson; who,
though not a person of extraordinary talents,
was peculiarly fortunate, either in his mode of
communicating instruction, or in the geniuses
of his pupils, as he had the honor of instructing three of the most eminent painters of the
age:—Sir Joshua Reynolds, Mortimer, and
Wright. With Mr. Hudson, young Wright
continued two years; upon the termination of
which he returned to Derby, where he practised
in the portrait line. Not satisfied, however,
with his own performances, he returned to
London in 1756, and pursued his studies for
fifteen months, under the direction of his for-

mer preceptor. He then came back to Derby,
after having made considerable progress in the
art, and executed several portraits in a superior
style. About the year 1760, he produced a set
of historical pictures, which deservedly rank
among the earliest valuable productions of the
English school: because prior to this time,
scarcely any paintings of consequence in the
historical line, had been produced. The principal in this set, were, the Gladiator, Orrery,
Air-Pump, Hermit, and Blacksmith's Forge;
paintings, whose excellency, established his reputation as an artist, on so firm a basis, that
neither the jealousy nor the calumnies of his
brethren in the profession, could ever over-
turn. The Royal Academy was established
some time after the production of these pieces,
but through the invidious jealousy of some of
the members, Wright was not elected a R. A.
This distinction, was afterwards gratuitously
offered him, by the hands of their Secretary,
Newton, who was deputed to visit him at
Derby, and solicit his acceptance of a diploma,
which he then indignantly rejected. In 1773,
at a mature age, he went to Italy, to visit the pre-
cious remains of art to be found in that country.
Here he resided two years, improving himself,
and studying the works of the greatest masters;

particularly, the inimitable productions of Michael Angelo, in the Capella Sistina of the
Vatican, from which he took several correct
copies. During his abode in Italy, he had the
good fortune to witness an extraordinary erup-
tion of Vesuvius, which increased his passion,
and very much improved his taste, for representing the superior effects of light: and his
different paintings of this sublime phenomenon, are deservedly ranked as *chef d' œuvres*,
in that style of colouring. His moonlights are
also particularly beautiful; and his mountain
and lake scenery superior to most similar productions:—for, unlike many artists who study
nature within doors, he passed his days and
evenings, in contemplating the beautiful and
delicate hues of objects under the various circumstances, attendant upon scenes of this description in the open air. On these kind of
subjects, his pencil was last employed; and his
view of *Ulls-water Lake*, from Lyulph's Tower,
may justly be considered as the finest of all his
landscapes, and a production, which alone
would rank him, among the most eminent
artists of the English school. On his return
from Italy; he settled in his native town, where
he died, on the 29th of August, 1797, esteemed
and lamented by all who were favored with his

friendship; but the time he devoted to his professional studies, prevented the circle of his
acquaintance from becoming extensive. " It is
pleasing to record," observes his biographer,[*]
" that in his works, the attention is ever directed to the cause of virtue; that his early historical pictures, consist of subjects either of rational or moral improvement; and he has succeeded admirably in arresting the gentler feelings of humanity; for what eye or heart ever
remained unmoved at the sight of Maria,
Sterne's Captive, or the Dead Soldier? In his
works, not 'one immoral, one corrupted thought'
occurs, to wound the eye of delicacy, or induce
a wish, that so exquisite a pencil had not found
employment on more worthy subjects."

The late celebrated Dr. ERASMUS DARWIN,
equally famed as a Physician and a Poet, spent
the last twenty-one years of his life at Derby,
and its vicinity. He was the son of a private
gentleman, of Elton, near Newark, Nottinghamshire; where he was born on the 12th of
December, 1732. He went through the usual
routine of Grammar-school education at Chesterfield, under the tuition of the Rev. Mr. Bur-
rows; and was sent to St. John's College;

* Rev. Thomas Gisborne: Monthly Mag. Oct. 1797.

Cambridge. There he continued until the
year 1755, when he took his batchelor's degree in medicine; and in his thesis on that occasion, maintained that the movements of the
heart and arteries, are immediately produced
by the stimulus of the blood. While at Cambridge, he composed a poem in 1751, on the
death of Frederic Prince of Wales: it was
printed among the Cambridge Collection of
Verses on that occasion, but in merit does not
rise above mediocrity. From Cambridge he
went to Edinburgh, to complete his studies;
which being finished, and having taken the
degree of doctor of medicine, he went to Litchfield, and there commenced his career of practice.

At this time he was four and twenty years of
age; " somewhat above the middle size; his
form athletic, and inclined to corpulency; his
limbs too heavy for exact proportion. The
traces of a severe small pox; features, and
countenance, which, when they were not animated by social pleasure, were rather saturnine
than sprightly; a stoop in the shoulders, and
the then professional appendage, a large full-
bottomed wig, gave him at that early period of
life, an appearance of nearly twice the years

he bore. Florid health, and the earnest of good humour, a sunny smile, on entering a room, and on first accosting his friends, rendered, in his youth, that exterior agreeable, to which beauty and symmetry had not been propitious."*

Soon after the arrival of Dr. Darwin at Litchfield, his skill and discernment as a physician were put to the test. Being sent for to a young. gentleman of family and consequence in the neighbourhood, who lay sick of a dangerous fever, and whose case had been pronounced hopeless by a celebrated physician, who had for many years possessed the business and confidence of the Litchfield neighbourhood; he, by a reverse and entirely novel course of treatment, gave his dying patient back to a fond and despairing mother, with renewed existence and renovated health. This success gave him so high a degree of reputation at Litchfield, and in the neighbouring towns and villages, that his competitor finding himself neglected, and his reputation eclipsed by his youthful and ingenious rival, gave up the contest and left the place. From that moment his practice became very extensive; and his future

---

* Miss Seward's Memoirs of the Life of Dr. Darwin.

efforts, were attended by a success equal to his
first fortunate exertion.

, In the year 1757, he married Miss Howard,
of the Close of Litchfield, who is represented
as " a blooming and lovely young lady of eighteen :" possessing " a mind, which had native
strength; an awakened taste for the works of
imagination; ingenuous sweetness; delicacy
animated by sprightliness, and sustained by
fortitude, made her a capable as well as fasci-
nating companion, even to a man of talents so
illustrious.—To her he could with confidence
commit the important task of rendering his
childrens' minds, a soil fit to receive, and bring
to fruit the stamina of wisdom and science.
But alas! upon her early youth, and a too delicate constitution, the frequency of her ma-
ternal situation, during the first five years of
her marriage, had probably a baneful effect.
The potent skill and assiduous cares of *him*,
before whom disease daily vanished from the
frame of *others*, could not expel it radically
from that of her he loved. It was however
kept at bay thirteen years. Upon the distinguished happiness of those years, she spoke
with fervor, to two intimate female friends, in
the last week of her existence, which closed at
the latter end of the summer 1770."* By this

* Memoirs; p. 11.

lady he had three sons, who lived to the age
of manhood: two of them he survived; the
third Dr. Robert Waring Darwin, is now in
considerable practice as a physician at Shrewsbury.   ‹

Dr. Darwin's house during his residence at
Litchfield, is represented as the resort of a knot
of philosophic friends, who frequently met together.   Among these are enumerated;—The
Rev. Mr. Michell, a skilful astronomer; the
ingenious Mr. Kier, of West Bromich, then
Captain Kier; Mr. Boulton, the celebrated
mechanic; Mr. Watt, the improver of the steam
engine; the accomplished Dr. Small, of Bir-
mingham, who bore the blushing honors of his
talents and virtues to an untimely grave; Mr.
Edgeworth, well known in the literary world;
Mr. Day, author of The Dying Negro, The
Devoted Legions, and the ingenious story of
Sanford and Merton; Sir Brook Boothby;
F. N. C. Mundy, Esq. of Markeaton; and Miss
Seward, who wrote the Memoirs of the Doc-
tor's Life.

In the year 1781, Dr. Darwin married a second wife; Mrs. Pole, the widow of Colonel
Pole, of Radburn, Derbyshire. This lady he
had first seen in the year 1778, when she had
brought her children, who had been injured
by a dangerous quantity of the *cicuta*, injudi-

ciously administered to them in the hooping
cough, by a physician in the neighbourhood,
to be under his care. Mrs. Pole remained with
her children at the Doctor's house for a few
weeks; till the poison was expelled from their
constitutions and their health restored: and by
her external accomplishments and internal qualifications she contributed to inspire Dr. Darwin's admiration, and to secure his esteem.—
In 1780 Colonel Pole died; and an opportunity was thus afforded the Doctor of disclosing an
affection, which he had long entertained, but
which he was obliged to confine within his own
breast. His addresses were accepted: and as
Mrs. Darwin had taken a dislike to Litchfield,
he removed directly on his marriage to Derby.
His reputation, and the unlimited confidence
of the public, followed him thither: and he
once more became a happy husband with a second family of children, springing up fast
around him. About the year 1801, Dr. Darwin removed from Derby to the Priory, a house
about two miles distant from the town, which
he had fitted up for the place of his future
abode. But alas! his residence there, was destined to be of no long continuance. On Sunday the 18th of April 1802, Derby and its vicinity, and the lettered world of genius, were

deprived by death of Dr. Darwin. During a
few preceding years, he had been subject to
sudden and alarming disorders of the chest, in
which he always applied the lancet, instantly
and freely: he had repeatedly risen in the
night and bled himself. The year preceding
his death, he had a very dangerous illness. It
originated in a severe cold, caught by obeying
the summons of a patient in Derby, after he
had himself taken some strong medicine. His
skill, his courage, his exertion, struggled ve-
hemently with his disease. Repeated and daring use of the lancet at length subdued it;
but, in all likelihood, irreparably weakened
the system.

He seemed to have a presentiment of his approaching dissolution; as on the evening preceding it, while in conversation in the garden
of his new residence, the Priory, with Mrs.
Darwin and her female friend, he remarked,
that it was not likely that he should live to see
the effect of those improvements he had planned. The following morning he arose in health
and spirits; and after taking a large draught
of cold buttermilk, according to his usual custom, he proceeded to write some letters. But he
had written no more than one page, of a very
sprightly one to Mr. Edgeworth, describing

the Priory, and his intended alterations there, when the fatal signal was given. He rang the bell and ordered his servant to send Mrs. Darwin to him. She came immediately, accompanied by one of her daughters. They saw him shivering and pale. He desired them to send directly to Derby, for his surgeon : but he was dead before he could arrive. It was the general opinion, that a glass of brandy might have saved him for that time. Its effects would have been more powerful from his utter disuse of spirits; and perhaps, on such a sudden chill of the blood, its application might have proved restoring. The body was opened, but no traces of a peculiar disorder were found; and the state of the viscera indicated a much more protracted existence. " Yet thus (to use the words of his fair memorialist, from whose work this sketch is principally taken) in one hour, was extinguished the vital light, which the preceding hour, had shone in flattering brightness, promising duration—such is often the ' cunning flattery of nature;' that light which through half a century, had diffused its radiance and its warmth so widely; that light, in which penury had been cheered, in which science had expanded: to whose orb poetry had brought all her images: before whose influence disease had

continually retreated, and death had so often
turned aside his levelled dart!"

Dr. Darwin died in his sixty-ninth year.—
As to his person it has been remarked, that he
was rather unwieldly in his appearance, having a slight lameness, caused by an incurable
weakness, proceeding from an accident which
befel him at Litchfield, of breaking the patel-
la of his knee. He stammered exceedingly,
and his tongue seemingly too large for his
mouth, made it rather difficult to understand
him. But whatever he said, whether gravely
or in jest, was always worth waiting for: and
the intelligence and benevolence, with which
his features were lighted up, in conversation,
did away every unpleasant sensation, which
might have been excited by an apparent defor-
mity. Conscious of great native elevation,
above the common standard of intellect, he
became, early in life, sore upon opposition,
whether in argument or conduct, and always
revenged it by sarcasm of very keen edge.—
Nor was he less impatient of the sallies of
egotism and vanity: even when they were, in
so slight a degree, that strict politeness would
rather tolerate than ridicule them. Dr. Darwin seldom failed to present their caricature
in jocose but wounding irony. He carried his

skepticism of human truth so far, that he often
disregarded, the accounts his patients gave of
themselves, and rather chose, to collect his information by indirect inquiry, and by cross-
examining them, than from their voluntary
testimony. Dr. Darwin avowed a conviction
of the pernicious effects of all vinous fluid, on
the youthful and healthy constitution, and totally abstained from spirits of all sorts, and
from strong malt liquor. Acid fruits, with
sugar, and all sorts of creams, and butter, were
his luxuries; but he always ate plentifully of
animal food. The Doctor was " not famous
for holding religious subjects in veneration:"
but however skeptical he might have been in
his belief; he exhibited in his conduct, what is
more beneficial to the world, than the tenacious
adherence to any speculative opinions—firm
integrity and a benevolent heart. Professional
generosity, distinguished his medical practice.
Diligently did he attend to the health of
the poor at Litchfield and Derby; supplied
their necessities by food, and every kind of
charitable assistance. In each of those towns,
his was the cheerful board of almost open-
housed hospitality, without extravagance or
parade; ever deeming the first unjust, the lat-

tor unmanly. Generosity, wit, and science,
were his household gods.

To these many rich endowments, which nature bestowed upon the mind of Dr. Darwin,
she added a highly poetic imagination. The
effusions of his early muse, were occasionally
sent, to one or other of the monthly publications; but without his name: conceiving from
the examples of Akenside and Armstrong, that
the reputation he might acquire by his poetry,
would operate as a bar to his advancement in
the practice of medicine. His " Botanic Garden," in which he celebrates what he calls, the
Loves of the Plants, (the first of his poems to
which he put his name) was not published until the year 1781; when his medical fame was
so well established, as to make it safe for him,
to indulge his taste in any way he should chuse.
This poem consists of two parts; the first contains the Economy of Vegetation, the second
the Loves of the Plants. Each is enriched, by
a number of philosophical notes; stating a
great variety of theories and experiments in
botany, chemistry, electricity, mechanicks, and
in the various species of air. They also contain explanations of every personified plant, its
generic history, its local situation, and the nature of the soil and climate to which it is indi-

genera; its botanick and its common name. By
an inversion of all custom, Dr. Darwin published the second volume of his poem first;
giving as a reason, is an advertisement, that
the appearance of the first part had been deferred till another year, for the purpose of re-
peating some experiments in vegetation. But
the real cause was, the consciousness he entertained, that the second part of his work, would
be more level than the first; to the comprehension, more congenial to the taste of the superficial reader; from its being much less abstract
and metaphysick, while it possessed more
than sufficient poetic matter, to entertain and
charm the enlightened and judicious few. The
novelty of the design, and the brilliancy of
the diction, full of figurative expressions, in
which every thing was personified, rendered
the poem for, some years, extremely popular.
But the fame which it acquired, has, in a great
degree subsided, and it is now but little noticed.

In 1794, the author published the first volume of " Zoonomia, or the Laws of Organic
Life," 4to. The second volume was printed in
1796. The purpose of this work, the gathered
wisdom of three-and-twenty years, was, to re-
form or entirely new model, the whole system

of medicine, professing no less, than to account for the manner in which man, animals,
and vegetables are formed. It was his opinion,
that they all took their origin from living filaments, susceptible of irritation, which is the
agent that sets them in motion. Archimedes
said, " give me a place to stand on, and I will
move the earth;"* so great was his confidence
in the power of the lever. Our author said,†
" give me a fibre susceptible of irritation, and
I will make a tree, a dog, a horse, a man."
The Zoonomia, has long ceased to be popular;
its doctrines are not always infallible; and its
sophisms are many. Nevertheless, it is an ex-
haustless repository of interesting facts, of curious experiments in natural productions, and
in medical effects.

About the year 1795, Dr. Darwin published
a small tract, in 4to. on Female Education. It
is said to contain some good rules for promoting the health of growing children; but on the
whole, to be a meagre work of little general
interest, and that consequently that it attracted
but little notice.

Early in 1800, Dr. Darwin published another

---

* Plutarch's Life of Marcellus.

† Zoonomia, vol. 1. p. 492.

large 4to. volume, intitled, " Phytologia, or
the Philosophy of Agriculture and Gardening."
Dr. Darwin's conviction, that vegetables are
remote links in the chain of sentient existence,
often. hinted at in the notes to the Botanic
Garden, is here avowed in a regular system.—
The Phytologia insists, that plants have vital
organization, sensation, and even volition; and
a number of instances are adduced to support
the theory. This work obtained but little attention from the public, and was suffered to
pass almost unnoticed.

The last poetical production of Dr. Darwin
is, " The Temple of Nature, or the Origin of
Society," 4to. with notes. This work, " the
setting emanation of this brilliant day-star,"
the Doctor had prepared for the press, a few
months before his death, and was published in
1803. It treats of the production of life; the
re-production of life; the progress of the mind;
and of good and evil. Its aim is simply to
amuse, by bringing distinctly to the imagination the beautiful and sublime operations of
nature, in the order, in which the author believed, the progressive course of time presented
them. This work contains, like all his productions, some beautiful and inimitable passages. These, together with some papers in

the Philosophical Transactions, and the share
he had in the formation of the System of Vegetables of Linnæus, published in the name of
the Botanical Society Litchfield, are all the
published works of Dr. Darwin. But if report
says true, there is yet a production, truly Dar-
winian, with which the admirers of learning
and genius, may at some future period be favored.

In perspicuity, which is one of the first excel-
lencies in poetic as well as prose composition,
Dr. Darwin has, perhaps, few equals. He is
clear, even when describing the most intricate
operations of nature, or the most complex
works of art; and there is a lucid transparency
in his style, through which we see objects in
their exact figure and proportion. He delights
the eye, the taste, and the fancy, by the strength,
distinctness, elegance, and perfect originality
of his pictures; and gratifies the ear, by the
rich cadence of his numbers. But the passions
are generally asleep, and seldom are the nerves
thrilled by his imagery, impressive and beauteous as it is, or by his landscapes with all
their vividness. The greatest defect in Dr.
Darwin's poetry, is the want of sensation;—that
sort of excellency, which, while it enables us
to see distinctly the objects described, makes

us feel them acting on our nerves. In the
notes to his different works, we discover the
botanist, the philosopher, and the man of an
exalted and daring genius: but though he
often appears to advantage, it must be confessed, that, in many instances, he sacrifices too
much to imagination.

The Derbyshire General Infirmary, is situated
a little way out of the town, on the southern
side, near the road leading to London.—
The ground on which it stands, was purchased
of the Corporation of Derby, at the price of
£200 per acre: and to prevent in future the
too near approach of offensive objects, the
committee have secured, for the exclusive use
of the institution, above fourteen acres of the
surrounding land. The healthfulness of the
situation has likewise been very particularly
attended to:—it is elevated, airy, and dry,
abounding with excellent water, and accessible
by a good road. The design of the building
was arranged by Wm. Strutt, Esq. according
to which, working plans were drawn by Mr.
Browne, who also superintended the construction of a model, executed with architectural
skill and ingenuity. The building is constructed of a beautiful, hard, and durable
whitish stone; of a cubical form, with an ele-

vation handsome, yet simple and unornamented; containing a light central hall with a double staircase. It is three stories high, and universally admired as well on account of the numerous conveniences it contains, as for its elegant simplicity. On a close inspection, the
workmanship is found to be excellent; and the
stability such, that in the whole building, there
does not appear to be the slightest shake or
crack. The iron dome, the wide stone gallery,
and the very large stone staircase, resting upon
the perforated floor of the hall, which covers
part of the basement story, excite admiration;
because, being the parts most difficult of execution, they appear nevertheless to possess the
most perfect strength and solidity.

The committee, before the erection began,
directed their attention to the means of obtain-
ing the best plan; and in order to form a correct judgment on the subject, endeavored to
learn from the experience of similar establishments, what were the principal objects to be
kept in view in the construction of an edifice
of this nature. The result of their enquiries,
suggested several improvements, which have
been carried into execution; and which have
brought this Infirmary to a degree of perfection unknown to similar establishments. One

considerable improvement, and which contri
butes much to the health and comfort of the
patients, is, the construction of two light and
spacious rooms, (one for each sex) called *Day*
(or convalescent) *Rooms;* in which those patients, to whom it may be agreeable, may eat
their meals and pass the day, instead of being
confined to the same room day and night, as is
the usual practice. Another very great improvement, is, the construction of a *Fever-
House*, a place where relief is administered, in
cases of infectious diseases. Such an establishment as this, has, generally' in large towns,
been separate from the Infirmary; but here a
portion of it is properly constructed, for the
reception, not only of those, whose infectious
diseases may commence in the Hospital, but of
those also, which may occur elsewhere. The
entrance to this Fever-House, is on the side of
the building, directly opposite to the front, and
has no internal connection whatever with the
Infirmary.

Beside the Convalescent Rooms, and Fever-
House, above mentioned, another circumstance
in which the plan of this Infirmary surpasses
others, is, in providing superior accommodation for patients labouring under acute dis-

cases. In general, the surgical and medical, the acute and chronick diseases, are assembled in one large ward, day and night; that this must be always painful, and in some cases highly prejudicial, cannot be denied. The better accommodation consists, in providing for each sex, a set consisting of four small wards, containing one, two, three, and four beds respectively, with a water-closet, nurse's bed-room, and scullery. This arrangement enables the medical attendants to separate the diseases from each other, as may best suit their natures; and the whole of each set of rooms being shut off from the body of the house by one door, these together, procure for the patient silence and darkness, (which is essential in some cases) as well as every other convenience, in a degree, perhaps, superior to many private houses.

This plan, however, might not be eligible, unless it was constructed with another improvement; one which is of great importance, and which has hitherto been a desideratum in all Hospitals; that is a cheap and simple, and, in every respect, unobjectionable method of warming and ventilating effectually in cold weather. Both these have been effected perfectly in this Infirmary; and thus the ventilation will be copious, while at the same time, the warmth may be regulated at pleasure; many lives will be preserved, which owing to a certain state of the air generally pervading Hospitals, might have been inevitable lost. Particular attention has been paid to the construction of the water-closets, which it is said have not yet been managed, so as to be unobjectionable in Hospitals; for if they are ventilated externally, the draft, which should be from the house outwards, is the reverse, especially if the house is warm. A mode of construction, has been invented for the occasion, in which every objection of this kind has been done away.

- A small steam engine has been erected, to pump water, wash, &c. Warm and cold baths have also been constructed;—in short, it is furnished with every convenience, while in the construction and arrangement of all the offices, every attention has been paid to adapt them to the various purposes with the greatest œconomy. A statue of *Esculapius*, emblematical of the object of the Institution, has been modelled by Mr. Coffee, and placed upon the centre of the dome.

The magnitude of the building, is equal to the accommodation of eighty patients, besides those with infectious diseases. This is doubtless a greater number, than are likely at present to want relief at any one time; but considering the increasing population of the county and town, it cannot be considered as too large.

The original estimate of the building was £10,500; but owing to some large expences, having been incurred which were not estimated, and other parts of the Institution being finished, which it was intended to defer to some future time, the expence of the erection very much exceeded the estimate. By the report of the committee, dated the 1st of June, 1809, it appears, that the expenditure, for land purchased and building the Infirmary, &c. amounted to £17,870 3s. 4d. From the same paper it also appears, that the donations, received by the treasurers for the institution, amount with their interest to £31,238 19s. 0d. so that the balance lodged in the different funds, &c. constituting the funds of the Infirmary, amount to £13,368 16s. 8d.

Three Physicians, four Surgeons, and a house Apothecary, have been appointed to the Institution. The Infirmary was opened for the reception of In, and the relief of Out-patients, on the 4th of June, 1810.

Not far from the Infirmary, and about the

some distance from the town, is the *Ordnance Depot*. The ground on which this building stands, being an acre and a quarter, was purchased for the purpose by the Board of Ordnance in the year 1803. The respective buildings, erected according to a plan by Mr. Wyatt, the Architect, were compleated in 1805. These consist of an Armory in the centre; the room on the ground-floor, being seventy-five feet long by twenty-five broad, is calculated to contain fifteen thousand stand of arms: these are disposed here in the same order as those are in the Tower of London, and present a very pleasing appearance, on the entrance to the room.— Above this is a room of the same proportions, containing accoutrements for the use of the army. On the North and South sides of the armory, are two magazines, capable of containing 1200 barrels of ammunition. These are internally arched with brick, to prevent accidents; and, for the same purpose, conductors have been erected at a little distance from each. Four dwellings are situated in the angles of the exterior wall; two of which are Barracks for a detachment of Royal Artillery, and the other two, are the residence of Officers in the Civil Department of the Ordnance.—

Besides these buildings, suitable workshops, &c. have been erected on the inside of the surrounding wall. The establishment is under the superintendance of an Ordnance Storekeeper, who is appointed by the Master-General of the Ordnance.

CHAP. VI.

Description of the Deanery of Derby.

THE first place worthy our attention in the Deanery of Derby, after the town itself, is the Roman city *Derventio*, now called LITTLE CHESTER. This *village* stands on the East bank of the Derwent, about half a mile from Derby, and contains from thirty to forty houses. There are several circumstances which combine to prove, that this spot was once a Roman station. The present name (Chester) is evidently derived from the Latin word *Castrum*, (a camp) from its once having been a Roman military situation. " Now," says Camden,* " where the Derwent turns its course to the eastward, stands Little Chester, *i. e: a Little City.*" But the vestiges of. its. Roman origin, though few, may be yet traced. Dr. Stukely; in the year 1721,· endeavored to ascertain its form and extent: and was so far successful, as to trace the track of the wall all round, and in some places

* Britannia, p. 491.

discovered under ground, its foundations in
the pastures, and some vaults along the side of
it. He discovered, that the cellar of one of the
then existing houses, was built on a side of the
wall, which was three yards thick. He observed, that the station was of a square form,
and that the *castrum* was five hundred feet by
six hundred: it was situated between the Roman
road called the *Rioning* and the river Derwent.
Within the walls, he found foundations of
houses; and in the fields, round what is called
the castle, he traced the direction of streets
overlaid with gravel. Near a Mr. Hodgkin's
house, he thought it probable that once a temple stood; a stag's head having been dug up
in his cellar. Besides the Roman road called
Rioning, he mentions another, which he was informed went up the hill, directly from the
street of the city by Chaddesden. Part of it,
he says, had been dug up near the town, and
its ridge was visible in 1725. These observations of the Doctor, might have been just and
accurate at the time they were made; but from
the alterations made since, no tracts of streets
are now to be discovered in the pastures; and the
only way, overlaid with gravel, is one, which
running East and West, nearly intersects the
station into two equal parts; and a second

which extends from the north-east corner, in a
direct line across the pastures towards Breadsall.

In one part of the station, human bones
have frequently been dug up; and about five-
and-twenty years ago, the bones of a body
were discovered, with all the teeth in the head,
as firmly fixed and undecayed, as if they had
been laid only a few days in the ground. All
the bodies are found without any stones, or
other covering to protect them from the earth.

"The antiquity of Little Chester is sufficiently attested," says Mr. Gibson,* "by the
many pieces of Roman coins found, both in
digging the cellars, and ploughing. Some of
them are of copper, some of silver, and some
few of gold, bearing the inscription and image
of several of the Roman Emperors." Of the
two former kinds, Mr. Pilkington saw several.
The copper ones were so much corroded and
defaced, that the legends were mostly destroyed. He was, however, able to make out the
following inscriptions upon some of the silver
coins:—*Tetricus Senior et Junior. Galianus.
Pictorinus. Posthumus. Julia—. Vespatianus.
Antoninus Pius. Hadrianus. Faustina Junior.*

8   к k

---

* In his Camden, p. 497.

Marcus. Strellius Antoninus. Aurelius Antoni-
nus. Crispina. Gordianus. Antoninus Augus-
tus. Co. Trajanus. Caurausius.

The date on one of these coins, is as early as
the year 14, and another as late as 318. It
cannot, however, be inferred from this, that
the Romans were stationed at *Derventio* for the
space of 300 years. But we may safely conclude,
that they were there, as late as the beginning
of the fourth century : about which time, they
began gradually to withdraw from every part
of Britain.

We have in a former chapter* taken notice
of the Ikenild-street, or greater Roman road,
which proceeds from Monk's-bridge near Burton, through Little Chester to Chesterfield. It
is said, that the foundations of an ancient
bridge, carrying this road across the Derwent,
was visible near a century ago when the water
was clear.† Some pains have been taken to
determine its precise situation : Some writers
have fixed it a little to the North of the walls
of the station : but it is the opinion of some of
the inhabitants of the place, that it was in the
same line with the street, which appears to
have been carried through the midst of it.

---

* Page 18.   † Gibson's Camden, 497.

At the time of the Norman survey, Little
Chester was a place of some note; as it is there
noticed,* under the name of *Cestre*. However, at present, no monuments of its ancient
grandeur remain. The camp of the Roman
Legions, has for ages been the pasture of cattle: and the peaceful plough has passed over
that ground, on which once stood a city famed
for its magnificence, and honored with the presence and genius of the mighty masters of
the world.

DERLEY or DARLEY, is a populous hamlet,
situated on the West side of the Derwent, about
one mile from Derby. Its population, has increased considerably, within late years, owing
to the erection of cotton and paper mills, belonging to the Messrs. Evans.

In our account of the Monastery of St. Helen,† we observed, that the Dean of Derby,
gave to the Master and Canons of that House,
his possessions at Darley, for the erection of a
church and habitation for themselves. This
being accomplished to his wish, he endowed
the new foundation, with his patrimonial estate
in Derby, and the patronage of the church of
St. Peter, with all appurtenances. This grant

was afterwards renewed and confirmed, by the
charters of the burgesses of Derby, and of king
Henry II. · But these endowments, constituted
but a very small part of the wealth of this religious House; for many valuable gifts were afterwards bestowed by other persons. In particular, it became possessed of the churches of
St. Michael, St. Werburgh, and the School in
Derby; also the churches of Crich, Uttoxeter,
Pentridge, Ashover, Wingfield, Bolsover, and
Scarcliff, together with the emoluments and
privileges, of which they were respectively
possessed.

" Derley Abbey was also endowed with many
tracts of land of great extent in various parts
of the county. Several entire manors were
granted to it. Of this number were Rippley,
Pentridge, Ulkerthorp, Crich, Lea, Dethic,
Ibol, Tanesley, Wistanton, Oggedeston, (Hognaston) Succhethorn, Aldwerk, and Sewelle-
dale. Lands in other places were likewise given
for the support of this religious house; in particular, nineteen ox-gangs in Chilwell, and five
in Aneleg, (Annesley,) a moiety of Blackwell,
a moiety of Kildulvescot, a moiety of Newton,
eight ox-gangs in Rutinton, and four in Her-
diwic, one manse in Nottingham, and two
hundred acres in Burley. It was endowed too

with the mill at Horseley, two mills upon Od-
debroc, near Derby, and two mills in the same
town. This religious house likewise held, by
various patents, tenements in Derby, Alvaston,
Normanton, and Wessington ;* in Crich, Hasle-
wood, and Duffield ; in Litchurch, Weston,
Muginton, Normanton, Spondon, Chaddesden,
and Little Chester ;† in Thurleston, Alvaston,
and Ambaston ;‡ in Rippley, Waring-grene,
Codnor, and Derby :§ The abbot also enjoyed
several peculiar privileges. All his lands in
tillage, and indeed all his other property were
exempt from tithe. He was appointed dean of
all the churches in Derbyshire, which were
given to the abbey, but more especially of
those situated in the town of Derby. He was
empowered to hold a chapter of the secular
clergy, and in conjunction with them to judge
of those things, which appertain to the office
of a dean, without the interference of any person whatever, excepting the bishop. Nor should
I omit to mention, that the abbot and canons
of Derley, were allowed as much wood as they
could draw from Chaddesden with one cart."‖

* " Pat. Edw. III.—† Pat. 44 Edw. III.—‡ Pat. Rich.
II.—§ Pat. 11 Hen. IV."

‖ Pilkington, Vol. II, page 162.

of £35. The church, according to Ecton, formerly belonged to the priory of Derlegh: but
it appearing from the charter of Hugh Earl of
Chester, that it was given towards the close of
the twelfth century, to the priory of Calke, he ,
is thought to have been mistaken in his statement.   The Earl of Huntington is the patron.
The liberty contains about sixty houses, and
the inhabitants are principally engaged in agricultural pursuits, though some of them are
employed in spinning jersey, and making stockings.

DALE ABBEY, was a religious house of the
Premonstatentian Order, and dedicated to the
Virgin Mary. The following particulars of this
foundation are related by Mr. Pilkington.

" A monk, who belonged to it, has left in
manuscript a history of its foundation as related
by Maud de Salicosamara, who built the church
belonging to the abbey.

" The following are the principal facts, and
circumstances recorded in this history.—We
are told, that there once lived in the street of
St. Mary in Derby a baker, who was particularly distinguished by his great charity and
devotion.   After having spent many years in
acts of benevolence and piety, he was in a dream
called upon to give a very trying proof of his

good principles; he was required by the virgin
Mary to relinquish all his worldly substance,
to go to Depedale, and to lead a solitary life
in the service of her son and herself. He accordingly left all his possessions and departed,
entirely ignorant of the place to which he should
go. However directing his course towards the
east, and passing through the village of Stanley, he heard a woman saying to a girl, take
with thee our calves, and drive them to Depedale, and return immediately. Regarding this
event as a particular interposition of Divine
Providence, he was overwhelmed with astonishment, and drawing nearer, he said, tell
me, where is Depedale; when he received this
answer, go with the girl, and she, if you please,
will shew you the place. Upon his arrival he
found it a very marshy land, and very distant
from all human habitations. Proceeding from
hence to the east, he came to a rising ground,
and under the side of the hill cut in the rock a
small dwelling, and built an altar towards the
south; and there spent day and night in the
divine service, with hunger, thirst, cold, and
want.

" It happened one day, that a person of great
consequence, by name Ralph, the son of Gere-

9   L l

mund, came in the pursuit of the diversion of
hunting, into his woods at Ockbrook; and
when he approached the place, where this hermit lived, and saw the smoak rising from his
cave, he was filled with indignation and astonishment, that any one should have the rash-
ness and effrontery to build for himself a dwelling in his woods, without his permission.—
Going then to the place, he found a man
cloathed with old rags and skins, and enquir-
ing into the cause and circumstances of his case,
his anger gave way to the emotions of pity, and
to express his compassion he granted him the
ground where his hermitage was situated, and
tythe of his mill at Burgh (Borrowash) for his
support.

" It is related, that the old enemy of the human race then endeavoured to render him dis-
satisfied with his condition, but that he reso-
lutely endured all the calamities of his situa-
ation.   One of the greatest evils, which he
suffered, was a want of water.   However from
this he was relieved by discovering a spring in
the western part of the valley.   Near this he
built a cottage and an oratory in honour of the
blessed virgin, and ended his days in the service of God.

" Serlo de Grendon, lord of Badely, a knight

of eminent valour, great wealth, and distinguished birth, who married first Margery, the daughter of the above Ralph, and afterwards Maud, lady of Celston, gave to his Godmother during her life the place of Depedale with its appurtenances, and some other land in the neighbourhood. She had a son, whom she educated for holy orders, that he might perform divine service in her chapel at Depedale, and herself resided at a small distance southward of this situation.

"But in a short time afterwards, with the consent and approbation of this venerable matron, the above Serlo de Grendon invited canons from Kalke, and gave them the place of Depedale.

"When these canons were settled here, they with immense labour and expence built a church and other offices: their prior also went to the court of Rome and obtained several important privileges for them, and the place was much frequented by persons of all ranks, some of whom were large benefactors to this religious establishment.

"However in process of time, when the canons, already mentioned, had been long separated from the social conversation of men, and became corrupted by the prosperity of their situation, they began to grow negligent of the divine service. They frequented the forest more than the church, and were more intent upon hunting than prayer and meditation. But the king, hearing of their insolent conduct, commanded them to resign every thing into the hands of their patron, and to return to the place, from which they came.

" Depedale was not long left desolate. For there soon came hither from Tupholme six white canons of the Præmonstratensian order. To them was given the park of Stanley, but how or by whom, the writer of this history acknowledges, that he cannot with certainty affirm. But I hope I shall be able to throw some light upon this doubtful point by means of the obliging information of the Rev. Robert Wilmot of Morley.

" One of the windows of the church at Morley consists of painted glass with inscriptions, which are plainly designed to record some remarkble event. The glass was brought from Dale abbey, when it was dissolved, and was intended to convey an idea of the following circumstances.

" According to tradition, the keepers of the park or forest, being disturbed by the encroachments of the monks, carried their complaints

to the king. And with a view of representing
this fact they are painted upon the glass in green
habits, standing before him, with this inscription, ' whereof we complain unto the king ;'
when they received this answer, ' go and tell
him come to me.' In another part of the window, the person, against whom the complaint
is lodged, appears kneeling before the king.
With a view of adjusting the matter in dispute,
and giving satisfaction to both parties, the king,
it is said, granted to the canons at Depedale as
much land as betwixt two suns could be encircled with a plough, drawn by deers, which were
to be caught from the forest. This is expressed by two other inscriptions. ' Go take them,
and tame them.' ' Go home, take ground with
the plough.' We find that this determination
of the king was afterwards carried into execution. For upon the glass is painted a man with
a plough drawn by deer, with these words underneath. ' Here St. Robert plougheth with
them.' What extent of land was incompassed
in this way cannot now be ascertained. But
it is probable, that it comprehended the pre-
cincts of the abbey, or the whole liberty of
Dale.

" The canons, in whose favour this grant was
made, experienced many difficulties and dis-

tresses in their new situation. Having spent
six years in excessive poverty, they cut the tops
of the oaks in the park, sold them and returned
to Tupholme,

"Now the church at Depedale was for a season deprived of its worshippers. To supply
this loss William de Grendon, whose name has
been already mentioned, sent for, and procured
five canons of the Præmonstratensian order
from Welbeck, But they experienced no less
grievous sufferings than their predecessors, and
were soon recalled by their abbot.

"We see, that every attempt, which had yet
been made to establish a religious house at Depedale, proved unsuccessful. But now by the
concurrence and pious zeal of several different
persons such steps were taken, as were effectual
for the execution of their purpose.

"Geffrey de Salicosamara or Saucemere, who
had married Maud the granddaughter of William
Geremund, had a promise of the village of Stanley as part of his wife's dower. But having no
children, they earnestly entreated their father
to offer it to God, and to build a religious house
in the park of the same village for an abbot of
the Præmonstratensian order. This request was
readily granted, and to carry their design more
effectually into execution, the father sent for

William de Grendon his sister's son, who was
lord of Ockbrook, and requested him to contribute towards the accomplishment of their
pious intentions. He told his nephew, that as
he was patron of the ancient place of Depedale,
where several different congregations of religious men had successively resided, but had
been driven away by extreme poverty, he wished him to resign it for the plantation of a new
society, and to join with him in providing for
its support out of the lands, possessions, and
goods, which God had granted them.—This
proposal was immediately complied with. The
nephew was ready to resign the house with all
its appurtenances, on condition, that divine service should be celebrated every day by a priest
in the chapel of Depedale for his own soul, and
the souls of his ancestors and posterity, and for
the souls of all those who rested in Christ there:
and that in an inn there should be placed upon
a large table a daily supply from the convent
of bread and beer, and distributed among the
poor of the neighbouring forest. This grant
was gratefully accepted by his uncle; and the
execution of the whole business was committed
to Geffrey and Maud Saucemere. Nor did
they delay a single moment the accomplishment
of a design, which they had themselves origi-

nally suggested. Having received charters and
other instruments necessary for the foundation
of a religious house, they departed by the order of their father to Newhouse in Lincolnshire,.
and brought from thence nine canons, who
were admitted into the order already established at Depedale.*

" Besides the endowments, which have been
noticed, the abbey at Dale received several
other valuable benefactions, of which the following are the principal:—Four ox-gangs of ·
land in Sandiacre; three ox-gangs with their
appurtenances in the same liberty; two ox-
gangs of lands with their appurtenances in Al-
waldeston (Alvaston) and Baletone; all the
possessions, excepting three acres of land, of
Jordan de Tuke in Hyltone; an ox-gang of
land with its appurtenances in the same village; -
the homage and service of the men of Robert
de Lexintone in Essoure (Ashover); eight
acres, and the moor below Paystanhirst; four
ox-gangs of land with their appurtenances in
Knyveton; two ox-gangs, and a messuage with ·
their appurtenances in the same place; forty
acres of land with their appurtenances in Brassington; land in Hallam; one ox-gang of land

---

* " Mon. Angl. vol. II. p. 620."

with its appurtenances in Selestone and Wan-
desleye, the same extent of land with twenty-
four shillings and eight-pence rent in the same
liberties; ten ox-gangs with their appurtenances
in Windesley, (Windley); land in Broydestone;
lands in Mushampe, Holme, and Baley; two
selions in the last of these liberties.; a moiety
of the mill of Backer, and three selions near
it; a moiety of a fishery in Trent, and an
island in the same river; land in Michelbergh;
thirty-eight acres of land in Croxton; a messuage and an ox-gang of land in Steyntone,
(Stanton); two ox-gangs of land in the same
place; five messuages, and nine acres and a half
of land in Derby; and all the land of Geffrey
de Salicosamara, and Maud his wife in Nottingham. These grants are recited and confirmed
in a charter of king Henry III.

" Dale abbey was also endowed with the advowson of the churches of Heanor, Ilkeston,
and Kirk-Hallam; with land in Eggington,
and Etwall; with Thoroton wood in Cossale:
and with tenements in Stanton, Alvaston, Thur-
lestone, Bolton, Stanley, Kirk-Hallam, and
Spondon.

" At the dissolution the whole yearly revenue
of this religious house was £144 12s. 0d.; and

9   M m

Gervas Kingstone, Esq. was the reputed patron. It was founded in the year 1204; and surrendered the eighth of October 1539, by John Staunton the last abbot, and sixteen monks.— The site of it was granted in the thirty-fifth year of Henry VIII. to Francis Poole, Esq.

" In the year 1650 the abbey clock sold for six shillings; the iron, glass, paving stones, and grave stones were sold for £18, and there were six bells 47 cwt.

" The whole number of the abbots of Dale was eighteen, and the period of their government was three hundred and twelve years, six weeks, and one day."*

The church belonging to this Abbey, was, according to tradition, a very grand and magnificent structure :—It contained several large windows on the North and South sides, and one at the East end in the chancel, which was very spacious and lofty. But hardly any part of it is now standing, except the arch of the East window, which is partially covered with ivy, and forms a pleasing object. The chapel, built by the godmother of Serlo de Grendon, still remains standing at a little distance from the abbey-ruins, and divine service is yet regularly per-

* " Mong. Angl. vol. III. page 72."

formed in it. It is said, that the abbey was formerly enclosed by a handsome stone wall, and that there was a grand entrance to the West. There is also a tradition, that all travellers and strangers, who passed that way, were entertained and lodged at the inn one night, and in the morning furnished with such supplies, as were necessary to assist them on their journey.

A little way beyond the abbey, on a pleasant wooded hill, is the hermitage or cave, cut in the rock by the poor baker. This is overhung with trees, and had originally a window on each side of the door-way. The abbey-buildings seem to have been of considerable extent, as various parts which yet remain have been converted into dwelling-houses and barns. Some of the windows of these houses, contain painted glass with inscriptions.

ASTON.—When the Norman survey was made " in *Æstune* (Aston) and *Serdelau* (Shardlow.)" there were " six ox-gangs and a half of land to be taxed. There is one plough in the demesne, and four villanes* and two bordars† with one

---

* *Villanes, Villeins,* or *Villains,* were so called because they lived chiefly in villages, and were employed in rustic works of the most sordid kinds. The *villanes* belonged to the

plough, and four acres of meadow. Uctebrand
holds this of the king. It is worth five shillings.* " In *Estune*, Levenot had two carucates
of land to be taxed. ' Land to two ploughs.
There are now three ploughs in the demense,
and eight villanes, and four bordars, having
two ploughs and twenty-four acres of meadow.
Wood pasture half a mile long, and half broad.
Value in king Edward's time sixty shillings,
now forty. Alcher holds it.† " In *Estune*,
Uctebrand had one carucate of land, and two

Lord of the Manor, and were transferable by deed from one
Lord to another. They could not leave their Lord without
his permission; but if they ran away, or were purloined·
from him, might be claimed and removed by action, like
rents or other chattels. A villane could acquire no property, either in lands or goods: and his children were born to
the same state of bondage as their parents. They held their
small portions of land upon *villane services*, that is, to
carry out the dung, to hedge and ditch the Lord's de-
menses, and any other mean office.

· † *Bordars*, boors or husbandmen, holding a little house,
with some land for husbandry, bigger than a cottage. They
were distinct from the villanes, and seem to have been of a
less servile condition. They held their cottage and land on
condition of supplying the Lord with poultry and eggs,
and other small provision for his board or entertainment.

* Domesday. Hammenstan Wapentake, *Orig.* 272. *b.* 1.
Trans. 296.

† Walecross Wapentake, *Orig.* 273. *a.* 1. Trans. 303.·

ox-gangs and a half soke,* to be taxed and five
acres of meadow. Value in king Edward's
time six shillings, now eight shillings.† "In
Estune, Tolf had five ox-gangs and a half of
land to be taxed. Land to one plough. There
are now two sokemen,‡ and six villanes, and
one bordar having three ploughs. There are
two acres of meadow. Wood pasture seven
quarentens long, and four quarentens broad.
Value in king Edward's time, and now, twenty
shillings. Lewin holds it under the king."§

At present the liberty of Aston contains
about one hundred houses, and five hundred
inhabitants. The living is a rectory, valued in
the king's books at £29 15s. and yearly tenths
£2 19s. 6d. The church is dedicated to All-
saints; and several of the Holden family have
been buried in it. From the charter of Robert
Ferrers, junior, Earl of Derby, it appears, that
two parts of the lordship and tithe of Aston,
were given to the priory of Tutbury. The
hamlets of Sharlow and Wilne lie within the

---

* *Soke* has the same signification as carucate, which see
page 128.
† *Orig.* 275. *b.* 2. Trans. 312.

‡ *Sokemen*, those that were free of blood, and fit for honourable service. In our days called *Yeomen*.

§ Land of the king's Thanes. *Orig.* 278. Tran. 326.

parish of Aston;—the former contains about
seventy houses, and the latter eighteen. A few
stocking-frames, are the only appearance of
manufacture to be met with in the parish; but
a considerable number of hands are employed
in navigating the barges up the Trent.

WESTON.—At the Norman survey, we find
that in *Westune* (Weston) " with the Berewicks,
Earl Algar had ten carucates of land, and
two ox-gangs and a half to be taxed. Land to
as many ploughs. There are now in the demense three ploughs and twenty-four villanes
and six bordars, having twelve ploughs, and
four farmers paying sixteen shillings. There
are two churches and a priest, and one mill of
nineteen shillings and four-pence, and a fish-
pond and a ferry of thirteen shillings and four-
pence, and fifty-one acres of meadow. Pasture half a mile long, and three quarentens
broad. Value in king Edward's time £8, now
£16."*

Weston was distinguished by some peculiar
privileges, in the reign of King John. By a
patent granted in the sixteenth year of his
reign, the inhabitants were exempted from all
services of counties, hundreds, tithings and

* Demesday *Orig.* 272. *s.* 1. Trans. 296.

wapentakes; from appearance of frank-pledge;
from aids, and charities; from demands, gra-
tifications, and complaints, to which villages
and bailiwicks are subject. The church is dedicated to St. Mary; and the living is a rectory, under the patronage of Sir R. Wilmot.
Its value in the king's books is £11 16s. 3d.
and yearly tenths £1 3s. 7¼d. The parish of
Weston is not very extensive, and the number
of houses not great. The village is situated
near the canal and the Trent, and the inhabitants have been much employed in the navigation upon each.

ELVASTON.—When Domesday* was composed, there were " in Æhwoldestune (Alvaston)
and Emboldestune (Ambaston) and Torulfestune
(Tharlston) and Alewoldestune (Alvaston) a
priest and a church; one mill of twelve shillings, and one smith, and fifty-two acres of
meadow, and an equal quantity of coppice
wood."

" The inhabitants of Elvaston and Ockbrook
were formerly required by mutual agreement
to brew four ales, and every ale of one quarter
of malt, and at their own costs and charges,
betwixt this and the feast of St. John the baptist

*.Orig. 276. a. 2. Trans. 316.

next coming. And every inhabitant of Ockbrook shall be at the several ales, and every
husband and his wife were to pay two-pence,
every cottager one penny, and all the inhabitants of the said towns of Elvaston, Thurlaston,
and Ambaston, shall have and receive all the
profits and advantages, coming of the said ales,
to the use and behoof of the said church of Elvaston; and the inhabitants of the said towns of
Elvaston, Thurlaston, and Ambaston, shall brew
eight ales betwixt this and the feast of St. John
the baptist, at the which ales, and every one of
them, the inhabitants shall come and pay as
before rehearsed, who if he be away at one ale
to pay at the t'oder ale for both, or else to send
his money. And all the inhabitants of Ockbrook shall carry all manner of tymber, being
in the Dale wood now felled, that the said
priest chyrch of the said towns of Elvaston,
Thurlaston, and Ambaston shall occupy to the
use of the said church."*

Elvaston, is the seat of Stanhope, Earl of
Harrington, and has long been the residence of
that family; though neither the situation nor
the house have any particular beauty. The

---

* " Inter. MSS. Dodsworth in Bib. Bod. vol. 158. p.
97.—This appears to be the ancient method of paying
money for the repair of country churches."

gardens and grounds are laid out in the ancient manner; but some of the apartments in the
mansion have been fitted up by the present
Lord, in the modern style. Several family
portraits, and a few other paintings of value,
are preserved here.

WALTER BLUNT, who was raised by Edward
IV. to the dignity of Baron of Mountjoy was
born at this place; he, as well as many of his
descendants, was eminent for learning. From
the family of the Blunts, the estate sometime
before the reign of Henry VIII. passed to the
Poles of Radburn; but about the end of the
same reign, it came to the possession of the
Stanhopes. William Stanhope, the first Earl
of Harrington, was a person of distinguished
abilities: and early in life was appointed envoy
extraordinary to the Court of Spain. His diplomatic talents were not his only qualifications, for his bravery appears to have been
equal. On the accession of George the first,
he had been made Colonel of a regiment of
dragoons; and in 1719 headed a detachment
to assist the English squadron, in the attack
made on the enemy's ships in Port St. Anthony.
His conduct greatly contributed to the success
of the expedition; for when the boats ap-

9   N n

proached the shore, he was the first who leaped
into the water; and the destruction of three
men of war, and a very large quantity of naval
stores, was chiefly effected through his contrivance and courage. By George the Second, he
was nominated ambassador and plenipotenti-
ary to the Congress at Soissons; and in 1729
advanced to the dignity of a British Peer, by
the style and title of Lord Harrington of Harrington, in the county of Northampton. In
the year 1742 he was created Viscount Peter-
sham, in the county of Surry, and Earl of
Harrington; and having filled some intermediate offices, was in November 1746, made Lord
Lieutenant-General, and Governor-General of
the kingdom of Ireland. In 1747, he was constituted general of his Majesty's foot forces, and
in 1751, was succeeded by the Duke of Dorset
as Lord Lieutenant of Ireland. He died in the
year 1756. The life of William, the second
Earl, offers nothing particularly remarkable:
that of Charles, the third and present Earl,
abounds with vicissitudes, and splendid actions; to display which, with their various connecting circumstances, will occupy the pen of
some future biographer.

BARROW.—" In *Barruue*," (Barrow) says

Domesday,* "Godwin and Colegrim, had three oxgangs of land and a half to be taxed. It is waste. One villane has there four oxen, and eight acres of meadow." " In *Bareue* are twelve oxgangs of land to be taxed. Soke to *Mileburne*, (Melbourne). There is a priest and a church, and one sokeman, with half a plough and eighteen acres of meadow."† The living is a vicarage; and the church is dedicated to St. Wilfred. Upon an alabaster slab, at the entrance into the chancel, is the effigy of a man in armour. The name of John Bothe, and the date MCCCLXXXII. are yet legible. On the windows on each side of the church, are painted different coats of arms. Six oxgangs of land in the village, and without it, with all their appurtenances, formerly belonged to the priory of Repton. Barrow contains the liberties of Arleston and Sinfin. The chapelry of Twiford, and the hamlet of Stenson, are also in the parish of Barrow. The inhabitants of these villages are principally supported by agriculture, and the navigation upon the river Trent, and the canal.

---

* Land of Henry de Ferriers, *Orig.* 275, *a.* 2. Trans. 310.

† Land of Ralph the son of Hubert, *Orig.* 277, *a.* 1, Trans. 320.

Osmaston, in Domesday* called Osmundestune, is a small chapelry, belonging to the parish of St. Werburgh in Derby. The chapel is dedicated to All-saints, and Sir Robert Wilmot is the patron.

At Osmaston is the seat of Sir Robert Wilmot, a descendant of a very ancient family.— Speed mentions a nobleman of this name who lived in Essex, in the reign of king Ethelred.— In the eleventh century a family of the name of Wyllimot, resided at Sutton-upon-Soar, in the county of Nottingham. The present Baronet is a descendant of a younger branch of the family, which settled at Chaddesden, early in the sixteenth century. The estate at Osmaston has been in the family of the present possessor for nearly two centuries. The house was erected in 1696, partly of brick and partly of stone; but the brick work has since been stuccoed. It has two fronts; that to the South measures 192 feet in length; that to the North 217: the latter has a very handsome appearance when viewed from the London road, which passes within half a mile of the mansion. This building is furnished with a well chosen library, and contains a variety of paintings.

---

* Land of Henry de Ferrieres, *Orig.* 275, *b.* 1, Trans. 397.

In the Hall, there are several original whole length portraits, but coloured in a hard dry style. The principal are; *Philip the Second of Spain*, with a distant view of the *Escurial* in the back ground; *Christian the Fourth*, king of Denmark; *Amedius*, Duke of Savoy; and *Monseigneur de Soubize*.

In the library is a very fine painting of *The Meeting of Hector and Andromache* at the *Scean-Gate*, by Cignaroti, nine feet in length, by seven in breadth. This was designed from the passages in the Iliad:

" With haste to meet him, sprung the joyful fair,
His blameless wife, with Aëtion's worthy heir:
The nurse stood near, in whose embraces prest,
His only hope hung smiling at her breast,
Whom each soft charm, and early grace adorn,
Fair as the new-born star that gilds the morn.

Silent the warrior smil'd, and pleas'd resign'd
To tender passion all his mighty mind.
His beauteous princess cast a mournful look,
Hung on his hand, and then dejected spoke;
His bosom labor'd with a boding sigh,
And the big tear stood trembling in her eye."

Pope's Trans.

The expression in the countenance of Andromache is remarkably forcible, and her whole attitude seems perfectly in accordance with the idea of the poet: the other figures are equally well conceived; and the colouring is executed in a uniformly masterly manner.

supposed to afford. The estate is tolerably
wooded; and the vicinity of the house improved by an ornamental fish-pond, and pleasure ground : the latter, with the kitchen garden, includes about five acres of land.*

SWARKESTON, called by the Norman surveyors, *Serchestun*,† is a small village, a few miles
to the South of Osmaston. The living is a
rectory; valued in the king's books at *£6*, and
yearly tenths 10s. The church is dedicated to
St. James. *Swarkeston-bridge*, which crosses
the Trent, and low meadows subject to be
overflowed by that river, stands near this place.
It was constructed several centuries ago, but
the particular time cannot be ascertained.—
According to the tradition of the neighbourhood, it was built at the expence of two mai-
den sisters. Their names, however, have not
been preserved; and when the great length of
the bridge, which extends to the distance of
above three quarters of a mile, is considered,
it renders the tradition improbable; as the expence of such an undertaking must, in former
ages, have exceeded the ability of private individuals. The number of arches, standing at

---

* Beauties of England, Vol. III. page 293.
† Domesday *Orig.* 275. *b.* 2. Trans. 311.

various distances from each other, is said to be
twenty-nine; of late years, that part of the
bridge which crossed the Trent has been rebuilt.

MACKWORTH, in Domesday* called, *Mach-
eworde*, is a place of some antiquity. The manor in the time of Henry VI. belonged to a
family of the name of Mackworth; one of
which, in the third and fourth years of that
king's reign, represented the county of Derby
in Parliament. There was formerly a castle
here, but the only remains of it now visible, is
the South-gate, which is nearly entire. The
time it was built is uncertain, as well as who
were its original proprietors; but its site is now
the property of Lord Scarsdale. In the fourth
of Philip and Mary, it was held under the
Crown, in the same manner as the honor of
Tutbury, by soccage and fealty. According
to the tradition of the village, it was demolished during the civil wars, between Charles
I. and the Parliament; and some high ground
in the neighbourhood, is still called Cannon-
Hills, because it is reported, that ordnance
were planted there, when the Castle was destroyed.

9   o o

---

* *Orig.* 278, a. 2. Trans, 298.

The living of Mackworth is a vicarage; the church is dedicated to All-Saints, and is said to have once belonged to the Monastery at Darley.

At MARKETON, a small hamlet, belonging to the parish of Mackworth, is the seat of F. N. C. Mundy, Esq. an able, diligent and respectable magistrate. The manor of Mark-eton (of which Mackworth and Allestry are members), belonged, at the Norman survey, to the Earl of Chester. Sometime afterwards, it was possessed by the *Touchets;* one of whom married the heiress of Lord Audley, of Audley, in Staffordshire, and acquired that title. In the time of Henry VIII. this estate was sold by Touchet, Lord Audley, to Sir John Mundy, Knight, a wealthy goldsmith; and sometime Lord Mayor of London. This was the lineal ancestor of the present possessor, in whose family the estate has now remained nearly three centuries.

WILLINGTON, called in Domesday* *Welle-dene* and *Willetune,* was then partly possessed by the king and partly by Ralph the son of Hubert. The living is a vicarage: the church

---

is dedicated to St. Michael, and according to
Ecton, formerly belonged to the priory of Rep-
ton. The patrons are, the governors of Etwall
Hospital.

MICKLE-OVER, or GREAT-OVER; the *Ufre*
of Domesday,* was when that book was compiled, included in the land belonging to the
abbey of Burton. The living is a vicarage, valued in the king's books at £9. 11s. 5½d. and
yearly tenths 19s. 1d. The church is dedicated to All-Saints: and in the presentation,
Lord Scarsdale has one turn, and —— Wilmot
two.

FINDERN and LITTLE-OVER, are connected
with Mickle-Over. It is said in Domesday,
" three berewicks belong thereto : *Parua Ufre*
(Little-Over), *Findre* (Findern), and *Potlac*
(Potlock),"† but there are only two now. The
living of Findern is a donative curacy. The
Presbyterians have also a place of worship
here. The Chapel at Little-Over is also a donative curacy, connected with the church at
Mickle-Over.

RADBOURN, at the time of the Norman survey, belonged to Roger of Poictou: but "Ralph

* *Orig.* 273, *b.* 1, Trans. 297.
† Domesday *Orig.* 273. *b.* 1. Trans. 297.

the son of Hubert claimed a third part of *Rab-burne*, and the jury of the wapentake gave their verdict in his favor."[*] Since that time, it has been the seat of several wealthy and respectable families. At an early period, Robert Walkelyne resided here; whose youngest daughter, a co-heiress, conveyed it by marriage to Sir John Chandos, Knight. Sir John, the fourth in descent from this nobleman, here laid the foundations of " a mighty large howse, withe a wonderful cost;"[†] but it seems doubtful, whether it was ever completed. From the Chandos family, the manor was conveyed to that of the Poles, by the marriage of its heiress to Peter de la Pole, of Newborough, in Staffordshire, sometime in the reign of Edward the Third; when Radbourn became the seat of the family of Pole, in which line it yet remains; Sacheverel Pole, Esq. being the present inheritor. The old family mansion stood near the church, and is now in ruins. The present house, was built by German Pole, Esq. about seventy years ago: its situation is elevated and pleasant, and commands some beautiful and extensive prospects of the adjacent country.

---

* Ibid. *Orig.* 275, *b.* 2, Trans. 311,
† Leland's Itenerary.

The parish of Radbourn is a single hamlet; the living is a rectory : The church is dedicated to St. Andrew, and contains several monuments, erected to the memory of the Poles; but some of the inscriptions are much injured, and almost defaced.

, KEDLESTON, in the Conqueror's time called *Chetelstune*,* and then included in the land of Henry de Ferrieres, is a parish of small extent. The living is a rectory, and the church is dedicated to All-Saints.

Kedleston is the celebrated seat of Nathaniel Curzon, Lord Scarsdale. " The first account we have" says Mr. Pilkington,† " of the family being seated at Kedleston, is in the time of Edward I. In the twenty-fifth of his reign, Richard de Cursun died, possessed of the manor of Ketleston, which was valued at twenty marks a year; and also the advowson of the church, which was estimated at £4. a year.— Robert Ferrers, Earl of Derby, made him a free and full grant of the manor and advowson of the church by his charter, on condition of rendering him homage and service." From him it has descended to his present Lordship,

* Domesday *Orig.* 275. a. 2. Trans. 310.
† Hist. Vol. II. p. 130.

whose father was raised on the tenth of April,
1760, to the dignity of a Peer, by the style
and title of Baron Scarsdale of Kedleston in
the county of Derby. His Lordship was, during three parliaments, chairman of the House
of Peers.

Kedleston-house, the splendid mansion of
Lord Scarsdale, is situated about three miles
to the north-west of Derby. On the road which
passes to the right of the mansion, a comfortable Inn has been erected, as well for the convenience of such strangers, as curiosity may
lead to view the house, as for the accommodation of those, who come for the benefit of the
waters in the neighbourhood. The house
(erected by the late Lord in 1761) stands half
a mile to the West of the inn, from whence it
is approached by a foot-path. This path is
carried through the park, which is about seven
miles in circumference, and displays some
flourishing plantations, together with a number of large and venerable oaks; some of which
are of the enormous size of twenty-four feet in
girth, one hundred and eighteen feet in height,
and are thought to have stood for more than
seven hundred years. Following the path
shaded by the antiquated arms of these "forest
monarchs," it conducts to an elegant stone

bridge of three arches, thrown over a piece of water, amplified to its present extent, by judiciously cutting away, the banks of the little brook Weston, which formerly rilled through the park in quiet insignificance. The surface of this wide sheet, above the bridge, is broken into several falls; and a handsome cascade falls' gracefully under the arches, which is advantageously viewed from the principal rooms on the North front of the building. From hence a gentle ascent leads to the house, whose front, measuring three hundred and sixty feet in length, is a grand specimen of Adam's architectural skill. The front, which is of white stone, hewn on Lord Scarsdale's estate, is divided into three parts:—a centre, and two pavilions, connected to it by corridors of the Doric order, taking a sweeping form : that on the right (as we approach it) comprising the kitchen and offices, that on the left, consisting of Lord Scarsdale's private apartments.

In the centre of the North front is a double flight of steps, leading to a grand Portico, whose pediment is supported by six pillars [several of them in one single stone] of the Corinthian order, three feet in diameter and thirty feet in height, which were proportioned from those of the Pantheon at Rome: These support the Tym-

panum, on which are three elegant statues of
Venus, Bachus and *Ceres;* and in niches within the portico, *Two Muses* and a *Vestal:* and
basso-relievo medallions, by Collins, of *Vin-
tage, Pasturage, Harvest, Ploughing,* and *Boar
Hunting.* From hence is a beautiful home-
view, of the improvements of the late Lord
Scarsdale; whose gigantic plan, included the
transplanting of a village that stood in front
of the house to a distant part; the removal of
a turnpike road, which ran within fifty yards
of it, to its present situation; and the extension of a trifling brook into a noble expanse of
water.

Descending the flight of steps, beneath the
portico, at the basement or rustic story, is a
door conducting into a large room, called Cæsar's Hall, from its containing busts of the Cæ-
sars. Hence the stranger is conducted through
the tetrastyle, which is furnished with busts of
Alexander, Marcellus, Antoninus, &c. and
ascending the great staircase, decorated with
busts from the antique, he is ushered into,

The Hall, a room the most striking that
fancy can picture, planned after the Greek
Hall of the ancients. Its dimensions are sixty-
seven feet three inches, by forty-two feet; and
forty feet high: the coved ceiling of this apart-

ment, illuminated with three sky-lights, rises
to the top of the house, and is supported by
twenty Corinthian columns of beautiful varigated Derbyshire alabaster, twenty-five feet
high, and two feet six inches in diameter; with
rich capitals of white marble, proportioned
from the three columns, in the *Campo-Vicino* at
Rome, which are supposed to have belonged to
Jupiter Stator. Behind the columns are the
following paintings, in chiaro oscuro, from
the Iliad :—

On the West side :—*Helen* going to the field
accompanied by *Paris*. The *Judgment of Paris*. The *Meeting* between *Hector* and *Andro-
machc*. *Juno* and *Minerva*, preparing to assist
the *Grecians*, are forbidden by *Iris* sent from
Jupiter.

On the East side :—*Helen* reproaching *Pa-
ris* for his retreat from *Menelaus*, is silenced by
Venus. *Achilles* receiving from *Thetis* the ar-
mour which *Vulcan* had made at her entreaty.
Achilles delivering his armour to *Patroclus*.
Mercury delivering a Message at the Throne of
Jupiter, in the presence of *Juno* and *Neptune*.

At the North end :—*Apollo* and the Hours.
Sacrifice to *Sylvanus*. Sacrifice to *Diana*.

At the South end :—*Night* distributing her

10 · P P

Poppies. Sacrifice to *Apollo*. Sacrifice to *Mars*.

In the circles over the doors:—Introducing the intended Bride. The *Grecian* Marriage. Washing the Feet. Retiring to Rest. Under these, Trophies.

Over the chimney pieces, which are of statuary marble:—*Apollo* and *Hyacinthus*—after Dominichino. *Ceres* and *Arethusa*—after Gravelot; in circles.

In the niches, are twelve casts from the antique:—*Apollo Belvidere. Meleager*—of Paulo Pichini. *Idol. Venus. Fawn. Apollo.* Vil. Medici. *Urania. Fawn. Venus. Ganymede. Antinous. Mercury.* Of these, the Apollo and Meleager are the best. There are also two tablets with Lord Scarsdale's Arms; twelve seats after the ancient Sarcophagus, and the grates are after the antique tripods.

The Music Room, thirty-six feet by twenty-four, and twenty-two feet high; finished with stucco, and Ionic entablature, antique ceiling, compartments and ornaments; contains,

At the West end:—An Organ. *Bacchus and Ariadne;* by Guido. *Holy Family;* Leonardi di Vinci. *Landscape;* Horizonti. *David's Triumph;* Guercino.

On the chimney side:—*Landscape* with *Fi-*

gures; Horizonti. *Flowers* and *Fruit*; Baptiest.
Flowers; Baptiest. *Port of Naples*; Gaspar Oc-
biali. *Horses, Figures*, &c. Giovanni di St. Giov.
Water flowing from the Rock struck by Moses;
Bassan.

At the East end:—A Harpsichord. *Triumph
of Bacchus*; Luc. Giordano. This is a fine
painting; the figure of Bacchus beautiful and
spirited, as described by Milton,

" with clus'tring locks,
" With ivy berries wreath'd, and blithe in youth."

Shipping; Vandist. *Old Man's Head*; Rembrandt. *Roman Charity*; Signora Pozzi. *Arm
of the Sea and Storm*; Tempesta. The chimney piece is of statuary marble; Tablet, an
Epithalamium from the Adm. Rom. in basso
relievo, by Spang.

Drawing Room, forty-four feet by twenty-
eight, and twenty-eight feet high, hung with
blue damask; antique ceiling coved; Venetian
window: and door-cases finished with Corinthian columns of Derbyshire alabaster. Here
are,

Olympia and *Orlando*; a noble picture, by
Annibal Caracci. *Alexander*, &c. Paul Veronese.
Naaman's Story; the joint composition of Mom-
pert, Brughel, Teniers, and Old Franks. The
composition of this picture is good, and the
distant mountains fine; but, altogether, it is

harsh, and the colours are too vivid. A *fine.
Landscape*, by Cuyp.. The *Salutation of Elizabeth*; Andrea del Sart. *Landscape*; Dominichino: *Death of the Virgin*; Raphael, his
earliest manner. *Landscape*; Suaneveldt.—
Magdalen; Ann. Caracci. *Holy Family*;
Guido. *Holy Family in Landscape*; Polem-
berg. *Time on the Wing*; Teniers. The *Woman anointing our Saviour's feet*, by Benedetto
Lutti : a painting, of which it is not possible to
speak in terms of praise too high. *Scripture
History*, the Woman of Samaria and St. John;
Bernardo Strozzi, *vulgo* Prete Genoese. A
small beautiful *Landscape*, by Claude Lorraine.
Holy Family; Raphael, probably a copy. *La
vie Champetre*; Dom. Fetti. *Cain* and *Abel*;
Benedetto Lutti. This is a masterly performance, in which the chain of light is powerfully
fine; and the horror and remorse of Cain, after the murder of his brother, horribly natural.
Holy Family; Tintoret. *Holy Family*; Gio-
seppi Chiari. *A sleeping Cupid*, by Guido; a
most admirable figure, possessing all the sweetness and grace of this artist. *Holy Family*;
Nic. Beritoni. *Virgin* and *Child*, by Parmegiano.

The chimney piece is of statuary marble :
two whole-length Figures, by Spang: Tablet—

Virtue rewarded with Riches and Honor, in basso relievo, by Spang.

The *Library*, thirty-six feet by twenty-four, and twenty-two feet high; finished with stucco, and mahogany book-cases; Doric entablature and Mosaic ceiling. The paintings are,

Diogenes, a powerful figure, by Lueca Giordano. *Adam* and *Eve*—*Lot* and his *Daughters;* Carlo Lotti. *Daniel* interpreting *Belshazzar's Dream.* This is one of the finest productions of the pencil of Rembrandt. The solemnity of Daniel's figure; the attention and alarm in the different faces; the grandeur of the King; and the splendid light emanating from the *mithra*, or emblem of the sun, behind the king's throne, are all indications of transcendent genius and skill. *Man's Head—A Man in Armour;* Guercino. *Shakspeare*, a copy, by Vandyck.*

* " It would have been desirable" says Mr. Warner, from whom the criticisms on the paintings are chiefly taken, " to ascertain from what picture this copy was made, since commentators have not differed more on the abstruse passages of our immortal bard, than collectors have done as to the originality of heads called Shakspeare. It was for some time *determined* that there was no *original* portrait of him, but that Sir Thomas Clarges, soon after his decease, caused a painting to be made from a person nearly resembling him. Then came Mr. Walpole (whose deep researches in all questions connected with the arts, entitle him to the character of an *arbiter*), with an opinion, that

Winter, represented as an aged man; Andrea Sacchi. *Old Man*, half-length, by Salvator Rosa, very fine and spirited. *Holy Family*; Nic. del. Abbatti. *Rinaldo* and *Armida*, from Tasso; Nic. Poussin. *Andromeda* chained to the Rock, by Guido: grave in the figure, but a want of expression in the countenance.

On the tops of the book-cases are the busts of, *Homer*, *Sappho*, *Socrates*, *Virgil*, *Anacreon*, *Pindar*, and *Horace*. The chimney piece is enriched with Doric columns of statuary marble. Sienna marble ground. Tablet from the plate of Raphael's Cupid and Psyche, in basso relievo, by Wilson.

Over the Door are,—*Continence of Scipio*,—*Rape of the Sabines*, by M. A. Buono Rotti.— Small bronze of *Neptune*, by Fiamingo.

The *Saloon*, is a most elegant apartment: exact in its proportions, magnificent in its ornaments, and containing an assemblage of rich and elegant design, perhaps, unparalleled.— This beautiful room in its figure is circular, crowned with a dome, ornamented with rich stucco work, finished with octagon compart-

ments with roses, by Rose: its dimensions
are, forty-two feet in diameter, twenty-four
feet to the cornice, (which is extremely rich)
fifty-five feet to the top of the cupola, and
sixty-two to the extremity of the sky-light.
Beneath, the saloon is divided into four recesses,
or alcoves, having fire places, representing altars, adorned with sphinxes in bass relief; and
as many doors: the whole painted and ornamented with white and gold.

The candle branches have bass relieves of
boys under them, after Raphael, Albano, Dominichino, Parmegiano, Poussin, Pietro di Cor-
tona, &c. The doors have scagliola pilastres,
verd-antique, by Bartoli.

Over the doors are, Pictures of Ruins, by
Hamilton:—their frames ornamented with recumbent figures of Friendship and Liberality.
Over the alcoves, are delineations in chiaro oscuro, by Rebecca; the subjects from the English History: viz.

The Dukes of *Northumberland* and *Suffolk*
entreating Lady *Jane Grey* to accept the Crown;
Cipriani. *Edward* the Black Prince, serving
the French King (when his prisoner) at supper.
Elizabeth, widow of Sir *John Gray*, (afterwards
Queen) imploring king *Edward* the Fourth to
restore her husband's lands; *Angelica.* *Elea-*

nora sucking the poison from her husband Edward the First's wound.

. The bases and capitals of the door pilastres, are after the Temple of *Erectheus*, king of Athens; 1409 years before Christ. .   . . ˈ

This noble room forms the South entrance, which is designed after the Arch of Constantine, and is adorned with statues of *Flora Farnese*, and *Bacchus*, in niches, with medallions of *Apollo* and *Diana* over the pillars, the statues of *Pastoral*, and *Comic Muse*, *Prudence*, and *Diana*, above: and, by the steps, the Medicean and Burghesian vases. On the pediment is the following hospitable and liberal motto :—

·A. D. 1765. N. BARRO DE SCARSDALE AMICIS ET SIBI.

The *Ante-Chamber*, is twenty-four feet by twelve, and twenty feet high. It contains,

A *Landscape*, by Grimaldi J. Bolognese. A fine *St. John*, by Carlo Maratti. Two *Landscapes*, by Heusch: and a pair of beautiful pieces, in chiaro oscuro, in imitation of ivory; representing a Cupid in a Car drawn by Cupids; and Cupid carried on the shoulders of the Loves.

Principal Dressing Room, twenty-four feet square, and twenty feet high; hung with blue damask. Paintings,

Nathaniel Lord Scarsdale, and *Catherine* his wife; Hobe. *Charles* 1. by Vandyck. *Ruper-ta*, natural Daughter of Prince Rupert, by Madame Haghes, an actress; Sir Godfrey Knel-ler. A *Landscape*, by Salvator Rosa. A *Blind Beggar*, &c. by Jean Stein. *Landscape* and *Figures:* Berghem.

James Duke of Ormond, by Lely; an active character in the reign of Charles I. by whom he was nominated, Lord-Lieutenant of Ireland; and faithfully attached to his son, whom he followed into exile; for which he was, on the Restoration, again appointed to the government of Ireland, and enjoyed other places and honors. He was created a Duke in 1682, and died in 1688.

Henry Jermyn Earl of St. Alban's, by Lely, was second son to Sir John Jermyn, of Suffolk. Of the many who evinced their attachment to the imprudent and unfortunate Charles, no one appears to have more readily risked life and fortune than this personage; whose zeal indeed has been construed into more than mere loyal-ty, as he is reported to have been early favored by, and finally married to, Queen Henrietta Maria: on whom, during the troubles of her husband, he faithfully and diligently attended

10   Q q

through great perils and dangers, for which he
was rewarded with the title of Lord Jermyn;
and was, for continued services to the family
previous to the Restoration, created Earl of St.
Albau's by Charles II. to whom he was appointed Chamberlain. If he were distinguished by his courage and intrepidity in the troubled reign of Charles I. he was not less able to
shine, from the elegance of his person and
manners, in the licentious court of his successor; therefore we are not surprised to find mention of him in Grammont's Memoirs.

Two Landscapes; Cimeroli. View of *Matlock High Torr,* by Zuccarrelli. *Banditti;*
Lougherbourgh.

Principal Bed-Chamber; thirty feet by twenty-two, and twenty feet high ; hung with blue
damask. The chimney-piece is of statuary
marble; with an oval tablet, containing a fine
specimen of Derbyshire Blue John. The paintings are,

Sir *Nathaniel* and Lady *Curzon,* grandfather
and grandmother of the present Lord Scarsdale; Richardson. Two whole-length *Portraits;* Lely. *Keswick Lake,* and a *View in
Cumberland,* by Barret. *Dutchess of York;*
Lely. *Dutchess of Portsmouth,* and *D'Aubigne,*
(by Vandyke) on whose son, the title of Duke

of Richmond, was conferred by his father
Charles II. together with a grant of one shilling per chaldron, on all coals shipped in the
river Tyne; which was commuted by his Grace
of Richmond in 1800, for a perpetual annuity
of £19,000. per annum, secured by Act of
Parliament on the consolidated fund.

Catherine Countess of *Dorset* (after Mytens,
by Hamilton) was daughter of Sir George Curzon, and Governess to the Princess Mary, and
the Duke of York. Her dress is extremely singular, being curiously worked, and put on,
over a large hoop; the waist contracted by a
close bodice; and her neck encircled by a
large ruff.

Two *Landscapes*; Zuccarrelli.

In the *Wardrobe:* twenty-two feet by fourteen, and twenty feet high; hung with blue
damask; are thirty-six small pieces in enamel,
after Albert Durer, representing a series of
events in the life of our Saviour. The paintings are,

A fine painting of *Turkeys*, &c. by Van
Utretcht. *Catherine Countess of Dorchester*, by
Sir Godfrey Kneller. This lady was daughter
of Sir Charles Sedley, and mistress to James
the Second; by whom she was raised to the
rank of Countess; a situation which her father

me the honor, to make my daughter

ever considered as a splendid indignity offered
to his family. ' An injury so sensible could
scarcely be forgotten, or remain unresented,
when opportunity offered, On the first agitation of the questions, which brought about
the Revolution, Sir Charles was a distinguished
partizan, and at once indulged the parent's resentment, and wit's spleen, when he said, " The
King did me the honor, to make my daughter
a Countess, and I should be ungrateful indeed,
not to assist in making his daughter, (Mary
Princess of Orange) a Queen." When the re-
monstrances of his confessors, had induced
James to break off the connection with the
Countess of Dorchester, she married David,
Earl of Portmore, and died 1717.

A *Lady;* Sir Godfrey Kneller. *Jupiter* and
Io; Andrea Sacchi. *Thieves Gaming;* Bam-
boccio. *Sir Peter Rycaut*, by Vandyck. He
was employed in the diplomatic line, by the
two last of the Stuarts, and their successor
William; and has left us, not only proofs of
his talents as a negociator, but also as an historical writer. Whilst secretary to the embas-
sy at Constantinople, he composed, " An Account of the Ottoman Empire, and a continuation of Knolles's History of the Turks."—
Whilst resident at Smyrna, he published, "The

present State of the Greek and Armenian Churches." Ob. 1700.

His Wife and Child, by the painter himself, Quintin Metsys. This artist was a native of of Antwerp, where he carried on the trade of a blacksmith; but becoming enamoured of the daughter of a painter, who was willing to unite his child only to one of his own profession, our son of Vulcan, quitted his forge for the easel, and soon made himself sufficiently master of the art, not only to entitle him to his wife, but to the character of a celebrated painter. His most esteemed picture is known by the title of *The Misers*, and is in the Royal Collection at Windsor.

Nathaniel Baron Crewe, Bishop of Durham, one of the most despicable characters in the annals of James II. by whom he was selected as grand-inquisitor of the ecclesiastical commission, at which he rejoiced, " because it would render his name famous (or rather infamous) in history." On the reverse of fortune which deservedly attended that misguided Prince, this obnoxious prelate, hoping to cancel the remembrance of his former offences, basely deserted the sovereign, who had raised him, and affected to espouse the cause of liberty, which he had so long, and so lately, insulted. Ob. 1721. Æt. 88.

wash-house, dairy, and other inferior offices.
The corridor which leads to the family pavilion,
is hung with green paper and prints, *Volterra*
vases, &c. three marble medallions, and several small statues, after Fiamingo. Tablet,
Cupid and *Psyche*, by Wedgewood. The kitchen corridor is finished with stucco, and ornamented with prints. There is also there, a
model of the *Victory* ship of war, and of a
French *Sloop*, constructed by French prisoners.
Medallions of *Annibal Carracci*, *Raphael*, *Michael Angelo*, and *Corregio*. Above this corridor, are cisterns capable of containing 120
hogsheads of water, for the use of the house.

Family Pavillion. *Anti-Room*, contains a
good picture of *Fish*. *Hercules* and the *Ery-
manthean Boar*. *Landscapes* and coloured
prints. The chimney-piece is of marble from
the Peak of Derbyshire.

The *Breakfast-Room*, is eighteen feet square;
finished with fresco paintings, and antique ornaments, after the Baths of Dioclesian. The
chimney-piece of statuary marble, partly gilt.

Lady Scarsdale's Dressing-Room, is twenty-
four feet by eighteen, hung with paper, and
contains the following paintings:—A *Landscape*, by C. Lorraine; and another by Gaspar
Poussin. Two pieces representing *Turkish*

Carmous, by Peters. A *Landscape*; Brughel. A *Landscape*, by Wooton. Another, by Ber- chem. *Nymphs* and *Fawns*; Van Uden. *Merry Making*; Pandolfo. *Villa Madama*; Wilson. Two Drawings of Dead Game. Plants and Blossoms in water-colours. *Santa Christiana*; Carlo Dolci. The *Nativity*; Jac. Bassan. The chimney-piece is of statuary marble, having an oval tablet of root of Emerald.

Lady Scarsdale's Bed-Chamber, is eighteen feet square, and contains,

Lord Milsintown, by Hone. Small pictures by Morland.

Lord Scarsdale's Dressing-Room, is twenty-four feet by eighteen, hung with green paper, and coloured prints upon it. *Landscape*, by Paul Brill. *Venus* and *Cupids*, a cartoon, by C. Maratti. *Christ* delivering the Keys to *Peter*; Old Palma. A *Badger* and *Fruit*, by Snyders. *Lady Scarsdale*; Hone and Hamilton. A *Flemish Fair*; Velvet Brughel. Two Heads of the *Venus* of Medici; G. Hamilton. Hon. *Juliana Curzon*; Hone. *Landscape*, by Marco Ricci. A *Dutch Landscape*; Varderneer.

Atticks. *Crimson Damask Bed-Chamber*, contains, a drawing in red chalk, from *Raphael's Panassus*. A *Lady* and *Child*, by Parmegiano.

10

Large Dressing-Room, has a *Cymon* and *Iphigenia*, by Claude: and in the *Smaller Dressing-Room*, a *Cato*, by Spagniolet; and a *St. Catherine*, by Kent.

In the *Green Bed-Chamber* are; *Holy Family*, by Contarini. *Prince of Orange;* Cornelius Jansen. View of *Caprea.* View of the *Coast of Baia.*

The *Dressing-Room*, contains, *Festa Floralia*, by Zuccarrelli, after Vandyck.

From the above short account of Kedleston-House, it will be seen, that elegance and taste characterize every thing within and about it; but to these let us not forget to observe, that *comfort* may be added : the apartments are not reserved for *shew* alone, but are constantly inhabited by the family, and the numerous friends, which his Lordship's hospitality invites. The state rooms are not many; and the rest of the house consists of excellent offices, and comfortable apartments. The plan of the whole is easy and intelligible; and the skill of the architect, *Adams*, was, perhaps, never better displayed than by this mansion.

Besides the extent of the Park, and the umbrageous dignity of the noble oaks, which adorn it, already noticed; the Lodge at the entrance, built by Mr. Adams, after the Arch of Octavia—the truly elegant manner in which the gardens are laid out—the admirable ingenuity with which the boundaries of the river are concealed—and the disposition and shape of the water, and the plantations, merit particular attention; insomuch, that the stranger will find his curiosity amply gratified, and his trouble delightfully recompensed, by a visit to Kedleston;* the amateur and the virtuoso, will experience the sublimest gratification.

In the Park, and almost in front of the House, are the *Baths*, a simple, elegant building, ambushed in fir-trees, having accommodations for hot and cold bathing:—Between fifty and sixty years ago, it was, that the late Lord Scarsdale erected this building, enclosing the spring. In the part fronting the house, is a portico supported by a colonnade; and on each side of the well, which is situated in the middle of the open area, are the baths, with suitable conveniences.

The spring is pretty copious; and the water, in a glass, looks very clear and transparent; but in the well, it appears of a blackish blue

---

* His Lordship generously gratifies the Public, by a permission of inspecting the interior of his Mansion, between the hours of eleven and two, every day, Sundays excepted.

colour, tinged with purple; and any substance thrown into it, assumes the same appearance. Its smell is fœtid, and though on its first being put in a glass, it appears clear, yet, when it has stood for some time, a duskiness comes on, which is soon followed, by a total loss of scent and taste. That it is impregnated with sulphur in some state or form, is not only evident from its strong taste and smell, but likewise, from its changing silver to a dark copper colour; and in its passage from the well, depositing a yellowish-green sediment, like alkalized sulphur, on the stones, and in the baths.— From the examination of Dr. Short, it appears, that it is impregnated with other substances also. He says, that eight pints of it evaporated, left two scruples of sediments, twenty-one grains of which, were a dark brownish earth, and the rest salt. Mr. Lipscomb says, that it contains thirty-eight grains of sea salt, and forty-two grains of calcareous earth, in a gallon. In these respects it appears similar to the waters at Harrowgate.

Kedleston water is principally valued for its anti-scorbutic qualities. When taken inwardly, it acts as a diuretic, and has afforded relief to persons afflicted with the gravel. By external application, it has been found efficacious in

various cutaneous diseases, but more particularly in ulcerous complaints: indeed, it has
been found highly serviceable in the cure of old
and indolent ulcers. In the summer, it is frequently used by the neighbouring inhabitants,
as a substitute for malt liquor at their meals;
the charge of carriage being but trifling, and
affording sustenance to a few poor people of
the vicinity. The temperature of the water in
the spring, is fifty-three degrees. Two or three
half-pint glasses may be taken in the course of
the morning.

QUARNDON, is a Chapelry in the parish of
St. Alkmund, Derby. The village contains
about sixty houses, is esteemed very healthy,
and is much frequented in the summer season,
on account of its chalybeate spring. The well
is situated by the road-side, and at the distance
of about three miles from Derby.

This water is a carbonated chalybeate, with
the addition of a saline substance. These waters
are known to be chalybeate, by their striking a
purple or black colour with an infusion of galls,
or other vegetable astringent; by their peculiar inky flavour; and by their depositing a
yellowish ochre, when exposed to the air. They
are impregnated with fixed air, iron, and such
ingredients as are found in the most common

springs. It is by means of the fixed air, that
these waters retain the iron in solution; if,
therefore, they lose the gas, which they gradually do, by mere exposure, and more quickly
by boiling, the iron is precipitated, in the form
of ochre, 'and the water loses all its virtues,
and peculiar properties. If well corked, they
may be kept good for some time.

Quarndon Water, is turned to a very deep
purple, with the infusion of galls, and at the
bottom of the glass a dark green colour is produced. From the experiments made by Dr.
Short, it appears, that a pint contains one
grain of fixed salt, and that two gallons, when
evapourated, left half a dram of light-coloured
sediment, half of which was nitrous earth.—
The temperature is nearly forty-nine and a
half.

This water, when taken in sufficient quantities, is found by some to be purgative; others,
however find, that without using a good deal of
exercise, it does not pass through the stomach
with ease. Its medical virtues, are chiefly as a
tonic, producing a genial glow, improving the
digestion, and giving strength and tone to the
whole system. It is particularly serviceable in
chlorosis, and other diseases of females; in fla-
tulency and indigestion, and in all cases of de-

bility from free.living or debauchery. Persons of a weak and relaxed habit, have been much benefited by the use of the Quarndon water. After drinking it a few days, they have found their spirits and strength return in a surprising manner: and in the space of a month, a cure has been enirely effected.

. The proper quantity to be taken is, from a a pint and a half, to three pints daily : and the use of the water, should not be continued, more than from six to eight weeks, without a considerable intermission.

. The Chalybeate at Quarndon, is a good deal frequented every summer. It is drank, not only by those, who take lodgings in the village for that purpose, but sometimes also, by company who resort to Kedleston, which is not more than a mile distant.

..Kirk Langley, in Domesday called *Langlei*, where, at that time, " Levenot had four carucates. of land to to be taxed. Land.to six ploughs. There is now one plough in the demesne, and two villanes, and four bordars have two ploughs. Wood pasture one mile long, and three quarentens broad, and an equal quantity of coppice wood. Value in king Edward's time, 100s. now 40s."*

* Land of Ralph the son of Hubert. *Orig.* 327, *a.* 1. Trans. 320.

The living of Kirk Langley is a rectory, valued in the king's books at £12. 2s. 1d. and
yearly tenths £1. 4s. 2d. In the church there
are several monuments of the Meynil and Beresford families. The parish, which is a single
hamlet, contains from sixty to seventy houses.

MUGGINTON. "In *Mogintun*," say the Norman surveyors, " Gamel had two carucates of
land to be taxed. Land to three ploughs. There
is now one plough in the demesne, and eight
villanes, and eight bordars have two ploughs.
There is a church and a priest, and one mill of
three shillings, and three acres of meadow.—
Wood pasture, one mile and a half long, and
one mile broad. Value in king Edward's time
forty shillings, now twenty shillings. Chetel
holds it."*

In the parish of Mugginton are included the
hamlets of Mercaston and Weston-under-Wood,
which, together with that of Mugginton, are
supposed to consist of about one hundred and
twenty houses. The living is a rectory. Its
value in the king's books is £9. 12s. 8½d. The
church is dedicated to All-Saints; and formerly
paid 6s. 8d. to the priory of Tutbury.

MERCASTON, called in Domesday,† *Merche-*

---

* Domesday, Land of Henry De Ferieres, *Orig.* 276. *a.*
1. Trans. 312.   † *Orig.* 276, *a.* 1, Trans. 312.

nestune, was held at that time by Gamel under the Earl of Ferrers. There was one plough in the demesne, and six villaines and four bordars, having one plough. There were fourteen acres of meadow, and the site of one mill.

It is thought to have been, in ancient times, a place of greater importance than it is at present. Several old coins have been found in one part of the village; and it is generally supposed to have once contained a seat of one branch of the Kniveton family. At a small distance from the village, a part of an ancient road may be traced, which probably led to some other eminent place in the neighbourhood.

SCRAPTON, which is situated near the banks of the Dove, lies detached from the other parishes of which the Deanery of Derby consists. At the conquest, *Scrotune* was a place of considerable consequence. There were thirty-two villanes and twenty bordars there. There were also a priest, and a church, and one mill, and the site of another mill: Valued altogether at ten pounds.* Henry de Ferieres† who then

10 s s

* Domesday. Trans. 303.

† He was one of the commissioners appointed to take a general survey of England, and received Tutbury Castle as a gift from the Conqueror. He possessed one hundred and fourteen Lordships in Derbyshire, besides several in other counties.— Dug. Bar. v. I. p. 275.

held the manor, bestowed the tithe of his
Lordship of Scrapton to the Priory of Tutbury,
in the eleventh century. The church is dedicated to St. Paul, and in former times, belonged to the chantery of Scrapton. The whole
parish consists of the liberties of Scrapton and
Foston.

At FOSTON, which is supposed to be the *Fa-
rulaeston* of Domesday, was born, in the year
1640, " Arthur Agard, forty-five years Deputy
Chamberlain of the Exchequer, who died in
1651. Mr. Camden calls him *Antiquarius in-
signis.* Walter Achard, or Agard, claimed to
hold by inheritance the office of Escheator and
Coroner of the whole Honor of Tutbury, in
the county of Stafford, and of the Balliwick
of Leyke, for which he produced no other evidence, than a white hunting horn, adorned
with silver gilt in the middle, and at each end
with a belt of black silk, set with silver gilt
buckles, and the arms of Edmund, second son
of Henry III. This horn is now in the possession of Mr. Foxlowe, of Staveley, in this county,
who enjoys the posts of Feodary, or Bailiff-in-
Fee, Escheator, Coroner, and Clerk of the
Market of Tutbury Honor, by this tenure, and
by virtue of his being in possession of this
Horn, which he purchased of Christopher Stanhope, of Elvaston, Esq. into whose family it

came by a marriage with the heiress of Agard. The arms, as represented by Mr. Pegge,* are really those of the House of Lancaster, impaling Ferrars of Tamworth, who probably held those offices before Agard; for Nicholas Agard of Tutbury, who was living in 1569, married Elizabeth, daughter and co-heiress of Roger Ferrars, eleventh son of Sir Thomas Ferrars of Tamworth."†

CHADDESDEN, called in Domesday *Cedesdene*, is a small Chapelry, of about the distance of two miles from Derby. The church is dedicated to St. Mary; and is said to have been built before the time of Edward the Third: For in the twenty-ninth year of his reign, a grant was made of one messuage and thirteen acres of land, to three chaplains in the church of Chaddesden; and in the fourth year of Richard the Second, were given by different persons, for the singers at the Altar of the blessed Mary in the chapel of Chaddesden two messuages, one toft, and sixty acres of land, held of the Duke of Lancaster.

At Chaddesden is the seat of Sir Robert Mead Wilmot, a descendant of the same family as the Baronet of the same name, mentioned

<hr>

* Archæologia, 3. 6.   † Gough's Additions to Camden.

before:* The mansion is pleasantly situated,
and has a handsome appearance.

- LOCKO, is a Chapelry, consisting of a few
houses. Here it is supposed, was situated the
Preceptory or Hospital of *Lockhay:* it was dedicated to St. Mary Magdalene, and is said to
have been of the order of St. Lazarus of Jerusalem, and subject to a foreign House in France,
to which was annually paid from hence, a rent
of £20. But upon a war breaking out between
France and England in the reign of Edward
III. the revenue of the Hospital was seized, and
given by the king to King's Hall, in the University of Cambridge.

Locko-Park, is the seat of W. Drury Lowe,
Esq. and anciently of the Gilberts and Coopers.
The surrounding grounds consist of agreeable
slopes, and pleasant inequalities, enlivened by
an extensive artificial lake. The style of plant-
ing, or rather of pruning, which was adopted
during the last century, is, however, too apa-
rent: the rows of trees in some places, forming
right-angled triangles, and the clumps appearing tasteless and formal.

STANLEY. During the Norman survey, *Stan-
lei†* belonged to Robert son of William, and

---

* Page 276.
† Domesday. *Orig.* 278. *a.* 1. Trans. 324.

was valued at ten shillings. The church at
Stanley is dedicated to St. Andrew, and its
' clear value is £10. The whole liberty contains
about fifty houses.

OCKBROOK, or *Ockbruke*, or (as it is in Domesday) *Ochebroc*, is a parish, including the hamlet of Borrowash. The living is a curacy, and
the church is dedicated to All-Saints. It formerly belonged to the Abbey at Derley. William de Grendon gave the village to Dale-
Abbey.

The Moravians,* have established a society,

* The *Moravians* arose, under Nicholas Lewis, Count
of Zinzerdorf, a German Nobleman, who died in the year
1760. They were for sometime called *Hernhuters*, from
Hernhuth, the name of a village, where they were first settled. The followers of Count Zinzerdorf are called Moravians, because the first converts to his system, were Moravian families: the society, however, assert, that, they
are descended from the Old Moravian and Bohemian Brethren, who existed as a distinct sect, sixty years prior to
the Reformation. They also style themselves *Unitas Fra-
trum*, or the *United Brethren:* and, in general, profess to
adhere to the Augsburgh confession of faith. When the
first Reformers were assembled at Augsburgh in Germany,
the Protestant Princes employed Melancton, a divine of
learning and moderation, to draw up a confession of their
faith, expressed in terms as little offensive to the Roman
Catholics as their regard for truth would permit: And this
creed, from the place where it was presented, is called, the
Confession of Augsburgh. It is not easy to point out the
leading tenets of the Moravians. Opinions and practices

d erected a place of worship, at Ockbrook;
:y have a minister of their own, to whose
pport they all contribute; and are under the
re and direction of a governor and governess.
ie Moravian brethren, are chiefly employed
the manufacture of stockings, and the sis-
s, in tambour, needle-work, and embroidery.
SAWLEY, in Domesday called *Salle*, is a very
tensive parish: containing the chapelries of
Ilne, *Long-Eaton*, *Breason*, *Risley*, and the
mlets of *Draycot* and *Hopewell*. At the time

re been attributed to them, of an exceptional nature,
ich the more sensible of them disavow. They direct
ir worship to Jesus Christ (addressing hymns even to the
und or *hole* in the side of the Saviour); are much at-
hed to instrumental as well as vocal music, in their reli-
us services; and discover a predilection for forming
mselves into classes, according to sex, age, and charac-
. They revive their devotion by celebrating *Agapæ*, or
e-feasts; and the casting of lots is used among them, to
ow the will of the Lord. The sole right of contract-
marriage lies with the elders. The men and women al-
ys sit separately at their places of worship. They have
distinct habitations, and all mutual intercourse is deem-
unlawful. The conduct of the Moravians as religionists,
in general, honorable to their virtue and piety: But to
tional observer their devotion seems to spring, more
m enthusiasm, than from just views of a supreme Being.
iong this sect, it is thought, Mr. Wesley first imbibed
se extravagant notions, which he afterwards preached
h such success; and which from their tendency to pos-
the minds of the ignorant and superstitious, bid fair to
clude every trace of rational religion from our country.

of the Norman survey, there were " in *Salle*, and *Dracot*, and *Opeuuelle*, a priest and two churches, a mill, one fishery, and thirty acres of meadow."[*] The living of Sawley is a curacy, and the church is dedicated to All-Saints. The church at Wilne is dedicated to St. Chad: that at Long-Eaton to St. Lawrence: and that at Breason to St. Michael.

Risley. " Henry de Laci Earl of Lincoln, at his death was seized of a certain Wapentake at Risley, in the county of Derby, held every three week of the manor of Knesale and Wapentake of Allerton, in the county of Nottingham." In the reign of Edward the Third, Risley was granted to Geffrey, son of Roger Mortimer, Earl of March, being part of the land of the Earl of Kent attained. Some time afterwards it became the property of the Lords of Sheffield, ancestors to the Duke of Buckingham; of whom it was purchased by the Willoughbys of Risley in the year 1587. Of this family was Sir Hugh Willoughby, who in the last year of Edward VI. was employed in seeking a north-east passage in the frozen ocean; but was starved to death with all his company; near *Wardhous*, in Scandia;[†] and whose me-

---

[*] Domesday. *Orig.* 273. *b.* 1. Trans. 296.

[†] Camden, p. 492.

lancholy fate is thus delineated by Thomson,
in his Seasons:

     - - - - - - - - - " Miserable they!
Who, here entangled in the gathering ice,
Take their last look of the descending sun ;
 While, full of Death, and fierce with tenfold frost,
The long, long night, incumbent o'er their heads
Falls horrible. Such was the BRITON's fate;
As with first prow, (what have not Briton's dar'd !)
He for the passage sought, attempted since
So much in vain, and seeming to be shut.
By jealous Nature with eternal bars.
In these fell regions, in Arzina caught,
And to the stony deep his idle ship
Immediate seal'd, he with his hapless crew,
Each full exerted at his several task,
Froze into statues ; to the cordage glu'd
The sailor, and the pilot to the helm."—Winter, 930.

The family of the Willoughbys, is now extinct: the last of them, a daughter, dying in
1720, or 1721, unmarried. She is represented
as a very charitable woman; and the foundress
of the free-schools at Risley.

Near the site of an ancient Manor-House belonging to the Lords Sheffield, in the mote at
Risley-Park, was found in the year 1729, a
large silver dish, or salver, of antique basso
relievo, and of Roman workmanship.   Dr.
Stukely, by whom an account of it was read
before the Antiquarian Society, observes, that
it was twenty inches long, and fifteen broad;
and weighed seven pounds. Upon the face,

there were a variety of figures, representing rural sports, employments, and religious rites.— It stood upon a square basis or foot; and round the bottom, and on the outside, this inscription was rudely cut with a sharp pointed instrument, in Roman characters of the fourth century:—

EXSVPERIVS EPISCOPVS ECCLESIÆ BOGIENSIS

DEDIT.

Intimating, that it "was given by Exsuperius, who was Bishop of Bayeux and Toulouse in the year 405, to the church of Bouges:" near which a battle was fought in the year 1421, between the Scots, under the Duke D'Alenson, who were quartered in the church, and the English, under Thomas, Duke of Clarence, brother to Henry the Fifth, who was slain there. At this time it is supposed to have been taken from the church as a trophy, and given to Dale Abbey.*

A few miles to the South of Risley is CAVEN-DISH-BRIDGE; so named from its having been built by the Cavendish family about fifty years ago. Formerly there was a ferry at this place, which, from the overflowing of the Trent, was

11 T t

* Stukeley's Dissertations on it, quoted by Gough.

sometimes very inconvenient. The present
bridge is a handsome modern fabric of three
arches, composed of free-stone, brought from a
neighbouring quarry : it crosses the Trent, and
unites the counties of Derby and Leicester.
Near the bridge, the great Staffordshire Navigation, or Grand Trunk Canal, falls into the
Trent, and, by its various connecting branches,
facilitates the removal of goods to every part of
the kingdom. Some good houses have been
erected here, by the gentlemen who have the
direction of the wharf; which, together with
other buildings raised near them, go under the
name of Cavendish-Bridge.

SANDIACRE. At the time of the Norman
survey, there were at *Sandiacre,* " a priest,
and a church, and one mill of five shillings
and four-pence, and thirty acres of meadow,
and an equal quantity of coppice-wood."[*]
" Near this" (Risley) says Camden,[†] " stands
Sandiacre, or as others would have it *Saint-
Diacre,* the seat of that noble family, the *Greys*
of *Sandiacre,* whose estate came to Edward
Hilary in right of his wife; his son took the
name of *Grey;* one of whose daughters and

---

* Domesday, *Orig.* 278. *a.* 2. Trans. 327.
† Britannia, 492.

heirs some years after, was married to Sir *John*
Leak, Kt. the other to *John Welsh*." The living of Sandiacre is a curacy, of the clear value of £23.   The Prebendary of Litchfield Cathedral, is patron and proprietor.

WEST-HALLAM, in Domesday called *Halen*,
is a small village, containing from seventy to
eighty houses.   The living is a rectory, and the
church is dedicated to St Wilfred.

HEANOR.   This parish contains the hamlets,
Codnor, *Loscoe*, *Langley*, *Milnhay*, and *Shipley*. When Domesday was compiled, there
was a church at *Hainoure* :* and it appears,
from the history of the foundation of Dale-
Abbey, that there was a chapel as well as a
church there, in the reign of Henry the Second,
belonging to the parish of St. Mary in the town
of Derby. In the thirteenth year of Edward
IV. the church was appropriated to the Abbey
at Dale. The living is a vicarage, and the
king is the patron.

Codnor, in Domesday *Cotenovre*, is a small
hamlet, remarkable for the ruins of a Castle.
In the early part of the thirteenth century there
was a Castle here; and in the reign of Henry
the Third, it was the chief seat of Richard de

---

* *Orig.* 276, *b*. 1. Trans. 314.

Gray, whose descendants, the Barons Grey of
Codnor, possessed it till the eleventh of Henry
the Seventh, when it passed to Sir John Zouch,
(the youngest son of William Lord Zouch of
Harringworth), who had married the aunt of
the last possessor of this family. John Zouch,
Esq. the last of the family who resided at Codnor, sold his land and coal in the neighbourhood about the year 1692, and leaving the
kingdom, settled in Ireland. It afterwards became the property of the *Masters*, one of whom,
it is said, inhabited the Castle in the year 1712:
but even then it was in a ruinous state, and
since that period, it has almost entirely fallen
into ruins.

Codnor Castle was situated on elevated ground
commanding an extensive prospect to the East.
The wall on the East side, is yet standing to a
considerable height; and in the inside are several recesses, formed in a singular manner.—
These remains indicate its having been a place
of considerable extent. To the South, there
appears to have been an extensive square court,
from which were two entrances, or gates, into
the Castle, The wall on the West side of the
court, which is yet entire, has two large recesses in it, supposed to have been used as watch-
houses. On the eastern side was a broad deep

ditch or moat; and on the bank grew a double
row of trees, which were cut down about the
year 1738. The park belonging to the Castle
was very extensive; comprehending about two
thousand and two hundred acres of land.

Shipley was formerly the seat of the *Vava-
sours,* and afterwards of the *Strelleys,* one of
whom was married to the heiress of Vavasour.
In the time of Charles the Second, Shipley was
the property of Sir Edward Leche, Knt. Master
in Chancery, whose heiress married one Miller;
and the heiress of Miller married Edward Mundy, Esq. (a younger branch of the Mundys
of Markeaton) whose only son, Edward Miller
Mundy, Esq. is the present possessor; and has
represented the county of Derby in several Parliaments.

, KIRK HALLAM. This parish contains the
hamlet of Maperley: The living is a vicarage;
and the church is dedicated to All-Saints. Its
clear value is £11. 6s. 2d. and yearly tenths
8s. 11½d. Sir Windsor Hunloke is the patron.
The church was formerly impropriated to the
Abbey at Dale.

ILKESTON, in Domesday called *Tilchestune,*
is an extensive village. The parish contains
the hamlets of *Cotmenhay* and *Little Hallam.*
Near the end of the fourth century, there was

£40. issuing out of the town of Derby.* John
de Holland,.third son of Thomas, earl of Kent,
in the fifteenth year of Richard II. had a grant
of Horseton castle for life.   In the thirty-fifth
year of Henry VI. Edmund Hallam, earl of
Richmond, died possessed of the castle and
lordship of Horeston.   In the year 1514, the
castle of Horeston and manor of Horsley were
granted, in special tail, to be held by the service of one knight's fee, by Henry VIII. to the
duke of Norfolk.   They were part of the reward, which was bestowed on him for the very
important service, which he had rendered the
king during his expedition into France, having
prevented the incursion of the Scots, and defeated them at Flodden, near the Cheviot hills.
On this remarkable occasion one archbishop,
two bishops, four abbots, James IV. king of
Scotland, and about ten thousand men were
slain, and their whole artillery taken.   Upon
the attainder of the son of the duke of Norfolk, these possessions most probably escheated
to the crown, and were granted to some of the
Stanhope family.   At least Thomas Stanhope
was possessed of the castle in the tenth year of
queen Elizabeth.   At what time it was destroy-

* Bar, Ang. vol. I. page 796.

ed, I have not been able to discover. At present a very small part of the ruins is visible. The scite of it belongs to the earl of Chesterfield."

PENTRIDGE, *Pencriz*, and in Domesday *Pentrice*, is a parish containing the hamlet of *Ripley*. The living is a vicarage, and the church is dedicated to St. Matthew. It formerly belonged to Derley Abbey. The Duke of Devonshire is the patron. Waingriff in this parish, was presented by Ralph Fitz-Stephen, to the Knights Hospitallers of St. John of Jerusalem, for the erection of a house of that order at this place. There is a Calvinists' place of worship at Pentridge.

RIPLEY, or *Ripelie*, is a very considerable hamlet, which owing to the extensive coal and iron works carried on in the neighbourhood, has of late years experienced a very great increase of population. The iron works at Butterley, belonging to the Messrs. Jessop and Co. employ a great number of hands, while the different collieries find occupation for several more. There is a Unitarian Chapel, and also a Methodist Meeting House, at Ripley.

CRICH. In the time of the Norman survey, Leuric and Levenot held a lead-mine at *Crice*.[*]

11   U u

---

[*] Domesday, *Orig.* 277. *b.* 1. Trans. 319.

In the reign of Stephen, Robert Ferrers, Earl of Derby, gave the church of Crich to the Abbey at Derley: and it is supposed, that it was about this time, that a church was first erected there. In the forty-second year of the reign of Edward the Third, a chantry was founded in the church. The living is a vicarage, and is dedicated to St. Mary.

The town of Crich has the appearance of antiquity; and is supposed to have been known to the Romans. Some years ago, a collection of ancient coins, was found in the neighbourhood; and by the superscription, it appeared, that some of them were coined in the reigns of *Domitian*, *Adrian*, and *Dioclesian*.

The inhabitants are supported, chiefly, by working lead-mines, burning limestone, and the manufacture of stockings.

A little to the North of the town is *Crichcliff*, one of the highest hills in the Low-Peak: on its summit, is a Tower of Observation, which was erected some years ago; it is seen from several points of the surrounding country, and from the top, the eye is gratified with a very extensive prospect, commanding a view of parts of the counties of Leicester, Stafford, and Salop.

The town and liberty of Crich, consists of about ninety houses; and the parish contains the hamlets of, *Codington*, *Fritchley*, *Wheat-croft*, *Edge-Moor*, *Wessington*, and *Tansley*.

BLACKWELL, in Domesday called, *Black-euuelle*, is a parish, containing but one ham-let of the same name. The living of Black-well is a vicarage, and the church is dedicated to St. Werburgh. In former times, it belonged to the priory of *Thurgarton*, in Nottingham-shire. The clear value is £10. 0s. and yearly tenths 10s. 5d. The Duke of Devonshire is the patron.

BRAMPTON,* *Brandune*, or *Brantune*,† is a

---

* About the year 1780, the Rev. Mr. CARTWRIGHT, well known as the inventor of that master-piece of mecha-nical ingenuity, the Machine for Combing of Wool, and as the author of that elegant and justly admired Poem *Armine and Elvira*, resided at, and (I believe) had the cu-racy of, Brampton: and it was here he made that most va-luable discovery, that yeast affords an antidote for the most dangerous disease, with which the human body can be af-flicted. The fact is thus communicated to the world, from himself, in the Gentleman's Magazine for September 1799.

"Seventeen years ago I went, " says this benevolent clergyman, " to reside at Brampton, a populous village near Chesterfield. I had not been there many months before a putrid fever broke out amongst us. Finding by far the greater number of my parishioners too poor to afford them-selves medical assistance, I undertook by the help of such books on the subject of medicine as were in my possession, to prescribe for them. I early attended a boy about four-teen years of age, who was attacked by the fever. He had

† See Domesday, Trans. p. 315, and 322.

very extensive parish, and the most northern
in the Deanery of Derby. The living is a curacy, and the church is dedicated to St. Peter.
King Henry II. gave it, with all its appurtenances, to the Cathedral at Lincoln; and the

---

not been ill many days, before the symptoms were evidently putrid. I then administered bark, wine, and such other
remedies as my books directed. My exertions were, however, of no avail; his disorder grew every day more un-
tractable and malignant, so that I was in hourly expectation of his dissolution. Being under the necessity of taking
a journey, before I set off I went to see him, as I thought
for the last time; and I prepared his parents for the event
of his death, which I considered as inevitable, and reconciled them, in the best manner I was able, to a loss which I
knew they would feel severely. While I was in conversation on this distressing subject with his mother, I observed,
in a small corner of the room, a tub of wort working. The
sight brought to my recollection an experiment I had some,
where met with, ' of a piece of putrid meat being made
sweet, by being suspended over a tub of wort in the act of
fermentation.' The idea flashed into my mind, that the
yeast might correct the putrid nature of the disease; and I
instantly gave him two large spoonfuls. I then told the
mother, if she found her son better, to repeat this dose
every three hours. I then set out on my journey. Upon
my return, after a few days, I anxiously enquired after the
boy, and was informed he was recovered. I could not repress my curiosity, though I was greatly fatigued with my
journey, and night was come on. I went directly to where
he lived, which was three miles off, in a wild part of the
moors. The boy himself opened the door, looked sur-
prisingly well, and told me, he felt better from the instant
he took the yeast."

Dean is now the patron. The church contains several ancient monuments, chiefly relating to the family of Clarke of Somersall. The parish contains three hundred and twenty-five houses; and in that part of it which lies near Chesterfield, there has been a considerable increase in population, owing to the iron works. This part of the country is said to be remarkably healthy, and the grave-stones in. the church-yard, afford many instances of great longevity.

ALLESTRY, *Allestree*, or as it is called in Domesday, *Adelardestreu*, is a village, situated about two miles to the North of Derby. The living is a donative curacy; and the church is dedicated to St. Andrew. It formerly was one of the churches belonging to the Abbey at Darley.

. BREADSALL. At the time of the Norman survey, " there was at *Braideshale* a church and a priest, and one mill of thirteen and fourpence, and twelve acres of meadow.*

There was a House of Friers Heremites founded here, in the reign of king Henry the Third; which, afterwards was converted into a small Priory, for the Order of St. Austin, and dedi-

---

* Domesday, *Orig.* 275, a. 2. Trans. 309.

cated to the Holy Trinity. It was endowed
with one messuage and twenty acres of land
in Horsley and Horston;* with tenements in
Derby, Chaddesden, Spondon, Duffield, Windley, Breadsall, Morley, and Hazzlewood;† with
tenements in Mugginton, and a moiety of the
church.‡

The Priory at Breadsall was also endowed
with three messuages, two cottages, and eleven
acres of land in Derby; with one cottage and
eight acres of land in Chaddesden; with one
toft and two acres of meadow land, and ten
acres of pasture in Windley; with one toft and
two acres of land in Breadsall; and with one
acre and a rood of land in Hazzlewood.

But at the dissolution, it was found, that the
revenue of all these possessions, did not amount
to more than £13. 0s. 8d. total, or to £10. 17s.
9d. clear. The Priory at Breadsall was given,
in the sixth year of Edward the Sixth to Henry,
Duke of Suffolk.

The parish of Breadsall is but small, consisting of a single hamlet. The living is a rectory, and the church is dedicated to All-Saints.

LITTLE EATON, is a chapelry, under St.

---

* Pat. 2nd, Edward III.   † Pat. 15th, Richard II.
‡ Pat. 2nd, Henry IV.

Allmund's Derby. It contains about forty houses; and has, of late years, experienced an increase of population, from its vicinity to the Derby canal.

DUFFIELD, in Domesday called *Duuelle*, where at that time, there were a priest and a church and two mills,* is a very extensive parish; comprehending the chapelries of *Heage*, *Belper*, *Holbrooke* and *Turnditch*; and the hamlets of *Makeney*, *Millford*, *Windley*, *Shottle*, and *Postern*.

In former times, Duffield was a place of great consequence; as it was the residence of the Ferrers, Earls of Derby. On elevated ground, at the north-west end of the village, stood their Castle: but a piece of ground, which now bears the name of *Castle-Orchard*, is the sole remaining help to point out its site. At the conclusion of the thirteenth century, or the beginning of the following, this fortress was destroyed. For Robert de Ferrers, the last Earl of Derby,† joining the barons in a rebellion against Henry the Third; that monarch, in 1264, sent his son, afterwards Edward the First, " into the county of Derby, in order to ravage with fire and sword the lands of the Earl

---

* Domesday, *Orig.* 275, *a.* 2. Trans. 309. † See p. 206.

of that name, and take revenge of him for his
disloyalty."* At this time, I think† it most
likely that this Castle was demolished: and so
complete was the ruin, that not a vestige can
now be traced of its ancient grandeur; not a

---

* Hume, vol. II. p. 203.

† Mr. Pilkington says, that " Robert de Ferrers the second Earl, in the nineteenth year of the reign of Henry
II. hearing that the territories of the king of France were
invaded by the adherents of young Henry, whom his father caused to be crowned during his own life, joined in
rebellion against his sovereign, and manned his Castle in
Duffield. However, some time afterward, to obtain the
favor and pardon of the king, he surrendered his fortress
to him, and he commanded it immediately to be demolished. This order was carried into execution in August 1325."
There must be some mistake in this statement: for " Robert de Ferrers the second Earl" was dead thirty-four years
before 1173 (the nineteenth of Henry II.) But if Mr. P.
means, the second Earl *of the name of Robert*, who *died* in
the nineteenth of Henry II. the account is still attended
with a difficulty; as he says, that he *some time afterward*
(after the nineteenth of Henry II., in which year he died,)
endeavoured to obtain a pardon. And besides all this, the
time when the king's orders for *immediate* demolishment is
carried into execution is August 1325, one hundred and
fifty-two years subsequent to the nineteenth of Henry II.
From the whole it appears, that the period which Mr. P.
assigns for the demolishment of Duffield Castle, which
seems to have taken place at the close of the reign of Henry
III., or the commencement of Edward the First's, is nearly
correct: and that the error lies in the assigning it to a
wrong reign,

stone remains, to tell the inquisitive antiquarian, where once it stood. And though a
haughty Ferrers might here have once plumed
himself upon the extent of his power, and the
splendour of his retinue,—

> " Now, what avails that o'er the vassal-plain,
>   His rights and rich demesnes extended wide?
> That Honor and her Knights compos'd his train,
>   And Chivalry stood marshall'd by his side?
>
> " Tho' to the clouds his castle seem'd to climb,
>   And frown'd defiance on the desp'rate foe;
> Though deem'd invincible, the conq'ror Time
>   Levell'd the fabric as the founder low."

CUNNINGHAM.

It appears from Domesday and some other
records,* that there was formerly in the neighbourhood of Duffield an extensive forest; and the
appearance of charcoal-hearths, now visible after
the ground is ploughed, confirms the tradition,
that the surrounding hills, were once entirely
covered with wood, These forests, appear to
have belonged to the Earls of Derby; for in the
twenty-sixth year of Henry III. William de
Ferrers, gave the Monks of Tutbury, for the
health of the soul of Agnes his wife, and those

11   X X

---

* See grant of Wood to the Monastery of St, Helens,
page 137.

of his ancestors, tithe of all pannage, venison, honey, and rent arising out of the forest of Duffield. William Lord Hastings, who was beheaded by Richard the Third, was constable of Tutbury, chief forrester of Duffield, and surveyor of that honor, with a salary of twelve pounds a year, for life.

Duffield was once the property of the Earls of Lancaster; and the manor, the advowson of the church, the whole forest, with other lands in Derbyshire, were given as a dower to the daughter of Edmund, Earl of Lancaster, second son of Henry III. The tithe of Duffield, with the exception of a third part, was given by Henry de Ferrers, in the reign of William the Conqueror, to the Priory at Tutbury.

The village of Duffield is partly situated in a fine semicircular plain, formed by the river Derwent flowing on the eastern side; and generally attracts the notice of those who pass through it, as well from its rural appearance, as from its containing several good houses. The church, which is dedicated to St. Alkmund, and formerly belonged to the college of Newark in Leicestershire, is situated a little out of the village; and its venerable spire, which is seen towering above the surrounding trees, attracts and gratifies the eye, while it wanders

over the beautiful scenery of the surrounding
vale. Duffield is a place of no trade; its population being principally made up, of that
class in society, which is termed, the middle;—
a class in which philosophers have, in all ages,
directed us to look for a true picture of human
life; and in which we often discover many true
ornaments to learning, many warm and practical friends to virtue and religion.

Besides the established church, the Unitarians, the General Baptists, and the Methodists,
have their respective places of worship here.

About a quarter of a mile to the South of
Duffield, in an enclosure, not far from the
road leading to Derby, there is a small chalybeate spring, of the same impregnation and
quality as that at Quarndon,* but not so strong.

MAKENEY, a small hamlet, situated on the
western side of the Derwent, was a place of
some consequence at the time of the Norman
survey, and is noticed there† by the name of
Machenie. It contains about twenty-five houses,
and one hundred inhabitants.

HOLEBROOKE, by the Norman surveyors written *Holebroc*, is situated on an eminence, at

* See page 310.
* Domesday, *Orig.* 275. *a. 2.* Trans. 309.

the distance of about a mile to the East of the last-mentioned place. Some years ago, a chapel was built here, and endowed by the late Mr. Bradshaw.

MILLFORD, in Domesday *Muleford*, has of late years, risen from a few houses, to a considerable hamlet. This increase in size and population, is owing to the erection of two large Cotton Mills, on the same construction as those at Belper, and an extensive Bleaching Mill, belonging to the Messrs. Strutts. The Cotton Mills employ about six hundred hands, and the Bleaching Mill sixty more.

Bleaching, which consists in removing the coloured matters intermixed with vegetable and animal substances, in their natural state, or such as have been subsequently imbibed by accident, or some artificial process, is accomplished in this mill, by the following operations:

The calico, when received from the weavers, is first steeped in lukewarm water for 60 hours, or in cold 144, until a fermentation takes place. It is then well washed, in what is called a *Wash-Wheel*, where the sizing and other materials used by the weavers, are entirely separated from it: by this operation, it is prepared for that of *Bucking* or *Boiling*, in a solution of pot, pearl, or combay ashes, soda, or lime, whichever the bleacher may think most proper. The cloth is to remain, during the process of bucking, for about eight hours in the solution, which at first is cold, but is gradually increased to 212 degrees of heat; after which, it is continued in for two hours. The calico is then taken, and well washed in cold water in a wash-wheel; and then it is taken out, unfolded, and left to drain for 12 hours. It is next immersed in oxygeniated muriatic acid, diluted to a proper strength. (This gas is produced by distilling six pounds of common salt, four pounds of manganese, four pounds of vitriolic acid, and five pounds of water.— The gas produced from these ingredients, is impregnated with lime and water, by continual agitation). In this mixture the calico is steeped for eight hours, when it is taken out; and the operations of bucking and steeping are repeated as often as the bleacher may think proper. Great care is requisite to wash the calico clean from the oxygeniated muriatic gas every time it is steeped in it. The next operation the cloth undergoes is *souring*, which consists in immersing it for ten or twelve hours, in a mixture of vitriolic acid and water; in a lukewarm state, and of such a strength as the

among the towns in Derbyshire, was, prior
to the year 1776, as low in population as it was
backward in civility; and considered as the
insignificant residence of a. few uncivilized
nailers.

BELPER was formerly written *Beaupoirs*; and
though not noticed in Domesday by that or any
name similar to the present, has yet some claims
to antiquity. About eight years ago, a small
gold coin of *Agustus Cæsar*, in high preservation, was found in the neighbourhood; and
military weapons, generally thought to have
been Roman, have been dug up in several places: these remains may lead us to suppose, that
though the Romans might not have had a settlement here, the place was not unknown to them.
It has been handed down, by immemorial tradition, that John of Gaunt, Duke of Lancaster, and son of Edward III. once resided at
Belper: but after every possible inquiry, no
confirmation of the tradition, or ascertainment
of the fact, has been acquired. A few fragments of old walls, of great thickness, buried
in the ground, are indeed discoverable near the
dwelling called the Manor-House, the spot
where this Duke of famed strength and stature's
mansion (the Manorial palace) once stood: but
this goes but a short way to prove, that John of

Gaunt, more than any other person, resided
here. The same tradition says, that the present chapel, and the old bridge, which had
arms (supposed to have been his) cut in stone
placed in front,* were built in his time, and at
his expence. However, whether the Duke of
Lancaster lived here or not, it certainly has,
some time or other, been the residence of some
person of note. Not far from the spot where
this mansion is thought to have stood, several
coins have been dug up; two of which I have
seen: they are silver; and judging from the
inscriptions, which are much defaced, I think
that one is, of the First Edward's reign, and
the other of Stephen's.

Whatever, therefore, might have been the
grandeur, or the extent of Belper in former
times, it appears now impossible to determine:
but its present flourishing state is discernible
to all, and, perhaps, interests us more. In
the year 1801 the population of Belper amounted to 4,500, and in 1809 to 5,635. This increase of population, is owing to the extensive

11   Y y

* This Stone, a wood-cut of which is given in the title-
page, was placed, when the old bridge was taken down, in
the wall of one of Mr. Marshall's premises, on Bridge-hill,
and may be seen there now.

Cotton Mills erected here, belonging to the Messrs. Strutts; where between 1,200 and 1,300 persons find daily employment.

These Mills are four in number, the first of which was erected in 1776, by the late Jedediah Strutt, Esq.[*] The principal of those now standing[†] is 200 feet long, 30 feet wide, and six stories high; and its floors being constructed of brick arches, and paved with brick, it is considered absolutely indestructible by fire, and therefore proof against the havoc of that dreadful element. This mill has three water-wheels attached to it; the largest one, which is used in floods only, is remarkable, as well for its magnitude, as for its singular construction. It is upwards of 40 feet long, and 18 feet in diameter. It being impossible to procure timber sufficiently large to form the axle, or shaft, of this wheel in the usual mode of structure, it is made circular and hollow, of a great number of pieces, hooped together like a cask : the shaft is between five and six feet in diameter. The other two, which are used when the water is at a common height, are composed principally of

---

[*] See an Account of this Gentleman's Life, under the head " SOUTH NORMANTON."

[†] The Mill built in 1776, was lately pulled down for re-erection.

iron, and are remarkable for their simplicity, strength, and lightness of appearance. They were constructed by Mr. T. C. Hewes, an ingenious engineer and mechanic of Manchester. Their diameters are 21 feet 6 inches, and length 15 feet. Each shaft is of cast iron, and the arms which connect them with the sole, (as it is commonly termed), or that part of the wheel to which the buckets or ladles are attached, are simply, round rods of wrought iron, an inch and a half in diameter. Each wheel has eight of these arms, and they are supported in the direction of the shaft or axis, by eight diagonal rods of the above dimensions.

The operations* which cotton undergoes in its passage from the raw material to the state of thread, are various and multiplied in proportion to the fineness required, and the different uses to which it is destined.

If we analize these operations, they resolve themselves into the following: Picking, carding, doubling, drawing, and twisting. The three latter are never performed singly, but

---

* For the following Description of Cotton Spinning, the Author is indebted to a Gentleman, whose acquaintance with the process, is best exemplified by a perusal of the correct and interesting account itself.

are variously joined in the same machine : and the same elementary processes are oftentimes repeated in different machines, with various and different effects.

With reference to these effects, the operations which cotton undergoes, may be denominated picking, carding, drawing and doubling, roving and spinning.

Picking is that operation which prepares the cotton for carding, by opening the hard compressed masses in which it comes from the bales, and in separating it from seeds, leaves, and other adventitious matter.

This operation was formerly, and is now in some degree, performed by beating the cotton with sticks on a square frame, across which are stretched cords, about the thickness of a goose quill, with intervals sufficient to allow the seeds, &c. to fall through.

When a hard, matted, or compressed mass of cotton, is smartly struck with a stick, the natural elasticity and resiliency of its fibres, gradually loosen and disengage them, and the cotton recovers, by repeated strokes, all its original volume. During this operation the seeds, &c. which adhere, are carefully picked out by hand, and the cotton rendered as clean as possible.

The operation of beating or batting *by hand*, is now almost entirely superseded by the invention of machines, which have the advantage of more completely separating the dirt from the cotton; and consequently much manual labour in picking is avoided.

The machines in general use for this purpose, are the Devil and the Batting machine. The former consists of two large cylinders, covered with spikes, which are made to revolve with great velocity. The cotton is applied in small quantities by means of a pair of rollers, and the lumps and hard masses of cotton are thus torn in pieces; and at the same time separated from a considerable quantity of dirt, which they generally contain.

The batting machine performs, by mechanical means, what was formerly done by hand: viz. beating or batting the cotton with sticks on a corded frame; and by a number of ingenious, but complicated movements, this object is completely attained; but on account of its complication and short durability, to which engines of this kind are particularly liable, from sudden jerks, and the irregular motion of their parts, this machine is daily growing into disuse.

Carding is that operation in which the first

rudiments of the thread are formed. It is performed by cylinders covered with wire cards,
revolving, with considerable swiftness, in opposite directions, nearly in contact with each
other, or under a kind of dome or covering,
the under surface of which is covered with similar cards, whose teeth are inclined in a direction opposite to the cylinder. By this means
the separation of almost every individual fibre
is effected, every little knotty or entangled
part is disengaged, and the cotton spread
lightly and evenly over the whole surface of the
last or finishing cylinder, from which it is stripped by a plate of metal, finely toothed at the
edge, and moved in a perpendicular direction
rapidly up and down by a crank. The slight,
but reiterated, strokes of this comb, acting on
the teeth of the cards, detaches the cotton in a
fine and uniform fleece; which being contracted by passing through a funnel and rollers, .
forms one endless and perpetual carding;
which is interrupted or broken only when the
can that receives it is completely filled.

Drawing and doubling, or passing three or
four cardings at once through a system of rollers, by which they are made to coalesce, is intended to dispose the fibres of the cotton longitudinally, and in the most perfect state of

parallelism, and, at the same time, to correct any inequalities in the thickness of the card- ings. The operation of carding effects this, in a certain degree, yet the fibres although paral- lel are not straight but doubled, as may easily be supposed from the teeth of the cards catch- ing the fibres, sometimes in the middle, which become hooked or fastened upon them. Their disposition is also farther disturbed by the ta- ker-off, or comb, which strips them from the finishing cylinder; and though the general ar- rangement of a carding is longitudinal, yet they are doubled, bent, and interlaced in such a way, as to render the operation of drawing absolutely necessary.

The drawing frame consists of a pair of cy- linders, slowly revolving in contact with each other, at a little distance from a second pair re- volving with greater velocity, the lower cylin- der of each set being furrowed, or fluted in the direction of its length, and the upper ones neatly covered with leather. If we suppose, the end of a carding to be passed through the first pair only, it may be readily imagined, that it will be gradually drawn forward, and pass through the cylinders without suffering any other sensible change in its form or texture, than a slight compression from the weight of the incumbent cylinder. But if from the first pair it be suffered to pass immediately to the second, whose surfaces revolve much quicker, it is evident, that the quicker revolution of the second pair, will *draw out* the cotton, rendering it thinner and longer, when it comes to be delivered at the other side.

Three or more cardings, coiled up in deep cans are applied at once to these rollers, in their passage through which they not only coalesce so as to form one single *drawing*, but are also drawn out, or extended in length.— This process is several times repeated: three, four, or more drawings, as they are now termed, being united and passed between the rollers; the number introduced being so varied, that the last drawing may be of a size proportioned to the fineness of the thread, into which it is intended to be spun.

Roving is that operation by which the prepared cotton, as it comes from the drawing-frame is *twisted* into a loose and thick thread.— In the state in which it comes from the drawing-frame, it has little strength or tenacity; and is received into similar deep cans from whence it was passed through the rollers. To enable it to support the operation of winding, it is again passed through a system of rollers,

similar to those in the last machine, and received in a round conical can revolving with
considerable swiftness. This gives the drawing a slight twisting, and converts it into a
soft and loose thread, now called a roving,
which is wound by the hand upon a bobbin,
by the smaller children of the mill, and then,
carried to the spinning, or twist-frame.

In some cases, where great evenness, or more
than ordinary fineness, is required in the
yarn, the roving undergoes another operation,
before it receives its final twist. This is called
stretching; and is performed on a machine
nearly similar to the mule. It consists of a
system of rollers like those of the drawing and
roving frames, through which the roving is
drawn and received upon spindles, revolving
like those of the mule; and from which it acquires the twist. The carriage on which the
spindles are disposed is moveable, and receding
from the rollers somewhat quicker than the
thread is delivered, draws or stretches it in a
slight degree: hence the name of *stretching-
frame.*

In other cases, where less nicety is required,
the operation of stretching is substituted for
that of roving, by the roving-frame above des-

cribed : the operation of winding by hand, by the smaller children of the mill, is thus rendered unnecessary.

The roving is now carried to the spinning-frame, on which it is to receive its final extension and twist. This machine consists of a system of rollers similar to, and acting upon principles the same as, those already described in the drawing, roving, and stretching frames, to which is connected, with little alteration, the fly, bobbin, and spindle, of the common flax wheel.

· The yarn is now reeled into hanks, each containing 840 yards, and being packed in bundles of 10lbs. each, is sent principally to Nottingham, Leicester, and Lancashire, for the use of the hosiers and calico manufacturers.

· Another branch of business carried on at Belper, and which once gave celebrity to the place, is the manufacture of nails; but within the few last years, it is supposed that the trade has been on the decline.

Belper is a market town, with a market on Saturday, which is, generally, well supplied with all kinds of provisions. Its chapel, which is dedicated to St. John, is valued in the king's books at £3. 0s. 6d. and yearly tenths 6s. 0d.

The *Unitarians*, the *Independents*, and the

Methodists, have also their respective meeting-houses. Four hundred children are taught at the Sunday-school, supported here by Mr. Strutt; who has adopted several of the plans of education recommended, and so successfully practised, by that benefactor to his country, Mr. Lancaster. The Independents and Methodists have also Sunday-schools, where about 700 more are instructed.

A little to the North of the mills, is a handsome stone-bridge of three arches, erected over the Derwent at the expence of the county; the old one, which from the arms placed in the centre, was thought to have been built by John of Gaunt, having been washed down, in the year 1795, by a great flood.

Of the remarkable events that have happened at Belper, there are but few upon record. The plague, that dreadful scourge of the human race, raged here in 1609. From the first of May to the thirtieth of September of that year, fifty-one persons died by it, and were buried near the chapel.

Sometime prior to the year 1686, Thomas Bromfield, a travelling beggar, was gibbeted on the bridge-hill, for murdering an old woman, with whom he lodged. This old woman lived in a house situated where Mr. John Gil-

lott's orchard now is; and the gibbet was erected at no great distance from that place.

December the eleventh, 1686, Matthew Har-
rison was killed in a coal-pit on gibbet-hill.

With its increase in extent and population,
Belper is also improving in civilization and respectability. Immorality and ignorance, which
were once thought the characteristics of the
place, have, in a great measure, disappeared;
and improved morals, and more enlarged views,
supplied their places.

About the centre of the town, is the mansion
of Jedediah Strutt, Esq. and a little above the
bridge, pleasantly situated, is Bridge-Hill, the
seat of G. B. Strutt, Esq. The wear above the
bridge is well worth attention; and the fine
expanse of water, extending for a considerable
way up the river, interspersed with islands covered with young trees, has a pleasing effect.

HEAGE is a small straggling village, containing, together with the whole liberty, about
two hundred houses. The clear value of the
established chapel there is £10.

In this liberty, near the road leading from
Crich to Belper, and about midway from both
places, is a *martial vitriolic* spring, the only
one of the kind that has yet been found in the
county. It is situated in a black boggy soil,

and was discovered about the year 1767, " by
a labouring man, who was employed in forming a sough, with a view of draining the ground
in its neighbourhood. He had been a long
time troubled with an ulcerous disorder in one
of his legs, but found, during the prosecution
of his undertaking, it gradually disappeared,
and that by the time it was finished, a cure
was entirely effected. This circumstance led
him to suspect, that the water was possessed of
some medicinal virtues, and upon examination,
he perceived the vitriolic taste, by which it is
distinguished."

This water affords very strong and decisive
evidence of its being impregnated with iron
and vitriol. Its taste is sour, and is thought
to contain fixed air in some quantity; not only
from the bubbles which may be seen in it,
when first poured into a glass at the spring,
but likewise from the circumstance, that when
tightly enclosed in a cask or bottle, it will
burst it with a slight degree of agitation; an effect attributed to the efforts of the fixed air to
escape. Besides the efficacy of Heage water
in ulcerous complaints, it has sometimes also
been found beneficial in stopping inward bleed-
ing; and when applied outwardly, it is said to
have this effect as soon, and as completely,

as the Extract of Saturn. It has also been
found efficacious in fastening the teeth, and in
healing sore and inflamed eyes. But its salutary influence is most conspicuous in certain
ulcerous disorders: and yet in these external
applications, it should be used with great
caution, as sometimes a paralytic stroke in the
diseased part, has followed, the too sudden
drying up of the humour.

TURNDITCH, contains about forty houses;
and its chapel is set down, at the clear value
of £4.

SHOTTLE. In the northern part of this hamlet, is a *sulphureous spring:* but from the scent
and taste, the impregnation seems to be but
small. The sulphureous quality of this water,
like that of Kedleston,* depends upon the presence of inflammable air holding sulphur, and
a small quantity of purging salts in solution;
but as these are found but in small quantities,
its medicinal virtues cannot be great. It has a
sharp acid taste, and when swallowed, occasions a dryness and irritation in the throat and
stomach. Its virtues, though not so powerful,
are similar to those of the Kedleston water.

---

* See page 307.

CHAP. VII.

Deanery of Repington.

HAVING taken a survey of the Deanery of Derby, and noticed the objects most worthy attention in its different parishes, we now return to a description of the Deanery of Repington.

CHILCOTE, in Domesday called *Cildecote*, and then belonging to Clifton in Staffordshire,[*] is one of the most southern parishes in the county of Derby. It is small, and contains but few houses. A large and ancient Hall, which was one of the seats of Godfrey Bagnall Clarke, Esq. who represented the county of Derby, in the early parliaments of the present reign, and who died about the year 1774, is situated in this parish. Having been uninhabited for many years, it is now in a very ruinous state.

APPLEBY. This parish, at the compilation of Domesday, belonged to the Abbey of Bur-

---

* Domesday *Orig.* 372, *b.* 2. Trans. 293.

ton ; whose Abbot held five carucates of land there. *Aplebi* was at that time a considerable village, and valued at sixty shillings.* It is situated partly in Derbyshire, and partly in Leicestershire ; the church standing in the latter county. The manufacture of stockings, and the pursuits of agriculture, form the principal support of the inhabitants.

STRETTON, is another small parish, containing about thirty houses. At the Norman survey, it was part of the lands of Henry de Ferrers ; and *Streitun*, at that time, consisted of some arable and meadow land, and one mill ; altogether valued at fifteen shillings.

The living is a rectory, and the church is dedicated to St. Michael. Its valuation in the king's books, is £9. 10*s*. 5*d*. and the yearly tenths, 19*s*. 0½*d*.

MEASHAM, in Domesday *Messeham*, which at that time belonged to the king, and was afterwards the property of the Priory at Gresly, is a considerable parish, containing nearly two hundred houses. The living is a donative curacy, of the clear value of £2. 7*s*. The church is dedicated to St. Lawrence.

DONISTHORP, is situated partly in Derby-

---

* Domesday *Orig.* 273, *b.* 1, Trans. 297.

shire and partly in Leicestershire. The number of houses in the former is about twenty: they belong to the different neighbouring parishes.

The village of OKETHORP, in Domesday *Achetorp*, is situated in the different parishes of *Measham*, *Stretton*, and *Gresley*.

WILSLEY, in Domesday called *Winlesley*, is a small village, containing but few houses. It was, for some centuries, the residence of the Abney family. They had a seat at Wilsley as early as the reign of Henry the sixth; and at a still later period, 1656, James Abney, of Wilsley, Esq. was High-Sheriff for the county of Derby. The living of Wilsley, is a donative curacy, of the value of £12. The chapel is dedicated to St. Thomas, and formerly belonged to the Abbey of Burton.

PACKINGTON, is a large village, situated in the two counties of Derby and Leicester: the greatest number of its houses standing in the former, and its church in the latter county.

LULLINGTON. " In *Lullituns*," say the Norman surveyors, " there is a priest, and one mill of six shillings and eight-pence, and twelve acres of meadow: value four pounds."* The

12 A 3

* Domesday *Orig.* 278, *b.* 2, Trans. 327.

living of Lullington is a vicarage, of the clear
value of £48. 16s. and yearly tenths, 9s. 2½d.
The church is dedicated to All-Saints, and was
presented by Edward III. to the Priory of
Gresley.

The hamlet of COTON, which was anciently
called *Coton Cotes*, and belonged to the Abbey
of Burton, is situated in the parish of Lullington. It is pretty considerable in size, but is a
place of no manufacture.

RAUNSTON, called at the time of the Conquest *Ravenstune*, was then the property of
Nigel de Statford. This village, though belonging to Derbyshire, is totally surrounded
by Leicestershire; and lies about three miles
south-east of Ashby-de-la-Zouch, in the latter
county. The living of Raunston, is a rectory,
valued in the king's books at £5. 1s. 0½d. exclusive of yearly tenths. The church is dedicated to St. Michael, and the king is the
patron.

CROXHALL, in Domesday, *Crocheshalle*, is a
small village on the borders of Leicestershire.
The living is a vicarage, and the church is dedicated to St. John the Baptist. The value in
the king's books is five pounds. It formerly
belonged to the Priory at Repton, and the king
is the patron.

Mr. Camden records,* that in his time a part of the family of the Cursons, dwelt at Croxton; and Mr. Pilkington, says, that " Richard Curson or Curzon, (second son of Giraline de Curson or Curzon, who came over with William the Conqueror) held a considerable estate in the county of Derby in the reign of Henry I. It is probable that Croxhall was part of this estate: for Thomas Curson died possessed of the manor, in 33d of Henry VIII. This branch of the family terminated in an heir female, Mary, daughter and sole heiress of Sir George Curson, knt. who was married in the reign of James I. to Sir Edward Sackville, knt. afterwards fourth earl of Dorset, and ancestor to the present duke.

" It is supposed, that cardinal Robert Curson was of this family. Having applied with great diligence to the study of sacred and profane learning, at the university of Oxford, he acquired a distinguished reputation in his own country. Afterwards meditating greater things, he went to Paris and Rome. At the first place he was honoured with the degree of doctor in divinity, and at the latter he was created a cardinal, by the title of St. Stephen in mount

---

* Britannia, p. 491.

Cellus. In the year 1218; when the city of Dalmatia in Egypt was taken in the reign of John Brenn, king of Jerusalem, Cardinal Curzon accompanied Pelagius the pope's cardinal. He wrote several books, and came into England as legate in the reign of Henry III."

CATTON, in this parish, is now but a very small hamlet; but at the time Domesday was composed, *Chetun* belonged to Henry de Feriers, and was valued at the very considerable sum of sixty shillings.

WALTON-ON-TRENT. At the time of the Norman survey, there were at *Waletune*, " a church and a priest, and a mill of six shillings and eight-pence, and forty acres of meadow, value ten pounds."* The living is a rectory, and the present church is dedicated to St. John the Baptist.

" In the fifteenth year of the reign of Edward II. Thomas, Earl of Lancaster, being pursued by the king, placed his foot on each side of the bridge at Burton, to prevent his passage over the Trent. By this precaution he obliged the king to ford the river at Walton.— When the earl discovered this, he drew his men out of Tutbury castle, expecting a reinforce-

* Domesday *Orig.* 272, a. 2. Trans. 292.

ment, but being disappointed, he fled towards
the North."*

ROLLISTON, is a chapelry belonging to the
parish of Walton. It was written *Redlauestan*
by the Norman surveyors; and in their time
there were, ". a church and a priest, and one
mill of six shillings and eight-pence, and forty
acres of meadow there, valued at ten pounds."
At that time it was the property of the king.—
The present chapel is dedicated to St. Mary,
and the whole hamlet contains about fifty
houses.

GRESLEY is an extensive parish, containing
the hamlets of *Church Gresley, Castle Gresley,*
Spadlincoat, (Siuardingescote) *Linton,* (Linc-
tune) and *Drakelow,* (Drachelawe). The living
is a donative curacy, and its clear value £6.

There was formerly in Church Gresley, a
Priory belonging to the Order of St. Austin,
which was founded by William, son of Nigel
de Gresley, in the reign of Henry the First,
and dedicated to St. Mary and St. George. In
the third year of Edward II. a patent was
granted, for appropriating the church of Lullington to it; and in the thirty-seventh of the
following reign, it was endowed with tenements

at Heathcote, Swardingcote, and Church Gresley; and in the third year of Henry VI. certain lands in Okethorp, and Donthorp, were given to this religious house. At the Dissolution, its revenues, were, according to Dugdale, £31. 6s. In the thirty-fifth year of Henry VIII. it was granted to Henry Crache. A small part of its ruins was lately remaining.

In the church is a monument to the memory of Sir Thomas Gresley, who was Sheriff of the county of Derby in the year 1668: he died in 1669; and is represented on the tomb in a kneeling posture, clad in the dress of his time. There is also, near this, another monument, to the memory of the Alleynes, who were buried in this church, and who once were possessed of a part of the manor. It appears from the long inscription, containing the genealogical account of the family from the time of Henry VIII. to the commencement of the last century, that the Alleynes of Gresley, were descended from Sir John Alleyne, knight, who was twice Lord Mayor of London, and Privy Counsellor to the above monarch.

The hamlet of *Castle Gresley*, derives its name from a castle, having been erected here by the Lords of Gresley. Camden says,* that in his

---

* Britannia, p. 400.

time, " *Greisley Castle* was a mere ruin;" and now, scarcely any traces of this ancient fortress can be found; the irregularity of the ground, alone marking out the spot where it stood.

. At *Drakelow* is the seat of Sir Nigel Bowyer Gresley, the present head of the family of that name. The pedigree of the Gresleys, is traced back to very ancient times; and they are said to have sprung from Malahulcius, whose brother was an ancestor of William the Conqueror. From him was descended, Roger de Toeni, standard-bearer of Normandy; whose two sons, Robert and Nigel, accompanied the Conqueror into England: and from the general survey made in 1079, it appears that Robert possessed 160 Lordships, of which Stafford, the place of his residence, was one. In Domesday book,[*] Drakelow is set down, among the lands belonging to Nigel de Stafford. At what period the family assumed the name of Gresley, is uncertain; but it is supposed to have been prior to the year 1200, for *William de Gresley*, at that time held the manor of Drakelow, *in capite*, by the service of finding a bow without a string, one quiver of Tutesbit, and thirteen arrows; twelve fledged, or feathered, and one

---

[*] *Orig.* 278. *a.* 1.

unfeathered.*   The present Sir N. B. Gresley,
was Sheriff for Derbyshire in the year 1780 ;
and some of his ancestors, have represented the
county of Derby in Parliament.

The residence of Sir N. B. Gresley at Drakelow, is situated rather low; but upon the whole
it is a pleasant situation, surrounded by the
luxuriant meadows bordering the Trent, opposite Staffordshire.   The house is a large irregular pile, of brick building, whitened over,
but not presenting any thing remarkable.   .

HARTSHORN.   *Heorteshorne* at the time of
Norman survey, belonged to Henry de Ferrers.
The living is a rectory : its value in the king's
books is £3. 12s. 1d. and yearly tenths 6s. 2½d.
and the church is dedicated to St. Peter.

STAPENHILL, or *Stapenhills.*   The living is
a vicarage; and the church, which was formerly part of the endowments of the Abbey of
Burton, is dedicated to St. Peter.   Many of
the houses, which compose the village of Sta-
penbill, stand within the parish of Burton.

NEWHALL, is a hamlet, lying within the parish of Stapenhill.   It contains but few houses ;
and the inhabitants are chiefly supported by
collieries, which are worked at the place.

* Veredict. de Singulis wapent. in com. Not. et Derby.
Blount's Tenures.

CALDWELL, is another small hamlet, situated in this parish. In Domesday it is said, " that the king gave the manor of *Caldewelle* to the Monks (I suppose, of Burton) in Benefice and not in Fee."* At Caldwell is the seat of ——— Mortimer, Esq.

CALKE or *Calc.* The number of houses in this parish is not many. The living is a donative curacy: the church is dedicated to St. Giles; and about the middle of the twelfth century, was given to the Priory of Repton.

A convent of regular canons of the order of St. Austin, was founded at Calke, sometime prior to the year 1161. " It was dedicated to St. Mary and St. Giles, and received endowments from various benefactors, but chiefly from Ranulph, second earl of Chester, Matilda his widow, and their son Hugh. These endowments were a wood betwixt Sceggebroc and Aldrebroc, a piece of land in tillage betwixt Aldrebroc and Sudwude, the little mill at Repindon, six ox-gangs of land in Ticknall, the chapel of Smithby, one manse of land in Tamworth, the liberty of fishing with one boat at Chester, and one manse of land for the convenience of the fisherman, a portion of land

12   B 3

---

* Domesday *Orig.* 273, *b.* 1.

extending from the well, as you descend from Repton, to the boundaries of the liberty of Milton, and the whole land of Erwin Esegar of Trengeston. The monks were to enjoy these possessions free from all secular service, and customs whatever. Besides these grants, Hugh, the third earl of Chester, gave them their court in Repindon, and as much wood as they wanted either for their buildings or for fire. He also appointed, that they should enjoy the above mentioned possessions and privileges in a free and quiet manner.*

" This religious house was also endowed with the working of a quarry at Repindon near the river Trent, and with the advowson of the church of St. Wicstan at the same place, together with all the appurtenances belonging to it. The countess of Chester made these grants on this condition, that the convent at Repton, when a convenient opportunity offered, should become the head, to which Calke should be only a member.

" The charter of Edward II. recites and confirms other privileges. It grants the canons at Calke possession of a plough-gate of land in Loke, and three acres of meadow land in the

---

* Mon. Ang. vol. iii, page 97.

same village. It also released them from an obligation of furnishing sixty men to labour one day every year, for the privilege of pasture at Stanton.*

" To all these endowments may be added the church at Leke. But afterwards they were transferred, and the canons removed to the priory at Repton. At the dissolution they were granted in the first year of Edward VI. to John earl of Warwick."

At Calke, is *Calke Abbey*, the seat of Sir Henry Crewe, (late Harpur) Bart. It is a spacious and handsome mansion, built round a quadrangular court; but the situation is bad; as the rising grounds which almost surround it, exclude the view of the adjacent country.

The Harpurs† are a very ancient family; and were, according to the first account we have of them, of Chesterton in Warwickshire; where Hugh, son of Richard le Harpur resided as early as the reign of Henry the First; and where his descendants continued to live during several succeeding generations. Dif-

---

* Mon. Ang. vol. ii. page 282.

† That is the name of the present Baronet's Ancestors, though he has lately taken the name of Crewe; which was that of his grandmother, who was the daughter of Thomas Lord Crewe, of Steneby.

ferent branches of the family, afterwards settled at Rushall, in Staffordshire, at Little-
Over, Swarkston, Twyford, and Calke in this
county: but all the family becoming extinct,
except the branch at Calke, the estates devol-
ved of course to the surviving one. The title
was first bestowed in the second year of king
Charles I. (1626) when Henry Harpur, Esq.
was created a Baronet by that monarch.

TICKNALL, in Domesday *Tichenhalle*, is an
extensive parish, and a large village, consisting of near two hundred houses. The living
is a donative curacy, of the clear value of £26.
The church is dedicated to St. Thomas Becket;
and in former times was part of the endowments of the priory at Repton. Sir Henry
Crewe is the patron. The lime kilns find employment for many of the inhabitants during
the summer season; while the pursuits of a-
griculture employ several more.

NEWTON-SOLNEY, *Newetun*, is a small village
situated on the banks of the Trent; consisting
of about fifty houses. The living of Newton
is a donative curacy; the church is dedicated
to St. Mary, and is supposed to have formerly
belonged to the Priory, either of Repton or
Gresley.

WINSHILL, *Wineshalle*, is a hamlet situated

in the parish of Newton-Solney, though it belongs to that of Burton, in Staffordshire. It contains fifty houses, and the inhabitants rely
entirely on agriculture for their support; no
manufacture being carried on in this part of
Derbyshire.   ~

FOREMARK, by the Norman surveyors written *Fornewerche,* is a parish including the
hamlet of *Ingleby* or *Englebi,* which contains
about thirty houses. The living is a donative
curacy; the church, which was built and endowed by Sir Francis Burdett, Bart. and consecrated by Bishop Haskett, in the year 1662,
is dedicated to St. Savior, and belonged in
former times to the Priory at Gresley. Sir
Francis Burdett is the patron.

  Foremark, in this parish, is the seat of Sir
F. Burdett, Bart. one of the present representatives of the city of Westminster. The mansion,
which is pleasantly situated on the southern
banks of the Trent, was built about fifty years
ago, by the late Sir Robert Burdett, on the
site of a very ancient one, belonging to the family. The present house, is a handsome stone
building, with a portico projecting from the
North front, which is in other respects uniform

---

* Domesday *Orig.* 278, *a.* 1.

with the South, consisting of a square centre, flanked with bows, terminating in dome roofs, which have a rather heavy appearance. Each front has an elegant double flight of steps. The offices are connected with the East end of the house, by a covered walk, leading through the enclosed court.

" A spacious handsome Hall, forty-seven feet long, by thirty broad, extends through the centre of the edifice from North to South; having windows, and an entrance at each end, opening on the steps before-mentioned. The spaces on each side of the hall, are occupied by various convenient apartments, and a stair-case of oak, very wide and handsome. This leads to the bed-chambers and dressing-rooms: over which is an attic story, distributed into commodious rooms. The internal, as well as the external, part of this building, is very neatly finished, and reflects considerable credit on the abilities of the architect. All the floors and doors are of the the best oak, nicely fitted. The rooms contain some good family portraits; but none of particular celebrity.

"On a rising ground, near the West end of the house, which is ornamented by a small lawn, shaded by a grove of young oaks, stands the village church; a plain humble fabric, with a

low tower; yet forming a pleasing object, in
connection with the contiguous scenery. from
several points of view. The old parish church
or chapel, stood in the hamlet of Ingleby, on
the banks of the Trent, about a mile to the
East: but when that fell into decay, the present edifice was erected.

" A pleasant secluded walk, between two
rows of aged oaks, runs from the East end of
the house, and is skirted on the North side by
a close thicket of underwood, interspersed with
willows, ash, and oak trees, through the intervals of which, the prospect of an irregularly
rising lawn is admitted, pleasingly varied by
scattered oaks, thorns, and beeches; and bounded by plantations. But the most striking ornament of the grounds is a grove of majestic
oaks, which extends from the vicinity of the
house to a piece of water at some distance, opposite the North front. Were the dimensions
of this pellucid sheet somewhat more enlarged,
it would become a very interesting feature in
the scenery: but it is at present too diminu-
tive; and except from the walk in the grove,
where its boundaries are not visible, conveys
an idea of insignificance rather than grandeur.
Beyond the grove, the land declines northward
to the rich meadows watered by the Trent.

" Opposite to the house, on the South, the ground gently swells into a hill; ascending which, and proceeding in a southerly direction, the road leads to Foremark-Park, where the country assumes a down-like appearance, consisting of green swelling eminences, which agreeably contrast with the flat meadows, enlivened with the silver winding Trent, on the North. These rising grounds were, formerly disposed in a spacious park, but are now enclosed.

" Foremark has been noticed by Burton in his ' Anatomy of Melancholy,' as particularly *pleasant, wholesome,* and *eligible;* and with reason, for, besides the agreeable disposition of the scenery, the soil is dry and fertile, it lying very near a stratum of gravel. It is also very favorable to the production of game, particularly pheasants.

" At the distance of somewhat more than a quarter of a mile from Foremark, in a northeast direction, is a singular rocky bank, which terminates abruptly above the extensive meadows on the margin of the Trent. The summit is only a continuation of the high grounds of Foremark; but from its rude and sudden break, singularity of form, and neighbouring objects, it constitutes a very curious piece of scenery, particularly when viewed from the low grounds at its foot. Its centre where the rock projects, and is most naked and precipitous, presents the appearance of a Gothic ruin, with openings to admit light, and a door-way rudely fashioned out of the rock, leading into several excavations, or cells, which communicate with each other, and give a probability to the tradition, of its having been the residence of an Anchorite; whence it has derived the name of *Anchor Church*. The rock is chiefly composed of rough grit-stone, and a congeries of sand and pebbles, possessing the appearance of having been formed by water. The river which now flows at a short distance, formerly ran close under the rock, as is evident from a dead pool of water yet remaining at its foot, and communicating with the present channel. The summit of the rock is crested by old oaks and firs, and is irregularly broken by deep fissures and abrupt prominences, half covered with brushwood and ivy, which mantling over the Gothic-like door and windows of the hermitage, give a very picturesque appearance to the whole mass. Human bones have been dug up on this spot; and the faint traces of a figure, somewhat sepulchral, are yet left beneath the rock."*

12   C 3

---

* TOPOGRAPHER, Vol. II. p. 40.

The family of Burdett is very ancient and
respectable. The first of them, that we have
an account of, is, Hugh Burdett, who came
into England with William the Conqueror.—
His descendant, William Burdett, Lord of
Lowseby, in Leicestershire, who lived in the
time of Henry II. founded the Priory of Aucote,
near Seckingdon, Warwickshire, to expiate the
murder of his wife, whom he had slain, on his
return from the Holy Land.   Sir Robert Burdett, Knt. lived at Arrow in Warwickshire, and
represented the counties of Warwick and Leicester in parliament, during the reigns of
Edward the First and Second.   Nicholas Burdett, Knt. served in the wars of Henry the
Fifth and Sixth, and was slain at Pontoise.—
Thomas, his heir, a person of great eminence,
was in the commission of the peace, from the
seventh to the fourteenth of Edward the Fourth;
but for his attachment to the Duke of Clarence,
and the utterance of some rash words, was beheaded as a traitor.   He was succeeded by His
grandson, Thomas Burdett; whose great-grandson Thomas Burdett of Seckingdon and Bram-
cote, Esq. was created a Baronet on the twenty-fifth of Feb. 1618.   This Baronet married
Jane, daughter and heiress of William Fraun-
cys, of Foremark, Esq. by whom Foremark,
and the estates connected with it, were con-

veyed to the Burdett family. The present benevolent and illustrious Baronet, and owner
of Foremark, is I believe the fifth in descent
from the above mentioned gentleman.

KNOWLE HILLS, a beautiful and retired spot,
surrounded by fine woods, and plantations of
oak and beech, is situated a little to the south-
east of Foremark. Here, at the entrance of a
narrow dell, once stood a pleasant house, built
by Walter Burdett, younger son to the first
possessor of Foremark, to whom it was bequeathed by his father. Walter, having dis-
agreed with his relations, either gave or sold
the estate at Knowle Hills, to a gentleman
named Hardinge, who inhabited the mansion
for some years. From his heir it was purchased by the late Sir Robert Burdett, who resided in it, while the Hall at Foremark was
re-building; and afterwards dismantled it.—
To a ruin of the upper part of the house, that
was left standing, a neat little room has been
attached, with ornamental doors and windows
opening upon a small grass-plat, or terrace.—
The prospect from this room is confined by a
grove of lime and beech trees, through which
a narrow walk leads to a pond surrounded by
alders, but admitting through their intervals,
a veiw of a wood of oaks, at some distance.—

From the terrace, the dell opens to the north, and north-east, and presents the eye with a rich view of the extensive meadows, which skirt the Trent, in which Swarkston Bridge, appears a very ornamental object. By the margin of a limpid pool, in one part of this charming retirement, is an ancient and venerable beech, of great beauty, and uncommon magnitude.

MELBOURN, in Domesday is included in the land belonging to the king; and at that time, there were " at *Mileburne*, a priest and a church, and one mill of three shillings, and twenty-four acres of meadow."* Henry the Second granted Melbourn to Hugh de Beauchamp, whose eldest son gave it to William Fitz-Geoffry with his daughter in marriage.

Edmund of Woodstock, Earl of Kent, second son of Edward I. obtained, in the nineteenth year of his father's reign, free warren, in *Meileburne*, in Derbyshire.† And Robert de Holland, obtained from the king a grant in fee, of the manor of *Meleburne*, together with several others in the county of Derby, with divers liberties and privileges, viz. returns of writs, pleas of Wythernam, felons goods, &c.‡

---

* Domesday *Orig.* 272, a. 2. Trans. 292.
† Dugdale's Baron. Vol. I. p. 779.   ‡ Ibid. Vol. I. p. 73.

Henry, Earl of Derby, brother to Thomas, Earl of Lancaster, obtained a grant for a market at Melbourn, in the second year of Edward III.

The vestiges of an ancient Castle may yet be traced in this village; but by whom, or at what period, it was built, it is now impossible to ascertain. That it existed in the time of Edward the Third is certain; as Thomas, Earl of Lancaster, died possessed of *Melbourn Castle*, in the first year of that monarch. Camden says,[*] " not far from the Trent stands *Melborn*, a castle of the king's now decaying; where John, Duke of Bourbon, taken prisoner in the battle of Agincourt, was kept nineteen years in the custody of *Nicholas Montgomery* the Younger." This Duke was committed by Henry V. and released by his successor, Henry VI. In the year 1460 this fortress was dismantled, by order of Margaret, queen to the last-mentioned monarch:[†] yet, Leland says, that in his time (about 1550) it was in tolerable, and in *metely good repair.*

Lord Melbourne has an agreeable seat, near the village.; but it is situated, in a rather confined situation: the family but very seldom reside here.

---

* Britannia, p. 491.   † Stowe's Annals, p. 413.

The parish of Melbourn is large, and includes the hamlet of *King's-Newton*. Its inhabitants, also, are numerous;—they are principally employed in combing and spinning jersey, and working on the stocking-frame: a small manufacture of scythe-stones, is likewise carried on here.

The living of Melbourn is a vicarage, valued in the king's books, at £9. 13s. 4d. and yearly tenths, 19s. 4d. The church is dedicated to St. Michael, and the Bishop of Carlisle is the patron. Sir Ralph Shirley, who died in 1516, bequeathed lands in Melbourn and Worthington to the Chantery of St. Catherine, in St. Michael's church Melbourn, for ever, to pray for his soul. The variety of religious sects, existing in so small a place as Melbourn has been remarked; as the Presbyterians, Calvinists, Baptists, Quakers, and Methodists, have each a place of worship here.

STANTON is a parish of small extent, containing from thirty to forty houses. The living is a rectory of the value, in the king's books, of £6. 12s. 8½d. and yearly tenths, 13s. 3½d. The church is dedicated to St. Michael; and Sir Henry Crewe, is the patron.

REPTON, though now but a small village, was once a considerable town. Some histori-

ans say; that it was an ancient colony of the
Romans, called *Rapandunum*, but this assertion cannot be proved by any authentic memorials. The earliest account we have of Repton, goes so far back as the year 660, previous
to which, " a noble monastery of religious men
and women, under the government of an abbess,"* was established here : but the Danes on
their arrival in England destroyed it.

Repton was called by the Saxons, *Hreopan-
dune*, and in ancient deeds, is written, *Reppen-
dune, Rapandon, Repindon*, &c. It is celebrated by antiquarians, as the principal city in
the Saxon kingdom of Mercia, and as the bu-
rial place of many of the kings of that nation.
About the year 750 Ethelbald, king of the
Mercians, after an attempt to march into Wes-
sex, in which he was opposed by Cuthred, with
all his forces, and driven back to Sceadune near
Tamworth, where the Mercians were routed,
after a decisive battle, was slain by one of his
own Chieftains, and buried in the cemetery
belonging to the above-mentioned monastery.
Merewala, another Mercian sovereign, and
Kynechardus, brother of Sigebert, king of the
West Saxons, were likewise interred there.

---

* Edburga filia Adulphi regis Orientalium Anglorum Ab-
batissa in Reopendune. Lib. Elinsis. MS. lib. I. c. 9.

acre in Dreth; and an acre in Wynnes; the mill at Willington with all their appurtenances; two tofts of land in the same village; five acres of land with their appurtenances in the liberty of Willington; an acre in Pilardescroft together with pasture for one horse, three cows, and their calves till they are two years old; all their water with the whole fishery in the river Trent from the divisions of the water of Newenton (Newton Solney,) as far as below Willington.* The impropriate rectory and advowson of the vicarage of Great Baddow, and the advowson of the church of Little Baddow, in Essex;† the advowson of the church of Leke, in Nottinghamshire;‡ free warren in Repton, Calke, Ingleby, and Ticknal, in Derbyshire, and Gransden M. in Huntingdonshire;§ and a fourth part of the manor of Repton."‖

In the thirty-second of Henry the Eighth, the priory, and its possessions at Repton, were vested in Thomas Thacker, Esq. who was servant to that monarch: When Mr. Thacker was put in possession of the fabric, there remained four bells unsold. At first he neglected

---

* All these grants are recited in and confirmed by a charter of Henry III. † Morant's Essex, vol. ii. p. 20, 25. ‡ 9 Edw. I. vol. I. § Cart. 25. Edw. I. w. 15. ‖ Pat. i. Hen. V.

taking the church down, but being alarmed by
a report, that queen Mary would re-establish
Abbeys, he hired, on a Sunday, all the car-
penters and masons, of the neighbouring county, and in a single day pulled down the most
beautiful church; saying, he would destroy
the nest, lest the birds should settle there
again.*

In the family of the Thackers, the possessions
continued till the reign of queen Anne, when
the property was divided, between two co-
heiresses; the elder of whom conveyed her
share, to the Stanhopes of Elvaston; but the
younger, at her death in 1728, devised her
part to Sir Robert Burdett, Bart. of Foremark,
whose grandson, Sir Francis, is now the proprietor. The site of the Priory, and Mansion
now used as the house of the head master of
Repton School, are included in the possession
of the latter.†

* Fuller's Church History, Book VI. p. 368.

† That part of the manor of Repton, which was not
vested in the priory, descended through the families of
Lord Segrave, and Mowbray, Duke of Norfolk, to the
Finderns, of whom, John de Findern was possessed of an
estate at Repton, in the first of Henry the Fifth. This, by
the marriage of the only daughter of Thomas Findern with
Sir Richard Harpur, Judge of the Common Pleas in the
reign of Henry VIII. was conveyed into that family, in

Mr. Gibson says, that " since the Dissolution, Sir *John Port*, of *Etwall*, in this county, by his last Will, order'd a Free-school to be erected at Repton, appointing certain lands in the counties of *Derby* and *Lancaster* for its maintenance."[*] In pursuance of this will, the school was founded. This gentleman, was, by a grant of Henry the Eighth, possessed of several estates belonging to the Priory at Repton, which in 1556, he devised for the support of a Grammar-school there, and for the foundation of an Hospital at Etwall. His executors purchased, of Gilbert Thacker, Esq. part of the Priory, and fitted it up for the reception of the scholars, and residence of a master and usher. By James the First, the master and poor men of Etwall Hospital, with the school-master, ushers, and poor scholars, of Repton, were incorporated; and the appointments, and hereditary government of these foundations, were vested in the families of the Earls, Chesterfield and Moira, and —— Gerrard, Bart.

Repton is a large village, situated upon the

---

which it still remains. The manor-house of the Findern and Harpur estate, was pleasantly situated a little above the town, where they had, till within these few years, a park, now converted into farms.—England and Wales.

[*] In his Camden, p. 495.

edge of a valley, through which the Trent flows. It consists, principally, of one street of scattered houses, extending from North to South, about a mile in length; and has a brook running through, emptying itself into the Trent. At the lower part of the village, pleasantly elevated above the meadows, stands the church, a large handsome structure, ornamented by an elegant spire, sixty-six yards in height. Tradition says, that this is the third church, that has stood on the same spot. The present edifice, has, evidently been erected at two different periods: by the style of the windows and arches, the nave and side isles, seem to be of the reign of Edward the Third; but the chancel appears to be more ancient, and to have been, formerly, higher than at present. The arches, which divide the aisles from the nave are pointed, excepting the two, that adjoin the chancel, which are circular.

" Beneath the chancel is an ancient *Crypt*,* discovered of late years, which is supported by two rows of round Saxon wreathed pillars, with passages at each corner of the West end, leading into the church, and another on the North.

---

* Crypt, is a subterraneous vault or chapel, used in ancient times for preserving the bodies of martyrs, or other saints; and for the performance of divine worship.

be opened, the lady of the manor having forbidden it.

"This was attested to us by several old persons, who had seen and measured the skeleton."

Near the same place, was discovered in 1749, an ancient grave-stone. It had an inscription upon it; but by exposure to the air, the characters were much defaced, and so imperfect, that they were scarcely legible. The legend appears to have been in verse, as is evident from the Hemistic, it bore, *iste tegit tumulatum*; and was undoubtedly ancient, there being a mixture of Saxon characters; but more recent than the Norman conquest,—probably of the twelfth or thirteenth century. The verse was of the Leonine kind, and the first line read thus—RVDVLPHVM GRATVM *LA*PIS IS-TE TVMLATVM, by substituting the three letters in italics. The rest was so imperfect, that nothing could be made out of it, though some detached words, such as—ABAT IPSVM, and AMABAT, could be read: There seemed also the name of a saint, BADEGES, which is not found in the Calendar.

" From the fields adjacent to the churchyard, may be traced many foundations of buildings leading to the north-end, and joining to the priory itself. In the area before the church, is an old stone-cross, consisting of eight octagonal steps, terminating in a column; and a large plain pointed arch, or gate-way, leading into the priory, or school-yard. On the east side of this inclosure, are the remains of the priory, now converted into the school, with habitations at each end, for the upper master and first usher. The school-room, as appears from the windows, and other traces, was the refectory, or hall of the priory. This is supported by a row of strong round Saxon pillars, evidently of very ancient date, which formerly extended to the end of the priory; but several were removed a few years ago, when some alterations were made in the house of the first usher. The dormitory was at the north end of the hall; and on the east side, was situated the cloisters, the area of which is converted into a garden for the master.

" Adjoining to the cloisters, stood the priory church, which, from the remains that have occasionally been laid open, appears to have been an elegant fabric, supported by pillars of alabaster, extending 180 feet, and upwards, from the school building.

" In the adjoining orchard, extending over several acres of ground, are the foundations of

13   B 3

the other buildings of the priory, which may be plainly traced in various directions. At the north end of the priory yard, on the banks of a piece of water, called the Old Trent, is a mansion that was rebuilt by the Thackers about a century ago, upon the foundation of the prior's lodging, and which of late years has been appropriated for the residence of the headmaster. This house exhibits towards the water, a curious brick tower, with battlements, and an ornamental cornice. This is one of the earliest specimens built with such kind of materials now remaining; and is of the date of Henry VI. as the rebus and initial letters of Overton, (one of the priors in that reign) evidently point out: the rebus, &c. is in the lower room. The number of houses in Repton, as returned under the late act, is 230: the inhabitants 1424; their chief employment arises from the operations of agriculture."*

MILTON, is a small hamlet belonging to the parish of Repton, and stands at the distance of a mile from the town. It contains about thirty houses.

BRETBY, is now but a small chapelry, belonging to the parish of Repton: formerly,

* Beauties of England.

however, it appears to have been more considerable in size, as vestiges of walls, foundations, wells, &c. have frequently been discovered, in the adjacent ground.

In former times, there was a castle at Bretby: In the reign of Richard II. it belonged to Thomas de Brotherton, Earl of Norfolk, and second son of Edward the First; from whom it descended to the Mowbrays, Dukes of Norfolk. The estate afterwards descended to the Berkleys, from whom, through a family of the name of Mee, it passed to the present possessor, the Earl of Chesterfield. The site of this castle, may be discovered from the unevenness of the ground, no other vestige remaining, as the walls were entirely levelled.

On the spot where BRETBY-PARK, the residence of the present Earl is built, formerly stood a venerable and magnificent mansion, which, according to tradition, was erected of the materials of which the castle consisted.— This ancient edifice, which his Lordship, in his youth, was, by an artful steward, persuaded to pull down, as being in a dangerous state of decay, though it was afterwards proved to have been very firm and substantial, was furnished with rich tapestry and fine paintings, and surrounded with gardens, disposed after the plan of those at Versailles, in the old grand style, with terraces, statues, and fountains.

STANTON, near DALE, at the time of the Norman survey, was called *Stantone*, and belonged to Gilbert de Gand. The parish is not extensive: The living is a curacy, and the church is dedicated to St. Michael, and formerly belonged to Dale Abbey : Mr. Thornhill is the patron.

SPONDON,* is called *Spondune* in Domesday,† at which time, there were, a priest, and a church, and one mill of five shillings and fourpence there. The living is at present a vicarage, and the church is dedicated to St. Mary. In former times it belonged to the *Hospital de Lazars*, at Burton, in the county of Leicester.

Spondon, is a large parish, including the chapelries of *Stanley, Chaddesden,* and *Locko*.‡ The village itself is large, containing nearly two hundred houses; and, standing in an airy, elevated, and pleasant situation, is inhabited by several genteel families.

* This parish ought to have been included in the Deanery of Derby, and inserted after Foston, page 315.

† *Orig*. 275. *a*. 2. Trans. p. 309.

‡ Which see p. 315.

CHAP. VIII.

Deanery of Castillar.

EGGINTON. At the time of the Norman survey, there were at *Eghintune*, " a priest and a church, and one mill of five shillings, and six farmers, paying fourteen shillings and four-pence."* The parish is not extensive; and the village though small, is pleasant.

Near it, on the banks of the Dove, is the seat of Sir Henry Every, Bart. This family came originally from Somersetshire; and Sir Simon, who was created a Baronet by king Charles the First, in the seventeenth year of his reign, was born at Chard in that county. He became possessed of the estates at Egginton, by marry- ing the eldest daughter, and co-heiress, of Sir Henry Leigh, of Egginton, Knt. The estate continued in the possession of his lineal de-

---

* Domesday, *Orig.* 276. *b.* 2. Trans, 316.

scendants, till about 1760, when, the Rev. John Every, the last direct heir, dying without issue, the property was claimed by Mr. Edward Every, an Attorney of Derby, who descended from a son of the first possessor, who lived at Burton; in his family the estate at present continues.

In the year 1736, a fire consumed the greatest part of the house, in which Sir Simon Every then lived, and the present mansion was erected in its place.

It is said, that Walcheline de Ferraries, and Margaret Peverel, his wife, formerly lived at Egginton.

MARSTON, called *Merstun* in Domesday, where at that time there were, a church and a priest, was held by the Monks, under Henry de Ferrieres. This living is a vicarage, and the church is dedicated to St. Mary. It formerly belonged to the priory of Tutbury; and the Duke of Devonshire is the patron. The parish contains also, the hamlets of Hilton, (*Hiltune*) Hatton, (*Hatune*) and Horne.

CHELLASTON, by the Norman surveyors written *Celerdestune*, and *Cellesdene*, is a small farming village; containing about fifty houses. The living is a donative curacy; and the church which formerly belonged to the priory of Dale, is dedicated to St. Peter. In the church is a raised tomb, with this inscription :—

Barredon quondam Cappelanus, A. D. M, D, XXIIIJ. cujus aio propitietur Deus. Amen.

ETWALL. There were at *Etewelle*, in the Conqueror's time, a priest and a church.[*]— John of Gaunt, granted a licence to Sir William Finchenden, Knt. and Richard de Ravenser, archdeacon of Lincoln, to give the manor of Etwall, to Beauvale priory, to pray for the soul of the said William whilst he lived, and the souls of him and his wife after their deaths. The church at Etwall was once, part of the priory at Welbeck: It was given in the reign of king Stephen, by Thomas Cukeney, who was the founder of this religious house.

We have before noticed, under Repton, that Sir John Port, who endowed the school at that place, lived at Etwall. In the reign of queen Mary, (about the year 1557) he left lands for the erection and endowment of an hospital at this place. It was at first built for the reception of six persons only ; but in consequence of the increased value of the lands, it has been considerably enlarged. It was taken down and rebuilt, in the year 1680, upon such a plan,

---

[*] Domesday, *Orig.* 276. *b.* 1.

that it will now accommodate sixteen persons: it now consists of sixteen distinct dwellings.— The government of this hospital is vested in the same persons, as that of Repton school.

At Etwall is the seat of Rowland Cotton, Esq. who is descended from an ancient and respectable family. His father represented the town of Newcastle in parliament, and died in the year 1753.

The parish of Etwall contains the hamlets of Burnaston, *(Bernulfestune)* and Barrowcoat, *(Beruerdescote)*.

DOVERIDGE, *Dovebridge*, or as it is in Domesday *Dubrige*, had, at the time of the Norman survey, a church and a priest. Doveridge was held by Edwine, the last Earl of Mercia, at the time of the Norman Conquest: but this prince being betrayed and slain, it was given to Henry Ferrers, under whom it was held by the Monks. Berta, founded a priory at Tutbury, in Staffordshire, and endowed it with lands of considerable value at Doveridge. When this religious house was dissolved, in the time of Edward the Sixth, those lands were granted to Sir William Cavendish, Bart.

At Doveridge is the seat of Sir Henry Cavendish, a descendant of the last-mentioned Baronet. The house, which is a modern and hand-

some building, was erected about the year
1770, and is pleasantly situated. It stands upon an eminence, commanding a view of the
town of Uttoxeter, the river Dove, the rich
pastures which extend along its banks, and of
a range of distant hills on the opposite side of
the valley.

The family of Cavendish, settled at Dove-
ridge, is supposed to have had its origin, in
William Cavendish, Esq. who was sheriff of
Derbyshire in 1591, and was nephew of Sir
William Cavendish, ancestor of the Duke of
Devonshire. The title was first bestowed on
Henry Cavendish, Esq. who was raised to the
dignity of a Baronet, in the year 1755.

At EATON HALL, in this parish, lived Sir
Thomas Milward, Chief Justice of Chester,
who entertained king Charles the First: The
house is now in ruins. Over the door is placed
the following inscription : —

*V. T. placet Deo sic omnia fiunt, anno Do-
mini, 1576, Junii 12.*

The living of Doveridge, is a vicarage; the
church is dedicated to St. Cuthbert; and was
given by Henry Earl Ferrers to the priory
at Tutbury. The Duke of Devonshire is the
patron.

13   F 3

SUDBURY. At the time of the Norman survey there were, a church and a priest at *Sud-
berie*. The living, at present, is a rectory, and
the church is dedicated to All-saints. It formerly belonged to the priory at Tutbury.—
Lord Vernon is the patron.

The manor of Sudbury, belonged, in the
time of Edward the Second, to the Montgomery family, who held it until the time of
Henry VIII, when the youngest daughter, and
co-heiress of Sir John Montgomery, conveyed
it, by marriage, to Sir John Vernon, son of Sir
Henry Vernon of Haddon-Hall; whose descendant, George Venables, Lord Vernon, is the
present proprietor.

The mansion, which is the seat of his present Lordship, was erected about the year 1610,
by Mary, widow of John Vernon Esq. grandson to the above Sir John. Though the house
is so ancient, yet it contains several good apartments, fitted up in a neat and elegant manner.
It is a respectable building of red brick, intermixed with others of a darker colour; and
though-not very large, is well proportioned,
and has two small wings. In the dining-room
are some good paintings; particularly, *The
Rape of the Sabines, Sloth and Industry*. In the
parlour are several family pictures. In the with-

drawing-room, are *Lord* and *Lady Effingham Howard*, a *Cleopatra*, and a *Mary Magdalene*. In the Library is an excellent painting of *The Miser*, which is said to. be a copy of Quintin Metsys's at Windsor-Castle. The Common parlour contains some family portraits. On the stair Case, is the *Battle of Alexander*; and in a good gallery which runs through the house, are portraits of Lords, *Cromwell* and *Stafford*, and *Sir John Vernon*, three of the favorites of Charles the first.

The family of the Vernons, is of great antiquity. They are descended from the Lords of Vernon in Normandy; one of whom, Richard de Vernon, accompanied William the Conqueror, into England, and was one of the seven Barons, created by Hugh Lupus, the great Earl of Chester. Sir Ralph de Vernon, who was alive in the reign of Edward II. was styled the *Long-Liver*, from his great age, which is said to have been 150 years. The first of this family invested with a peerage, was the late George Venables Vernon, who was raised to that honor by his present majesty, in the year 1762, by style and title of Lord Vernon, Baron Kinderton, in the county of Stafford.*

---

* For a further account of the Vernons, see " HADDON HALL."

Sudbury Church is an ancient fabric, standing in the garden near the house; and being
luxuriantly covered with ivy, becomes a picturesque object. Here the ancestors of the family, for more than two hundred years, have
been deposited, and several monuments have
been erected to their memories. An inscription on a neat mural monument, raised to the
memory of *Catherine*, daughter of the late Lord
Vernon, is a very elegant tribute to her worth;
is was written by Whitehead, Poet Lau-
reat:—

> " Mild as the opening morn's serenest ray,
>   Mild as the close of Summer's softest day;
>   Her form, her virtues, (form'd alike to please
>   With artless charms, and unassuming ease;)
>   On every breast their mingling influence stole,
>   And in sweet union breath'd one beauteous whole.
>   This fair example to the world was lent
>   As a short lesson of a life well spent:
>   Alas, too short!—but bounteous heaven best knows,
>   When to reclaim the blessings it bestows."

HILL SOMERSAL, is a hamlet, which belongs
to the parish of Sudbury, and contains about
twenty houses.

CHURCH BROUGHTON, *Broctune*, is a pretty
considerable parish, containing upwards of fifty
houses. The living is a vicarage, and the
church is dedicated to St. Michael. According
to Ecton, it formerly belonged to the priory at

Tutbury. Dugdale* says, that Robert de Fer:
rers, second Earl of Derby, gave the village of
Brocton to this religious house.

SUTTON ON THE HILL; when Domesday was
compiled, *Sudtune*, was a part of the lands of
Henry de Ferrers, and there were a church and
a priest there, at that time.† The living of
Sutton is a vicarage, and the church is dedicated to St. Michael.

DALBURY, called by the Norman surveyors,
Dellingeberie, and *Delbebi*, is not a very extensive parish. The living is a rectory, and
the church is dedicated to All-saints. It formerly belonged to the priory at Trentham.
—— Cotton, Esq. is the patron.

BARTON; at the Conquest, there were at
Bractune, a church and a priest, which were
the property of Henry de Ferrers.

Barton once belonged to the family of Le
Blunt.‡ In the ninth year of Richard the Second, Walter le Blunt, obtained a charter for
free Warren, in all his demesne lands, at Al-
kemonton, Sapperton, and Hollington. William le Blount, Lord Mountjoy, by his will,
bearing date, the thirteenth of October, in the
year 1534, directed, that in case he should die,

---

* Mon. Angl. Vol. I. page 354.
† Domesday, *Orig.* 274. *b.* 2.   ‡ See page 273.

within the counties of Derby or Stafford, his body should be conveyed to the parish church of Barton, there to be buried under an arch, on the South side of the altar.

During the civil wars, in Charles the First's time, an engagement took place, (February 15th, 1646,) between the Parliamentary Army stationed at Barton-Blount-house, and a detachment of the Royalists quartered at Tutbury.

The parish of Barton contains but very few houses. The living is a rectory, and Samuel Crompton, Esq. is the patron.

TRUSLEY, supposed to be the *Toxenai* of Domesday,* is a small parish, not containing many houses. The living is a rectory, and the church is dedicated to All-saints.

A very respectable family of the name of Coke, formerly resided at Trusley. Sir Francis, who lived here in the time of Charles the First, had a brother, whose name was John, who was Secretary of State in that king's reign. He spent many years at Cambridge, and there acquired such high reputation for his learning, that he was chosen public Professor of Rhetoric to the University. He afterwards accompanied a person of consequence, in his travels on

---

* See *Orig.* 274. *b.* 2. Trans. 304.

the continent, and on his return, retired in the capacity of a private gentleman. When he was arrived at the age of fifty years, he was appointed Secretary to the Navy, then Master of Requests, and in the year 1620, Secretary of State. The honor of Knighthood was, shortly after, conferred upon him, and he was chosen the Representative of the University of Cambridge in Parliament.

In the third parliament of Charles the First, Sir John Coke made a considerable figure; and in the important business transacted at this time, he appears to have conducted himself with such moderation, that though he was often obliged, from his official character, to deliver messages which were far from being agreeable to the members of the house at that time, he yet, by his discretion and lenity, took care to secure himself from their personal resentment and displeasure. After having continued Secretary of State for about twenty years, he was removed from his office, and died on the eighth of September, 1644.

George, another brother of Sir Francis Coke, was, successively, Bishop of Bristol and Hereford. He was involved in the same condemnation with the rest of the Bishops, passed, for their signing the protest in parliament, in order to secure the preservation of their privileges; and is said to have died in reduced circumstances, on the tenth of December, 1646.

BOYLSTON. The manor of *Boilestun* was given by William to Henry de Ferrers, and was then valued at thirty shillings. The present parish, contains from forty to fifty houses. The living is a rectory; and the church is dedicated to St. John the Baptist. Its clear value is £49. 0s. and yearly tenths, 12s. 0½d.

SOMERSALL. In Domesday, *Sumersale*, is a parish containing the hamlets of *Church Somersall*, and *Herbert-Somersall*. The living is a rectory; the church is dedicated to St. Peter, and the Earl of Chesterfield is the patron.

The mansion of —— Fitzherbert, Esq. stands in the liberty of Herbert-Somersall, and is supposed to have been built with the materials, which were collected from the ruins of an ancient seat of the Montgomery family, which was situated near the church at Cubley.

CUBLEY. In Domesday it is said, " there is now at *Cobelei*, a priest and a church, and one mill of twelve pence, and eight acres of meadow." The living is a rectory, and the church is dedicated to St. Andrew: The Earl of Chesterfield is the patron. The number of houses in the liberty of Cubley is thought to be about eighty.

Marston Montgomery, is a chapelry belonging to Cubley, containing, nearly, one
hundred houses : The chapel is dedicated to St.
Giles. Here the site of the house, where the
family of Montgomery once lived is shewn.—
It is said that dame Margaret Stanhope was the
last who inhabited it. In the year 1659 a new
house was built with its ruins.

No manufacture of any consequence, is carried on, in this part of the county of Derby,
and, therefore, the inhabitants, are principally
engaged in the pursuits of agriculture, and rely,
chiefly, upon its produce for their support.

Longford, or *Laganford*, is a parish containing the hamlets of, Longford, Hollington
(Holintune) Rodsley, *(Redlesleie)* Alkmonton
(Alchementune) and Bentley *(Benedlege).*—
The living of Longford is a rectory; and the
church is dedicated to St. Chad. It was given
by Nicholas de Griesly, alias, de Longford, and
Margaret his wife to the Monastery of Kenil-
worth, in Warwickshire, Edward Coke Esq. is
the patron. There was formerly a Chapel at
Alkmonton, but the font is the only present remains of it. Walter le Blount,* by a will da-

18   G 3

* See page 273.

ted the eighth of July 1474, " directed that his
executors should purchase lands to the yearly
value of ten pounds, and appropriate them to
the hospital of St. Leonard situated betwixt
Alkmonton and Bentley, to pray for the souls of
his ancestors, for his own soul, and for the souls
of his wife and children, for the souls of Hum-
phrey, Duke of Buckingham, Richard, earl Rivers, Sir John Wodoyle, knt. and for the souls
of the ancient lords of that hospital.

" Moreover he appointed, that the master of
the above hospital should continually find seven
poor men, who were either to be chosen from
his own domestics or dependants, or were old
servants of the lord and patron, of the lord, of
the manor of Barton and of the same hospital
of St. Leonard. But in case they could not be
met with in this way, they were to be collected
from the old tenants of all the lordships of the
said lord, and patrons within the counties of
Derby and Stafford. And he was required to
pay weekly to these seven poor men two shillings and four-pence. But no persons were to
be considered as proper objects of this charity,
till they had attained to the age of fifty-five
years. When these seven men were chosen,
they were to have seven kine (cows) going
within his park at Barton, and seven load of

wood yearly for their fewel, which were to be
taken within his lordships of Barton, Alkmonton, and Bently, or other lordships in Appletree hundred, in the county of Derby.

"The master of the hospital was also obliged,
every third year, to give to each of these seven
poor men a gown and an hood of white or rus-
set of one suit, and of these two colours alternately; the gown was to be marked with a
Tayewe cross of red, and none of these poor
men were allowed to ask alms upon pain of
removal from the hospital.—Moreover every
one of them was obliged to repeat our Ladies
psalter, twice every day, within the chapel of
the hospital.—It was also appointed, that there
should be a mansion with a square court adjoining to the same chapel without any back door,
that the roof of the chapel should be raised, the
wall heightened, the windows made with strong
iron work, with a quire and perclose, and altars without the quire.—Moreover the master
was forbidden to wear either red or green, but
upon his gown of other colour, a Tayewe cross
was to be placed upon his left side, and he was
allowed to enjoy no benefice but the Parsonage
of Barton.

"Lastly he directed, that a chapel of St. Nicholas should be built at Alkmonton, that the

master of the above hospital should say mass there yearly on the feast of St. Nicholas, and at other times, when he thought proper.*"

LONGFORD HALL, is the seat of Edward Coke, Esq. one of the representatives of the town of Derby in Parliament. It is an ancient and spacious fabric; with wings, which have the appearance of being more modern, than the body of the house. The surrounding grounds are pleasant, and the neighbouring country furnishes a variety of agreeable prospects.

The estate at Longford, passed through several families, before it became the property of its present respectable possessor. It was, formerly, the seat of a family, who seem to have derived their name from the place. As early as the seventeenth parliament of Edward the Second, about the year 1321, Nicholas de Longford, represented the county of Derby. Sometime after the year 1620, when the last of the Longfords died, it became the seat of a descendant of Sir Edward Coke, Lord Chief Justice of England, in the reign of James I. In this family Longford continued till the year 1727, when, Sir Edward Coke dying without issue, it became the property of Edward Coke,

---

* Dugdale's Bar. vol. I. p. 520.

Esq. of Holkam, Norfolk, a descendant of another branch of the Lord Chief Justice's family. Dying unmarried, in 1733, he left his estate to his younger brother, Robert Coke, Esq. who was vice-chamberlain to queen Caroline. He died in the year 1750, and Wenman Roberts, son of his youngest sister, Anne, was his heir; who, upon succeeding to his uncle's estates, in the counties of Derby and Lancaster, took the name of Coke, and in the year 1772 was chosen one of the representatives of the town of Derby in parliament. From this gentleman the present Edward Coke, Esq. is descended.

BRAILSFORD, in Domesday,* called *Brailesford*, and also, *Breilesfordham*, and where there were then, a church and a priest, is a considerable village. It is situated on each side of the road leading from Derby to Ashburn, and nearly midway between those places. The inhabitants are chiefly engaged in the pursuits of agriculture.

The manor of Brailsford, was held in the twenty-fifth year of Edward I. by H. de Brailsford. In the reign of Edward IV. it was held by Ralph Shirley, under Duke Clarence of Tutbury. In this family it continued till it was

---

* *Orig.* 274. *b.* 2. and 280. *a* 2.

disposed of by the late Earl Ferrers, to a Mr.
Webster, formerly of Derby.

The living is a rectory; the church is dedicated to All-saints; and the Rev. Mr. Gardiner
is the patron.

SHIRLEY; at *Sirelei* there were at the compilation of Domesday, a church and a priest,
and one mill. The living is at present a vicarage; the church is dedicated to St. Michael.—
It formerley belonged to the Monastery at Derley; it has the same patron as Brailsford.

At Shirley stood, some years ago, the ancient seat of the Etendon family, which assumed
the name of Shirley, in the reign of Henry the
Third; at which time, James Shirley had free
Warren granted him, in all his demesne lands
in this place. The manor, passed through the
same persons as Brailsford, to the late Earl
Ferrers, when the farms, of which it consisted,
were sold to different purchasers.

YEAVELY, in Domesday, *Gheveli*, is a chapelry under Shirley, consisting of about fifty
houses. Here there was formerly a Hermitage,
which in the reign of Richard I. was given by
Ralph le Fun, with all its appurtenances and
revenues, to the Knights Hospitallers of Saint
John at Jerusalem, and afterwards became a
preceptory to that order. Sir William Meynil,

Lord of the town, was, in the year 1268, a great benefactor to this religious house: It was dedicated to St. Mary, and St. John the Baptist.

At the Dissolution, its revenues, together with those of another preceptory at Barrow, in Cheshire, were valued at £98. 3s. 4d. This house, was granted, in the twenty-fifth year of Henry VIII. to Charles, Lord Mountjoy.

OSMASTON, in Domesday, written Osmundestune, is a small hamlet in the parish of Brailsford, containing, together with the whole liberty, about fifty houses. The chapel is dedicated to St. Martin, and valued at £15.

DENBY, is a parish, containing a single hamlet of the same name: This village is large, containing about one hundred and sixty dwellings. The living is a curacy; and the church is dedicated to St. Mary:—Its clear value is £9.

Denby appears to have been a place of some importance, about the commencement of the fourteenth century; as in the eighth year of Edward the Third, Richard, Lord Grey of Codnor, obtained a charter, for holding a market at Denby, with a fair, on the eve and nativity of the blessed Virgin. The inhabitants are, chiefly, supported by working the collieries, and the manufacture of stockings.

Denby, disputes with Derby, the honor of giving birth, to that great and celebrated Astronomer, *John Flamstead;* but, as it cannot be ascertained to which it is due, and the probability being in favor of Derby, we have given a sketch of his life, in our account of that Town.*

* See page 211.

CHAP. IX.

Deanery of Ashbourne.

EALASTON, *Edolveston,* and supposed to be the *Duluestune* of Domesday, is a small parish, containing about forty houses. The living is a rectory; and the church is dedicated to St. James. It is set down in the king's book, at the clear value of £46. and yearly tenths, 7s. 10d. The Dean of Lincoln is the the patron.

NORBURY. At the time of the Norman survey, there were a priest and a church at *Nortberie.** The liberty of Norbury is but small: it includes the hamlet of *Roston,* and the chapelry of *Snelson, (Snellestune)* whose chapel is dedicated to St. Peter. The living of Norbury is a rectory; and the church is dedicated to St. Mary.

At Norbury was the ancient seat of the *Fitzherberts,*† to whom the manor was given, in

14   B 3

---

* Domesday *Orig.* 275. *b.* 2. Trans. 307.

† Camden, page 491.

1125, by William de Ferrers, Prior of Tutbury;
and in whose possession, it has continued to
the present time. Several of this family, have
been celebrated for their learning, but none
more so, than Sir Anthony Fitzherbert. He
was born at Norbury, and educated at Oxford,
from whence he removed to one of the Inns of
Court. In 1523, he was made a Judge in the
Court of Common Pleas, where he presided
during part of the reign of Henry VIII. and is
reported to have opposed Cardinal Wolsey, in
the plenitude of his power. He wrote, 1. The
Grand Abridgment of the English Law; 2. A
Collection of Laws; 3. The Office and Authority of Justices of the Peace; 4. The Office of
Sheriffs; and 5. New Natura Brevium; works
which are still in repute among the students of
his profession. He is also supposed, to have
written a book on the Surveying of Land; and
another on Husbandry. He died in 1538, and
was buried in Norbury church.

· There were, also, two of Sir Anthony's grand-
sons, who signalized themselves, in the republic of letters. Thomas Fitzherbert, whose
writings are wholly controversial, was a Jesuit,
and rector of the English College at Rome,
where he died in 1640. Nicholas Fitzherbert, wrote, 1. A Description of the University

of Oxford; 2. On the Antiquity and Continuation of the Catholic Religion in England; 3.
The Life of Cardinal Allen. He went to Italy
in 1572, where he resided with Cardinal Allen,
till 1612, when he was drowned.

The last possessor of the estate was, William
Fitzherbert, Esq. whose death was occasioned,
by imprudently venturing into a cold bath, after having heated himself by walking. This
gentleman's widow, is the celebrated Mrs. Fitzherbert, so well known in the fashionable world,
for having excited the admiration of an illustrious Personage.

BRADLEY, *Braidelei*, is a parish containing
from fifty to sixty houses. The living is a rectory; and the church is dedicated to All-saints.
The Dean of Lincoln is the patron.

At Bradley is the seat of the family of the
Meynells. In the year 1625, Sir Gilbert Kniveton, resided here; but in the year 1655, the
manor was purchased by Francis Meynell, Esq.
Alderman of London, from whom it has descended to the present proprietor. The ancient family seat at Bradley has been taken down,
and the stables converted into a dwelling-
house. It is now seldom used by Mr. Mey-
nel, except for the convenience of hunting in
the neighbourhood.

Near this gentleman's seat there is a spring
of chalybeate water, which bears a great resemblance to those at Chesterfield and Duffield.

ASHBOURN.

—▸◆◂—

ASHBOURN, *Ashbourne*, or *Ashburn*, is a neat
Market town, imbosomed amid hills, which
rise around it on every side, and confine within them a rich valley, through which, the river
Dove, rolls its water. The view of the town,
from the top of the hill, on approaching it
from London, is particularly delightful. In
the deep rich valley below, the town is seen,
overhung with beautiful high grounds, at the
back, as well as the front. The descent to it
by the turnpike road, is the finest walk imagi-
nable, being fenced on the inner steep side with
a handsome railing, and having a thorn hedge
on the outer side. A small rivulet, called the
Henmore, divides the town into two parts,
the most southern of which is denominated
Compton, anciently *Campdene*. The houses,

are, chiefly built of brick, and rise on the side of a hill.

At the time of the Norman survey, Esseburne was a royal manor, and had "a priest and a church."* At this time, the town also was the property of the king. King John granted it to William de Ferrers, Earl of Derby; but on the rebellion of his son William Ferrers, in the succeeding reign, it was seized by the crown — Edward the First bestowed it on his brother, Edmund Crouchback, Earl of Lancaster. Roger Mortimer, Earl of March, procured from Edward III. for his son, a grant of the Wapentake of Risley and Ashbourn in the Peak, being parcels of the lands of the late Edmund, Earl of Kent, attainted.

The manor of Ashbourn then became the property of the Cockaynes, a very ancient family, whose principal seat, was at this place for many generations: the last of this family, died at the end of the seventeenth century without issue.

The manor of Ashbourn then became the property of the Cokes of Melbourn, from whom it was purchased, in the reign of Charles the Second, by Sir William Boothby, Knt. and Bart. The family of Boothby is thought to be

* Domesday, Orig. 272, a. 2

of great antiquity, and is supposed to have
sprung from a person of that name, mentioned
in the reign of king Egbert, who lived near a
thousand years ago. The first who is ascertained with certainty to be an ancestor of the
present Baronet, is Richard Boothby, who was
living in the third year of queen Elizabeth.
His grandson, Henry Boothby, was created a
Baronet by king Charles the First, by letters
patent, dated November the fifth, 1644: but,
owing to the civil wars, the title did not pass
the great seal. However, his son William, was
knighted by Charles II. in the field; and at
the restoration, the king renewed his patent
gratis, by the name of Sir William Boothby, of
Broadlow-Ash, the former patent being of
Clator-Clote. The present Sir Brooke Boothby, (well known as a great classical scholar and
an elegant poet,) is a lineal descendant and
the male heir of the above.

The present church of Ashbourn, which is a
fine specimen of Gothic building, was erected
in the thirteenth century, as appears from a
memorial in brass, commemorating its dedica-
tion to St. Oswald, discovered a few years ago,
on one of the walls of the church. The inscription is in Latin, in ancient abbreviated
characters: the following is a translation;—

" In the year from the incarnation of our Lord, 1241, on the twenty-fourth of April, this church was dedicated, and this altar consecrated, in honour of St. Oswald, king and martyr, by the venerable Hugh de Patishul, lord Bishop of Coventry."

. This church at Ashbourn, together with the chapels, lands, tythes, and other appurtenances, belonging thereto, were given in the time of Edward the Confessor, by William Rufus, to the Cathedral church at Lincoln.

. In former times, there stood in the neighbourhood of Ashbourn, a chapel dedicated to St. Mary. Some years ago its remains were taken down, by Sir Brooke Boothby; prior to which time, it had been used as a malthouse.

. The present church is built in the form of a cross, with a square tower in the centre; terminated with a lofty octagonal spire, enriched with ornamental workmanship, and pierced by twenty windows. The roof is supported by several pointed arches; the interior is spacious, but not commodiously disposed, though galleries have been erected for the convenience of the congregation. It contains several monuments, erected to the memories of the *Cokaines*, *Bradburnes*, and *Boothbys*; and in the windows are numerous shields of the arms of different families, in stained glass.

The beautiful monument erected in this church a few years ago, executed by the classic chisel of Banks, in remembrance of the daughter of Sir Brooke Boothby, his only daughter, a child, six years of age, does as much credit to the abilities of the artist, as to the feelings of the parent. Nobody ought ever to overlook this tomb, as it is, perhaps, the most interesting and pathetic object in England. Simplicity and elegance appear in the workmanship; tenderness and innocence in the image. On a marble pedestal and slab, like a low table, is a mattress, with a child lying on it, both being cut out of white marble. Her cheek, expressive of suffering mildness, reclines on a pillow; and her little fevered hands, gently rest on each other, near to her head. The plain, and only drapery, is a frock, the skirt flowing easily out before, and a ribbon sash, the knot twisted forward, as it were, by the restlessness of pain, and the two ends spread out in the same direction as the frock. The delicate naked feet, are carelesly folded over each other, and the whole appearance, is, as if she had just turned, in the tossings of her illness, to seek a cooler or easier place of rest. The man whom this

does not affect, wants one of the finest sources
of genuine sensibility; his heart cannot be
formed, to relish the beauties, either of nature
or of art!

The inscriptions round this pleasing memorial of evanescent life, frail beauty, and departed innocence, are in, English, Latin, French,
and Italian. The English has;—

1. Left hand on the slab.

I was not in safety, neither had I rest, and the trouble came.

Beneath on the pedestal;—

TO PENELOPE,

Only child of Sir Brooke Boothby, and Dame Susannah
Boothby,

Born April 11th, 1785, died March 13th, 1791.

She was, in form and intellect, most exquisite.

The unfortunate Parents ventured their all on this frail Bark,
and the wreck was total.

2. Latin side at her head, on the slab;—

Omnia tecum una perierunt gaudia nostra.*

Beneath on the pedestal;—

Tu vero felix
Et beata
Penelope mea,
Quæ tot
Tantisque
Miseriis una
Morte perfuncta es.†

14   r 3

* All our joys are perished with thee alone.

† But thou art happy and blessed, my dear Penelope,
who, by one touch of Death, hast escaped so many and
so great miseries.

3. French side the other end of the slab;—
Beauté c'est donc ici ton dernier azyle!*
Beneath on the pedestal;—

Son cercueil
. Ne la contient pas
. Toute entiere;
Il attend le reste de sa proie:
—Il ne l'attendra pas
Longtems.†

4. Italian side;—

Lei che'l ciel ne mostra terra n'asconde.‡

Beneath on the pedestal;—

Le crespe chiome d'or puro lucente,
E'l lampeggiar dell Angelico riso,
Che solean far in Terra uh Paradiso,
Poca polvere son che nulla sente.§

There are also, three other monuments, to
persons of the same family, inscribed with some
beautiful verses by Sir Brooke Boothby, and
the late Miss Seward.

Near the church, a noble monument of phi-
lanthropy presents itself, in the Free-Grammar-
School, which was founded, in the time of queen
Elizabeth, by the voluntary contributions of
Sir Thomas Cokaine, Knt. William Bradburne,

* *Beauty*, this then is thy last asylum!
† Her tomb does not yet contain all; it waits for the
rest of its prey :———it will not wait long.
‡ Those that descend into the grave are not concealed
from Heaven.
§ Thy curling locks of pure shining gold, the lightening of thy angelic smile, which used to make a Paradise
on Earth, are now become only a little senseless dust.

Esq. and " divers well-disposed citizens of London, being born in, or near to Ashbourne on the Peak, combining their loving benevolence together, built there, with convenient lodging for a master, and liberal maintenance allowed thereto."

This school is under the patronage and direction, of three governors and twelve assistants, to be chosen from among the resident householders of Ashbourn, who are incorporated according to the patent of Queen Elizabeth. The head Master is to be of the degree of Master of Arts, and has a house and garden for himself and family, adjoining to the school, with about one hundred pounds a year salary : the under-master has, also, a house, and about thirty pounds per annum. The children admitted into this school, must be those of the town, or its immediate neighbourhood. There is another Free-School at Ashbourn, for educating poor boys and girls, the master and mistress of which, have a salary of about ten pounds each.

There is also, at the south-east of the town, a neat chapel, and a row of alms-houses, for the admission of six poor men or women, erected and endowed, in 1800, by a native of Ashbourn of the name of Cooper. This person,

when a boy, followed the humble occupation
of brick-making, but having been disgusted
with the employment, he went to London, and
by frugality and persevering industry, acquired
a considerable property. Hospitals for the reception and support of aged and decayed house-
keepers, have also been founded here; as well
as one for the maintenance of four clergymen's
widows.

The town of Ashbourn, according to the
ascertainment of the late population act, contains 459 houses, and 2006 inhabitants. The
markets, which are held on Saturday, supply
an extensive neighbourhood. It has also a considerable support from its cattle-fairs, of which
no fewer than seven, are held here yearly, to
which great numbers of horses, oxen, sheep,
pigs, and wares of various descriptions, are
brought for sale. The trout caught in its
river, the Dove, afford a delicious treat, of
which most travellers choose to partake. Its
fame for cheese, it is unnecessary to mention;
an article supplied by the dairy-farms in its
neighbourhood, which are chiefly engaged in
the manufacture of it.

The parish of Ashbourn, extends partly in
the Wapentake of Wirksworth, and partly in
the Hundred of Appletree. In the latter are

the hamlets of *Clifton, Offcote, Underwood, Yeldersley,* and *Hulland,* together, containing about 105 houses.

Near the town, is ASHBOURN-HALL, a seat belonging to Sir Brooke Boothby. It was from remote antiquity, the residence of the *Cokaines,* one of the most eminent families in Derbyshire. Their residence here may be traced, with certainty, from the time of Henry the Third, to that of Charles the Second, when they sold the estate to Sir William Boothby. No architectural beauties adorn the exterior of this mansion, though within, every part is disposed with taste and elegance. Many of the pictures are valuable; and the books are a judicious collection of classic and polite literature. The situation is low; but the park and gardens, are laid out in a style of beauty and gracefulness, which compensates for the want of more picturesque scenery.

Of its ancient possessors, the Cokaines, we find a John Cokaine, who represented this county in several parliaments and councils during the reign of Edward the Third. Another John Cokaine, was knighted by Henry the Fourth, at the battle of Shrewsbury, (1403) and killed in that conflict. His younger son, was Chief Baron of the Exchequer in the third of Henry the Fourth; and a Justice of Common Pleas in the sixth of the same king, and second of Henry the Sixth. He lies buried in the church at Ashbourn; his tomb being decorated with the effigies of himself and his lady, carved in alabaster: the latter is adorned with a Turkish head-dress. The family of Cokaine, resident till of late years at *Cokaine-Hatley* in Bedfordshire, descended from this famous Judge. Thomas Cokaine, of Ashbourn, the representative of the eldest branch, was knighted for his valour at the battle of Spurs, under Henry VIII. Sir Charles Cokaine, in the time of Charles the Second, was the last of this family who resided at Ashbourn. He was a considerable sufferer for his loyalty to Charles I. and gave the finishing blow to an old venerable inheritance, which began to decline in the reign of James. He was a great writer of verses, the chief merit of which consists in genealogical history; a subject but ill-adapted to accord with the smooth current of the Pierian spring. Sir William Cokaine, of a younger branch of this family, was Lord Mayor of London in the year 1619; and his son Charles was raised to an Irish peerage, by the title of Viscount Cullen, in 1642.

The following article is found inserted in the

church register at Ashbourn;—" 1645 August, king Charles came to the church, and many more, and talked with Mr. Peacock."

About half a mile to the left of the road leading from Ashbourn to Wirksworth, and about three miles from the former place, are two Sulphureous springs, known in the neighbourhood by the names of *Agnes* and *Mudge Meadow Springs*. They are situated at the distance of nearly a quarter of a mile from each other; and in their qualities and virtues resemble the Kedleston water.

MAPPLETON, *Mapletune*, is a small village, lying in a valley to the North of Ashbourn, on the banks of the Dove. The living is a rectory; and the church is dedicated to St. Mary. The liberty is thought to contain, about one hundred and seventy inhabitants.

THORPE, in Domesday called *Torp*, is a very agreeable little village, with a small church, seated upon the brow of a hill, and so surrounded with trees, as to be rendered highly picturesque. The living is a rectory, and the church is dedicated to St. Leonard: the Dean of Lincoln is the patron.

A little to the North of the village, is *Thorp Cloud*, a conical hill, of very steep ascent, which rises to a great height. Near this is a

tolerably good descent, into a deep hollow
called, *Bunster-Dale;* one side of which is
bounded by a steep acclivity, finely covered
with wood; and the other by a range of lofty
crags, of wild, uncouth appearance. Passing
through this narrow ravine (where the eye is
prevented from excursion, and the mind thrown
back upon itself) for half a mile, a sudden turn,
presents the eye, with the southern entrance,
of the far-famed, and romantic, DOVE-DALE,
a name it has received from the river *Dove,* pouring its waters through the valley.

On entering *Dove-Dale,* it is impossible not
to be struck with the, almost instantaneous,
change of scenery, so different from the surrounding country. Here, instead of the brown
heath, or the rich cultivated meadow, rocks
abrupt and vast, their grey sides harmonized
by mosses, lichens, and yew-trees, their tops
sprinkled with mountain-ash, rise on each
side. The mountains that enclose this narrow
dell, rise very precipitous, and bear on their
sides fragments of rock, that, at a distance,
look like the remains of some ruined castle.—
After proceeding a little way, a deep and narrow valley presents itself, into whose recesses
the eye is prevented from penetrating, by the
winding course it pursues, and the shutting-in

of its precipices, which fold into each other, and preclude all distant view.

On proceeding, the scenery of Dove-Dale, gradually increases in majesty and rudeness.— Now, those objects which at a distance seemed to have been ruins, are found to be huge pyramids of rock, and grand isolated masses, ornamented with ivy net-work, rising in the middle of the vale; and were the scene on a sandy desert, divested of its woods, it might delude the mind with the fancied plains, in the neighbourhood of Cairo. The rocks which enclose the Dale, rise perpendicularly to a very great height, forcing themselves into the clouds, their scathed and uncovered heads overhanging the narrow path, that winds through the dark recesses of the Dale; and frowning with craggy grandeur, and shaggy with dark oaks that grow out of the chinks, and cling to the asperities of the rock, form a scene in romantic beauty, unrivalled. The mind regards it as a sequestered solitude, where contemplation " to the crowd unknown," might take her seat, and extend her musings through the wide range of existence, neither interrupted by jarring sounds, nor distracted by discordant images. The loneliness and silence that reigns here, entitle it to

14   K 3

the appellation of the Vale of Fancy or another
Vaucluse; and as there is but one rugged, narrow
footpath, it has more the air of being the haunt
of imaginary beings, than human ones.

After proceeding about a mile in the Dale,
the walk perpetually diversified by new fantas-
tic forms, and uncouth combinations of rock on
all sides, a vast mural mass of detached rock,
extending along the edge of the precipice on
the right, is seen: this is called *Reynard's
Hole.* It consists of three parts;—a mass of
mural rock, in front of the *Hall*, perfectly detached from it, and perforated by nature into
a grand arch, nearly approaching to the shape
of the sharply-pointed Gothic, about forty-five
feet high, and twenty wide. After climbing
the rock, and passing through this arch, a steep
ascending path leads to the first cavern called
Reynard's Hall. This is a natural cave, of
forty-five feet in length, fifteen in breadth, and
thirty in height. From the mouth of this cavern, the scene is singular, beautiful, and impressive. The face of the rock which contains
the arch, rises immediately in front, and would
effectually prevent the eye from ranging beyond its mighty barrier, did not its centre
open into the above-mentioned arch, through
which, is seen a small part of the opposite side

of the Dale, a mass of gloomy wood, from
whose shade a huge detached rock, solitary,
craggy, and pointed, starts out to a great
height, and forms an object truly sublime.—
This rock is known by the appellation of *Dove
Dale Church*, and is pleasingly contrasted by
the little pastoral river, and its verdant turfy
bank below. At the end of this cave, there is
a narrow opening, which some of the country-
people, in the neighbourhood, suppose, leads to
other very extensive caverns, and terminates
in a place called Parwich, about two miles and
a half distant.

· To the left of this cavern, and a little above
it, is another, called *Reynard's Kitchen*. This
is about forty feet in length, fourteen in breadth,
and twenty-six in height. From the inside of
this, a pleasing view is presented, of the upper
part of the Dale, its river and rocks.

The approach to these natural excavations,
is very difficult of access even on foot, but impracticable on horseback: the latter however,
was unfortunately tried about forty years ago.
The Rev. Mr. Langton, Dean of Cloger, in
Ireland, being on a visit to a family in the neighbourhood of Ashbourn, a party was formed, to
make an excursion into Dove-Dale. As they
were proceeding along the bottom of the val-

ley, Mr. Langton proposed to ascend on horseback, a very steep precipice, near Reynard's
Hole, apparently between three and four hundred feet high; and Miss La Roche, a young
lady of the party, agreed to accompany him
on the same horse. When they had climbed
the rock to a considerable height, the poor animal, unable to sustain the fatigue of the task
imposed upon him, fell under his burden, and
rolled down the steep. The Dean was precipitated to the bottom, where he was taken up so
bruised and mangled by the fall, that he expired in a few days, and was buried in Ashbourn
church: but the young lady, whose descent had
been retarded by her hair entangling in a bram-
ble bush, slowly recovered; though when disengaged, she was insensible, and continued so for
two days. The horse, more fortunate than its
riders, was but very slightly injured.

After passing Reynard's hole, the Dale becomes narrower, admitting only a foot-path
between the river and the rock, which now
rises more abruptly on either side, and appears
in shapes more wild and singular; but softened
and diversified with shrubs and brush-wood.
This scenery continues to the northern extremity, when two vast rocks, rising sublimely
to the right and left of the brook, form the jaws

or portals of this wonderful valley, which now
drops at once the grand picturesque, its bottom gradually widening into an indulated flat,
and its rocks sinking into round stony hills.
The rock on the right hand of the termination
of the Dale, has two large natural excavations
called the *Dove-Holes*. The first is a regular
arch of about sixty feet in span, and thirty-four
in height; and a few yards higher up, is the
other hole of the same shape, but of much less
dimensions. Neither of these penetrate far into the rock. Opposite the Dove-Holes, on the
Staffordshire side of the river, is the other mass
of rock, which is called *Dove-Hole-Church*,
bearing a very strong and striking resemblance
to such an edifice.

.· The length of Dove-Dale, is, nearly three
miles, but the views are more limited from the
sinuosity of its course and its projecting precipices. Through the whole of this majestic feature of country, the river Dove leads his stream,
murmuring innocently and transparently over
its pebbly bed, in the halcyon days of summer,
but swelling into rage during the winter months:
little tufts of shrubs and underwood, form
islands in miniature in the river, that enlarge
and swell the rest of the objects.

On the right, or Derbyshire side of the Dale,

the rocks are more bare of vegetation, than on
the left, or Staffordshire side, where they are
thickly covered, with a fine hanging wood of
wild pear, apple, and cherry trees, the nut, the
yew, the buck-thorn, the birch, and a great
variety of other trees and odoriferous shrubs
and plants, which from its various combinations with the surrounding objects, presents a
succession of beautifully picturesque and romantic views. But the character of the scenery
is greatly diversified by the varying forms of
the rocks, and the changing current of the
Dove, the motion and appearance of which is
perpetually changing. " It is never less than
eight, nor so much as twenty, yards wide, and
generally from three to four feet deep; and
transparent to the bottom, except when it is
covered with foam of the purest white, under
falls which are perfectly lucid. These are numerous, but very different: in some places they
stretch straight across, or aslant, the stream;
in others, they are only partial, and the water
either dashes against the stones, and leaps over
them, or, pouring along a steep, rebounds upon those below: sometimes it rushes through
the several openings between them, and at other
times it is driven back by the obstruction, and
turns into an eddy. In one particular spot, the

valley, almost closing, leaves hardly a passage
for the river, which, pent up, and struggling
for vent, rages, and roars, and foams, till it
has extricated itself from confinement. · In
other parts, the stream, though never languid,
is often gentle, flows round a little desert island, glides between aits of bulrushes, disperses
itself among tufts of grass and of moss, bubbles
about a water-dock, or plays with the slender
threads of aquatic plants which float upon the
surface."*

The rugged, dissimilar, and frequently grotesque and fanciful appearance of the rocks,
distinguish the scenery of this Dale from, almost every other in the kingdom. "On the
whole" to use the words of Mr. Gilpin,† "it
is perhaps, one of the most pleasing pieces of
scenery of the kind, we any where meet with.
It has something peculiarly characteristic. Its
detatched, perpendicular rocks, stamp it with
an image entirely its own, and for that reason,
it affords the greater pleasure. For it is in
scenery as in life:—We are most struck with the
peculiarity of an original character, provided
there is nothing offensive in it."

---

* Wheatley's Obser. on Modern Gardening. p. 114.
   † In his Northern Tour.

At Wooton-Hall near Dove-Dale, Hume procured a place of retreat, for that singular character and ingenious writer, *Jean Jacques Rousseau*. Flying from a persecution which his exuberant imagination 'pictured, as thickening around him on the continent, he arrived in London in January, 1766: he first intended taking up His residence in Wales, but about the latter end of March, he settled in Derbyshire. "Here," says he, " I have arrived at last, at an agreeable and sequestered asylum, where I hope to breathe freely, and at peace."* The spot was, indeed, every way adapted to his melancholy and romantic mind, and suited to his genius, affording him scope for his favorite study, Botany.— From this abode, however, he issued in April, 1767, with his usual eccentricity, inflamed by an imaginary affront, and heaping reproaches on persons, to whom he stood most indebted, for their attention to his welfare and felicity, and returned to the continent. While Rousseau lived at Wooton-Hall, he planted a number of curious seeds in Dove-Dale, the scenery of which he much admired, and often visited.†

* Correspondance avec. M. Peyron Tom. II. Lettre, 45.

† To those who visit Dove-Dale (and who that has an opportunity will not do so?) it may be acceptable to know✗

FENNY BENTLEY, in Domesday called *Ben-edlege*, is a parish containing about thirty houses, and one hundred and forty inhabitants. The living is a rectory; the church is dedicated to St. Mary Magdalen; and the Dean of Lincoln is the patron.

that there are in its immediate vicinity several objects worthy their attention: but being on the western side of the Dove, they are situated in the county of Stafford, and therefore cannot be introduced into the body of this work.

After inspecting the Dale, and returning to its southern extremity, a small winding of the Dove to the right, will lead to the road leading to Islam, a small ancient village, one mile from the Dale; situated upon the united rivers, Manifold and Hamps, which join their streams in the pleasure grounds of Mr. Port. This gentleman's mansion is an old Hall, surrounded with pleasing walks, and commanding a very fine prospect.

Proceeding one hundred yards from the house, a little wooden bridge, is arrived at, thrown over an abyss in the rock, out of which boils up, with surprising force, the river Manifold, after having pursued a subterraneous course for five miles, from the point where it ingulphs itself in the earth, called Weston-Mill. At the distance of twenty yards further, a similar phænomenon occurs; for here there is another fissure in the rock, from whence the river Hamp throws its waters into day. This river disappears at Leek *Water Houses*, a place half-way between Leek and Ashbourn; thus pursuing a subterraneous course of seven miles, before it again emerges into light. On their emer-sion, the temperature of the two rivers differs two degrees and a half; the Hamps being thus much colder than the Manifold.

14 L 3

Towards the end of the fifteenth century,
Fenny Bentley was the residence of the *Beresfords*, of which the Marquis of Waterford, is
a junior branch. The family came originally
from Beresford in Staffordshire, and settled
here about the reign of Henry the Sixth; when,

Ascending from this place, a flight of stone-steps conducts to a higher walk, which pursues a zig-zag course,
through the wood that covers the face of the rock, and
overhangs the river just quitted. In this solemn abstrac-
ted scene, safe from the obtrusion of the busy crowd, and
secure from every discordant sound, lulled to peace by the
river that flowed beneath him, and the sacred whisper of
the wood which waved above his head, *Congreve*, when
scarcely nineteen, in a little grotto, (his favorite and accustomed retreat) wrote his comedy, called the " Old
Bachelor." This recess is built with gray stones, having a
stone-table in the middle, and an elegant drapery of ivy,
privet, young beech, and laurel branches, crown the roof,
and hang from above;—the whole is so romantic, that we
might expect to perceive, " inspiration breathe around."

In the church at Islam, are some ancient monuments of
the Cromwell family; but two of still greater antiquity
are found in the church-yard, which, from the Runic
knots, and other Scandinavian ornaments carved on their
faces, are supposed to be Danish, and attributed to the tenth
century.

At *Oakover* also, which is not far from Dove-Dale, there
are several of the best paintings of Raphael, Titian, Ru-
bens, Luca Giordano, Varelst, Vandervelt, &c. The
visitor is permitted to see one room only in this house; but
in this one the exquisite pictures by the above masters are
to be found.

a Thomas Beresford Esq. is said to have mustered a troop of horse in Chesterfield, consisting of his sons, and his, and their servants, for the service of the king in the French wars.—He lies buried in the chancel of the church, with a Latin, and an English inscription on his tomb; from which it appears that he died in 1473. The ancient Manor-House, of which the little that is left, retains somewhat of a castellated appearance, passed by an heir general, into the family of *Cotton*, of Beresford; but the male heir, of Thomas Beresford, still posseses some landed property here. Bentley church, contains several monuments to the memory of the Beresfords.

KIRK IRETON, anciently *Hiretune*, contains about one hundred and fifty houses, and above seven hundred inhabitants. The living is a rectory; the church is dedicated to the Holy Trinity; and the Dean of Lincoln is the patron.

HOGNASTON, in Domesday, *Ochnauestun*, is a village containing about fifty-five houses, whose inhabitants are chiefly supported by agriculture. The living is a rectory; but not in charge; the king is the patron.

Not far from the last-mentioned place, is KNIVETON, anciently *Cheniueton*, a pretty considerable hamlet, lying on the road to Ash-

barn. " Kniveton," says Camden, " hath given both name and seat to the famous family
of *Kniveton*, from whence the Knivetons of
Mercaston and *Bradley*, of whom is S. Louis
Kniveton, to whose study and diligence I am
much indebted." .

TISSINGTON, *Tizinctun*. The liberty contains
about forty-four houses ; and one hundred and
ninety-two inhabitants. The living is a curacy ;
and the church is dedicated to St. Mary. It
formerly belonged to the priory at Tutbury.

Near Tissington is, *Tissington-Hall*, the ancient seat of the Fitzherberts, who have resided
here, since the end of the fifteenth century.
The estate, in more remote times, belonged to
the *Savages*, and from them descended to the
Herthulls and *Meynells*. That portion of the
estate which belonged to the latter, came by
inheritance to the Fitzherberts, (who came originally from Norbury) through the families of
Clinton and *Fraunceys*, about the commencement of the fifteenth century. The part that was
in possession of the Herthulls, descended from
them to the Cokaines of Ashbourn, who sold
it to the Fitzherberts, in the reign of James
the First. William Fitzherbert, Esq.. of this
place, who died in 1772, left two surviving sons,
William and Alleyne. William, who was Re-

corder of Derby in 1783, was raised in the same
year to the dignity of a Baronet, and died in
1791. He left several children, the eldest of
whom, Sir Henry Fitzherbert, Bart. is now possessor of the estate and title.

Alleyne, the brother of Sir William, has attained some degree of political eminence. He
has been minister at Brussels, Petersburgh, and
Madrid; secretary to the Marquis of Buckingham, when Lord Lieutenant of Ireland; and
in 1782 negociated the peace of which prelimi-
naries were signed at Paris, in the January of
the following year. He was raised to an Irish
Peerage in 1791; and to a Peerage of Great
Britain and Ireland in 1801, by the title of
Baron of St. Helen's.

BRADBOURN; at the time of the Norman survey there were at " *Bradeburne,* a priest and a
church. and twelve acres of meadow." The
village of Bradbourn, is pleasantly situated on
a hill, and contains about thirty houses. The
living is a vicarage, and the church is dedicated to All-saints: the Duke of Devonshire is
the patron. It formerly belonged to the priory
of Dunstable, in Bedfordshire.

The parish of Bradbourn, includes the chapelries of Atlow, *(Etelauue),* Ballington, Brassington, *(Brazinctune),* and the township of

Aldwark; containing, altogether, about two hundred houses, and eight hundred inhabitants.

Near the road leading from Brassington to Pike-Hall, an ancient monument, called *Mininglow*, has been noticed. It is situated in the centre of a plantation, and is a low barrow, supposed to have been an ancient burial-place. The higher part of the mount seems to have been removed, as several of the vaults were exposed to view. The diameter of the barrow is about forty yards, and the vaults appear to have been carried around the whole circumference. The stones with which they are formed, are very large; and one of the vaults, was from six to seven feet long, three wide, and six deep: it consists of five stones, one on each side and end, and the other for the cover.

CARSINGTON, *Chersingtune*, is a parish containing about forty-six houses, whose inhabitants are chiefly supported by agriculture and the mines. The living is a rectory; the church is dedicated to St. Margaret; and the Dean of Lincoln is the patron.

WIRKSWORTH.

WIRKSWORTH is thought to be a town of great antiquity; but its existence cannot be traced back beyond the Conquest. At the Norman survey (1083) there were in " *Werchefuorde*, a priest and a church, and sixteen villanes, and nine borders, having four ploughs. There are three lead mines there, and twenty-six acres of meadow."* At this time, the manor was included in, the Wapentake of *Hammenstan*, and the property of king William. In the reign of king John, it became the property of the Earl of Ferrers's family, at the same time as Ashbourn. It was afterwards annexed to the Earldom and Duchy of Lancaster, of which the Manor and Wapentake of Wirksworth are still members. The present lessee is, Richard Paul Joddrell, Esq. a gentleman well known in the literary world, as an elegant classical scholar.

The Dean of Lincoln has a manor within the town, in right of his church; and the *Gells* of Hopton, have another manor in the town and neighbourhood, called the Holland or Rich-

---

* Domesday, *Orig.* 272. *a.* 2. Trans. 291.

mond Manor, from its having belonged to the
Hollands, Lords Holland, and Dukes of Exeter;
and afterwards to the Countess of Richmond,
mother to Henry the Seventh. In the Holland
Manor-House, the manufacture of Porcelain
was attempted, about forty years ago, but proving unsuccessful, it was relinquished.

Wirksworth lies in a low valley, almost surrounded by hills: generally enveloped in the
smoke, issuing from the neighbouring lead and
calamine-works. Here the features of the country, begin to assume a bold and prominent appearance; cultivation becomes less general, and
the enclosures, instead of being encompassed by
hedges, are, chiefly, fenced with stone walls.

The church, which is dedicated to St. Mary,
is a handsome Gothic building, apparently of
the fourteenth century. It consists of a nave,
and side aisles, a North and South transept, a
chancel, and a square tower, supported on four
large pillars in the centre. On the northern
side, is the dormitory belonging to the Gells of
Hopton, in which are the tombs of Ralph Gell,
and his son Anthony, who, in the time of
Queen Elizabeth, was a Bencher of the Inner-
Temple, and Feodary of Derbyshire; there are
also tablets, to the memory of three Baronets
of the same family. The church contains, also,

monuments of the *Lowes*, and *Hurts*, of Alderwasley, and of the *Wigleys*, of Wigwell.—
On the tomb to the memory of *Antonye Lowe*,
Esq. who, from the inscription, appears to have
been employed by the sovereigns, Henry the
Seventh, Edward the Sixth, and Queen Mary,
is placed a recumbent figure of the deceased,
having round the neck, a representation of a
chain of gold, and a medallion of Queen Mary,
now in the possession of Francis Hurt, Esq. of
Alderwasley, his lineal successor.

Near the church-yard, is a Grammar-school,
founded by Anthony Gell, Esq. of Hopton, in
the reign of Queen Elizabeth; to which, one
Agnes Fearne, was a very considerable contributor. The lands left for the maintenance of
this charity, produce a rental, equal to the support of a better establishment, than is at present kept up.

There is an Alms-house, established by the
same Anthony Gell, at Wirksworth, for six
poor men, and endowed with twenty pounds
per annum.

The Moot-Hall, is a respectable structure of
brick, erected in the year 1773: here all causes
respecting the lead mines within the Wapentake are tried; and here is also deposited, the

ancient brass dish,* which is the standard from which others are made, to measure the lead ore.

The weekly market at Wirksworth, which is held on Tuesday, was obtained in the year 1307, by Thomas, Earl of Lancaster, grandson of Henry III. The number of houses, within the township, is thought to be about 674, with a population of about 2979 inhabitants. The latter derive their chief support from the working of the lead mines; but between 200 and 300 hands are employed in the cotton-mill in the neighbourhood. The town contains some good houses, and is the residence of a few genteel families.

Wirksworth, has scarcely any supply of common water, but has a strong medicinal water of the sulphureous kind. This spring is situated at a small distance from the town, near the road leading to Ashbourn. It contains both sulphur and iron, and is said to be also impregnated with a purging salt; but the quantity of each is very inconsiderable.

ALDERWASLEY, is a chapelry belonging to the parish of Wirksworth: the village contains about sixty houses; and the inhabitants are,

---

* For the curious inscription on this dish, see page 78.

chiefly, engaged in the pursuits of agriculture.
Not far from the church, on an eminence, is
the mansion of Francis Hurt, Esq.; it is pleasantly situated, and commands an extensive
prospect. The manor of *Alderwasley*, together
with *Ashley-Hay*, and part of *Crich-Chase*,
were granted by Henry the Eighth, to Anthony
Lowe, Esq. In the reign of Charles the First,
Alderwasley, was a seat of a descendant of the
above-mentioned gentleman, who by his fidelity and attachment to that unfortunate monarch, became a considerable sufferer, from
the civil wars, which then distracted the kingdom. Tradition says, that a party of the parliamentary soldiers from Hopton, paid this ancient house three different visits, and stripped
it of every thing that was valuable.

HOPTON, in Domesday, *Opetune*, is another
small hamlet in the parish of Wirksworth; consisting, but of a small number of houses. This
hamlet is planted in the bottom of a deep valley, embowered in wood, and guarded by lofty
gray rocks, under whose projecting heads, the
cottagers have built their little crouching dwellings.

Here is the seat of Philip Gell, Esq. the
present Member in Parliament for Malmes-
bury. The family of Gell, has been resident

here since the time of Queen Elizabeth. In the
seventh year of her reign, died R. Gell, Esq.
who was succeeded by his son Anthony. John
Gell, who was Sheriff of Derbyshire in the
year 1634, and in 1643 created a Baronet by
Charles the First, was a very active partizan, in
the cause of Parliament, during the civil war,
and performed several spirited actions in its
service. When the royal standard was erected
at Nottingham, he marched into the town of
Derby, and placed a garrison in it. The year
following, he took Wingfield Manor by assault,
and was attended with such success, that at
length, no part of the county of Derby, had
the courage to declare in favor of the king. It
appears, however, that his conduct was not always satisfactory; for having been appointed
receiver of the money, arising from the seques-
tration of the effects of those persons, who were
suspected of being friendly to the king, an order was issued, to enforce the payment of six
thousand pounds. He was tried in 1650, for
misprison of high treason, and sentenced to
forfeit his estate, and to be imprisoned for life;
but within two years he received a pardon.

The ancient Manor-House, occupied in former times, by the Gells, was, a few years ago,
pulled down, and a neat modern building erect-

ed on its site. The grounds also have been
very much improved; and a new road, distinguished by the name *Via Gellia* from its maker,
has been carried towards Matlock through a
romantic valley, which affords several beautiful
views. High and steep hills, covered with
young firs, like a nursery, and, sweeping in
bold bases, guard it on all sides. Down the
hills, numerous narrow falls devolve, and at
their feet, all the way along the road side, frequently gray seats appear, covered with turf.
The little river in the valley, is formed by art,
for the purpose of angling, into several large
basins. Falling from these, over walls of gray
stones, having appertures formed for the discharge, it forms many pleasing cascades. Cottages among the wood, and mills at the verge,
add to the picturesqueness of this charming
road, whose projector, and executor, deserves
unusual praise for his public spirit* in bringing
a new road, through such delightful scenery.

* It is to be deplored, that this spirit is not more prevalent among the Gentlemen, and Proprietors of Land in Derbyshire; as it certainly does them no credit, that the roads
in their native county, a county if equalled, not surpassed
in beautiful scenery by any other, should be carried over
precipitous and barren hills, while they might have been
directed through the most charming vales, and thus be rendered capable of affording both facility and delight to the
traveller.

In making this road, an iron dagger, and some iron heads of spears, were found, covered to the depth of three feet beneath the surface by small stones. About one mile South from the valley, on a rising ground, is a large barrow, 196 feet in circumference, in which an urn of coarse baked earth, full of bones and ashes, was discovered by some labourers, who were preparing the ground for a plantation.— The urn fell to pieces, on endeavouring to take it up; its circumference was four feet, three inches. It was covered with a piece of yellowish free-stone, much corroded, on which the following lines, forming part of a Roman inscription, were legible:

. . . .

GELL

PRÆ C. III

L. V. BRIT

which has been thought to signify: *Gellius Præfectus Cohortis Tertiæ Legionis Victrices* Britannicæ.* The finding a rough stone with a Roman inscription, covering an urn in a barrow,

---

* Others have read *Quintæ* here; but it does not appear that the fifth Legion, ever was in Britain, and therefore it is supposed to signify *Victrices*, " the title of the sixth Legion, which probably remained sometime in Derbyshire before they marched to the north."

is, perhaps, the only instance of the kind upon record.

MIDDLETON, *Middeltune*, is a hamlet, situated near the summit of a lofty hill, belonging to the parish of Wirksworth. It contains about sixty houses. The inhabitants are chiefly supported by the lead mines.—The inhabitants of Ibol *(Ibeholon)* and Grange, which contain about twenty-three houses, are supported in the same way.

CROMFORD, in Domesday called *Crunford*, is another hamlet in Wirksworth parish. It lies low, surrounded by the beauties of nature, and enlivened by the busy hum of human labour.

The Manor of Cromford was purchased of Peter Nightingale, Esq. by Sir Richard Arkwright, in the year 1789. Soon afterwards, the population of the place began to increase, owing to the extensive cotton mills erected here by the last-mentioned gentleman, the first of which had been built about twelve years before. At present about 1200 hands are employed at these two mills; "whose operations," to use the words of Mr. Warner, " are so elegantly described by Dr. Darwin, in a work which discovers the art, hitherto unknown, of cloathing in poetical language, and decorating

with beautiful imagery, the unpoetical operations of mechanical processes, and the dry de-
tail of manufactures :"—

" So now, where Derwent rolls his dusky floods,
Through vaulted mountains, and a night of woods,
The Nymph GOSSYPIA,* treads the velvet sod,
And warms with rosy smiles the watery God;
His ponderous oars to slender spindles turns,
And pours o'er mossy wheels his foamy urns;
With playful charms her hoary lover wins,
And wields his trident,—while the monarch spins.
—First with nice eye emerging Naiades cull
From leathery pods the vegetable wool;
With wiry teeth *revolving cards* release
The tangled knots, and smooth the ravell'd fleece;
Next moves the *iron hand* with fingers fine,
Combs the wide card, and forms the eternal line;
Slow, with soft lips, the *whirling can* acquires
The tender skeins, and warps in rising spires;
With quicken'd pace *successive rollers* move,
And these retain, and those extend the *rove;*
Then fly the spoles, the rapid axles glow,
And slowly circumvolves the labouring wheel
below."

Botanic Garden, Canto 11. line 85.

The building where this process is carried
on, has one hundred and twenty windows in
front, and is full of the improved machinery
for making cotton into thread, all of which is
moved by two master-wheels. Adjoining to
this, is a paper manufactory, employing about

---

* Gossipium : the Cotton Plant.

forty people, in making the brown, blue, and writing paper. Old ropes cut into small pieces, untwisted, and ground, form the material of which the first article is made; coarse cotton and white rags are used for the second and third. Here it is manufactured, pressed, separated, sized, dried, and packed; and the process is so rapidly performed, that two men can make ten reams a day.

According to the returns made in the year 1801, the number of inhabitants at Cromford, was 1115, and that of houses, 208; but the increase in both, has been considerable since that period. The village has a good Inn, and a few respectable shops, built around an open space, where a market is held every Saturday.

At a little distance from the village is the Chapel; a small, but very neat structure of a reddish hewn stone, began by Sir R. Arkwright, and completed since his decease by his son Richard Arkwright, Esq. It was opened for divine service, on the fourth of June 1797, and consecrated, on the twentieth of September the same year. It contains a handsome marble font, an organ, and two small galleries, at the West end, for the use of the children, that attend the Sunday Schools. On the left of the

road leading up Cromford towards Wirksworth,*
stands an Alms-house, or as it is generally called, a Bead-house, which was founded in the
year 1651, for six poor widows, by Dame Mary
Talbot, widow of Sir William Armyne, Bart.
and daughter and co-heir of Henry Talbot,

* "Near the road leading from Cromford to Wirksworth, is a mine called *Godbehere's Founder*,† in which the
following remarkable event occurred at the commencement
of the year 1797. Two miners, named Job Boden and
Anthony Pearson, went into the mine on the morning of
the thirteenth of January, and while they were at work,
Pearson at the depth of forty-four yards, and Boden at the
depth of twenty, the earth above them, together with a
quantity of water, suddenly rushed in, and filled the mine
to the depth of about fifty-four yards. The other miners
immediately began to draw out the rubbish in search of
their lost companions, and on the third day after, Pearson
was discovered, dead, in an upright posture. The miners
would have discontinued their exertions, as there seemed
little probability of their labors being of any avail; but
being encouraged to proceed, (chiefly by the influence and
persuasions of Charles Hurt, Esq. of Wirksworth) they
at length discovered Boden, about three o'clock in the morning of the twentieth; and though he had not received any
kind of nourishment during the eight days of his confinement, he was still living, but greatly emaciated. On being
taken out, and treated with proper care, he so far recovered, as to be able to return to his work, in the space of fourteen weeks.

"To render the particulars of this extraordinary escape
more intelligible, it should be observed, that the entrance
to the mine is by a perpendicular shaft, forty-four yards,

† This is generally pronounced Godber's Founder.

Esq. fourth son of George, Earl of Shrewsbury.
At *Scarthin-Nick*, a perforated rock near
Cromford, about 200 Roman copper coins were
found about ten years ago. They were chiefly
of the lower empire: and several of them were

deep, from the bottom of which extends a *gait*, or *drift*,
(a passage in an horizontal direction) eight yards in length,
at the end of which descends a second shaft, (or as the miners term it, a *turn*,) to the depth of sixteen yards. At
the bottom of this is another gait, about, twelve yards in
length, from the extremity of which another shaft extends
to the depth of nearly twenty-four yards. At the top of
every shaft a windlass was placed, for the purpose of drawing up whatever might be extracted from the mine; and
Pearson's employment was to draw up to the top of the second shaft the ore, &c. that was obtained by Boden at the
bottom.

" At the distance of twenty yards from the entrance to
the mine was a pool of water, which, though generally
containing but a small quantity, had, at the time of the
accident, been much increased through wet weather. The
ground between the mine and the pool, had been under-
mined in searching for lead ore; and it is supposed, that
the additional weight of water over the vacuity, had forced
down the earth, which filled the mine to the depth of ten
yards in the second shaft. As the earth that rushed in descended below, Pearson's station at the mouth of this shaft,
was closed, he was consequently jammed in there, and was
discovered dead, as already mentioned. The remarkable
circumstance, that the rubbish did not sink into the mine
so low as to reach Boden, but stopped in its descent a few
yards above him, may in some measure be accounted for,
by observing, that the part of the mine where the fall
ended, was somewhat straightened by the projection of a

in good preservation, and are now in the possession of Charles Hurt, Esq. junior, of Alderwasley.

The parish of Wirksworth, contains, besides
the before-mentioned chapelries, the hamlets of

large stone, an obstacle which Boden had ineffectually attempted to remove.

" It appears from a conversation lately held with the man
thus strangely preserved from death, that after contemplating his horrid situation awhile, during the first hours of his
imprisonment, he lay down and slept. On awaking, the
idea of perishing for want of food rushed upon his mind,
and he recollected that he had four pounds of candles with
him in the mine: with these, when pressed by hunger, he
endeavoured to appease his appetite; but after two or three
vain attempts to swallow such loathsome food, he desisted;
and the candles were found after his release: his thirst,
which he had no means of alleviating, was excessive.—
Feeling extremely cold, he tried to remove this inconve-
nience, by exercising himself in turning the windlass at
the further end of the drift; but having the misfortune to
let the handle fall into the shaft below, he was deprived of
this resource.

. " After the space of three or four days, as he imagines,
being almost in a state of distraction, he ascended, by means
of a rope that hung down. to that part of the mine where the
rubbish had stopped in its descent, and by laboring hard,
caused a large quantity of it to fall to the bottom of the
shaft. He was employed in this manner, when, at length
he heard the miners at work above him, and by the expedient of knocking with a stone, continued to apprise them
that he was still alive. Though it is evident from this circumstance, that he retained his senses, he can hardly be persuaded but that he was deprived of them, and fancies that

Caulow, Biggin, Halton, Hitheridge-Hay, and *Ashley-Hay*, consisting altogether of about eighty houses. In the middle of Biggin, there is a considerable sulphureous spring, of the same impregnation as that of Kedleston.

he was prompted to make the signals by some friendly voice, receiving from it an a-surance, that if he did so, he should be rescued from his dreadful prison.

" The signals he made were heard by the miners about eight hours before they reached him; and he describes himself as so much terrified by their noise, and by apprehensions that persons were coming to murder him, that he should certainly have destroyed himself, if he had not been closely confined by the earth which he had drawn down, and which so filled the lower part of the shaft, that he was almost prevented from moving. In the midst of the panic that agitated him, he swallowed a considerable quantity of earth, which was afterwards expelled by proper remedies. He complained most that his legs were benumbed and dead; but their natural heat being restored by friction, no bad consequence ensued. When the accident happened, he was forty nine years of age, and then weighed upwards of twelve stones; but imagines that he was reduced to half that weight by his confinement in the mine: yet, as he was not weighed, this account cannot be affirmed with certainty. The anniversary of his deliverance from his subterraneous prison, he regards as a day of thankfulness and jubilee; and surely few individuals have ever had more reason than this man, to express their gratitude to a protecting Providence."

Beauties of England, Vol. III. page 524.

MATLOCK.

The name, Matlock, includes, both the village of MATLOCK, and MATLOCK-BATH. The
former is as ancient as the Conquest, and is
chiefly situated on the eastern bank of the river
Derwent. When Domesday was compiled,
Matlock (then called *Mesluch*) was a hamlet of
the Manor of *Mesterforde,** which was part of
the demesnes of the crown. It afterwards became a part of the estates of William de Ferrers,
Earl of Derby, who had a charter of free Warren granted to him, for his demesne lands here.
On the attainder of his son Robert de Ferrers,
for espousing the cause of Simon de Montford,
Earl of Leicester, Matlock, which was then
become a Manor, reverted to the crown; and
was granted in the seventh of Edward the First,
to Edmund Earl of Lancaster, and continued a

---

* Although this place was the head of the Manor, in the
time of the Conqueror, it is not now known. There is a hill
near Matlock-Bath, called *Nestes*, which was formerly celebrated for having several rich lead mines upon it, from whence
it is supposed, there was a *ford* across the river Derwent,
which was at the foot of this hill; which ford, or the houses
of the miners which were built near it, probably gave the name
to the Manor of *Metesforde* or *Netesforde*.

part of the possessions of the earldom and
duchy of Lancaster, until the fourth of Charles
the First, when it was granted by that king, together with a great number of other manors
and estates, to Edward Ditchfield and others,
in trust, for the mayor and citizens of London;
and in the following year it was sold by Ditchfield, and the other trustees, to the copyholders
of the Manor of Matlock, and is now divided
into several small shares. According to the returns made under the late act, the parish contains 492 houses, and 2354 inhabitants.

The living is a rectory; and the church is
dedicated to St. Giles. The Dean of Lincoln
is the patron. It stands on the verge of a romantic rock, and is a small edifice, unornamented, and destitute of monumental records.
It contains a nave, side aisles, and a small chancel; the outside is embattled, having an ancient
tower with pinnacles.

On a hill above the church, called *Riber-
Hill*, are the remains of what has been supposed to have been a Druidical Altar. It is
called the *Hirst-stones*, and consists of four
rude masses of grit-stone, one of which, apparently the smallest, is placed on the others,
and is thought to weigh about two tons. In
the upper stone is a circular hole, six inches

deep, and nine in diameter, wherein about half
a century ago, stood a stone pillar.

MATLOCK-BATH, is nearly a mile to the
south west of this village; and in approaching
it from Cromford, a specimen is presented, of
the scenery by which the dale is distinguished.
The entrance, is through a rock, which has
been blasted for the purpose of opening a convenient passage:—and here a scene bursts at
once into view, impossible to be described;—
too extensive to be called picturesque, too diversified to be sublime, and too stupendous to
be beautiful; but, at the same time, blending
together all the constituent principles of these
different qualities. Through the middle of this
narrow plain the Derwent flows along, overhung by a profusion of luxuriant beech, and
other drooping trees: on the eastern side of the
river, stands the elegant mansion of Richard
Arkwright, Esq. backed by rising grounds,
whilst the huge mural banks of the Matlock
vale, stretch themselves on the West, the white
face of the rock which compose them, occasionally shewing itself through the wooded clothing of their sides and head; this magnificent
scenery is singularly contrasted by the vast manufactories and lodging-houses at the bottom
of the vale.

But to see this magic spot to the greatest advantage, it should be entered at its northern extremity, as its beauties then succeed each other in a proper gradation, and their grandeur and effect are rendered more impressive. The first object that attracts the attention, is the grand and stupendous rock, called the *High-Tor*, appearing like a vast abrupt wall of limestone, rising almost perpendicularly from the river, to the height of more than 850 feet. The lower part of this majestic feature is shaded by yew-trees, elms, limes, and underwood of various foliage; but the upper-part, for fifty or sixty yards, presents a rugged front, of one broad mass of perpendicular rock.—From the summit of the High-Tor, the vale is seen in all its glory; diversified by woods of various hues and species; the windings of the Derwent, the greyish coloured rocks, and whitened houses imbosomed amidst groves of trees, which sprouting from every crevice in the precipices, give variety and animation to a sense of wonderful beauty.

Directly opposite to the High-Tor, is *Masson-Hill*, a very high eminence, rising with a less steep ascent than the Tor. The summit of this mountain, is called the *Heights of Abra-*

ham, and overlooks the country to a vast extent, and furnishes a view of almost the whole
length of the valley. Being considerably elevated above every surrounding object, their
general size and appearance are greatly changed :. even the High-Tor is considerably diminished in grandeur and sublimity; but this effect is in part compensated, by the extent of
the prospect, and the variety of objects which
it includes. The height of this eminence is
about 750 feet: the path to its summit has
been carried in a winding, or zig-zag direction,
through a grove; and about half-way up is an
alcove, from which an extensive view of a great
part of Matlock-Dale may be seen through an
opening avenue.

On proceeding towards the Bath, the features
of the vale assume still more majesty; the left-
hand side forming itself into rocky crags, which
overhang the Derwent. The screen to the
right is formed by steep meadows, surmounted
by naked downs. In front is a mountainous
bank, at whose roots is the lodging-house called
the Temple, a few other residences, and what

---

* This name, it is supposed, was given it, from its si-
milarity to the Heights of Abraham near Quebec, rendered
so memorable by the enterprise of the gallant Wolfe, in
1759.

was the Hotel. Following the road the plat-
form before the latter house is arrived at, where
the Derwent loses its peaceful character, and
its foaming waters roar over the obstructing
masses of disjointed rock, with restless rapidity and considerable noise. A small cascade
is seen falling down the bank in front; and in
the rear, is a grand face of white rock, richly
netted with ivy, and decorated with shrubs.

Following the lower road, which leads to
the Old Bath, another house of public reception, a new and most pleasing point of view is
reached. Here the river recedes in a curve from
the road, forming a little meadow as a fore-
ground to the picture. This is firmly opposed
and backed, by a line of rock and wood, a mass
of trees rising to the right, and shutting out,
for a short time, all the other features of the
scenery; amongst which the stream is lost, while
its murmurs are still heard. A broader face of
white rock quickly discovers itself, and the
road ascending to Saxton's Bath, affords, not
only an indiscribable fine prospect of the track
that has been passed, but opens another in
front, still superior;—a reach of alternate rock
and wood, nearly half a mile in length, contrasted to the right by desert downs, scarred
with crags.

On crossing the river near the Old Bath, it may be observed, that the natural beauties of the place, have received some improvements from art. On landing, three walks are seen pointing through the wood, in different directions. Two of them, by various and frequent windings, along the side of the dale at last lead to the summit, which is attained with little difficulty, through the judicious mode observed in forming the slopes; though the acclivity is exceedingly steep. The other path, which is called the *Lover's Walk*, has been carried along the margin of the river, and has been cut through the wood, and is beautifully arched by the intermingled branches of the trees which enclose it.

Some have thought that Matlock, some years ago, was infinitely more deserving of admiration, than since the increase of its buildings, and its having become the resort of gay and fashionable visitors. Be that as it may, it still possesses a thousand charms, of which it is scarcely possible for pen or pencil to convey a just representation: and to use the words of Mr. Lipscomb, " Matlock must be allowed to possess superior advantages to the generality of watering places. It has gaiety without dissipation, activity without noise, and facility of

communication with other parts of the country
undisturbed by the bustle of a public road. It
is tranquil without dulness, elegant without
pomp, and splendid without extravagance. In
it the man of fashion may at all times find
amusement, the man of rank may meet with
society by which he will not be disgraced, and
the philosopher a source of infinite gratification; while they who travel in search of health,
will here find a silver clue that leads to her
abode."

Diversified beauty, is the prevailing characteristic of the country around Matlock; and
the valley in which Matlock-Bath is situated,
is enclosed, and completely shut in, by two
ranges of bold and romantic eminences, washed
by the Derwent. The village is but small, and
consists principally of the Old Bath, the New-
Bath, two Lodging-Houses, a Museum for the
Derbyshire spar, and a few shops and private
houses, all of them situated on the south-west
side of the river.

Although the scenery of Matlock be so beautiful, it was not until the discovery of its warm
springs, that it began to attract notice. Prior
to the year 1698, it was the residence of a few
miners only; but at that period, "the original
bath was built and paved by the Rev. Mr.

Fern, of Matlock, and Mr. Heyward, of Cromford; and put into the hands of George Wragg,
who to confirm his title took a lease from the
several Lords of the Manor, for ninety-nine
(some say 999) years, paying them a fine of
£150, and the yearly rent or acknowledgment
of six-pence each. He then built a few small
rooms adjoining to the bath, which were but a
poor accommodation for strangers. The lease
and property of Mr. Wragg were afterwards
purchased for about £1000, by Messrs. Smith
and Pennel of Nottingham, who erected two
large commodious buildings, with stables and
other conveniences; made a coach-road along
the river's side from Cromford, and improved
the horse-way from Matlock-Bridge. The
whole estate afterwards became the property of
Mr. Pennel by purchase; and on his death,
about 1733, descended to his daughter and her
husband;" and since that time has become the
property of several individuals.

The judicious means thus exerted to render
the accommodations attractive, and the increased celebrity of the waters, occasioned a great
influx of visitors; and a second spring having
been discovered, within the distance of about a
quarter of a mile, a new bath was formed, and
another lodging-house erected, for the recep-

tion of company. At a still later, period, a third spring was met with, three or four hundred yards eastward of that which was first noticed; but its temperature being some degrees lower than either of the other springs, it was not brought into use till a level had been made in the hill, and carried beyond the point where its waters had intermingled with those of a cold spring. Another bath and lodging-house were then erected. These buildings are respectively named, the Old Bath, the New Bath, and the Hotel. They are, like all the other buildings at Matlock, of stone, neatly finished; and the general cleanliness of the inns, lodging-houses, and inhabitants, cannot escape the notice of travellers. The number of persons that may, at the same time, be accommodated at these, is upwards of 400; and since the taste for contemplating beautiful scenery, has become so general, more than this number has been frequently entertained.

The warm springs at Matlock, issue from between fifteen and thirty yards above the level of the river: higher or lower, the springs are cold, differing in nothing from common water. The quality of these springs has been examined by several medical gentlemen, who have borne testimony of their beneficial effects. The late

Dr. Perciyal of Manchester, has observed that Matlock water is grateful to the palate, of an agreeable warmth. (68 degrees of Fahrenheit's thermometer) but exhibits no proof of a mineral spirit. He adds that it is impregnated with selenite, or earthly salts, and also thinks it probable that a small portion of sea-salt is contained in it. Dr. Pearson says, " It has been reported to contain, in a gallon of water, forty grains of sediment which is called nitre, alkaline earth, and sea-salt." He observes himself that " it is impregnated with rather more fixed air than Buxton water, and that a pint weighs eight grains heavier than distilled water." Mr. Pilkington concluded, " that it contains a small quantity of fossil alkali." Dr. Pennington of Cambridge, concurs with Dr. Elliott, in fixing the degree of its heat at 69 degrees; and found that alkalies made the water cloudy and milky; and that when a gallon was evaporated, thirty-seven or thirty-eight grains of sediment were deposited; of this, about twelve or thirteen were saline matter, composed of calcareous nitre, (vitriolated magnesia) and twenty-four or twenty-five grains of calcareous earth. Dr. Short examined the residuum, and discovered some particles in it, which were attracted by the loadstone.

Several theories have been advanced in order to account for the natural heat of the Matlock and Buxton waters; the most ingenious of which is proposed by Dr. Darwin, in his letter, inserted in Mr. Pilkington's History. He particularly notices the phænomenon which takes place at Matlock, in the production of a spunge-like calcareous stone in the course of the springs, which he considers as strongly corroborative of his theory, that the origin of these waters is, in " the steam raised from deep subterranean fires, and not from the decomposition of pyrites," as had been affirmed by Mr. Tissington. The Doctor refers to Whitehurst's Theory of the Earth, in proof that " the strata in this part of Derbyshire consist of beds of limestone and lava (toad-stone) which lie reciprocally on one another," and sums up the whole argument by stating the supposition, that " the steam rising from subterraneous fires is owing partly to water slowly subsiding upon those fires, and to limestone gradually calcined by them; from whence, (he supposes) it must happen, that this steam rising through the perpendicular clefts in the superincumbent rocks, must be replete with calcareous (carbonic acid) gas, and so the phlogisticated air. If," continues he, " this steam so impregnated be conden-

15   P 3

sed in limestone strata, the fixed air in this hot
steam will suppersaturate itself again with calcareous earth, which is what precisely happens
at Matlock, where the waters are-replete with
calcareous particles, as appears by the copious
deposition of tupha, or calcareous incrustation along the channels in which they flow."

To this theory it has been objected, that it
is difficult, to admit that a subterranean fire
can be maintained for a long series of years, so
as to keep up a regular and undiminished heat,
capable of producing the effect above described: and that whatever validity there may be
in such an argument, it will be quite as difficult to imagine, that a bed of pyrites should be
more inexhaustible than a body of enkindled
fire: and, besides, we have positive proof of the
existence of beds of pyrites of vast magnitude
and extent; while the idea of central, or subterranean fire, at least in the present instance,
is merely a vague conjecture, and cannot be
proved.

A new theory, has, therefore been advanced,
by Mr. Lipscomb of Birmingham, in his Description of Matlock. This gentleman commences by observing, " First, it is well known
from the experiments of Dr. Percival and
others, that a portion of saline matter is detec-

ted in these waters.—Secondly, It is well known
that the acid of sea-salt will dissolve lime in
considerable quantity:" from which he con-
jectures, that the water of these springs, being
previously impregnated with salt, becomes saturated with lime in its passage through the
strata before described, and is afterwards decomposed by the addition of pyrites dissolved
in the rain water, which percolates through the
supercumbent strata: for pyrites containing
sulphur, the heat which takes place during the
solution of the pyrites, will necessarily disengage a certain proportion of acid: and sulphuric acid will immediately unite with lime,
when held in solution by the weaker acids, and
when united with it, fall down in what is che-
mically denominated calcareous sulphate; and
heat is again generated during the process.*

---

* To support this hypothesis the following circumstances
are brought forward;—

" 1st. That there is present in the *Matlock* water a much
greater quantity of calcareous matter than common water
is known to be capable of holding in solution, without the
assistance of an acid.

" 2ndly. That muriate of iron, which would be necessarily formed by the marine acid uniting with the iron of
the pyrites, after the former had been disengaged from the
lime, by the sulphuric acid which had previously existed
in combination with the pyrites, is perfectly soluble in
water, but may be detected therein by the purple colour,

The diseases in which Matlock Waters are recommended, and in which their beneficial tendency has been chiefly experienced, are glandular affections, rheumatism, and its consequent debility; the first stages of consump-

which is communicated by the addition of the infusion of galls, as in Dr. *Pennington's* experiment.

"3dly. That on a chemical analysis of the calcareous encrustations deposited by the water, they have been found to contain a small portion of iron mixed with sulphate of lime: and Dr. *Short* detected the presence of iron also, in the residuum procured by evaporating the water, as before mentioned.

" In this manner all the phenomena observable at *Matlock* and in similar springs, may, I think, be reasonably accounted for, on principles well understood, and capable of the clearest demonstration; without resorting to mere hypothetical conjecture, which is both difficult to be comprehended, and incapable of proof.

" I must beg leave to add, that since the above remarks were committed to paper, a circumstance has been presented to my observation, which so strongly corroborates them, that it may be considered as little short of the demonstration resulting from a synthetical experiment.

" Having at the suggestion of my learned and ingenious friend Dr. *Bache*, been induced to investigate the effects of carbonic acid upon lime water;—by blowing through a small tube into a glass containing a portion of that liquid, carbonate of lime was speedily produced in considerable quantity:—we then dropped in a little sulphuric acid, which occasioned the precipitate to be re-dissolved with great facility: and the liquid thus restored to its original transparency was suffered to stand undisturbed for several days, at the end of which, the sides and edge of the glass were covered with a transparent crystallization exactly similar to the spar and stalactite found in the subterranean caverns near *Matlock*."

tion, scrofula, calculous complaints, diabetes, gout, cachexy, obstructions from biliary concretions, hœmoptoe, and those indispositions which are promoted and continued from relaxation of the muscular fibres.

The usual time of bathing 'and drinking the water, is, before breakfast, or between breakfast and dinner. A small quantity, is at first' taken, increasing it gradually as the stomach will bear. "The best and strongest recommendation of this excellent bath," says Mr. Lipscomb, " is the acknowledgment of the numerous patients, who, for more than seventy years, have annually resorted to it, have tasted largely of its efficacy, and returned convalescent to their families and friends, after hanging up the votive crutch, an impressive trophy of the victory which Matlock had obtained for them over disease.". The Matlock season commences about the latter end of April, and continues' till November. But even in Winter, Matlock is not devoid of charms: when its hills are clothed in snow, and the drooping woods covered with rime and spangled ice, the scene is beautiful beyond expression; and will furnish ample materials for contemplation, to the mind who loves to admire,

"Nature, great parent, whose unceasing hand
Rolls round the seasons of the changeful year."

The western bank of the Derwent, for the whole distance between the turnpike at Matlock and the old Bath, is one vast bed of tuphus, or petrified moss, as it is vulgarly called, a strata of calcareous incrustation, about twenty feet in thickness. It seems to have had its formation from water which had passed through limestone, and thus become replete with earth; and had then formed itself upon a morass, or collection of moss, shrubs, and small trees, which having incrusted, the vegetable matter gradually decomposed, and left nothing but the stony evelopement. The *Petrifying Spring*, near the New Bath, has afforded innumerable specimens of these kind of transmutations of vegetable, animal, and testaceous substances, which have been exposed to its influence. The collection exhibited by the person, who shews the spring, contains several extraordinary specimens of its petrifying powers.

On the side of a hill to the west and northwest of the village, are three appertures in the rock, which are respectively named, the *Cumberland*, the *Smedley*, and the *Rutland Caverns*. The Cumberland Cavern,* formerly communi-

---

* The following description of *Cumberland Cavern*, was written by my respected friend the Rev. J. Evans, A. M.

cated with the entrance of a lead-mine: the
other, named Smedley Cavern from its proprietor, was first discovered by searching for lead-
ore. The entrance is near the top of the hill,

_____

of Islington, on his return to the inn after he had visited
it; and which he calls "a sketch warm from the heart."

"Cumberland Cavern is situated on the brow of a steep
hill, and its mouth is closed with a white-washed wooden
door, which being opened, the man took his taper out of
his lanthern, with which he lighted three candles to guide
our steps through the bowels of the earth! Whilst this
ceremony was performing we stood at the entrance, and
surveyed with pleasure the scenery which surrounded us.
We were taking, as it were, a farewell of the light of day,
when our leader informed us that the lights were ready, and
having taken them into our hands, we followed him in slow
procession. The first thirty yards of the way were partly
artificial, he having himself piled up stones at each side,
that the entrance into the cavern might be gained with facility. We now descended into this abode by steps, fifty-
four in number, which seemed as if we were going down
towards the centre of the earth! At the bottom of this descent the cave opened upon us in solitary grandeur. The
profoundest silence reigned in every corner of the recess.
Huge masses of stone were piled on each other with a tremendous kind of carelessness, evidently produced by some
violent concussion, though at a period unknown to any
human creature. From this place we ascended, as it were,
the side of a steep hill, and at the top came to a long regular passage of some extent. The roof had all the regularity of a finished ceiling, and was bespangled by spars of
every description. From above, from below, and from
the respective sides, the rays of our candle were reflected
in a thousand different directions. Our path had so brilliant a complexion, that my eyes were for some time fixed

and keeps tolerably level for about twenty
yards, when the way begins to descend, and
then winds irregularly to the right and left,
and sometimes ascending and descending, you

upon it, though I trust not with the same temper of mind
with which Milton has made one of the fallen angels contemplate the pavement of heaven:—

> " Mammon, the least erected spirit, that fell
> From heav'n, for e'en in heav'n his looks and thoughts
> Were always downward bent, admiring more
> The riches of heaven's pavement, trodden gold,
> Than aught divine or holy, else enjoy'd
> In the vision beatific ?

"When I withdrew my attention from this enchanting
object, I was shewn little cavities on every hand, which
contained spars in their innumerable forms of crystallization. The wantonness of nature in these her operations is
wonderful, and oftentimes exceeds our conceptions. The
part of the cavern that is ornamented by the brilliancy of
the spars and ores, we were assured delighted the ladies,
who, notwithstanding their characteristic timidity, have
ventured into this dark abode for the gratification of their
curiosity! Proceeding onwards a few yards we came to
large flat stones, which lay on one another, not altogether
unlike flitches of bacon. How they came there, and for
what reason they could be thus laid together baffled our
comprehension. In the next compartment we observed
rocks heaped on rocks, in terrible array, and on descending from this part, these rocks assume a threatening aspect,
seeming as if they would *slide down* and crush you to atoms!
Another scene surprises you, and is peculiarly gratifying
to the senses. An apartment is decorated with what is here
called the *snow fossil.* This species of stone is, both from
its figure and colour, a resemblance of snow. Its fairness
and delicacy cannot fail to please. One portion of this was

proceed forward, each person having a candle
in his hand, through this dark and surprising
work of nature, where art has only smoothed
out the roughness beneath, and hewn out steps
in the alabaster spar or jet rock; here and there
is also a rude branch to lean on or hold by, in
descending the most rapid declivities, that the
penetration into this abode of silence and wonder might be effected with proper security.—
The visitor is lead for several hundred yards,
through a number of vaults, or hollows, the
largest of which is about fifty feet long, twen-

_____

so stained by this fossil, that it possessed peculiar charms.
It had just the appearance of a cavity, into which the snow
had been drifted by the winter storm! This apparent imitation of nature is certainly a beautiful curiosity. Near the
extremity of the cavern was shewn a part of it, which
might, on account of its internal appearance, be denominated the *piscatory hall!* Here are seen, fishes petrified and
fixed in the several strata, which form the surrounding recess. What kind of fish they were could not be ascertained,' but they were clearly discernible. One of the fishes
had its back *jutting out* of the side of the earth, as if petrified in the act of swimming! What an indisputable proof
that the earth was once in a state of fluidity! We might
have seen another branch of the cavern, where was to be
found a well of considerable depth; but waving any further re-search, we returned the way we came. After many
an ascent and descent, together with *numerous* meanderings,
we reached the entrance, and hailed the cheerful light of
day with renovated satisfaction!"

16 Q 3

ty wide, and twenty-two in height. The bottom consists of immense masses of rock broken,
stupendous and grotesque in their shape, lying
in all directions, and forming a rugged ceiling
for another vault below, into which is a descent by a flight of natural rude steps. A candle, judiciously placed at a distance, gives to
the snow fossils that line some of these vaults,
the appearance of immense mountains of snow,
piled one upon another, and gives to the whole
an effect truly grand and sublime. The proprietor, cleared away with his own hands, by an
Herculean toil of seventeen years, all the obstructions, and numerous projections of rock,
which impeded the passage, and thus rendered
the way through it safe and easy.

Pursuing Matlock Dale in a southerly direction, WILLERSLEY-CASTLE, the spacious and
elegant mansion of Richard Arkwright, Esq.
presents itself to the view; together with the
numerous dwellings of the persons he employs.
This is indeed a different scene from the calm
and sequestered environs of Matlock; but it is
by no means an unpleasing one; for industry
and neatness are combined to give an air of
comfort and animation to the whole surrounding district: and cold and unfeeling must be
the heart which does not experience gratifica-

tion at the sight of happy human faces, or
know a sentiment of delight at hearing the
sounds of merriment and cheerfulness amongst
the poorest of their fellow mortals.

Willersley-Castle, is beautifully situated on
a verdant knoll; and though the native beauties of the place, may in part eclipse the pride
of art, yet this structure cannot less than command admiration. At the back, or to the North
of the house, is a commanding eminence, which
runs from East to West, and terminates the
extensive range of rocks, that forms the eastern
boundary of the Derwent in its course through
the dale. Round the foot of the hill, the river
flows in a grand sweep for some distance to the
East, but afterwards resumes its former direction to the South, and pursues its course through
a more open country. In front of the castle,
on the western side of the Derwent, rises a
lofty perpendicular rock, through which is the
passage before mentioned into the dale. From
this spot the view of the building is highly impressive; its castellated appearance, judicious
proportions, exact symmetry, and beautiful surrounding scenery, form, altogether, a most
pleasing prospect.

" The Castle consists of a body, in the form
of an oblong square, having a circular tower

rising from the centre of the roof, and a semi-
circular tower projecting from the front on each
side of the entrance, and two wings, with a
round tower at each angle: the whole structure
is embattled; and the walls are of white free-
stone. The spot on which it stands, was originally occupied by a large rock, in the removal of which about three thousand pounds
were expended by the late Sir Richard Arkwright, who purchased the estate of the late
Thomas Hallett Hodges, in the year 1782. The
Architect was Mr. William Thomas, of London. This edifice was covered in 1788; but
before it was inhabited, it was set on fire by a
stove that was over-heated, and all that was
combustible in it consumed: this accident occurred on the eight of August, in the year
1791.

"The interior of this mansion is furnished
with great taste and neatness: indeed it cannot
be more graphically characterized than in the
expressive words of the Poets, *simplex mundi-
tiis;* the general arrangement being more for
use than ornament. It contains several excellent family portraits by Wright of Derby, particularly a whole-length of Sir Richard Arkwright; and also some smaller pieces by the
same ingenious artist, as well as the sublime

view of *Ulls-water-Lake*, already noticed as one
of his best performances, and which is, perhaps,
equal to the greatest efforts of art in landscape
painting that this country has ever produced.
This was purchased by Mr. Arkwright for 300
guineas.

"The grounds of Willersley possess great
variety and beauty. Between the Castle and
the Derwent is a verdant lawn, which slopes
somewhat precipitously from the house, but afterwards inclines more gently to the river. The
east-end of the lawn extends to Cromford Bridge
which stands about a quarter of a mile from the
Castle, near the entrance to the grounds, which
open by a small, but very neat lodge. The
summit of Cromford rock, which has been noticed as rising directly in front of Willersley,
is beautifully fringed with trees and underwood; and though towering to a considerable
height, it does not terminate the prospect from
the castle, which being elevated in situation
almost as much as the top of the rock, commands a view of the hill that rises beyond it,
to a great height above the village of Cromford.
Near the summit of the latter eminence, are
several rude masses of grit-stone, which are
piled on each other in a very singular manner.
The adjacent parts being formerly moorish,

and having a naked, uncheerful appearance, have been planted with a great number of trees; which, when arrived at maturity, will greatly improve this portion of the scenery. Towards the west, the prospect includes the river, an eminence beautified with trees and copses, and a sharp indented ridge of rocks; with here and there a cottage perched on the summit of a cliff, half hidden in a deep recess, or emerging from a thicket.

" The hill behind the Castle, rises to a considerable height, and is covered with wood to its summit, as is also that portion of it which extends eastwardly. The coach-house, stables, bath, &c. which stand near the mansion on this side, though in a somewhat more elevated situation, are almost concealed by the trees. In the midst of the wood are several romantic rocks, round which, and on the acclivity of the hill, the principal walk winds in a circuit of almost a mile. The walk leading from the castle on the west, gradually turns to the north, taking a direction parallel to the course of the river, and passes under some perpendicular rocks, though yet elevated to a great height above the stream. The rocks are in some parts bare of vegetation, but are occasionally fringed to their tops with trees, particularly the yew

and ash, the roots of which insinuate themselves into the clefts and fissures in a singular
manner. Advancing up the walk, towards
the point called the *Wild Cat Tor*, the eye is
delighted by one of the finest scenes that nature ever produced. It consists of the long
rampart of rocks opposite Matlock; the wood
that clothes the declivity from their bases to
the river; and the tall trees on the opposite
side, that stretch their branches down to the
water, which appears dark, gloomy, and almost motionless, till it reaches a weir, down
which it rushes in an impetuous torrent, almost
immediately under the feet of the spectator,
by whom it cannot be contemplated without
some degree of terror as well as admiration.—
The Baths, the Heights of Abraham, the body
of Masson-Hill, and the summit of the High-
Tor, are also seen from this part of the grounds;
through which various other walks extend in
different directions, and lead to a diversity of
scenery, that can hardly be paralleled within
a similar extent in any part of the country.—
The green-house, gardens, and hot-houses, are
all worthy of notice: the latter are plentifully
stocked with ananas, and a great variety of excellent vines. The walks were laid out under

the direction of Mr. Webb, and are kept with the greatest neatness."*

The late proprietor of this elegant seat, SIR RICHARD ARKWRIGHT, Knt. was one of those great characters, which nature seems to have destined, by the endowment of superior powers, to be the benefactor of their fellow-creatures. Born of parents, who were classed among the inferior rank of society, and brought up to one of the most humble occupations in life, he yet, by the aid of genius and perseverance, rose to affluence and honor. Richard Arkwright, who was the youngest of thirteen children, was born at Preston in Lancashire, sometime in the year 1732. In that neighbourhood, there was a considerable manufactory of linen goods, and of linen and cotton mixed, carried on; and his acquaintance with the operations he witnessed there, seems, in early life, to have directed his thoughts to the improvement of the mode of spinning. This however he did not accomplish till many years had elapsed; for prior to the year 1767, he followed his trade, which was that of a barber; but at that period, he quitted his original business and situation at Wirksworth, and went about the country buy-

* Beauties of England and Wales.

ing hair. Coming to Warrington, he projected a mechanical contrivance, for a kind of perpetual motion. A clock-maker of that town,
of the name of John Kay, dissuaded him from
it, and suggested that much money might be
gained by an engine for spinning cotton, which
Kay promised to describe. Kay and Arkwright
then applied to Peter Atherton, Esq. of Liverpool, for assistance in the construction of such
an engine, who, discouraged by the mean appearance of the latter, declined; though he
soon afterwards agreed to lend Kay, a smith
and watch-tool maker to prepare the heavier
part of the engine, whilst Kay himself undertook to make the clock-maker's part of it, and
to instruct the workmen. In this way Arkwright's first engine, for which he afterwards
took a patent, was made.

· Mr. Arkwright experienced many difficulties
before he could bring his machine into use:
and even, after its completion had sufficiently
demonstrated its value, its success would have
been for ever retarded, if his genius and application had been less ardent. His circumstances were by far too unfavorable, to enable him,
to commence business on his own account, and
few were willing to risk the loss of capital on a
new establishment. Having at length, how-

ever, the good fortune to secure the co-opera-
tion of Mr. Smalley of Preston, he obtained
his first patent for spinning cotton by means of
rollers : but their property failing, they went
to Nottingham, and there by the assistance of
wealthy individuals, erected a considerable
cotton-mill turned by horses; but this mode of
procedure being found too expensive, another
mill, on a larger scale, was erected at Cromford, the machinery of which was put in motion by water.

This patent-right was contested about the
year 1772, on the ground that he was not the
original inventor. He obtained a verdict, however, and enjoyed the patent without. further
interruption, to the end of the term for which
it was granted.

Soon after the erection of the mill at Cromford, Mr. Arkwright made many improvements
in the mode of preparing the cotton for spinning, and invented a variety of ingenious machines for effecting this purpose in the most
correct and expeditious manner; for all which
he obtained a patent in the year 1775. The
validity of this second patent, was tried in the
court of King's Bench, in 1781, and a verdict
was given against him on the ground of the in-
sufficiency of the specification; but in 1785,

the question was again tried in the court of Common. Pleas, when he obtained a verdict.— This verdict, however, raised up an association of the principal manufacturers, who instituted another cause by writ of *scire facias*, in the court of King's Bench, when Mr. Arkwright was cast, on the ground of his not being the original inventor. Conscious that this was not the case, he moved for a new trial, the rule, however, was refused, and on the 14th of November 1785, the court of King's Bench gave judgment to cancel the letters patent.

The improvements and inventions in cotton spinning, for which we are indebted to the genius of Sir Richard Arkwright, and which complete a series of machinery so various and complicated, are so admirably combined and so well adapted to produce the intended effect in its most perfect form, as to excite the admiration of every person capable of appreciating the difficulty of the undertaking. And that all this should have been accomplished by the single efforts of a man without education, without mechanical knowledge, or even mechanical experience, is most extraordinary, and affords a striking instance of the wonderful powers displayed by the human mind, when its powers are steadily directed to one object.

Yet this was not the only employment of

this eminent man; for at the same time that
he was inventing and improving the machinery,
he was also engaged in other undertakings,
which any person, judging from general experience, must have pronounced incompatible
with such pursuits. He was taking measures
to secure to himself a fair proportion of the
fruits of his industry and ingenuity; he was
extending the business on a large scale; he was
introducing into every department of the manufacture, a system of industry, order, and
cleanliness, till then unknown in any manufactory where great numbers were employed together, but which he so effectually accomplished,
that his example may be regarded as the origin
of almost all similar improvements.

When it is considered, that during this
entire period, he was afflicted with a grievous
disorder (a violent asthma) which was always
extremely oppressive, and threatened sometimes
to put an immediate termination to his existence, his great exertions must excite astonishment. For some time previous to his death,
he was rendered incapable of continuing his
usual pursuits, by a complication of diseases,
which at length deprived him of life, at Cromford on the third of August 1792, in the six-
tieth year of his age.

He was knighted by his present majesty, on

the 22nd of December, 1786, on occasion of presenting an address, as high sheriff of the county of Derby.

In the infancy of the invention Sir Richard Arkwright expressed ideas of its importance, which to persons less acquainted with its merits appeared ridiculous; but he lived long enough to see all his conceptions more than realised in the advantages derived from it, both to himself and to his country; and the state to which those manufactures dependant on it have been advanced since his death, makes all that had been previously effected appear comparatively trifling. The merits of Sir Richard Arkwright may be summed up by observing, " that the object in which he was engaged, is of the highest public value; that though his family were enriched, the benefits which have accrued to the nation, have been incalculably greater; and that upon the whole he is entitled to the respect and admiration of the world." The portrait of him by Wright, is esteemed a very characteristic and striking likeness. He is represented sitting in his study, with one hand resting on a table, whereon is placed a set of rollers for spinning cotton, in allusion to the most essential part of his ingenious machinery.*

* Vide DR. REES's Cyclopædia. Articles, ARKWRIGHT and COTTON.

BONSALL, in Domesday *Bunteshale*, is a rectory, of which the Dean of Lincoln is the patron: the church is dedicated to St. James.
It contains about two hundred and fifty houses.
Its inhabitants are employed in the mines, and
at the works at Cromford. Here is a Free-
school, built and endowed by Robert Ferne of
this place, ancestor of the Fernes of Snitterton.

PARWICH, written in Domesday, *Pevrewic*,*
is a chapelry belonging to the parish of Ashbourn. The church is dedicated to St. Peter.
At the time of the Norman survey, Parwich
was a royal manor, and passed in the same manner as Wirksworth, till the time of Charles the
First. In this manor, was included a subordi-
nate, yet more valuable one, which belonged
to the Fitzherberts of Norbury, and afterwards
to the Cokaines of Ashbourn, who sold it in
the time of James the First; in whose reign
it was purchased by the family of *Levigne*, a

---

* To this Manor there belonged then " three berewicks,
Elleshope, (Alsop) *Hanzedone*, (Hanson Grange) and *Eitun*,
(Eaton); and five manors, *Derelei*, (Darley) *Mestesforde*,
Werchefuorde, (Wirksworth) *Esseburne*, (Ashbourn) and
Peureuuic, (Parwick), which with their berewicks, paid
in king Edward's time thirty-two pounds, and six secta-
ries† and a half of honey, now forty pounds of pure sil-
ver."—Domesday, *Orig.* 272. *a.* 2.

† A sectary is four pounds.

descendant of which, Sir Richard Levigne, is the present possessor of the estate.

Half a mile to the North of this village, there are some faint vestiges of a Roman encampment or station. The spot is called *Lombard's Green*, and is a level piece of ground, on the summit of a very high eminence. It is of an oblong form, and occupies about half an acre of ground. It consists of about twelve divisions, made by walls, the foundations of which are in many places still visible. The size and shape of the remaining divisions are various, some being oblong, some semi-circular, and others square. The ground has been much disturbed by searching for lead ore; and it was by a miner, about forty years ago, the discovery was made, which led to suppose that it was occupied by the Romans. About the depth of two feet and a half, a military weapon, a considerable number of coins, and an urn of great thickness, in which the coins, had, most probably, been deposited, were found. The coins, consisted, principally, of Roman *Denarii*, in good preservation. They were altogether about eighty, and stamped in the Upper empire, and were some of them as high as the Trium-virate of *Octavius*, *Lepidus*, and *Marc Antony;* and others as low as the emperor *Aurelian*. Near this ancient station, on the summit of the hill, is a bank about two feet high, and three broad, which extends nearly two miles and a half, in a direction East and West: at the western extremity it enters the road leading from Ashbourn to Buxton. About four hundred yards below is a second narrow ridge of earth, which extends about half a mile to the West in a direction nearly parallel to the former. Whether these banks were formerly connected with the station, or only intended as boundaries, it seems impossible to ascertain.

ALSOP, anciently *Elleshope*, is another chapelry in the parish of Ashbourn. The church is dedicated to St. Michael; and the whole liberty contains about fourteen houses.

HARTINGTON, in Domesday called *Hortedune*, is a large parish, extending nearly twelve miles, along the western boundary of Derbyshire, and comprehending all that tract of land, which lies between the manors of Buxton and Thorpe. It is divided into, the Hartington town quarter, the Lower quarter, the Middle quarter, and the Upper quarter; altogether containing about three hundred and forty houses. The village itself contains about 370 inhabitants: the living is a vicarage, and the church is dedicated to St. Giles: it formerly belonged to De-

nus Minoress, in London, but the Duke of Devonshire is the present patron.

This Manor gives the title of Marquis to his grace the Duke of Devonshire, who is possessed of a large estate in land here, and indeed of almost all the surrounding country. In the village of Hartington, the entrance of which has some interesting rocky scenery, there was, in former times, a castle; and some remains of ancient works may be discovered in several places in the vicinity. The manor formerly belonged to the Ferrers' family, and afterwards to the Duchy of Lancaster. In Charles the First's time, it became the property of Villiers, Duke of Buckingham; but in the reign of king Charles the Second, it belonged to the Cavendishes, Earls and Dukes of Devonshire.

There are several traditions handed down, respecting battles which have been fought in this neighbourhood. It is said, that the Britons had a most bloody and obstinate conflict, with the Roman General Agricola, on Hartington-common; and that when it was finished, the blood ran down the hill into the town. It is also reported, that the Republicans and Royalists during the Civil Wars, had a severe engagement on a hill near the village. The for-

16   s 3

mer tale is not supported by any according circumstances; but the latter has been corroborated, by the finding many musket balls, which
had been washed down with the soil, from the
high grounds, after heavy rains.

"About a mile and a half to the south-east
of Hartington, is a high eminence, called *Wolf's-
Cote-Hill*, on the summit of which is a *Barrow*
or *Low*.* This ancient remain, is a large heap
of stones of various sizes. The smallest are
the most outward, and over them is a thin covering of moss and grass. It rises about three
yards above the common surface of the ground
around it, and is exactly circular. The circumference at the base, is nearly seventy yards:
at the top, the diameter is about ten yards; and
in the middle is a cavity one yard deep, and
three wide. This Low has been opened a small
way towards the centre; and in its inward con-

---

* BARROWS, or *Tumuli*, or *Lows*, or *Cairns*, are the
monuments, which the ancients used to raise over their illustrious dead. They consist of hillocks or mounds, raised
of earth, or stones, and are considered as the most ancient
sepulchral monuments in the world. The custom may be
traced to the remotest antiquity, and instances of it occur
in all quarters of the globe. Those that are found in Derbyshire, are generally supposed to have been raised by the
Britons, before the Roman invasion, over their deceased
heroes, and persons of distinguished characters.

struction appears greatly to resemble that, which will be described at Chelmorton, near Buxton."

In the Lower quarter division of Hartington, at a place called *Castle-Hills,* situated on the banks of the Dove, is a sharp ridge of rocks, supposed to have been reared by human labor, and rising to the height of six or eight yards in the shape of a sugar-loaf. Adjoining to this, there are some embankments, and several Lows of different shapes. Near a place called *Crowdicote,* are the foundations of a building, erroneously supposed to have been an Abbey. The ground about it has been searched for treasure, but none could be found.—In the Middle quarter of Hartington, there is a chapel, called *East-Sterndale.*

About three miles to the East of Hartington, is, NEWHAVEN, where the Duke of Devonshire has erected, a large, handsome, and commodious inn, where travellers may meet with excellent accommodation. The country around this place is very bleak, and was, formerly, an open and barren waste; but a bill of inclosure having been obtained some years ago, it begins to assume a less wild appearance, and several hundred acres are now in a state of cultivation. Many extensive and thriving plantations, which have been made, near the inn, will in a few years occasion a change in the appearance of this tract, and may cause similar improvements to be effected in the neighbourhood. There is an annual fair held here for the sale of horses, cattle, sheep, &c. which is generally attended by a great concourse of people. The spot of ground where the booths are erected, and pot-houses established for the entertainment of the company, is so broken and diversified, as to have the appearance of the site of an ancient encampment. At a little distance from this place, is a lead-mine, now not worked, wherein rich specimens of *wheat-stone*, or white ore of lead, have been frequently obtained.

About three miles to the West of Newhaven-house, the Dove rolls along: and though the scenery here is not quite so romantic as that of Dove-Dale, it yet partakes of a great deal of its character. The rocks are not so elevated, but the singular and rude forms into which they are broken, have a very striking effect; and the frequent changes in their appearance, are particularly interesting. One rock distin-guished by the name of the *Pike*, from its spi-ral form, and situation in the midst of the stream, has been noticed in the second part of the *Complete Angler*, by Charles Cotton, Esq.

who resided at BERESFORD-HALL, an ancient, but extremely pleasant mansion on the Staffordshire side of the river. The *Hall*, now looks old and ruinous; and the adjoining gardens and grounds exhibit a scene of neglect and desolation; but in Mr. Cotton's time they were kept in excellent order.

Below the house, the stream (famous for trout fishing) flows in a rapid current betwixt the craggs of steeps which form its boundaries, for some distance; when it looses itself under ground, " and after a mile's concealment, appears again with more glory and beauty than before, running through the most pleasant vallies, and fruitful meadows that this nation can justly boast of."*

Hither it was that the venerable *Isaac Walton*, the father of anglers, came from London, that during the summer months, he might with his friend Cotton, enjoy the sport of angling.— In return for these friendly visits, Mr Cotton built a small fishing-house, on a kind of peninsula on the banks of the Dove, the remains of which are still visible.† It was erected in the

* Complete Angler.
† Sir John Hawkins, in his edition of Walton's Complete Angler, gives two Views of this Fishing-House, and writes, that several years ago, he employed a person to visit

year 1674, and having been taken little care of
for several years past, it has fallen into decay.
Here, are, however, to be seen the cypher over
the door, containing the initials of the names
both of Cotton and Walton, interwoven in each
other, and the inscription above it, SACRUM
PISCATORIBUS (*sacred to fishermen*) half filled
with moss, and almost obliterated. It was in
this little deserted temple of friendship, that
the pleasing dialogue found in the *Complete
Angler*, respecting the formation of an artificial fly, took place.

In one of the rocks which hang over the river, is a small cavity, only to be approached by

it, and send him a description of it. From that account
the following paragraph is extracted; by which some idea
may be formed of its former condition :—

" It is of stone, and the room in the inside a cube of
about fifteen feet; it is also paved with black and white
marble. In the middle is a square black marble table, supported by two stone feet. The room is wainscotted with
curious mouldings that divide the pannels up to the ceiling; in the large pannels are represented in painting, some
of the most pleasant of the adjacent scenes, with persons
fishing; and in the smaller, the various sort of tackle and
implements used in angling. In the further corner on the
left is a fire-place, with a chimney ; and on the right a large
beaufet with folding doors, whereon are the portrait of
Mr. *Cotton* and boy servant, and *Walton* in the dress of the
times. Underneath is a cupboard, on the door of which
are the figures of a *Trout*, and also of a *Grayling* well pour-
trayed."

an intricate and hazardous path, in which Mr.
Cotton is said to have eluded the pursuits of
the officers of justice, after some offence of
which he had been guilty. The depth of it is
about fifteen yards; but even in this small
space are several windings, which render it
difficult of access, and · well adapted for the
purpose of concealment.

CHAP. X.

Deanery of Chesterfield.

SOUTH WINGFIELD or WINFIELD, called
in Domesday *Winefield*, and *Winnefelt*, is an
extensive parish, including a part of the manor
of Lea, and the whole manors of Ufton and
Okerthorpe; in the latter of which stands the
parish church, though it bears the name of
Wingfield church. The living is a vicarage, the
church, which formerly belonged to Derley
Abbey, is dedicated to All-Saints, and the
Duke of Devonshire is the patron. The whole
parish contains about eight hundred inhabitants, who are employed in the pursuits of
agriculture, working at the stocking-frame, and
at the cotton-mill. The number of houses is
about 170. The commons and waste grounds
of Wingfield, were enclosed under an act of
parliament, in the year 1786.

South Wingfield appears to have been the
seat of several distinguished persons, at different periods of time. Prior to the Norman

Survey, Roger of Poictou held it, but at that
period it was held by William Peverel, under
Earl Allan, who accompanied the Conqueror
into England, and commanded the rear of his
army at the battle of Hastings. About the
eight of Henry the Sixth, it came to the possession of Ralph, Lord Cromwell, who claimed
it as a cousin and heir at law of Margaret, wife
of Robert de Swyllington, Knt. to whom it
had descended through the families of *Heriz*
and *Bellers*, the former of whom had held it
for several generations from the time of com-
piling Domesday-book. The right of the Lord
Cromwell to Winfield, was contested by Henry
Pierpoint, Knt. the heir at law of John de Heriz, who died in the third year of Edward III.
but, on a compromise, was allotted to the former, and by him the reversion was sold to John
Talbot, second Earl of Shrewsbury. In this
family it continued till the decease of Gilbert,
the seventh Earl, in the year 1616, when it became the property of William, Lord Herbert,
Earl of Pembroke; Henry Grey, Earl of Kent;
and Thomas Howard, Earl of Arundel and Surry; who had married the three daughters, and
co-heirs of Earl Gilbert. The manor being divided between these noblemen, became still

16　　　T 3

further divided in succeeding years, and now belongs to several persons; but the greatest share is the property of Wingfield Halton, Esq. by whose ancestors it was purchased in the reign of Charles the Second. In the year 1666, Emanuel Halton, who was the first resident of that name, lived at Wingfield Manor; he was a good Mathematician, and some of his pieces are published in the appendix to Foster's Mathematical Miscellanies: in the Philosophical Transactions for 1676, is an account of an eclipse of the sun observed here by him: but the principal of his manuscripts were destroyed through carelessness.

The ancient Lords of this manor, had two extensive parks, on the border of one of which nearest Okerthorpe, are a moat and other vestiges of an ancient mansion, said by tradition, to be called *Bakewell-Hall.* These parks, which contained above 1000 acres of land, are now disparted into farms. The early mansion-house of the Lords of Wingfield, (unless it were at the place already mentioned, Bakewell-Hall) was near to the Peacock-Inn, on the turnpike road between Derby and Chesterfield: for the site of Ufton-Hall, *(Uftune)* which was unquestionably one of the houses of the Lords of Wingfield, is within a hundred yards of the inn;

which is believed to have been built on the site of the offices belonging to it, and is sometimes called *Ufton Barns*.

The Manor-house, the remains of which are still seen, and which even in its ruins, exhibits many specimens of its original magnificence, was (according to Camden) built by Ralph, Lord Cromwell, in the reign of Henry the Sixth. This stately and noble mansion, consists of two square courts; one of which to the North, has been built on all sides, and the South side of it forms the North side of the South court, which has also ranges of buildings on the East and West sides, and on part of the South : the latter court seems, principally, to have consisted of offices. The first entrance is under an arched gate-way, on the East side of the South court : from hence the communication with the inner court, is under an arched gate-way, in the middle of the North side of the South court. One half of this range of building seems, originally, to have been used as a hall, which received light through a beautiful octagon window, and through a range of Gothic windows to the South, now demolished, and a correspondent range to the North, altered into two ranges. This hall, measuring twenty-four yards, by twelve, is, like the other

parts of the building, completely dilapidated.
Beneath the hall is a vault of nearly the same
dimensions, curiously arched with stone, having
a double row of pillars running up the middle.
This part of the house, subsequent to the first
erection, was divided and subdivided into several apartments, which have suffered the same
fate, as the noble hall, whose magnificence their
erection destroyed. In the other part of this
range, are, the portal, and the remains of the
chapel, and of the great state apartment, lighted through another rich Gothic window. No
part of the building on the East side of the
court, except a low wall, now remains: and
of the range of buildings on the West side of
the North court, only the outer wall, and some
broken turrets survive.

This mansion was castellated and embattled;
at each corner stands a tower; but that at the
south-west rises higher than any of the rest, and
commands a very extensive prospect. Its situation, though the neighbourhood of Wingfield
has not those romantic features, by which Derbyshire landscapes are generally characterised,
is bold and majestic, with the advantage of
beautiful prospects in almost every direction.
The distant approach to it from the North, when
assisted by a sun nearly sunk in the horizon,

has a most affecting air of grandeur:—Here
imagination eagerly plunges into the facinating
scenes of antiquity, and the mental eye gazes
in rapture on the splendid and hospitable revels
of the days of chivalry: but a nearer approach
calls us back to contemplate the sad devasta-
tions of time:—we see walls which erst reared
their heads in proud defiance of the tempest,
spread in disorder and confusion:—and here,

> " . . . . the pilgrim oft',
> At dead of night, 'mid his oraisons, hears
> Agast the voice of Time, disparting towers."
> DYER's Ruins of Rome.

During the reign of queen Elizabeth, Wingfield was, at different times, made the place of
confinement of Mary queen of Scots, first under the Earl of Shrewsbury, and afterwards
under Sir Ralph Sadler.* Her suit of apartments, tradition informs us, was on the West
side of the North court: this, in the memory
of persons lately living, was the most beautiful
part of the building: it communicated with
the great tower; from whence, there is also a
tradition, she had an opportunity of seeing
the friends approach, with whom she held a secret correspondence. It is impossible to justify

---

* See his State Papers and Letters, lately published, by
Arthur Clifford, and Walter Scott, Esqrs.

Elizabeth's conduct towards the beautiful, though imprudent, Mary: and while we view the remains of her prison, the bosom that can feel, must recal the memory of a great and unfortunate Princess, indulged in her youth in the soft enjoyments of pleasure; but, owing to female jealousy, tasting in the succession of years, a succession of refinements on misery. The mind here yields, alternately, to the impressions of sorrow and indignation: and here the Englishman, in despite of his enthusiastic regard for his sovereign, cannot recal the memory of Elizabeth, amidst her parade of mercy and justice, without pronouncing it detestable.

Her imprisonment here probably commenced in 1569; in which year an attempt was made by Leonard Dacre, to liberate her from her confinement at Wingfield. On the 6th of December, 1584, the Earl of Shrewsbury obtained permission to resign his charge into the hands of Sir Ralph Sadler, after he had been her jailer for sixteen years; and in the execution of this revolting employment for so long a period, he had experienced a multiplicity of troubles and vexations. Elizabeth, though she had no reason to doubt his fidelity, yet her own malevolent jealousy, made her perpetually mistrust-

ful of every person who had the custody of
Mary, who was so much her superior in personal attractions. In Shrewsbury's wife, Elizabeth found a convenient instrument for gratifying her spleen against her rival, and for ob-
taining secret information respecting the beha-
viour of Shrewsbury towards his charge. The
Countess of Shrewsbury appears to have been
a narrow-minded, peevish, and suspicious woman; and hence we may suppose, that the
domestic feuds which the Earl had to encoun-
ter, while they aggravated the punishment of
Mary, constituted no small portion of his own
infelicity.

The length of the time which tradition says
Mary was confined at Wingfield, is nine years.
She was certainly in the custody of the Earl of
Shrewsbury from 1568 to 1584, when she was
removed* to Tutbury; but in that time she

* Sir Ralph Sadler's State Papers, Vol. II. In No.
XLIX. of this work, " we have several questions proposed
and answered relative to the custody and domestic establishment of the Queen of Scots. From these we learn that
there were in all 210 gentlemen, yeomen, officers, and soldiers employed in the custody of the queen at Wingfield, in
Nov. 1584. Sir Ralph Sadler says that 150 men would
suffice for a guard at Tutbury, and not less, as 15 or 16
must watch nightly. The domestic establishment of the
Queen of Scotland is said to have consisted of ' 5 gentilmen,
14 servitours, 3 cooks, 4 boyes, 3 gentilsmens men, 6 gen-

was at Buxton, Hardwicke, Chatsworth, and
other places as well as Wingfield; and if her
confinement here continued any thing near so
great a length of time as nine years, it must
have been with many intervals of absence.

The Manor-House is supposed to have first
suffered from an attack of the Royalists, in the
time of Charles the First, a party of whom,
under the command of William Cavendish,
Marquis of Newcastle, in the month of November 1643, took it by storm. But shortly

---

tilwomen, 2 wyves, 10 wenches and children.' The diet
of the queen of Scots on ' both fishe days and fleshe days,'
is said to have been ' about 16 dishes at both courses, dressed after there awne manner, sometymes more or lesse as the
provision servithe. The 2 secretaryes, master of her hous-
hold, the physician, and de Preau, have a messe of 7 or 8
dishes, and do dyne alwayes before the quene, and there
own servants have there reversion; and the rest of her folk
dyne with the reversion of her meat. Also her gentilwo-
men and the 2 wyves, and other mayds and children, being 16, have 2 messes of meate of 9 dishes at both courses
for the better sort, and 5 dishes for the meaner sort.'

"A queston is proposed respecting the price of provisions at the time, and it is answered,

' Wheat is about 20s. a quarter; malt about 16s. a quarter;
beef, a good oxe, 4l.; muttons, a score, 7l.; veal and other
meates reasonable good charge, about 8s.; hay about 13s. 4d.
a lode; otes, the quarter, 8s.; pease, the quarter, about 12s.'

" The queen and her train are said to consume about ten ton
of wine in a year. These particulars are of no great importance; but several of our readers, who will never see these
volumes, will regard them as matters of curiosity."

afterwards, Sir John Gell, of Hopton, having raised a regiment of horse for the service of Parliament, sent Major Sanders, one of his officers, with the horse, to attack the party who kept garrison at Wingfield, where they took prisoners, two Captains, and several other officers and soldiers of John Fitz Herbert, a Colonel on part of the king. The assault was begun on the East side with cannon, planted on Pentridge common,* and a half-moon battery raised for its defence in this quarter, was soon carried. But a breach being found impracticable, the ordnance were removed to a wood on the opposite side. From thence they played with terrible effect; and a considerable breach being soon opened, the besieged were compelled to an immediate surrender. " I saw," says Mr. Pilkington, " the breach by which the assailants entered, and several of the cannon-balls which were employed on this memorable occasion—one, which was lately found in the hills, weighs thirty-two pounds. Colonel Dalby, who was governor of the place, was killed by a deserter who knew him, as he was walking, disguised as a common soldier, in the sta-

---

* On this Common is a Roman encampment. It is nearly square, and consists of a double vallum.

ble. The hole through which he introduced
his musket is still to be seen near the porter's
lodge."

The papers of the neighbouring gentry, and
the traditions of the inhabitants about Wingfield, intimate it to have been the scene of
some other trifling skirmishes. A few years
after it had been taken possession of by the
Parliament, an order was issued, dated June
the twenty-third, 1646, for dismantling it.—
From this time for many years it was neglected;
and it had been fortunate for the admirers of
so venerable an edifice, had that negligence
been uniform from thence to the present time:
but a small part of it having been occupied by
the family of Halton, and a partition of the
estate taking place some years ago, under a de-
cree of the Court of Chancery, the mansion
was allotted to the late Mr. Halton, who began
to build a house at the foot of the hill, near to
the manor; and, since that time, some of the
most beautiful parts of the old building have
been pulled down for the sake of the materials,*

---

* See " History of the Manor and Manor-House of
South Winfield," by T. Blore, F. S. A.

ALFRETON.

ALFRETON, in Domesday called *Elstretune*, was at the compilation of that record included in the lands belonging to Roger de Busli; and the manor was held by one Ingram, at the annual rent of thirty shillings. Tradition says,[*] that this town was built by Alfred the Great; and that its name is derived from its founder: It is also said that he resided here, and even the spot is shewn on which the palace stood.

In former times, the town and liberty belonged to a family, that took its name from the place; one of whom, Robert, son of Ranulph, Lord of Alfreton, was the founder of Beauchief Abbey, and has erroneously been noticed as a participater in the murder of Thomas Becket, Archbishop of Canterbury. Mr. Camden says that " a few years after the building of the Monastery *de Bello Capite*, commonly *Beauchief*, (about the time of Henry III.) the estate of the Lords of *Alfreton*, for default of heirs male, went with two daughters to the family

---

* And so does Camden, p. 493.

of the *Cadurci* or *Chaworths*, and to the *La-
thams* in the county of Lancaster.* The share
of the latter, was sold to Chaworth, in whose
family and name the estate continued till the
time of Henry the Seventh, when it was conveyed, by the marriage of an heir general, to
John Ormond, Esq. whose heir general carried
it in marriage to the *Babingtons* of Dethick,
by whom it was sold to the *Zouches* of Codnor-
Castle. It was afterwards purchased by the
Morewoods, and in that family it continued from
the early part of the seventeenth century to the
death of the late possessor, who left it to his
widow, since married to the Rev. Mr. Case,
who afterwards assumed the name of More-
wood. The family seat stands in a high and
pleasant situation.

The living of Alfreton is a vicarage; and
the church, which is dedicated to St. Mary, is
an ancient rude structure, having an embattled
tower, with pinnacles. It is a market-town,
with a market on Friday. The number of
houses in the parish, is about 472, of which
about 200 are situated in the town, and contains
2400 inhabitants; they are chiefly employed
in weaving stockings, and in the neighbouring

* Britannica, p. 493.

collieries; and a few derive support from the manufacture of brown earthen-ware.

SWANWICK, is a small hamlet a little to the South of Alfreton. Here there is a Free-school for twenty-four poor children, who are instructed in reading and writing. This school was built in the year 1740, at the expence of Mrs. Elizabeth Turner, and by her endowed with £500. for the support of a master. At a place called *Greenhill-Lane*, at some distance from this place, an urn, containing about seven hundred Roman coins, was discovered some years ago, by a laboring man, who was repairing a fence.

PINXTON, is a parish containing about ninety houses, and four hundred and twenty-five inhabitants. The living is a rectory, and church is dedicated to St. Helen. There is a considerable porcelain manufactory at Pinxton, which finds employment for several hands.

SOUTH NORMANTON, is a small parish, including a village of the same name. The number of houses in the parish is, one hundred and twenty-one, and of inhabitants, five hundred and ninety; who are chiefly employed in the collieries, and the manufacture of stockings.

JEDEDIAH STRUTT, Esq. the ingenious inventor of the machine for making *ribbed stock-*

. About the year 1771, Mr. Strutt entered into partnership with the celebrated Sir Richard
Arkwright, who was then engaged in the improvement of his judicious machinery for cotton spinning. But though the most excellent
yarn, or twist, was produced by this ingenious
machinery, the prejudice which often opposes
new inventions, was so strong against it, that
the manufacturers could not be prevailed upon
to weave it into callicoes. Mr. Strutt, therefore, in conjunction with Mr. Samuel Need,
another partner, attempted the manufacture
of this article in the year 1773, and proved
successful; but, after a large quantity of callicoes had been made, it was discovered that
they were subject to double the duty (viz. six-
pence per yard) of cottons with linen warp,
and when printed, were prohibited. They had,
therefore, no other resource, but to ask relief
of the legislature, which after great expence,
and a strong opposition from the Lancashire
manufacturers, they at length obtained. In
the year 1775, Mr. Strutt began to erect the
cotton works at Belper, and afterwards at Millford, at each of which places he resided many years. These manufactures were carried on
for a number of years by Mr. Strutt himself,
and are continued to the present period, by the

Messrs. Strutts, his three sons. A little before his death, Mr. Strutt, feeling his health
declining, removed to Derby, where he died
surrounded by his family in the year 1797, and
lies buried with his brother, in the burying
ground of the Chapel which he erected at Belper. At *Thurlston-Grange*, the residence of
Samuel Fox, Esq. is a fine whole length portrait, by Wright, of this eminent mechanic,
whose daughter that gentleman married.

SHIRLAND, writen in Domesday *Sirelunt*, is
a parish, which includes part of the hamlets
of Stretton *(Streitun)* and Higham, and contains about one hundred and eighty houses.—
The living is a rectory, and the church is dedicated to St. Leonard.. There was a church
here, as early as Edward the Second's time : for
in the first year of his reign, Reginald de Grey,
was possessed of the manor, and advowson of
the church. This person was one of the Greys
de Wilton, who once resided at Shirland, which
was the seat of their barony, before they were
styled, de Wilton. The estate was sold to Talbot, Earl of Shrewsbury, about Edward the
Fourth's time ; and rather more than a century
after, was divided among the heirs general of
that family. In the church is a monument of

17   x 3

one of the Lords Grey, of the time of Edward
the Third, with many shields of arms.

Morton; at the compilation of Domesday
there were at *Mortune* a church and a priest.
The liberty of Morton is but of small extent,
containing about twenty-five houses. The living is a rectory, and the church is dedicated
to the Holy-Cross.

Brackenfield, is a hamlet belonging to this parish, containing about thirty houses: its chapel
is dedicated to the Holy Trinity.

Tibshelf, is by the Norman Surveyors written *Tibecel*. In the ninth of Edward the Second, there was a church at this place, the advowson of which, was appropriated to the
priory of Brewood. The present living is a
vicarage, and the church is dedicated to St.
John the Baptist. The number of inhabitants
in Tibshelf is about six hundred and eighty,
who are principally employed in a colliery, and
in the manufacture of stockings.

There is a chalybeate spring at Tibshelf;
but the impregnation is not very great. About
a century and a half ago, it was in great repute, and drank throughout the summer season: now, however, it is not much frequented.

Ashover, is thought to be a place of great

antiquity, as in Domesday* Essovie, had a
church and priest. The living is a rectory,
and the church is dedicated to All-Saints. In
this church, is a very ancient font, supposed
to be Saxon: the pedestal upon which it stands,
is of stone; the lower part is hexagonal, the
upper part circular, and surrounded with twenty figures, in devotional attitudes, embossed in
lead, which are cast in small compartments.
There are in the church, also, several monuments, coats of arms, and inscriptions, relating chiefly to the ancient family of the Babingtons, one of whom was knighted by Edward
the Third, at Morleux in Brittany, of which he
was appointed governor.

· The number of houses in the liberty of Ashover is about 321; the inhabitants are, chiefly,
employed in the mines, and the manufacture of
stockings.

On the declivity of a hill on Ashover common is a rocking-stone, called *Robin Hood's
Mark*, which measures about twenty-six feet
in circumference; and, from "its extraordinary
position, evidently appears not only to have
been the work of art, but to have been placed
with great ingenuity. About two hundred

* *Orig.* 277, *b.* 1, Trans. p. 318.

yards to the North of this, is a singularly shaped rock, called the *Turning Stone,* nine feet in height, and supposed to have been a rock idol."*

DETHICK, a small chapelry in this parish, was during a long period the seat of the Babington family. Anthony, who was a principal actor in the conspiracy formed against the life of Queen Elizabeth in 1586, resided here. This young gentleman possessed a plentiful fortune, had discovered an excellent capacity, and was accomplished in literature, beyond most of his years or. station. Being zealously devoted to the catholic religion, he had secretly made a journey to Paris some time before; and had fallen into intimacy with Thomas Morgan, a bigoted fugitive from England, and with the Bishop of Glasgow, the Queen of Scots' ambassador at the court of France. By continually extolling the amiable accomplishments of that Princess, they impelled the sanguine mind of young Babington to make some attempt in her service; and they employed every principle of ambition, gallantry, and religious zeal to give him a contempt of those dangers which attended any enterprize against the vigilant government of Elizabeth. They succeeded too

---

* Archæologia, Vol. XII. 43.

well: he came to England, bent upon the assassination of Elizabeth, and the deliverance of
the queen of Scots. In the prosecution of these
views, he employed himself in increasing the
number of his associates; and secretly drew into the conspiracy, many catholic gentlemen
discontented with the government. But their
desperate projects, did not long escape the vi-
gilance of Elizabeth's council, particularly
Walsingham, who procured the names of all
the conspirators, and obtained intelligence of
every motion they made: at last they became
aware that their designs were discovered, and
fled, covering themselves with different dis-
guises, and lay concealed in woods or barns;
but were soon discovered and thrown into prison. In their examinations, they contradicted
each other; and the leaders were obliged to
make a full confession of the truth. Fourteen
were condemned and executed in September
1586.* John Ballard, a priest of the English
Seminary at Rheims, the primary instigator of
this rebellion in England, suffered first; and
Babington undauntedly beheld his execution,
while the rest, turning away their faces, fell
upon their knees. He ingenuously confessed his

* State Trials, Vol. I. p. 135, Hume Vol. V. p. 284.

offence; and being taken down from the gallows, and about to be cut up, he cried aloud
several times, *parce me domine Jesu*—have
mercy upon me Lord Jesus.*

One of the houses at Dethick, which bears
the appearance of antiquity, is thought to be
made up of a part of the original seat of the
Babington family. But from this, it is impossible to ascertain the form or the size of the original building. Traces of walls, which are
now levelled, and of windows and doors which
have been blocked up, are visible 'in several
places. Some old arches are still entire, and a
little ornamental work, over what is now the
principal entrance, remains.

Lea, in Domesday *Lede*, is another small

---

* Queen Elizabeth and her ministers wished to persuade
the nation, that Babington and his associates, were instruments employed by the Queen of Scots, against her life
and the peace of her kingdoms. Mr. Pilkington, following Hume, and other historians, has believed this tale. But
the impartiality of succeeding ages, has rescued the memory
of the unhappy Mary from this foul calumny; and her
elegant historian, Robertson (see History of Scotland, Vol.
III. p. 37.) has proved that she was not privy to the conspiracy. Unfortunately, however, it answered the end of
her enemies: Mary was irregularly tried as an accomplice
in the conspiracy, most unjustly condemned, and beheaded
at Fotheringay Castle, in Northamptonshire, on the seventh of February, 1587, in the forty-fourth year of her
age, the last nineteen of which, she passed in captivity.

hamlet in the parish of Ashover. Here there
is a cotton mill, erected about two-and-twenty
years ago, by the late Peter Nightingale, Esq.;
it now belongs to ——— Shore, Esq. Near this
cotton mill is a cupola furnace for smelting
lead, belonging to Mr. Alsop. Above these, is
Lea-Hall, a large house, with a stone front,
formerly the residence of Mr. Nightingale: and
at a little distance from it, is a small Unitarian
meeting-house.

In the vale below, is *Lea-Wood*, the residence and manufactory of Thomas Saxon,
Esq. who employs about 120 hands at the hat-
factory adjoining the house. " The dwelling-
house stands by the side of the road from Cromford to Nottingham, and immediately behind it,
the workshops, warehouses, and some of the
dwellings of the workmen—all are constructed
of the stone of the country, and, together, form
a considerable cluster of buildings.

" Hills covered with wood, rise very near the
front and the back of the house, and at a greater distance, this is the case on *all sides*—it is
literally imbosomed amidst hills and hanging
woods. The multitude of trees is really wonderful, when one considers, that a very little
below the surface, the whole country seems to
be a stone quarry. From the garden, the aque-

duct, a handsome, well-arched bridge, which
carries the canal over the river, is seen to great
advantage. The canal and the Derwent run
for a considerable way side by side, and both
pass through a narrow valley, the sides of
which, are the wood-covered hills before mentioned.

" The villages of *Lea* and *Holloway* are scattered over a considerable extent of rising ground,
to the North and West; and from various parts
of them, command delightful and extensive
views into the vales below. Lead mines and
lime works are scattered over all the neighbourhood."*

At a little distance from Ashover, is *Overton
Hall*, a small but pleasant seat belonging to
Sir Joseph Banks, the intelligent President of
the Royal Society, whose continued exertions in
promoting the best interests of science and
philosophy, have rendered his name deservedly
illustrious. The ancestors of this Baronet, became possessed of this estate, by marriage with
the heiress of the Hodgkinson family.

NORTH WINGFIELD. When Domesday was
written, *Winnefelt* was included in the manor
of *Pinnesley* (Pillesley); and there were a

---

* Butcher's Excursion from Sidmouth to Chester, p. 233.

church and a priest belonging to it.* The
living is a rectory, and the church is dedicated
to St. Lawrence. In the liberty of North
Wingfield, are the hamlets of Williamthorpe,
(*Wilemesterp*), Pilsley, (*Pinneslei*), Stretton,
(*Streiton*), Ford, Hanly, (*Henlege*), Clay-cross,
Tupton, (*Tapetune*), Woodthorp, and Ainmoor,
containing, altogether, about 1335 inhabitants.

PLEASLEY, is a parish and hamlet containing
about ninety houses. As early as the time of
Edward the Second, there was a church at this
place: for in the tenth of that, reign, Roger
Willoughby, died possessed of the manor and
advowson of the church. The present living
is a rectory, and the church is dedicated to
St. Michael.

HAULT-HUCKNALL; this parish includes the
hamlets of Rowthorn, (*Rugetorn*), Stanesby,
(*Steinesbi*), Astwood, Arstaff, and Hardwick;
containing, altogether, about one hundred
houses.

The living is a vicarage, and in former times
belonged to the priory of Newstead, in Nottinghamshire: the Duke of Devonshire is the
patron.

---

* Domesday *Orig.* 276, *a.* 2, Trans. 315.

17 Y 3

In the chancel of this church are several monuments, among which there is a slab, with a
Latin inscription, in memory of the celebrated
Thomas Hobbes. This gentleman, whom the
bigotry and ignorance of his age set down as
an atheist, and another Machavel, was born at
Malmsbury in the year 1588, and educated at
Magdalen-Hall, Oxford. In 1608 he became
tutor to a son of the Duke of Devonshire; and
in 1643, was appointed mathematical tutor to
the Prince of Wales. He returned, however,
to the Devonshire family, under whose patronage he lived till the year 1679, when he died
at Hardwick, in the ninety-first year of his
age. He was well known at home and abroad
by his reputation for learning. The most famous of his works are, 1. his book *De Cive;* 2.
that on Human Nature; 3. one *De Corpore Po-
litico;* 4. his well known work called the *Levi-
athan;* 5. his translation of Thucydides, &c.

HARDWICK-HALL, a celebrated seat belonging to the Duke of Devonshire, is situated in
the parish of Hucknall. This stately mansion
is situated on a ridge of elevated ground, near
the eastern borders of the county. It stands in a
fine and extensive park, well wooded; and between the trees, the towers of the edifice emerge
with great majesty, their summits appearing

covered with the lightly shivering fragments of
battlements: these, however, are soon discovered to be carved open-work, in which the letters E. S. frequently occur under a coronet;
the initials and memorials of the vanity of Elizabeth, Countess of Shrewsbury, by whom this
edifice was built. The house is of stone, and has
a lofty tower at each corner: in the front is a
spacious quadrangular court, surrounded by a
high stone wall. This building, which affords a
specimen of English architecture in the 16th
century, was built by the Countess of Shrewsbury, daughter of John Hardwick, Esq. who
died in the nineteenth of Henry VIII. she had
been twice married before she became the wife
of the Earl of Shrewsbury—first to Robert
Barley, Esq. and, secondly to Sir William
Cavendish.* This house was erected after she
became Countess of Shrewsbury.

Hardwick-Hall, it is generally supposed, was
one of the prisons of Mary Queen of Scots; and
it has been thought, that it was originally fitted up for her reception, and with a view to a
visit, which though long talked of, it is very
probable Elizabeth never seriously intended
paying her. Several of the apartments derive

* See Inscription on her Monument, p. 146.

great interest from the furniture, and other articles preserved in remembrance of that injured Princess.

The *Hall*, which is large, is hung with tapestry, containing the history of the *Patient Grizzle*, and has a pair of gigantic elk's horns, placed between the windows opposite the entrance. Ascending the grand stair-case, you enter the chapel, where the chairs and cushions used by Mary still remain. It is hung with tapestry, in which are wrought several pieces of scripture history; particularly, the conversion of Paul, the punishment of Elymas the sorcerer, Paul pleading before Agrippa, and his shipwreck at Melita.

In the *Dining-Room* are several family pictures:—the first is *Sir William Cavendish*, husband to the Countess, Æt. 42, dressed in a fur gown, with a small flat cap, a glove in his left hand, a long pointed beard and whiskers.— *Elizabeth, Countess of Shrewsbury*, represented in a close black dress, a double ruff, long chain of five rows of pearls, reaching below her waist, sleeves down to her wrists, turned up with small pointed white cuffs, a fan in her left hand, and brown hair.* *William, the first*

* " Mr. Walpole records a tradition concerning this lady, which if founded on truth, proves the rage for building

Duke of Devonshire in armour. *Colonel Charles Cavendish*, his brother, taken when asleep; *Lord Harry Cavendish*, brother to the second Duke; one of the Earls of Devonshire; *Lord Treasurer Burleigh; Lord Burleigh*, son to the Countess of Exeter ; *Robert Cecil*, third son of the Earl of Salisbury, a small whole-length; a picture marked *Erasmus*, but having the Cavendish arms over it. Over the chimney-piece, are the arms of the Countess of Shrewsbury, with this inscription beneath ; *The conclusion of all things is to fear God, and keep his commandments. E. S.* 1597.

The *Drawing-Room* is wainscotted, to a considerable height, and hung above with tapestry. Here is another picture of the *Countess*, wherein she is portrayed of a more advanced age than in the former. From this an engraving was made by *Vertue*. Over the chimney-piece are her arms, in a lozenge, and two stags for supporters, under which is this inscription ;

—SANGUINE CORNU CORDE OCULO PEDE CERVUS
ET AURE NOBILIS AT CLARO PONDERE NOBILIOR.

that distinguished her conduct, to have originated in a superstitious weakness. The tradition is, that she was told by a fortune-teller, that her death should not happen while she continued building; and accordingly she employed a great deal of wealth in that way; yet she died in a hard frost, when the workmen could not labor."

In one of the Bed-chambers on this floor, is a bed, a set of chairs, and a suit of hangings, all worked by Mary and her attendants, when she was in the custody of the Earl of Shrewsbury: on these hangings is a figure adoring a cross, and various other figures, with these allusive mottos;—*Constans*—*Artimesia*—*Pietas* —*Chastity*—*Lucretia*, &c. These have been preserved with great care, and, considering the length of time since they were worked, are comparatively fresh and entire.

On the grand stair-case leading to the state-apartments, is a portrait of the first Duke of Devonshire on horseback, in an embroidered coat, a large wig, and a feather in his hat.

" The second floor is that which gives its chief interest to the edifice, as nearly all the apartments were allotted to Mary, (some of them for state purposes;) and the furniture is known by other proofs than its appearance, to remain as she left it. The chief room or that of audience, is of uncommon loftiness, and strikes by its grandeur, before the veneration and tenderness, which its antiquities, and the plainly told tale of the sufferings they witnessed, excite. The walls, which are covered to a considerable height with tapestry, are painted above with historical groups. The chairs are

of black velvet, which is nearly concealed by a
raised needle-work of gold, silver, and colours
that mingle with surprising richness, and remain in fresh preservation. The upper end of
the room is distinguished by a lofty canopy of
the same materials, and by steps which support two chairs. In front of the canopy is a
carpeted table; below which, the room breaks
into a spacious recess, where a few articles of
furniture are deposited used by Mary: the cur-
tains are of gold tissue, but in so tattered a
condition, that its original texture can hardly
be perceived: this, and the chairs which accompany it, are supposed to be much earlier
than Mary's time. A short passage leads from
the state apartment to her own chamber, a small
room, overlooked from the passage by a window, which enabled her attendants to know
that she was contriving no means of escape
through the others into the court. The bed
and chairs of this room are of black velvet,
embroidered by herself; the toilet of gold tissue; all more decayed than worn, and probably used only towards the conclusion of her
imprisonment here, when she was removed
from some better apartment, in which the ancient bed, now in the state-room had been

placed."* Over the door of this room, are the Arms of the Queen of Scots carved in wood, with M. R. in a cypher, and round it—*Marie Stuart, par le grace de Dieu, Royne d' Ecosse, Douariere de France.* Crest, a lion; the motto—*In my defens.*

The gallery of portraits occupies the whole extent of the East front of the house; it is 195 feet long, and is lighted from windows fixed in deep square recesses, and projecting beyond the wall. It contains portraits of several illustrious characters, the principal of which are the following;

On the right hand side of the entrance is a portrait of *Queen Elizabeth*, in a gown painted with serpents, birds, a sea-horse, swan, ostrich, &c. the hair golden: a whole-length of *James V.* of Scotland, in the 28th year of his age, and his Queen, *Mary of Lorraine*, in her 24th, in rich dresses, with long thin faces, both in one piece: *Countess of Exeter: Henry VII.*, and *William*, Second *Earl of Salisbury.*

On the South side of the chimney-piece;— *Charles I.; Catherine Countess of Salisbury; Henry VI.; Countess of Shrewsbury; Henry VIII.; Queen Mary; Sir William Cavendish;*

* Mrs. Radcliffe's Tour to the Lakes.

aged forty-four; *Edward VI.;* Cardinal *Pool;*
Hobbes, aged eighty-nine; *James I.* in the 8th
year of his age; *Stephen Gardiner,* the cruel
and sanguinary bishop of Winchester; *Lady
Jane Grey,* seated before a harpsicord, on which
a psalm-book is opened; on this picture is inscribed, *Mors potius quam dedecus* 1691, *æta-
tis* 19.; *Sir Thomas More,* in a fur gown and
black cap; *Mary Queen of Scots,* in black,
" her countenance much faded, deeply marked
by indignation and grief, and reduced as to the
spectre of herself, frowning with suspicion upon all who approached it; the black eyes looking out from their corners, thin lips, somewhat
aquiline nose, and beautiful chin." Under it is
inscribed—*Maria D. G. Scotiæ piissima regina.
Franciæ Doueria* 1578, *ano regni XXXVI.
Anglicæ captivæ X.* At the end of the gallery
and near the window are some pictures greatly
injured, and others nearly defaced: of this number are, *Arrabella Stuart—Lord Darnley—Sir
Thomas Wyat*—and *King Richard III.* Most
of the paintings in this gallery have suffered,
in a more or less degree, from the damp.

By ascending another flight of stairs, which
are of solid oak, you come to the roof of the
house, which is covered with lead. From this

17   z 3

elevated situation, there is a very extensive prospect into the adjacent country; and in a clear day the cathedrals of York and Lincoln may be faintly distinguished.

At the distance of a few yards from the present Hall, are the dilapidated remains of the more ancient seat of the Hardwick family. A few apartments, though approached with great difficulty through the fragments of others, are yet almost intire:—one of them, fancifully called the Giant's Chamber, has been remarked for the beauty of its proportions; and is said, by Kennet, in his *Memoirs of the family of Cavendish*, to have been " thought fit for a pattern of measure and contrivance of a room at Blenheim." At what time this ancient mansion was built, is uncertain, but it is known to have been the residence of the Hardwicks in the time of Henry the Eighth : for John Hardwick died here in the nineteenth year of his reign. In this house Cardinal Wolsey lodged one night in his way from York to Leicester Abbey, where he died November, 1536.

HEATH, the whole parish contains about sixty-four houses. The living is a vicarage, and the church is dedicated to All-Saints: it formerly belonged to Croxton Abbey. The manor of Heath was presented by Robert Ferrers, Earl of Derby, to the monastery of Grendon, in Leicestershire; but it now belongs, together with the patronage of the church, to the Duke of Devonshire. It is supposed that it came into the possession of the present proprietor, when in the sixth year of Edward the Sixth, Mr. Cavendish had, in exchange for his estates in Hertfordshire, several lands and manors belonging to dissolved priories and abbeys in Derbyshire.

WINGERWORTH, in the time of the Conqueror, was a soke of the manor of *Newbold*, and is written *Wingreurde*. In the twenty-fifth year of Edward I. there was a church here; as Henry de Brailsford was possessed of its advowson. The living is a curacy, under the patronage of the Dean of Lincoln. The parish is thought to contain about 310 inhabitants, many of whom find employment at the works, carried on here, for smelting iron ore.

WINGERWORTH-HALL, the mansion of Sir Windsor Hunloke, Bart. is a spacious building, standing in an elevated situation, and commanding several extensive prospects into the neighbouring country. The family of Hunloke is of considerable antiquity; and in the reign of Henry VIII. was possessed of some considerable estates in Middlesex and Nottingham-

shire. The Wingerworth estate was anciently
the property of the *Brailsfords*, and descended
from them to the *Curzons* of Kedleston, who
sold it, in the time of Queen Elizabeth, to Nicholas Hunloke.   Henry, the fourth in descent
from the first possessor, was distinguished for
his attachment to Charles the First; He lent
the king a considerable sum of money: raised
and accoutered a troop of horse for his service:
and in the twenty-second year of his age, signalized himself at the battle of Edge-Hill, where
he was knighted: soon afterwards he was created
a Baronet.   During the Common-wealth, the
family were obliged to quit Wingerworth, which
was converted into a garrison for the forces of
Parliament: but Sir Henry Hunloke's widow,
marrying one of Cromwell's Officers, the mansion did not suffer any great injury, and the
estate was preserved in the family.   Since that
period, the family have regularly resided here,
with the same title as the original proprietor,
to the present time.   The Hall, now standing,
was built between the years 1726 and 1730, by
Sir Thomas Windsor Hunloke, grandfather to
the present possessor.

On *Stainedge Cliff*, which forms a part of
the Wingerworth estate, are several rock-basins,

and two seats, supposed by Mr. Rooke* to have
been appropriated to the purposes of augury.

SCARCLIFF, in Domesday *Soardeclif*, including the hamlet of Palterton, *(Paltretune)* contains about ninety houses. Anker de Fretch-
ville was proprietor of the manor of Scarcliff,
at the commencement of the reign of Henry
the Third; but about its close, it was seized by
the king, because the castle and town of Northampton were, in a hostile manner, detained
from him, by the above Anker, Simon de
Montford, Hugh de Spenser, and others. Some
time after, the town of Scarcliff was presented
by Robert Lexington to the prior and canons
of Newstead. The advowson of the church
was given to Derley Abbey, by Hubert the son
of Ralph; but the Duke of Devonshire is the
present patron. The living is a vicarage, and
the church is dedicated to All-Saints.

OVER-LANGWITH. This parish is small, containing but a few houses, whose inhabitants rely
entirely upon agriculture for employment and
support. In the time of Henry the Second,
Langwith church was given to Thurgaston Priory, in Nottinghamshire. The living is a rectory; the church is dedicated to St. Helena;
and the Duke of Devonshire is the patron.

---

* Archæologia, Vol. XII. page 43.

BOLSOVER, is a small market-town, containing together with the whole liberty, about two
hundred and twenty houses, and eleven hundred inhabitants, who are chiefly employed in
agriculture. The living is a vicarage, the church
is dedicated to St. Mary, and the Duke of Portland is the patron. In the time of Henry the
Second, there was a church at Bolsover; as it
was in that reign given by William Peverel of
Nottingham, to the Abbey at Darley. In the
church, is a noble monument to the memory of
Sir Charles Cavendish, the father of the first
Duke of Newcastle, with a long and remarkable inscription, expressive of his virtues,

At the time of the Norman survey, the manor
of *Belesover*, was the property of William Peverel, who is supposed to have built a castle here.
In the reign of Richard the First, this fortress
passed to the hands of John, Earl of Montaigne; when Richard del Pec was appointed
governor. How long it remained under him is
uncertain; but early in the following reign,
king John made his favorite, Briuere, possessor
of it: it was, however, soon afterwards seized
by the rebellious Barons, who retained it till
the year 1215, when it was retaken for the king
by William Ferrers, Earl of Derby. In recompence for this service he was appointed go-

vernor, and, with the exception of an interval
of a short time, when it was held by Bryan de
L'Isle, and Hugh de Spenser, he enjoyed the
honor for six years.' In the reign of Henry the
Third, the Manor and Castle of Bolsover, were
granted to John Scot, Earl of Chester, who
dying without issue, it was allotted to Ada, his
fourth sister and co-heir, who married Henry
de Hastings, Lord of Abergavenny. About
this time it became again vested in the Crown,
and was not afterwards in the possession of a
subject, till the year 1514, when Henry VIII.
granted it to Thomas Howard, Duke of Norfolk, in reward for his service in the expedition
against France, to be held by the service of one
knight's fee : but on the attainder of his son,
in the thirty-eighth of the same monarch, it
escheated to the crown. In the reign of Edward
the Sixth, George Talbot, Earl of Shrewsbury,
had a grant of it in fee-farm : it continued in
this family until the reign of James I., when it
was sold by Earl Gilbert to Sir Charles Cavendish. Henry, second Duke of Newcastle, grandson of Sir Charles, dying without issue, the
estate became the property of Margaret, his
sister, who had married John Hollis, Earl of
Clare, afterwards Duke of Newcastle : their
daughter, married Harley, Earl of Oxford, from

whom, by a daughter also, Bolsover was conveyed to the Bentincts, Dukes of Portland, in whose possession it still continues.

In the time of Leland (about 1550) this ancient fortress was fast decaying; when it was purchased by Sir Charles Cavendish in 1613, it was in ruins; and now, not a vestige of it remains. Its exact situation cannot be exactly ascertained; but it is supposed that it stood near the same spot as the present mansion. The building which is now called Bolsover-Castle, stands upon a point which projects a little into the valley below, and overlooks a great extent of country. It was built in the years 1613—14—15, by Sir Charles Cavendish, and is a square and lofty fabric of brown stone, having a tower at each angle; that to the north-east being much larger and higher than the rest.— The entrance is by a flight of steps on the. east side, and leads through a passage to the hall, which is of a moderate size, and has its ceiling supported by stone pillars. The only other room on this floor designed for habitation is the parlour; this apartment has an arched ceiling, sustained by a pillar in the centre, around which is a plain circular dining table. There are, also, a smaller apartment, and two lodging rooms on this floor; and eight on the attick story, which are all very small: the floor of every room is of stone or plaister: on the whole, it is an ill-contrived, and very inconvenient domestic residence.

Sir Charles Cavendish, died about two years after he had finished this house, and was succeeded by his son, William Cavendish, Duke of Newcastle, a warm friend, and steady supporter of Charles the First. This nobleman was honored with two, if not three, visits from the King and Queen; for whom he fitted up his house at Bolsover, and provided superb entertainments. All the neighbouring gentry were invited to partake of the festival, and to pay their respects to the royal guests: Ben Jonson was employed in devising speeches, and fitting-up scenes; and the whole entertainment was conducted in such a magnificent style, that the expences of the second visit only, amounted to £15,000.

On the breaking out of the Civil Wars, the Duke, owing to his attachment to the royal cause, was obliged to leave the country, and resided at Antwerp till the restoration; when he returned, and began to build extensive additions to the old house at Bolsover to the West of the former mansion: but these were never completed, and the outside walls only, are now standing. In front was a fine terrace, from which a spacious flight of steps, led to the entrance. The proposed extent of this structure, may be conceived from the dimensions of the gallery, which was 220 feet in length, and 28 feet wide. At the South-end of the garden, is a very curious decayed fountain, standing in an octagon reservoir, six feet deep, ornamented with satyrs, masks, birds, and other figures. On the pedestal is a figure of Venus in alabaster, represented holding wet drapery, and in the action of stepping out of a bath.

GLAPWELL, anciently *Glapewelle*, is a hamlet in the parish of Bolsover, containing about twenty houses. Here, is, also, the seat of Brabazon Hallows, Esq.

CHESTERFIELD.

CHESTERFIELD, is thought to be a place of some antiquity, though not one of the most ancient towns in the county. The late Dr. Pegge,* supposes it to have originated in a Ro-

* Essay on the Roman Roads.

man station, on the road from Derby to York, which he thinks was fixed on an eminence called Tapton or Topton, at the point named Windmill-Hill, but distinguished in several old writings by the appellation of *Castle-Hill.*— "As to the site of Chesterfield," he says, "it lies so under the Castle-Hill, at Tapton or Topton, that when it became a place of note, it would rationally be called, *The field of the Chester, or Castle.*"

At the time of the Norman survey, *Cestre-feld* was a place of so little importance, that it is only noticed as a bailiwic, belonging to the manor of Newbold. Soon after this, however, it began to increase in size and importance: in the eleventh century there was a church at *Chesterfelt;* for William Rufus gave it at that time, to the Cathedral at Lincoln. In the reign of king John, the manor was presented by the sovereign to his favorite William Briwere or Bruere, through whose influence with that monarch, the town was incorporated: by the same grant, the same liberties were procured for Chesterfield, as were enjoyed by Nottingham; and an annual fair to continue eight days, and two weekly markets, on Tuesday and Saturday, obtained. From the *de Brueres*, the manor, went by the marriage of an heiress to the family of

Wake; and afterwards became the property of
Edmund Plantagenet, Earl of Kent, who married Margaret Wake; and was inherited by
his descendants for several generations. In the
twenty-sixth year of Edward the Third, it was
held by John, second son of Edmund Woodstock, and grandson of Edward I.; and in the
year 1366, by Sir Thomas Holland. In 1443,
Chesterfield belonged to William Neville; and
in the reign of Queen Elizabeth, to George
Talbot, Earl of Shrewsbury. It afterwards
became the property of the Cavendishes, by
purchase; from whom it descended to the late
Duke of Portland; but has since passed in exchange to the Duke of Devonshire. The Stanhopes, derive their title of *Earl of Chesterfield*
from this town. " Philip, lord Stanhope of
Shelford, in Nottinghamshire, was created earl
of Chesterfield in the fourth year of king Charles
I. The title has been continued in the same family ever since to the present day."

The charter originally granted by king John,
has been confirmed and enlarged in several
succeeding reigns. The government of the
town, till the reign of queen Elizabeth, was
exercised by an alderman and twelve brethren;
but the charter of incorporation granted by
that sovereign, vests it in a Mayor, six Alder-

men, six Brethren, and twelve capital Burgesses, who are assisted by a Town-Clerk.

The present church is supposed to have been erected about the beginning of the thirteenth century. In one of the windows, are the arms of Edmund Plantagenet and Margaret Wake, impaled together. It is built in the form of a cross, and is a spacious and handsome building: it is particularly remarkable for the appearance of its spire, which rises to the height of 230 feet, and is so singularly twisted, that it seems to lean in whatever direction it may be approached. Among several other antiquated monuments, there are in the chancel, two large altar-tombs, belonging to the respectable family of *Foljambs*, whose ancient seat was at Walton, in this parish. In the transept is an inscription recording a charitable legacy of £1800, for putting out boys to trade, or sea-service; including a clause, limiting the benefit of the charity to those who reside in the borough, and do not receive alms.

From another inscription it appears, that there was formerly a Guild at Chesterfield, dedicated to St. Mary and the Holy Cross, founded by Richard the Second, who maintained two or three priests in this church:—several other guilds are mentioned in ancient wri-

tings belonging to the Corporation, endowed
with considerable revenues: from the chapel of
one of them, called St. Helen's, the grammar-
school is supposed to have received the name
of *Chapel School*, by which it is generally distinguished. This school was founded in the
reign of Elizabeth, and was formerly the largest
in the North of England. The present school-
house was erected in the year 1710.

An ancient hospital for Lepers, was founded
in this town, before the tenth of Richard the
First, and dedicated to St. Leonard. John
Earl of Kent, held it *in capite* in the twenty-
sixth of Edward III.: but in the ninth year of
king Richard II. it was seized by Joan Princess
of Wales; it flourished, however, until the
time of Henry the Eighth.

Chesterfield, is not a place of great trade,
nor is there any considerable manufacture carried on in it. By an enumeration made in 1788,
it was found, by Mr. Pilkington, that Chesterfield contained 801 houses, and 3,626 inhabitants Since that time both the size and population have increased, as appears from the returns made under the late act, by which the
number of houses, was ascertained to amount
to 920, and of inhabitants to 4,267. The support of the latter is principally derived from

the iron-works in the town and neighbourhood,
and the manufacture of stockings. Some additional employment arises from three potteries,
for the manufacture of coarse earthen ware;
also from a carpet manufactory.; and from the
making of shoes, a large quantity of which, are
annually sent.to the metropolis.

In the market-place, is a neat Town-Hall, built
a, few years ago, under the direction of Mr.
Carr, of York; the ground floor of which is
converted into a gaol for debtors, and a residence for a gaoler : and on the second floor, is
a large room for holding the sessions, and trans-
acting the town's business. Several Alms-
houses have been endowed in different parts of
the town. At the Castle-Inn, an elegant Assembly-room has been recently built, for the
amusement of the more respectable inhabitants
of the town and neighbourhood.

In the reign of Henry the Third, the church
at Chesterfield, was made use of as a place of
refuge by Robert Ferrers, the last Earl of Derby. After the discomfiture of the rebellious
Barons at Evesham, in the year 1265, this Earl
bound himself by an oath, to a forfeiture of his
estate and honors, if ever he joined their party
again; but after some proceedings in the Parliament, held at Northampton, which were

particularly obnoxious to the Barons, he, in
the spring of the ensuing year, again assembled
his followers, in his castle at Duffield, and being
joined by several disaffected nobles, advanced
and took post at Chesterfield. Here he was
surprised by the forces of Henry, the eldest son
of the king of Almaine, and, after a severe
conflict, was defeated, and all his forces routed:
the Earl was one of those who escaped; he
at first was concealed in the church under
some bags of wool; but by the treachery of a
woman the place of his retreat was discovered,
and he conveyed in irons to Windsor: but after
a confinement of three years, he was set at liberty, on certain conditions,* which he proved
unable to perform, and was, at length, deprived of his estate and earldom. From the register of the church it appears, that the Earl of
Newcastle, was at Chesterfield with his forces
in May 1643, and again in December following. It is not improbable, that at one of these
times he engaged the forces of Parliament: but
it is certain, that during the civil wars, he obtained a victory over them at this place.

The Unitarians, Independents, Quakers, and
Methodists, have their respective places of worship at Chesterfield.

* See page 206.

The parish of Chesterfield contains the following chapelries and hamlets;—Brimington (*Brimintune*), Temple Normanton, Newbold, Dunstone, Walton,* (*Waletune*), Tupton, Calow, and Hasland; containing altogether about 500 houses.

There is a chalybeate spring at Chesterfield, but it is weak; however, when drank in sufficient quantity, it is purgative, and has been found useful in disorders, arising from weakness and relaxation.

SUTTON-IN-LE-DALE, which was in former times connected with the living of Duckmanton (*Dochemanestun*), is a rectory, and the church is dedicated to St. Mary. The church at Duckmanton, which is not now standing, was dedicated to the Saints, Peter and Paul; and belonged, in former times, to the monastery of Welbeck. The liberty of Sutton contains about twenty-three houses; and Duckmanton fifty-three. The inhabitants are chiefly supported by agriculture.

SUTTON-HALL in this parish, is a large and ancient mansion, standing upon elevated ground

---

* " Walton," says Mr. Camden, " descended from the Bretons, by *Loudham* to the *Folijambs*, a great name in these parts."

18   B 4

and commanding some beautiful views over the
adjacent country. At different times, it has
been the seat of several respectable families.—
In the time of Henry the Third, it belonged to
the family of *Harstone*, whose heir general married a *Grey*, a descendant of a younger branch
of the Lords Grey of Codnor Castle. In the
fourth year of Henry IV. the heir general of
Grey was married to Jo. Leak, whose descendant, Francis Leak was raised by king James
the First, to the dignity of a baronet; afterwards created a baron of the realm, by the
title of Lord D'Eincort of Sutton : and in con-
sideration of his services to Charles the First;
was, by that monarch, advanced to the degree
of Earl of Scarsdale. After the death of Nicholas, the fourth and last Earl of this family,
who succeeded his uncle in 1707, the Sutton
estate was sold, and again re-sold to Godfrey
Clarke, Esq. of Chilcote : it is now the property and residence of Thomas Kinnersley, Esq.
who succeeded to the estate, under the will of
Godfrey Bagnall Clarke, Esq.

ELMTON. At the time of the Norman survey, there were at *Helmetune*, a church and a
priest. Ralph de Aincurt gave it to the priory
of Thurgaston, in the time of Edward III. The
living is a vicarage, and the church is dedicated

to St. Peter. The parish of Elmton, together with the hamlet of Creswell, contains about sixty houses.

In this parish was born, in the year 1707, JEDEDIAH BUXTON, a person deserving to be recorded on account of his singular memory and powers of calculation. He was the son of a schoolmaster, who lived at Elmton; but notwithstanding the profession of his father, his education was so much neglected, that he never was taught to read or write; and with respect to any other knowledge, but that of numbers, seemed always entirely ignorant. How he first came to know the relative proportions of numbers, and their progressive denominations, he did not remember; but to this he applied the whole force of his mind, and upon this his attention was constantly fixed, so that he frequently was entirely regardless of external objects; but when he did pay attention to them, it was only with respect to their numbers. If any space of time was mentioned, he soon after would say it was so many minutes: and if any length of way, he would assign the number of hair-breadths, without any question being asked, or any calculation expected by the company. When he once understood a question, he began to work with amazing facility, after his own method, without the use of a pen, pencil, or chalk, or even understanding the common rules of arithmetic as taught in the schools. He would stride over a piece of land or a field, and calculate the contents of it, almost as exactly, as if it had been measured by a chain. In this manner he measured the whole lordship of Elmton, of some thousand acres, and gave the contents, not only in acres, roods, and perches; but even in square inches. His memory was so great, that, while resolving a question, he could leave off, and resume the operation again where he left it, the next morning, or at a week, a month, or at several months, and proceed regularly till it was completed.—His memory would doubtless, have been equally retentive with respect to other objects, if he had attended to them with equal diligence; but his perpetual application to figures prevented the smallest acquisition of any other knowledge. He was sometimes asked, on his return from church, whether he remembered the text, or any part of the sermon; but it never appeared that he brought away one sentence: his mind, upon a close examination, being found to have been busied, even during divine service, in his favorite operation; either dividing some time, or some space, into the smallest

known parts, or resolving some question that
had been given him as a test of his abilities.

His celebrity for extraordinary facility in
making arithmetical calculations,* and solving
the most difficult problems in arithmetic, by a
recondite method peculiar to his own mind, attracted the notice of Sir George Saville, who
had him brought to London, in 1754, when he
was introduced to the Royal Society, and answered various arithmetical questions so satisfactorily, that his dismissal was accompanied
with a handsome gratuity. In this visit to the
metropolis, the only object of his curiosity except figures, was a sight of the king and the
royal family; but they being just removed to
Kensington, Jedediah was disappointed. During his stay in London, he was taken to see
king Richard III. performed at Drury-lane;
and it was expected, either that the novelty and
splendour of the show, would have fixed him

* A person once proposed to him this question;—In a
body the three sides of which, are, 23,145,789 yards,
5,642,732 yards, and 54,965 yards, how many cubic
eighths of an inch? In about five hours, Jedediah accu-
rately solved this intricate problem, though in the midst of
business, and surrounded by more than one hundred labor-
ers. Even mixed company, conversation, and confused
noises, could not distract his mind, when intent on a problem.

in astonishment, or kept his imagination in a
continual hurry; or that his passions would, in
some degree, have been touched by the power
of action, if he had not perfectly understood
the dialogue. But Jedediah's mind was employed in the theatre, just as it was employed
in every other place. During the dance he
fixed his attention upon the number of steps :—
he declared after a fine. piece of music, that the
innumerable sounds produced by the instruments, had perplexed him beyond measure;
and he attended even to Garrick, only to count
the words that he uttered, in which he said he
perfectly succeeded.

, Jedediah returned. to the place of his. birth,
where, if his enjoyments were few, his wishes
did not seem to be more. He applied to his
daily labour, by which he subsisted, with cheerfulness; he regretted nothing that he left behind him in London; and it continued to be
his opinion, that a slice of rusty bacon, afforded
the most delicious repast. This extraordinary
character, living in laborious poverty, his life
was uniform and obscure. Time with respect
to him, changed nothing but his age; nor did
the seasons vary his employment, except that
in summer, he employed a ling-hook, and in
winter, a flail. He prolonged his life to the age

of seventy years : he was married, and had several children. His portrait has been engraved
from a correct drawing of him by Miss Hart-
ley in January 1764, at which period, according to his own calculation, he had existed
1,792,230,823, seconds.

WHITTINGTON : at the compilation of Domesday, *Witintune*, was a bailiwick in the manor
of Newbold. The living is a rectory, and the
church is dedicated to St. Bartholemew. The
village is small.

Whittington had the honor of witnessing the
beginning of that association, which does so
much credit to those who embarked their lives
and fortunes in it, and the happy result of
which we are feeling at the present time. No
longer able to bear the arbitrary measures of
James the Second, nor the destruction of the
protestant religion, which he evidently meditated, a few *Worthies*, whose names will ever
be dear to the lovers of British freedom, in the,
year 1688, met each other on Whittington-moor,
for the express purpose of devising some means,
for resouring their country from the double sla-
very with which it was threatened. The only
persons who are certainly known to have been
at this meeting, were, the Duke of Devonshire,
Earl of Danby, (afterwards Duke of Leeds,)

and Sir John D'Arcy, son and heir of Conyers, Earl of Holderness. The spot on the moor where they met, according to the tradition of the country, was "at a middle place between Kiveton, Chatsworth, and Aston; and that a shower of rain happening to fall, they removed to the village for shelter, and finished their conversation at a public-house there, the sign of the *Cook and Pynot*,"* The cottage thus distinguished, stands, where the road from Chesterfield branches off for Sheffield and Rotherham, and has ever since been called the *Revolution-House.* The small apartment within, wherein the noblemen sat, had the name of *Plotting Chamber;* but this appellation being thought opprobrious, has been changed to the *Revolution Parlour.* An ancient chair is preserved here, in which the Duke of Devonshire is believed to have been seated.

On the 5th of November, 1788, the centenary commemoration of the Revolution, was celebrated with great magnificence at Whittington and Chesterfield. The commemoration commenced at Whittington, with divine service in the church. The Rev. Dr. Pegge, the late learned antiquary, being rector of the parish,

* The provincial name for a magpie.

delivered a sermon, and the descendants of the
illustrious families who were concerned in effecting this memorable event,—the houses of
Cavendish, Osborn, Booth, and D'Arcy, were
present, as well as a great number of other
persons. After the service, they went in procession to view the old *Revolution-House*, and
the chair; and then partook of a very elegant
cold collation, which was prepared in the new
rooms annexed to the cottage: the procession
moved afterwards in regular order to Chesterfield, where the remainder of the day was
spent with the utmost cordiality and rejoicing,

On the day previous to the Jubilee at Whittington, the committee appointed to conduct
the proceedings, dined at the Revolution-
House; and a considerable sum was afterwards
subscribed, for defraying the expences of a monumental column, proposed to have been erected on the spot, as a lasting memorial of the
measures by which the liberties of the kingdom were so happily preserved. The subscription remained open several months; but the
breaking out of the French Revolution, and its
consequent horrors, occasioned the erection of
the column to be deferred.

In an enclosure not far from the village, is a

18   C 4

chalybeate spring, which from the tests employed, has been found to contain about the same
quantity of iron, as those, situated at Quarndon and Buxton.   The respect in which it differs from them most materially, is, that it parts
more freely with the fixed air, with which it is
impregnated.

STAVELY, is a parish, containing the chapelry of *Barlow*, and the hamlets of *Netherthorp*,
Woodthorp, and three of the name of *Hanly;*
containing, altogether, about 408 houses.   At
the compilation of Domesday, there were a
church and a priest at *Stavelie*.   The living is
a rectory, the church is dedicated to St. John
the Baptist, and the Duke of Devonshire is the
patron.

In the time of Edward the First, the Manor
of Stavely belonging to John Musard; after
which it became the property of the family of
Frescheville, a branch of the family of that
name, who were barons of Crich, in the reign
of Henry the Third.   John Frescheville, Esq.
of Stavely, was, as a reward for his attachment
to Charles I. advanced by Charles II. to the
dignity of a Baron of the realm, by the title of
Lord Frescheville of Stavely.   There are in this
parish some valuable beds of iron-stone; and
furnaces have been built for converting it into
metal, which employ many hands.

,CLOWN, contains about eighty-five houses:
the living is a rectory, and the church is dedicated to St. John the Baptist, and the king is
the patron. In Domesday it is written *Clune.*
In the reign of Richard the Second, Ro. Fol-
ville, held some land in this parish.

WHITWELL. In the time of the Conqueror,
there were a church and a priest at *Witeuuelle.*
The living is a rectory, the church is dedicated
to St. Lawrence, and the presentation belongs
to the Duke of Rutland. The parish contains
about 142 houses; and the inhabitants rely
chiefly on agriculture for support.

BARLBOROUGH. *Burleburg,* is in Domesday
included in the same manor as the last-mentioned place; and in common with it, had a
considerable population. The living is a rectory, the church is dedicated to St. James, and
—— Rodes, Esq. is the patron.

The family of *Rodes,* who resided here for
many centuries, was of great antiquity: they
were lineally descended from Gerard de Rodes,
a baron who lived during the reigns of Henry
II. and the three succeeding monarchs, and
was employed by king John, as an ambassador
to foreign courts. Sir John Rodes, who was
living in 1727, was the last lineal descendant
of this ancestor, and the last that enjoyed the

title. The estate, after his death, went by the marriage of his sister to a Mr. Heathcote, whose descendants assumed the name of Rodes, and are in possession of the estate at this period.

DRONFIELD, *Dronefeld*, is a small, but neat town, pleasantly situated in a valley, and is the residence of many respectable inhabitants. The church, which is dedicated to St. John the Baptist, is a handsome building, 132 feet in length, having a tower at the West end, terminated by a spire: most of the windows are pointed. The rectory of Dronfield, before the reformation, was appropriated to Beauchief Abbey; and that fine and lofty building the chancel, which is equalled by very few, in our common parochial churches, was erected by the Abbot and convent of that house, long before the year 1535, when that religious foundation was dissolved; but, however, not till after the 13th of Richard the Second, or 1390, when this rectory was appropriated to the Abbey.

Henry Fenshaw, Esq. a native of the town, and Remembrancer of the Exchequer, founded a free-grammar-school here in the time of queen Elizabeth. The number of houses in the parish, is about 245, and of inhabitants 1,190.

In this parish, are the chapelries of *Dore*, and *Holmesfield*; and the hamlets of *Hilltop*,

Stubley, Woodhouse, Cowley, Totley, Unstone, Cole-Aston, and Little-Barlow.

ECKINGTON. The manor of *Eckintone*, belonged, in William's time, to Ralph the son of Hubert. At which period, there was a priest, but no church there:[*] however, about the beginning of the fourteenth century, there was one there. The present living is a rectory, and the church is dedicated to St. Peter and St. Paul. In the time of Edward I. the manor of Eckington was held by J. Langford. The township of Eckington contains, nearly 200 houses.

This parish includes the chapelry of Killimarsh, (*Chinewoldmarese*), and the hamlets of Renishaw, Trowey, Ridgeway, and Mosborough, containing, altogether, about 621 houses.

BEIGHTON, *Bectune*, was, at the compilation of Domesday, a soke in the manor of Eckington. The living is a vicarage, the church is dedicated to St. Mary, and the Duke of Kingston is the patron. Beighton contains the hamlets of Hackenthorp, Southwell, and Berley; containing, together with the whole liberty, about 120 houses.

NORTON, in Domesday *Nortune*, is a parish,

---

[*] Domesday, *Orig.* 277, a. 1. *Trans.* p. 317

consisting of several hamlets, and containing about 300 houses. The present living is a vicarage, and the church is dedicated to Saint James. As early as the conclusion of the 12th century, there was a church at Norton: for Robert son of Ralph, Lord of Alfreton, Norton, and Marnham, who founded the abbey of Beauchief, gave it to that religious house. Jeffery Blithe, bishop of Litchfield and Coventry, who died in 1534, built a chapel at Norton, and an alabaster tomb over his parents; and appointed a chantry for them.

In former times, two great courts were held at Norton every year; where a variety of business belonging to the parish was transacted.*

* "The principal business transacted on these occasions was examining into, and punishing offences, by which the inhabitants of the manor were or might be injured. The following in particular are noticed; incroachments upon the waste, altering water courses, neglecting to scour or cleanse ditches, turning a scabbed horse on to the common, shutting up a bridle road, giving an account of wafes and strays, examining those, who baked or brewed for sale without a licence from this court and amercing them for such offences, fixing the assize of bread and ale, and also the price of the latter (which appears about the thirty-fourth year of queen Elizabeth to have been one penny per quart), and fining such as broke the assize. Two men were sworn in as frank pledge, two as tithing-men, and one as constable for the year ensuing.

" Two ale tasters were also appointed at the court; and

There is a congregation of Unitarians* at Norton; who, as early as the reign of Charles the Second, performed divine service in a private house in the village.

it appears, that there were brewed in the parish love-ale, help-ale, and unwholsome-ale, for all which fines were levied.—Those who had committed an assault, and drawn blood, were fined seperately for each offence. Some also were fined for carrying staves or clubs, lodging suspicious persons, and remaining in alehouses after eight o'clock at night.

" The inhabitants of the parish were also obliged to make two butts to shoot at, and keep them in repair under certain penalties; and to provide their sons and men servants with bows and arrows, as late as the thirtieth year of queen Elizabeth. The stocks were to be kept up, and every gap in their fences to be made up before Lady-day.

" In the thirty-fourth year of queen Elizabeth, upwards of one hundred and thirty suitors were amerced for non-appearance, and other offences. Of this number were eleven brewers for selling ale unlawfully, and twenty-one persons for playing at unlawful games, as huddlings. If a frank pledge neglected to appear at court, heavy penalties were inflicted.

" There is no appearance of cock-fighting, horse-racing, throwing at cocks, no cards, or dice, nay what is more wonderful, no ducking of witches, or even a ducking stool is noticed."

* This body of religionists, like most others now called UNITARIANS, were formerly improperly termed PRESBYTE-RIANS, though the Scotch mode of church government was not adopted by them. Until about the middle of the last century, most of the Presbyterians adhered to the Calvinistic tenets; but since that period, the major part of their congregations have changed their creed, and, as their denomination implies, believe in the Unity of God.

The village of *Great Norton*, is pleasantly situated, and contains several large and good houses. Here is Norton-Hall, the residence of Samuel Shore, Esq. who is possessed of the manor of Norton. Norton-House, in the same village, is the seat of —— Newton, Esq.: and at a small distance from it, is an ancient mansion of John Bagshaw, Esq. The manufacture of scythes, is carried on to a great extent in this parish.

BEAUCHIEF, is an extra-parochial hamlet, deriving its name from a religous house, of the order of Præmonstratensian, or white canons.

The Abbey of Beauchief, or de Bello capite, was situated at this place, in a beautiful little vale, near the northern boundary of the county, within a short distance of Sheffield. It was founded, between the years 1172 and 1176, by Robert Fitz-Ralph, Lord of Alfreton. It was dedicated to Thomas a Becket, and the Virgin Mary; and from the former patron, has erroneously been supposed, to have been erected in expiation of his murder, by its founder, who has been represented as one of the executioners of the proud archbishop of Canterbury. Besides the endowments of its original founder, many other grants and privileges were bestowed on it, by various other persons, in different

parts of the country. On the dissolution of
this house, in the twenty-sixth of Henry the
Eighth, its revenues, according to Speed, were
estimated at £157. 10s. 2d. The Abbey was
granted, in the twenty-eighth year of the same
reign, to Sir Wich. Strelley; and several of the
lands belonging to it, were purchased by Sir
William West. Of this extensive building,
only a small part of the chapel is now remaining.

CHAP. XI.

Archdeaconry of Derby.

ONE, of the most southern parishes in this division, is DARLEY, in Domesday called *Dere-leie.* The living is a rectory under the Dean of Lincoln, and the church is dedicated to St. Helen. The whole parish contained about 400 houses, when an ascertainment was last made; but their number has increased very much of late years, owing to the erection of a cotton-mill, belonging to the Messrs. Dakeynes.

. The village of Darley is small, pleasantly situated on the banks of the Derwent, in the beautiful dale leading from Matlock to Bakewell, furnishing a most enchanting ride. The church is ancient, and in the church-yard stands one of the oldest and largest yew-trees in the kingdom. No traveller, can pass without noticing its appearance, which gives solemnity to the lonely cemetry which it oversha-

-dows. This venerable tree, is now robbed of a
great part of its pristine honors, but still exhibits a specimen of unusual vegetation, measuring in girth 33 feet. It is supposed that it
has been decaying for more than 300 years,
and in its prime to have covered a space of 100
feet in diameter. The church contains several ancient monuments: against a window on
the South side, is a recumbent statue of a Knight
Templar, with his feet crossed, a sword by his
side, and his hands crossed on his breast: tradition says his name was John of Darley, and
that he lived at a place in the neighbourhood
called Darley-Hall. Beneath this is an alabaster slab, with an inscription in old English,
now defaced. There are also some old monuments to the memory of the Rowsley family.
There is likewise in the church a stone fountain,
inscribed with letters, and coats of arms, which
is supposed to be very ancient. An antiquated
stone coffin is seen in the church-yard, probably belonging to some great family in the neighbourhood.

SNITTERTON-HALL, formerly the property of
the *Sacheverels*, is a curious old mansion, standing near the summit of a hill to the West of
the village, on the western bank of the Derwent. The front has two projecting wings,

with pointed gables, embattled sides, and large
bowed windows.   The entrance instead of being in the centre, as customary, is on one side;
the whole structure is of stone, enclosed within
high walls.

YOULGRAVE, by the Norman surveyors called *Giolgrave*, is a parish and village, containing about 140 houses, and 650 inhabitants, who
are principally supported by agriculture and
the mining business. The living is a rectory,
and the church is dedicated to All-Saints.   In
the reign of Henry the Second, it was given,
with its chapels, to the Abbey at Leicester;
but it was presented by Edward VI. to William
Cavendish; whose descendant, the Duke of
Devonshire, is the present patron.   The whole
parish contains the chapelries of Winster and
Elton; the hamlets of Alport, Birchover, Stanton, Stanton-Leys, Middleton, Gratton, and
some other smaller places.

WINSTER, anciently *Winsterne*, is a small
town, where a weekly market is held; it contains about 230 houses, whose inhabitants, are
employed in working the lead mines, and in
preparing cotton for spinning.   On the common, near the town, are several *cáirns*, or stone
barrows, and also, two or three barrows of earth.
One of the latter was opened in the year 1766,

and in it were found two glass vessels, between
eight and ten inches in height, containing about
a pint of light-green coloured limpid water.—
At the same time were discovered, a silver col-
lar or bracelet, studded with human heads, together with some other small ornaments; one
of which was of fillagree-work of gold and silver gilt, and set with garnet or red glass. There
were also, several square and round beads of
various colours, of glass and earth; and some remains of brass clasps and hinges, with a piece of
wood, which appeared to be a part of a box in
which the ornaments had been deposited. Several of these are now in the possession of a
gentleman of Bakewell. From the above antiquities, it is supposed, that the barrow was
raised over some Briton of distinction, shortly
after the Roman invasion.

Near the hamlets of BIRCHOVER, and STAN-
TON, the former of which contains about eighty
houses, and the latter seventy, there are several objects well worthy of particular notice.

At ROWTOR, near Birchover, is a remarkable assemblage of grit-stone rocks, extending
in length between seventy and eighty yards,
and rising to the height of from forty to fifty.
This massive pile is distinguished by the name

of *Router*, or *Roo-tor-rocks*.* Its general position, is, undoubtedly natural, and was, perhaps, occasioned by the sinking of the surrounding strata; but the forms and arrangement of many of the stones on the upper-part,
display evident traces of their being placed
here by design.

Near the East end of this pile, is a large stone
of an irregular shape, twelve feet high, and
thirty-six in circumference, and estimated to
weigh about fifty tons: its bottom, has somewhat of a convex form; and the rock on which
it stands, appears to have been hollowed to receive it.   When Mr. Pilkington wrote, this
stone was so exactly poised upon one end, that
a child might easily give it a vibratory motion;
but it is now immoveable, through having been
forced from its equilibrium by the mischievous
efforts of fourteen young men, who assembled
for the purpose on Whit-Sunday, in the year
1799.   At a little distance to the North, is a
second rocking-stone, resembling an egg in
shape, which may be moved by the strength of

---

* " This appellation appears to have been derived from
the various rocking-stones near the summit; as it is a common expression in the provincial dialect, that a thing *roos*
backward and forward."—Archæologia, Vol. VI. p. 110.

a single finger, though twelve feet in length,
and fourteen in girth. Farther to the North, is
another rocking-stone, resembling the latter
both in figure and facility of motion; and to
the West, are seven stones piled on each other,
various in size and form, but two or three very
large; all which may be moved by the pressure
of one hand, and this at various places.

"It should be observed, that the huge masses which occupy the summit of Router-rocks,
range from east to west along the middle of the
hill, and fiave a narrow passage, and two chambers or caves, cut within them. The largest
cave has a remarkable *Echo;* its length is sixteen feet, its width twelve, and its height about
nine. The origin of these excavations cannot
have been very remote, as the marks of the pick
on the sides, are very visible and fresh. They
were, probably, formed about the same period
as an elbow-chair near the west end of the
North side, which has been rudely shaped on
the face of a large mass of stone, and has a
seat for one person on each side of it. This,
we have been informed, was executed by the
direction of Mr. Thomas Eyre, who inhabited
the ancient manor-house, called *Router-Hall,*
near the foot of the hill on the south, about
sixty years ago, and used frequently to enter-

tain company on this elevated spot. A hollow
in the stone, which forms the highest point of
these rocks, Mr. Rooke supposes to have been
a rock-basin; he also mentions a second rock-
basin, on the north-west side.

" Nearly a quarter of a mile west of Rowtor,
is another assemblage of large rocks, forming
a similar kind of hill, called *Bradley-Tor;* on
the upper part of which, is a rocking-stone,
thirty-two feet in circumference, of an orbicu-
lar shape, and raised above the ground by two
stones, having a passage between them. Its
conformity to the description of the *Tolmen*
given by Dr. Borlase in his antiquities of Cornwall, has induced an opinion of its having been
a rock idol."

STANTON, *Stantune,* is a manor, the joint
property of the Duke of Rutland, and Bache
Thornhill, Esq. the latter of whom has an elegant mansion here, on a demesne, that has
been the property of his ancestors, of the sur-
names, of Bache and Thornhill, for more than
two centuries.

Near the south-west side of *Stanton-moor,*
(a rocky uncultivated waste about two miles in
length, and one and a half in breadth), is an
elevated ridge, which rises into three craggy
eminences, respectively called, *Carcliff-Rocks,*

Graned Tor, and *Durwood Tor*. On the top of the former, are several basins, varying in diameter from two to three feet; and about midway to the bottom, towards the west, is a small cave, called the *Hermitage*, supposed to have been, in former ages, the abode of some mistaken and zealous devotee. To the right hand on entering it, is seen a crucifix about a yard high; it is in relief, and almost perfect: in the inner part is a seat and a recess, apparently intended for a sleeping place.

" *Graned Tor*, called also *Robin Hood's Stride*, and *Mock Beggar's Hall*, is a singular heap of rocks, which Mr. Rooke supposes to have been anciently a curious group of Druidical monuments.* On one rock, that seems, from its position, to have fallen from the top, and is twenty-nine feet in circumference, are four rock-basins; and at the bottom of another a rock-basin of an oval form, four feet in length, and two feet ten inches wide, which ' evidently appears to have been cut with a tool.'† This basin is sheltered by a massive stone, placed in a sloping direction against the rock. The uppermost points of this Tor, are two vast stones,

19   E 4

---

* Archæologia, Vol. XII. p. 47.   † Ibid.

standing upright, each eighteen feet high, and about twenty-two yards asunder, which at a distance resemble the chimneys of an ancient mansion-house, from which circumstances the pile obtained the appellation Mock Beggar's Hall. Round the bottom of the hill there seems to have been a fence of broken masses of stone. On the top of Durwood Tor, are three rock-basins, artificially formed; and an impending crag, or rock-canopy, which overhangs what has been denominated an ‘augurial seat.’ At *Durwood*, on removing a large stone, an urn was discovered half full of burnt bones; and near it, two ancient *Querns*, or hand-mill-stones, flat at top, and somewhat convex on the under sides, about four inches and a half thick, and nearly a foot in diameter; the upper stone so much less than the under, that being placed on it, it could be turned round within its rim.* Similar stones have been found in Yorkshire and such are yet in common use in the Hebrides.

" In a field north of Graned Tor, called Nine-Stone-Close, are the remains of a *Druidical Circle*, about thirteen yards in diameter, now consisting of seven rude stones of various dimensions; one of them is about eight feet in

* Gough's Additions to the Britannia.

height, and nine in circumference. Between
seventy and eighty yards to the south, are two
other stones of similar dimensions, standing
erect.

"About a quarter of a mile west of the little valley which separates Hartle-moor from
Stanton-moor, is an ancient work called *Cas-
tle-Ring*, which Mr. Rooke supposes to have
been a British encampment. Its form is ellip-
tical; its shortest diameter from south-east to
north-west, is 165 feet; its length from north-
east to south-west, 243. It was encompassed
by a deep ditch and double vallum, but part
of the latter has been levelled by the plough.

"In a small enclosure, adjoining the north-
west end of Stanton-moor, are some remarkably situated rocks; on two of which the following inscriptions were cut in Roman capitals,
about 170 years ago, by an ancestor of the *Cal-
ton* family, who possessed the estate. '*Res
rustica quæ sine dubitatione proxima et quasi
consanguinea sapientiæ est, tam discentibus eget
quam magistris.*"—"*Nihil est homini libero dig-
nius, et quod mihi ad sapientis vitam proxime,
videtur accedere.*'

"About half a mile north-east from the Row-
tor-Rocks, on Stanton-moor, is a Druidical
Circle, eleven yards in diameter, called *The*

Nine Ladies, composed of the same number of rude stones, from three to four feet in height, and of different breadths. A single stone, named *The King*, stands at the distance of thirty-four yards. Near this circle, are several cairns or barrows; most of which have been opened, and various remains of ancient customs discovered in them. In one of the barrows, opened by Mr. Rooke, an urn of coarse clay was found, three feet three inches in height, having within it a smaller urn, covered with a piece of clay; in both of them were burnt bones and ashes: two other urns, similar to the former, were discovered in the same barrow.— Urns with burnt bones, &c. have likewise been met with in some of the other barrows. Under one of the cairns human bones were found, together with a large blue glass bead.

" On the east side of Stanton-moor, near the edge of a declivity overlooking Darley Dale, are three remarkable stones, standing about a quarter of a mile from each other, in a north and south direction. One of these, called *Cat's Stone*, is on the verge of a precipice, and has a road leading to it, cut through a surface of loose stones and rock: the second is named *Gorse**

* Archæologia, Vol. VI. p. 113, 114. Mr. Rooke supposes this name to have been derived from the British *Gorseddau*: but is it not more likely from the shrub, *Gorse ?*

Stone: and the third, which is the largest, is called *Heart Stone*, and measures eighty-three feet in circumference. Several other stones of singular forms may be observed on different parts of the moor; and particularly one called the *Andle Stone*, about a quarter of a mile eastward of the Rowtor Rocks: this is nearly fifteen feet high, and appears to have been shaped by art. At a little distance is another larger stone, named *Thomas Eyre's* chair, which has been rudely cut into the figure of a chair, and was formerly elevated on some smaller stones; but has been thrown down."

ALPORT is a hamlet, containing about twenty-two houses, whose inhabitants are chiefly employed in the pursuits of agriculure.

MIDDLETON, *Middeltune*, is a village, situated in a deep and narrow valley, and containing about fifty houses. Near this place, is one of the most remarkable monuments of antiquity to be found in Derbyshire. This is the ARBE-LOUS, or ARBOR-LOWS, a circle of stones, within which the ancient British Bards,[*] were accustomed to hold their assemblies. ·

* *Bardism:* by this is meant, what is generally conceived amongst the English of the term *Druidism*, which is a mistake, by giving the appellation of a particular branch to the whole of the order; for a matter of conve-

This interesting remain consists of an area, encompassed by a broad ditch, which is bounded by a high mound or bank: its form is that of an ellypsis, or imperfect circle, measuring forty-six yards. from East to West, and fifty-

nience an appropriate set of Bards,† were distinguished by the name of *Derwiddion* or *Druids.* The Bards were divided into three essential classes;—the *Bardd Braint, Derwidd,* and *Ovydd.*

The *Bardd Braint* was the title of the corporate degree, or fundamental class of the order. On all occasions when he acted officially, he wore the unicoloured robe of sky-blue, which was the distinguishing dress of the order, being emblematic of Peace, and also of Truth, from having no variety of colours.

The *Derwiddion* or *Druids,* were such of the Bards of either of the three orders, that were set apart to, or employed peculiarly in, the exercise of religious functions. The dress of the Druid was white, the emblem of Holiness, and peculiarly of Truth, as being the colour of light, or the sun.

The *Ovydd,* was an honorary degree, to which a candidate could be immediately admitted, without being obliged to pass through the regular discipline. The requisite qualifications for an Ovydd were, in general, an acquaintance with valuable discoveries in science; as the use of letters, medicine, languages, and the like. Thus *Bardd Braint* was peculiarly the ruling order; *Derwidd* the religious functionary; and the *Ovydd,* was the literary, or scientific order.

BARDISM was instituted long before the Christian æra, in a very early period of the world; and we must attribute

† The present vulgar acceptation of BARDD, whence the English word BARD, is, simply, a Poet. The literal meaning of the word is, one that maketh conspicuous; and the idea intended to be conveyed is, a TEACHER or PHILOSOPHER: and its import is well defined in MASON's epithet- MASTER OF WISDOM.

two from North to South. The width of the ditch, which surrounds the area, on which the stones are placed, is six yards; the height of the bank, or vallum, on the inside, is from six to eight yards; but it varies throughout the whole circumference. The bank seems to have been formed from the earth thrown up from the ditch; which is not carried entirely round the area: but both at the northern and southern extremities, they terminate, and allow a level passage or entrance of about fourteen yards wide. On the East side of the northern entrance, is a barrow standing in the same line of circumference, but entirely detached from it. This barrow was opened some years ago, and in it were found a stag's horns.

The stones which compose the circle within the area, are rough and unhewn masses of limestone, about thirty in number. Most of them are about five feet long, three broad, and one

its formation, to an age now deemed, by the learned world, to have been involved in barbarity. The principal doctrines of the order were ;—the belief in one God, the Creator and Governor of the Universe—Universal Peace and Good-will :—in short, it was a system embracing all the leading principles, which tend to spread liberty, peace and happiness among mankind; and for that reason, perhaps, too perfect to be generally adopted by any nation, or body of people. Vide Owen's Llywarch Hên.

thick; these, however, are variable, and their respective shapes are different. They all lie on the ground, and generally in an oblique position; but the representation of the narrowest end of each being pointed towards the centre, in order to represent the rays of the sun, which the Bards are erroneously supposed to have made an object of worship, must have arisen from an inaccurate observation; for they as frequently point towards the ditch as otherwise. In the middle of the area are three large stones, which it is probable composed originally but one, the *Maen Gorsedd* (Stone of Assembly). Within the circle are some smaller stones, scattered irregularly.

Whether the stones that compose the circle ever stood upright, as most of the stones of the Bardic circles do, is an enquiry not easy to determine; though Mr. Pilkington was informed, that a very old man living at Middleton, remembered, when a boy, to have seen them standing obliquely upon one end. This secondary kind of evidence, does not seem entitled to much credit; as the view of the stones themselves, and their relative situations, are almost demonstrative to the contrary.

This, most probably, was one of the provincial places of meeting of the ancient Bards.

They held their *Gorseddau*, or meetings, in the
open air, and (to use one of their own mottos)
in the face of the sun, and eye of the light. All
their places of assemblage were, like this, set
apart by forming a circle of stones around the
Maen Gorsedd; and at their meetings, the
Bardic traditions were recited, and the most
interesting topics discussed. The Bards always
stood bare-headed and bare-footed, in their
unicoloured robe, at the *Gorsedd*, and within
the *Cylch Cyngrair*, or Circle of Federation.
The ceremony used on the opening of a meeting,
was the sheathing of a sword, on the *Maen Gor-*
sedd, at which all the Bards assisted; and this
was accompanied with a very short pertinent dis-
course.* When the business was finished, the
meeting was closed by taking up, but not un-
sheathing, the sword, with a few words on the
occasion, when all covered their heads and

---

* The following is the purport of what was said at the
opening of one;—" THE TRUTH AGAINST THE WORLD:
Under the protection of the *Bards of the isle of Britain*, are
all who repair to this place, where there is not a naked
weapon against them; and all who seek the privilege apper-
taining to science and Bardism, let them demand it from:
Iolo Morganwg, *W. Mechain*, *Hywel Eryri*, and *D.Ddu Eryri*,
and they being all *graduated Bards*, according to the privilege of the *Bards of the Isle of Britain*. THE TRUTH AGAINST
THE WORLD."

19   F 4

feet. At the meeting there was always one, called the *Dadgeiniad*, or the reciter, whose business was, to recite the traditions and poems, to make proclamations, announce candidates, open and close the *Gorsedd*, and the like.

The spot on which this British place of Assembly was held, though considerably elevated, is not so high as some eminences, in the neighbouring country; it however commands an extensive view, more especially towards the East, and seems to be well suited to the purpose, to which it was undoubtedly appropriated: and the contemplative mind, feels a sensation approaching to veneration, when he treads the ground, rendered so interesting, by having been the theatre on which the Briton, perhaps, some thousands of years ago, displayed his eloquence, his knowledge, and his love of his country.

. " About the distance of half a mile from Arbor-low, to the West, is another large barrow, called *End-low*, in which ashes and burnt bones have been found. From this, numerous barrows may be seen, on the distant eminences; and in some of them, urns, human bones, ashes, and other memorials of the customs of remote ages, have been discovered. The names of several places in the neighbourhood are indicative of antiquity, though the places themselves are now of little account: as *Aldwark*, five miles from the Arbor-low, on the Roman road from Buxton to Little-Chester; *Aldport,* on another ancient way leading from Aldwark towards Bakewell, and some others.

" On a waste piece of ground between Moneyash and Arbor-low, about one mile and a half from the latter, is a huge block of limestone, lying on the heath, and having a circular cavity on the top, which those who discover remnants of Druidism in every singular shaped or hollow stone, would probably denominate a rock-basin. Its diameter is, about nine or ten inches, and its depth eighteen or twenty. The interior is rugged and uneven; and has somewhat the appearance of a corkscrew; though the hollows do not all run into each other. Scarcely a doubt can be entertained of this excavation being natural, though the particular cause of it cannot perhaps be assigned."*

BAKEWELL.

BAKEWELL, is the most extensive parish in Derbyshire; measuring in length from north-west to south east, more than twenty miles, and

---

* Beauties of England, Vol. III.

in breadth eight. It contains, nine chapelries, besides several large hamlets; containing altogether, about 1200 houses.

The town of Bakewell is of great antiquity. It is generally granted, that it existed in the time of the Saxons: for in the year 924, Edward the Elder, marched from Nottingham into *Peaclond*, as far as a place called *Badecanwyllam*, which he converted into a borough, and ordered a city to be built in its neighbourhood, and to be strongly fortified.* From this circumstance, it is supposed that there was a town here before that period, which derived its name *(Bath-quelle)* from a Bath situated in the place, which had been in use long before the visit of this monarch. The place where this ancient bath was situated, is now occupied by the residence of Mr. White Watson, who forms mineralogical collections for private cabinets; and whose own *Collection of Fossils* attracts many inspectors.

At the time of the Norman survey, there were "at *Badequella* two priests and a church,"† at which period the manor belonged to the king, with the exception of one carucate in *Hadune*, (Haddon) claimed by Henry de Fer-

* Gibson's Saxon Chronicle, p. 110.
† Domesday, *Orig.* 272, *b.* 2. Trans. p. 294.

rieres. Sometime afterwards, it became the property of William Peverel, whose son gave two parts of his tithe of his demesne of Bakewell, to the monastery of Lenton, in Nottinghamshire. The remaining part of the tithes, with the glebe and patronage of the church, was given to the Dean and Chapter of Litchfield, by John Earl of Montaigne, in whom the estates of the Peverels became vested. The manor afterwards belonged to the *Gernons* of Essex, one of whom, had a grant of a fair to be held here, from Henry the Third. In this family it continued till the reign of Henry the Seventh, when it was sold to the *Vernons* of Haddon, from whom it has descended to his Grace the Duke of Rutland, the present possessor.

Bakewell church is situated on an eminence, above the principal part of the town; it is an ancient structure, and built in the form of a cross, with an octagonal tower in the centre, terminated by a lofty spire. The various styles of architecture which may be observed in this church, prove it to have been erected at three different periods. The western part of the nave, is of plain Saxon architecture; but the external arch of the West door-way, is enriched with Saxon ornaments, and supposed to be the most

of arms, containing many quarterings with those of Vernon: his ladies are so much alike, that, a trifling variation in their dresses excepted, they appear as if cast in the same mould. The other monuments are large and costly; but there is nothing particularly excellent in the workmanship.

This church has lately been endowed with eight new bells, of the value of £500.; and an organ has just been erected which cost £300. The living is a vicarage, and the church is dedicated to All-Saints; and the Dean and Chapter of Litchfield are patrons. In the churchyard is an ancient stone cross, said to have been conveyed hither from some other place. The sides are diversified by ornamental sculpture. On the front are several rudely carved figures; the upper compartment appears to have represented a crucifixion; but as the top of the cross is broken off, the intention can hardly be determined: this ancient remain is supposed to be nearly eight hundred years old.

Bakewell is a Market town, standing on the western banks of the river Wye: its market, which is now on Friday, was formerly held on Monday, and at present is but very thinly attended. The *Town-Hall*, an obscure building, was erected in 1709: near it are six *Alms-*

houses, for six bachelors, or *sole-men*, endowed
by the Manners, with an estate in Wensley, in
Darley, and a rent-charge on an estate in Nottinghamshire.

Near the entrance into the town from Ashford, is a large cotton mill, belonging to R.
Arkwright, Esq. in which from 300 to 350 persons of both sexes, are employed, inclusive of
the mechanics, who keep the works in order.
The number of houses at Bakewell is about
240; that of inhabitants nearly 1400. Between
the grit-stone and limestone strata about Bakewell, is a thick stratum of shale, which being
of an argillaceous nature, and retentive of
moisture, the pasturage on it is remarkably
good.

About two miles to the South of Bakewell,
is HADDON-HALL, a venerable mansion belonging to the Duke of Rutland: it is situated on
a bold eminence, rising on the eastern side of
the river Wye, and overlooks the pleasant vale
of Haddon. When the desolate turrets, and
the princely ruins of Haddon, are first seen
amid a luxuriantly swelling group of old and
dark trees, they appear to be those of a strong
fortress; and even on a nearer approach, the
idea is apparently confirmed: but though thus

castellated, it does not appear ever to have
been furnished with the means of effectual resistance. The mansion consists of several apartments and offices, erected at different periods,
round two quadrangular courts. The most
ancient part, is the tower over the gateway, on
the East side of the upper quadrangle, and was
the grand entrance in the time of the Peverels:
this part, was probably built, about the reign
of Edward the Third—this, however, cannot
now be exactly ascertained. The chapel was
erected in Henry the Sixth's time; and the
tower at the north-west corner, on which are
the arms of the Vernons, Pipes, &c. may be
assigned to the same reign. The gallery on
the South front was built in the reign of Elizabeth, by Sir John Manners; and the North side
by the first Earl of Rutland, of the second
branch: over this are the arms of Manners and
Vernons.

The principal entrance is at the north-west
angle, under a high tower, through a large
arched gateway, leading by a flight of angular
steps into the great court:—From the great
court is a flight of steps, leading to the great
porch, over the door of which are two shields
of arms carved, in stone—the one containing
those of *Vernon*, and the other, of *Fulco de*

Pambridge, Lord of Tong, in Shropshire, whose daughter and heiress Isabella, married Sir Richard Vernon, and considerably increased the family estate by her possessions. On the right of the passage leading from the porch is the *Great Hall*, having a communication with the grand staircase and state apartments; and on the left, ranging in a line, are four large door-ways, with great pointed stone arches, which connect with the kitchen, buttery, wine-cellar, and numerous small apartments, that appear to have been used as lodging-rooms, for the guests and their retainers. In the kitchen are two large fire-places, with irons for a prodigious number of spits; various stoves, great double ranges of dressers, and an enormous chopping-block, whereon an ox might lie with ease. "The contiguous larder," says an entertaining Tourist, " has a leaden bathing tub, sufficient to hold meat for a garrison, together with a place like a tun for smaller provision: the dairy is of equal dimensions."

" The Hall must have been the great public dining-room, for no other apartment is sufficiently spacious for the purpose. At the upper end is a raised floor, where the table for the Lord and his principal guests was spread; and on two sides is a gallery, supported on pillars.

From the south-east corner is a passage, leading to the great stair-case, formed of huge
blocks of stone rudely jointed; at the top of
which, on the right, is a large apartment hung
with arras, and behind it a little door, opening
into the hall-gallery.

" On the left of the passage, at the head of
the great stairs, are five or six semicircular steps,
formed of solid timber, that lead into the *Long
Gallery*, which occupies the whole south side
of the second court; and is 110 feet in length,
and seventeen wide. The flooring is of oak
planks, affirmed by tradition to have been cut
out of a single tree, which grew in the garden.
The wainscotting is likewise of oak, and is curiously ornamented : on the frieze are carvings
of boars' heads, thistles, and roses; these, with
the arms, &c. prove it, in the opinion of Mr.
King, to have been put up *after* the house came
into the possession of Sir John Manners, yet
before the title of Earl of Rutland descended
to that branch of the family. In the midst of
the gallery is a great square recess, besides several bow windows, in one of which are the
arms of the Earl of Rutland, impaling Vernon,
with its quarterings, and circled with a garter,
&c.; and in another, the arms of England, si-
milarly encircled, and surmounted with a

crown. Near the end of the gallery is a short
passage, that opens into a room, having a frieze
and a cornice of rough plaister, adorned with
peacocks, and boars' heads, in alternate succession: an adjoining apartment is ornamented in the same manner; and over the chimney
is a very large bass-relief of Orpheus charming
the beasts, of similar composition.

. "All the principal rooms, except the gallery, were hung with loose arras, a great part
of which still remains; and the doors were concealed every where behind the hangings, so
that the tapestry was to be lifted up to pass in
and out; only for convenience, there were great
iron hooks (many of which are still in their
places,) by means whereof it might occasionally be held back. The doors being thus concealed, nothing can be conceived more ill-fa-
shioned than the workmanship; few of these
fit at all close; and wooden bolts, rude bars,
and iron hasps, are in general their best and
only fastenings."*

.. The chapel is in the south-west angle of the
great court; from whence the entrance leads
under a sharp pointed arch. It has a body and

* Archæologia, Vol. VI. p. 353. Beauties of England,
Vol. III.

two aisles, divided from the former by pillars
and pointed arches. In the windows are some
good remains of painted glass, bearing the date,
Millesimo CCCCXXVII. By the side of the
altar, is a niche and a basin for holy water: an
ancient stone font is likewise preserved here.—
Near the entrance into the chapel, stands the
Roman Altar mentioned by Mr. Gibson.*—
" It was digged up," says he, " in the grounds
belonging to *Haddon-house*, near *Bakewell*, and
is cut in a rough sort of stone, such as the
house itself is built of."—The inscription is
now nearly obliterated; but according to the
above-mentioned antiquaries, was the following;—

DEO
MARTI
BRACIACÆ
OSITTIVS
CÆCILIAN
PRÆFECT
TRO : : :
V. S.

Haddon-Hall, is considered as one of our
most complete baronial residences now remaining; and though not at present inhabited, nor
in very good repair, is extremely interesting to

* In his Camden, p. 497.

the antiquary, from the many indications it
exhibits of the festive manners and hospitality
of our ancestors; and of the inconvenient, yet
social, arrangement by which their mode of life
was regulated. This ancient mansion would
have been still more interesting, had it not,
about fifty years ago, been stripped of its furniture, which was, at that time, conveyed to
Belvoir Castle, in Leicestershire, another seat of
the Duke of Rutland.

The extensive park, which belonged to this
house, was ploughed up and cultivated, about
the same time as the removal of the furniture.
The gardens consist entirely of terraces, ranged
one above another; each having a sort of stone
balustrade. The prospects from one or two
situations, are extremely fine; and in the vicinity of the house, is a sweeping group of luxuriant old trees.

In Domesday Haddon, is set down as a be-
rewick in the manor of Bakewell, and as belonging to the king: but soon after it was constituted into a manor, and became the property of the *Avenells*, whose co-heirs married to
Vernon and *Bassett*, in the reign of Richard the
First. In the family of Bassetts, half the estate continued in the time of king Edward the
Third. The heiress of Vernon married to

Franceys, who assumed the surname of Vernon; and the whole estate, was the entire property of Sir Richard Vernon, in Henry the Sixth's time. This gentleman was speaker of the parliament held at Leicester, in the fourth year of Henry the Sixth (1425) by whom he was afterwards constituted treasurer of Calais, and died in the year 1452. He was succeeded by his son, who was also appointed Constable of England, and was the last that held that important office. Sir Henry Vernon his son and successor, was governor and treasurer to Prince Arthur, the eldest son and heir apparent of king Henry the Seventh. There is a tradition that the Prince frequently lived with Sir Henry at Haddon, where there was an apartment called the Prince's Chamber, with his arms cut in several places. Sir George, the son of Sir Henry Vernon, was so much distinguished for his magnificent port and hospitality, that he acquired the name of, *King of the Peak*. On his death, in the seventh year of Queen Elizabeth, his possessions, which amounted to thirty manors, descended to his two daughters, Margaret and Dorothy: the former was married to Sir Thomas Stanley, Knt. second son of the Earl of Derby, and the latter to Sir John Manners, Knt. second son to Thomas, first Earl of Rutland of that name. By this marriage, Haddon, with several manors in Derbyshire, that had been held by the Vernons, became the property of the Manners; and have regularly descended to the present Duke of Rutland.

The heirs and descendants of Sir John Manners, continued to reside at Haddon, for some centuries; but at the beginning of the last, it was quitted for Belvoir Castle. In the time of the first Duke of Rutland, (so created by Queen Anne,) seven score servants were maintained here; and the house was kept open, in the true style of Old English Hospitality, during twelve days after Christmas. Since that period, it has, occasionally been the scene of mirth and revelry; and the cheerful welcome of former ages, so far as the despoiled condition of the mansion would admit, has not been wanting to increase the pleasure of the guests. The joyous festive board was spread here, shortly after the conclusion of the Peace with America, when nearly 200 couples danced in the long gallery.

Ashford, Aisseford, is a chapelry in the parish of Bakewell; the village is situated on the banks of the Wye, and frequently from its lowness, called Ashford in the Water. The whole liberty contains, about 130 houses, and 600 inhabitants, who are employed in cotton spinning, agriculture, and at the marble manufactory.

Here, Edward Plantagenet of Woodstock, Earl of Kent, and after him, the *Hollands*, Earls of Kent, and more recently, the *Nevilles*, Earls of Westmoreland, had a residence; of which the only vestige now remaining, is the moat that surrounded the castle. This estate was sold by the Earl of Westmoreland, to Sir William Cavendish, the favorite of Wolsey, and still continues in the Cavendish family, being the property of the Duke of Devonshire.

" The *Marble Works* in this village, where the black and grey marbles found in the vicinity are sawn and polished, were the first of the kind, ever established in Great Britain. They were originally constructed about seventy years ago, by the late Mr. Henry Watson, of Bakewell; but though a patent was obtained to secure the profits of the invention, the advantages were not commensurate with the expectations that had been formed. The present proprietor is Mr. John Platt, of Rotherham, in Yorkshire, who rents the quarries at Ashford, where the black marble is obtained, of the Duke of Devonshire; as well as those where

the grey marble is procured, at Ricklow Dale,
near Moneyash. These are the only quarries
of the kind now worked in any part of Derbyshire. The machinery is somewhat similar in
construction, to that described in the marble and spar works at Derby; but it is worked
by water. One part, called the *Sweeping Mill*,
from its circular motion, is also different; by
this, a *floor*, containing eighty superficial feet
of marble slabs, is levelled at the same time."

MONSAL-DALE, is a most pleasing sequestered retreat, at a little distance to the West of
the road leading from Ashford to Tideswell:
On entering this Dale from the above-mentioned
road, the river Wye is seen, winding its current, through a rich and verdant valley. In
some places, the scenery is diversified by dark
rocks, which jut out on the South side, like the
immense towers of a strong fortress, with the
stream of the river sportively flowing at their
feet. Lower down, the crags soften into verdure; the Dale expands, and the eye dwells,
enraptured, on the rich prospect that presents
itself. The mountainous banks on each side,
are diversified, with fine masses of wood, which
occasionally slope down to the margin of the
river: in other places, the grey colour. of the
rocks, is beautifully harmonized by shrubs, un-

derwood, and green turf, which intermix their
varying tints, and increase the general richness
of the scenery. More distant, the bosom of
the Dale spreads wider; and the stream softly
meanders through luxuriant meadows, having
its margin occupied by a small farm-house, encompassed and partly concealed with wood—
and with its accompaniments, of a rustic wooden
bridge, broken rocks, and green turf, composing a very picturesque scene. The scenery
of Monsal-Dale, is in some places romantic;
but its general character is picturesque beauty,
which it possesses in a most enchanting degree—
and the man must be destitute of taste for the
beauties of nature, who can travel this way,
and look into it, without being filled with the
highest degree of admiration and delight.—
Standing upon the edge of a high and steep
precipice, which forms the back ground, and
casting the eye down into the valley, almost
every object is beheld, which can contribute to
render a small scene beautiful; and the sight is
delighted with one of the most pleasing views,
that the plastic hand of Nature ever arranged.
" Peaceful Monsal-Dale! let us look down on
thy sequestered hamlets, and thy huts of happiness! long, long may it be, ere the emissaries
of darkness create among thy inhabitants, en-

vies, anxieties, and wretchedness, or lucre lead them from their native paradise!"

. " On the summit of the eminence that over-looks Monsal-Dale, and is here called the *Great Finn*, was a large barrow, about 160 feet in circumference, chiefly composed of broken mas-ses of limestone, to obtain which, the barrow was destroyed, at different times, in the years 1794, 1795, and 1796. Within this tumulus, various skeletons were discovered, as well as se-veral urns of coarse clay, slightly baked, con-taining burnt bones, ashes, beaks of birds, &c. Two of the skeletons were of gigantic size, and lay in opposite directions, with their feet point-ing to an urn placed between them. In one part, at the bottom, was a cavity cut in the solid rock (two feet nine inches broad, and two feet one inch in depth,) wherein lay the bones of a skeleton with the face downward; and on the top of the skull, where it appeared to have been fixed by a strong cement, a piece of black Derbyshire marble, dressed, two feet in length, nine inches broad, and six inches thick: under the head, were two small arrow-heads of flint. In another cavity formed in the soil, with flat stones at the sides and bottom, were ashes and burnt bones. A spear-head, and some other memorials of ancient customs, were also found

here. It should be noticed, that, excepting
the side next the precipice, the summit of the
Great Finn, is surrounded by a double ditch,
with a vallum to each: the distance between
the valla, is 160 yards.

" Mr. Hayman Rooke, from whose letter, inserted in the twelfth volume of the Archæologia,
some of the above particulars are extracted,
imagines this barrow to have been of very remote antiquity, and quotes a passage in confirmation, from the *Nenia Britannica;* the
learned author of which, when speaking of
arrow-heads of flint observes, ' they are evi-
dences of a people not in the use of malleable
metal; and it therefore implies, wherever these
arms are found in barrows, they are incontestibly the relics of a primitive barbarous people, and preceding the æra of those barrows,
in which brass or iron arms are found."*

BASLOW, *Basselau*, is a chapelry in the parish of Bakewell, containing about 130 houses.
The liberty of Baslow includes, the hamlets of
Bubnal, Froggat, and Curbar, containing altogether about 90 houses.

GREAT LONGSTONE, *Langesdune*, is a chapelry, containing about 80 houses: the church

* Beauties of England, Vol. III. p. 483.

is dedicated to St. Giles. *Little Longstone*, an adjoining hamlet, contains about 25 houses.

The church at SHELDON, *Scelhadun*, is dedicated to All-Saints: the number of houses in this liberty is about thirty-five.

TADDINGTON, *Tadintune*, is another chapelry under Bakewell. The church is dedicated to St. Michael; and the number of houses in the hamlet is about seventy. These villages are situated in a part of the High-Peak, which is but little cultivated; and therefore, the inhabitants depend chiefly upon the working the lead-mines for their support.

MONYASH, *Maneis*, is also a chapelry in the parish of Bakewell: it consists of about fifty-five houses, scattered irregularly over a large portion of ground, and surrounded with distant elevated tracts of country. In the reign of Edward the First, the Archbishop of Canterbury ordered, that, to the twelve acres of fertile land, which the inhabitants gave, at the foundation of the chapel, to the priest celebrating divine worship there three times in a week, they should add one mark every year, and the chapter should pay the remainder, in order that for the honor of God, and the increase of his worship, divine service might be continually performed there. The church is dedicated to St. Leonard.

William de Lynford, who held the manor of Moneyash in the reign of Edward the Third, had a grant of a market and fair to be held here, in reward for the good services he had performed for the king in Scotland; but the place being now but very thinly inhabited, the market and fair are discontinued. At the distance of a mile and a half, in a narrow dale, which presents some pleasant scenery, are the quarries where much of the Derbyshire marble is obtained. The rocks from which it is blasted, seem almost wholly composed of etrochæ.

CHELMORTON, is a village situated at the foot of a high eminence, and containing about forty houses. The inhabitants are employed, chiefly, in the lead mines, and in the pursuits of agriculture. The manufacture of ribands has also been introduced here.

In the reign of Edward I. (1282) the revenue of the chapel of Chelmorton, was estimated at sixty marks; two parts of which, the Prior of Lenton in Nottinghamshire received, and the remainder belonged to the chapter at Litchfield; and the Archbishop of Canterbury ordered, that the prior and chapter should provide ornaments and books in the same proportion. The chapter was also obliged to furnish a priest, and to allow five marks for his support, which were to be taken from the tithes, before they were carried out of the liberty.

On the summit of the hill above the village, are two considerable barrows, within a short distance of each other. The circumference of the largest, is nearly eighty yards,—that of the smallest about seventy: on the top of both is a circular cavity or basin. Another barrow, described by Mr. Pilkington, as situated about a quarter of a mile to the north-east of Chelmorton, was examined in the year 1782. It measured at the base about seventy-five yards in circumference, and in height, seven feet. A knowledge of its inward construction was obtained by some labouring men, who were searching for stone to build a walled fence in the neighbouring field. After removing a thin covering of moss and soil from the lower extremity of the mount, they discovered a kind of breast-work, or regular wall of single stones, formed without mortar. Not apprehensive of meeting with any thing more extraordinary beyond this wall, they proceeded in their work, but were soon surprised by the sight of several human bodies. They found that the wall was at the end of a cell or coffin, in which the bodies had been deposited. The breadth of the cell within, was two feet, but its depth was not fully ascertained—it was supposed to be about a yard. The sides consisted of stones eight inches thick, and about two feet wide, placed on their edge, and forming a kind of wall or partition: the stones used for the covering, were from one to two inches thick, but not large.

Though some of the stones, and a small quantity of the soil had fallen into the vault, yet several of the human bodies or skeletons, might be clearly distinguished, lying at full length, with their heads towards the centre of the barrow. The bones had never been disturbed, and were apparently united together at the different joints; but on the slightest motion, they were found to be entirely loose and unconnected: upon examination, they were discovered to be remarkably strong and sound—the ribs in particular, were so little decayed, that they would easily bend without breaking. Those who saw the bones, thought that they were uncommonly large; and it was imagined that the persons to whom they belonged, must have been when alive, at least, seven feet high: the teeth also, were sound and perfect. From the number of bones and skulls, and the dimensions of the vault, it was supposed, that it contained four or five human bodies: and though only one vault was opened and examined, it was thought that others, were carried throughout the whole circumference of the mount, which, according to the calculation made, might contain twenty.

There is at Chelmorton, a stream, attended with some singular circumstances. The water which rises out of the ground at the head of the village, appears at first in a very considerable current, but, as it proceeds, gradually diminishes, till at length, it intirely disappears. Formerly it ran the whole length of the street; but since the very severe frost, in 1740, it flows only about half the distance from its source, it did before. This phænomenon is thus accounted for;—The soil is a light calcareous earth, through which moisture will easily pass; and, as this country abounds with chasms and fissures, it is not improbable, that the course of the stream may lie over one of these openings, which will readily receive the water, after it has passed through the soil, with which it is covered.

Between Chelmorton and Buxton, within about a mile of the latter, near a hill called *Staden-low*, are the remains of some ancient earth-works, which Dr. Stukely has noticed in the second volume of his Itinerary. Since his time, the ground has been enclosed and cultivated, but sufficient vestiges may yet be distinguished to ascertain the form of these memorials of antiquity. They consist of two divisions—an ellipsis, and an oblong square. The former, supposed by that learned antiquary to have been a place of public exhibitions and games, is encompassed by a shallow ditch, nearly a yard and a half wide; and a mound or bank, about one foot high, and seven yards and a half broad: the enclosed area measures, forty-five yards from south-east to north-west, and sixty-six, from north-east to south-west.— The square division is bounded by a vallum, now nearly levelled by the plough, and extends in length forty-five yards, and in breadth twenty-four. A small semi-circular cove of earth, is mentioned by Dr. Stukeley as being at the side of the circle farthest from the square.

BUXTON.

Buxton, lies in a hollow, surrounded by dreary hills, and extensive barren heaths: and so uninviting, and cheerless is the scenery

around it, that were it not for the deserved reputation of its mineral waters, it would never
have attracted any notice, and perhaps never
have become the residence of human beings.
On approaching this celebrated watering place,
the country appears naked and forlorn; and
nothing but extensive tracts of bleak, elevated
moor-lands present themselves to the eye.—
Long before Buxton is approached, its site
may be discovered, by the singular appearance
of the hill a little beyond, whose declivity is
scarred by innumerable limestone quarries; the
rubbish from which, contrast strikingly with
the black heath around, and produce a very
remarkable effect. Owing to the hills which
rise to a considerable height all round, the
town is not discovered, till it is almost reached;
and its appearance, when the public walks and
rides are thronged with carriages, persons on
horseback, and parties of gay pedestrians,
must produce a striking effect upon a stranger,
who, after travelling several hours, over moors
and steril heights, suddenly advances, within
view of this sequestered spot, rendered gay
and lively in its appearance, by its stately
buildings, and its showy, dashing, temporary
inhabitants.

It appears from a manuscript of the late Dr.

Gale, quoted in Gough's Additions to the Britannia; that that antiquary placed the *Aquæ* of Ravennas at Buxton. That its warm springs were known to the Romans, and its tepid waters used by that people, with whom warm-bathing was, not only a pleasurable, but a necessary practice, is evident from various concurring circumstances. Several ancient roads concentrate at this spot, particularly one called the *Bath-way*, or *Bathom-gate*, which commences at Brough, a Roman station near Hope, and was traced by the late Mr. Pegge; and another, that came from Manchester, and is known in different parts of its course, by the appellations of, *High-Street*, *Street-Fields*, *Street-Lane*, *Old-Gate*, &c. Specimens of Roman workmanship have also been discovered here at different times. Bishop Gibson mentions a Roman wall " cemented with red Roman plaister, close by St. Anne's well, where are the ruins of *the ancient bath*." This wall taken down in the year 1709, when Sir Thomas Delves, of Cheshire, in memory of a cure he had received from the water, erected a small stone alcove over the well; some capacious leaden cisterns, and different articles apparent-ly Roman, were found in digging the foundation. The shape and dimensions of the ancient bath, which was about six yards from the present, were clearly discovered when the building of the Crescent commenced in the year 1781. Its form appeared to be an oblong square, or parallelogram; it measured from East to West, thirty feet, and fifteen from North to South. The spring was situated at the West end, and at the East might be plainly perceived a flood-gate, by means of which the water was let out. The wall was built of limestone, covered on the outside with a strong cement; the floor consisted of a composition of lime, mixed with coarse sand, saturated with blood. Near one end, a cavity was formed in the floor, resembling a boat in shape, extending circularly in length almost from one side of the wall to the other; its breadth was about six feet; and its depth below the level of the floor, at the deepest point of curvature, about eighteen inches: the water was conveyed into this room by a leaden pipe.*

Though we have no accounts that the Buxton waters were used in the middle ages, it seems probable that they were never entirely forsaken; and it is not until the beginning of the sixteenth century, that we have certain

---

* Pegge's Essay on Roman Roads, pp. 35, 36, 41.

evidence, that they were in any high degree of
reputation. Dr. Jones, who in 1571, published
Observations on Buxton Baths, gave them celebrity, by his account and recommendation
of them. The first convenient house for the
reception of visitants, was erected a short time
previous to this publication, by the Earl of
Shrewsbury, on the same spot as the house
called at present the *Hall*, stands; which is
composed of a part of the old building. This
building occasioned the waters to be much
more resorted to than heretofore, by all ranks
of people. Mary queen of Scots, being, at that
time in the custody of the Earl of Shrewsbury,
was brought along with him, and his wife Elizabeth, in one of his visits to this place; on
which occasion this unfortunate Princess took
her farewell of Buxton in this distich, which
excepting a trifling alteration, are Cæsar's lines
upon Feltria :—

Buxtona *quæ calidæ celebrabere nomine lymphæ,*
Fortè mihi posthac non adeunda, vale.

Buxton, whose fame thy tepid waters tell,
Whom I, perhaps, no more shall see—farewell.

Buxton was much frequented in the reign of
Elizabeth; and since that period, the number
of persons resorting to it, and the buildings
erected for their accommodation, have been

continually increasing. About the year 1670, the old Hall was taken down, and a new and enlarged edifice was erected on the spot, by William, third Earl of Devonshire. This building, has, since that time, undergone several improvements, and is still one of the principal hotels for the reception of company, The baths are enclosed in this building; they are five in number, all adjoining each other, but in different apartments. The gentlemen's bath is in a close room, ten yards in length, and five and a half wide: along one end and side, is a stone bench, for the use of the bathers; and at each corner are steps leading into the bath.— This is twenty-six feet and a half long; twelve feet eight inches broad, and at a medium four feet seven inches deep. On the south-east side is a stratum of black limestone, through which the two principal springs rise; but the water also bubbles up in various lesser springs, through the chinks between the stones with which the bath is paved. In the bath for ladies, and that appropriated to the use of the poor, the water issues through several seams in the floors. The two other baths are private. It has been calculated, that all the springs throw out the water at the rate sixty gallons in a

minute; the gentlemen's bath having been filled to the height of five feet in fifty minutes;'
and two hours and fifty minutes being required
to fill the three baths.

On a chemical analysis, Buxton waters have
been found to be slightly impregnated with
mineral matter, particularly calcareous earth,
sea-salt, selenite, and acidulous gas, with perhaps some other permanently elastic vapour.—
The almost invariable temperature of the water is 82 degrees of Farenheit's thermometer;
and is clear, sparkling, and grateful to the palate.   The temperature of the baths is extremely agreeable to the feeling; a slight shock is
felt at the first immersion, which is succeeded
by a pleasant warmth. The beneficial tendency
of the waters, is particularly apparent in gout
and rheumatism ; many persons, every year,
absolutely crippled by these disorders, being
restored to the use of their limbs: they are
found beneficial also in nephritic and bilious
disorders, and debility of the stomach and in-
testines: In these, as usual in the administration of mineral waters, much of the benefit
must be imputed to the air, exercise, and change
of living.   The water, when drank in any considerable quantity, occasions many feverish
symptoms, such as a sort of giddiness, attend-

-ed with a sense of universal fulness and drow-
siness, and is found to possess a binding and
heating quality ; but in a few days these sen-
sations go off; and it often happens, that the
patient does not feel the full benefit of the waters till he has left the place.

Dr. Denham considers the Buxton waters, as
a more active remedy than is generally supposed ; and not only dissuades from its use in
all inflammatory and feverish complaints, but
likewise limits the quantity to be taken in cases
where it is proper, to a moderate portion. " In
common," says he, " two glasses, each of the
size of a third part of a pint are as much as
ought to be drank before breakfast, at the distance of forty minutes between each ; and one
or two of the same glasses between breakfast
and dinner will be quite sufficient." With respect to bathing, he recommends for invalids,
the time between breakfast and dinner as the
most proper, and directs that the prescribed or
usual exercise should be taken before going
into the bath : and that the water must never
be drank immediately before bathing. But the
most general time at present for bathing, is in
the morning before breakfast, which is thought
the best. In this respect, the company at the
Duke's Inns, have an advantage, as they are

permitted to bathe before nine o'clock, a privilege not allowed to the other houses.*

The place where the water is usually drank, is *St. Anne's Well;* (to whom it was anciently consecrated) an elegant classical building, in the Grecian style; to which it is conveyed into a white marble basin, from the original spring by a narrow grit-stone passage, so close and well-contrived as to prevent it from losing but a small portion of its heat; its general height being from 80¼ to 80¼ degrees of Farenheit.

The principal part of Buxton, is situated near the springs. The *Crescent* is a noble and magnificent range of building, erected here by the Duke of Devonshire, about thirty years ago, from a design and under the superintendance of Mr. Carr, the Architect. Its name describes its form—it is of stone dug on the spot, and faced with a fine free-stone, from a quarry one mile and a half from Buxton on the

---

* The poor at their bath, are not only exempt from t : charge, but also meet with great assistance and suppi;   .i the charitable contributions of the company; it being cus.   ,-- ary for every new comer, if he stays more than a day, to give one shilling for their use. And on bringing a certificate from the minister of their parish, and medical attendant, vouching for their being proper objects of charity, they are admitted to partake of the benefit of the fund; from which, necessary medicines are purchased, and fourteen indigent persons supplied with six shillings weekly for one month.

Disley road. It consists of three stories, the lowest rustic, forming a beautiful colonnade or piazza, as a shelter from the sun and heat; extending the whole length of the front, and is seven feet wide within the pillars, and eleven feet high. Ionic pilasters form the divisions between the windows above, and support an elegant balustrade that surmounts the front, the span of which is 257 feet. In the centre are the arms of the Cavendish family, neatly cut in stone, and surmounted with a pair of natural stag's antlers. The Crescent consists of one private Lodging-house, and three Hotels, in the largest of which, is the Ball-room, a very elegant and well proportioned apartment, lighted curiously by small semicircular windows just above the large projecting cornice, which prevents them from being seen, and gives an effect without an apparent cause. The lower rooms of some of the houses composing the Crescent, form a series of shops. The number of windows in the whole Crescent is about three hundred and seventy-eight; but as this noble edifice is situated so low, it cannot be seen to advantage from any station

A little to the North of the Crescent, are the *Stables*, an extensive pile, forming on the outside, an irregular polygon, but having a cir-

colar area within, sixty yards in diameter.—
They are commodious and extensive; colonna-
ded round the inside, for the convenience of
the grooms in wet weather, and in the centre
there is a spacious ride. The pillars which
support these arches are about ten feet in height.
The *Coach-houses* are also on an extensive scale,
a little detached from the stables, and capable
of containing about three score carriages. The
whole building is admirably planned and executed, and the public are greatly indebted to
the taste of the architect, as well as to the mu-
nificence of the noble proprietor, who is said
to have expended the sum of £120,000 in completing the Crescent and its appurtenances.

Besides the Hall, and the Hotels in the Crescent, there are several good inns and lodging-
houses in the other parts of the town; and also
a number of inferior boarding-houses, generally
crowded with persons in the less elegant walks
of life, who resort hither for amusement and
health, from the different populous manufac-
toring towns in the neighbouring counties.*

* The charge for bathing at the public baths, is one shilling each time; private ones, two and three shillings The
expences at the different houses where company are received during the season, do not differ materially. Dinner at
the ordinary, is two shillings and six-pence; tea, one shil-

. The Buxton season commences about the
end of May, and concludes in October; during
which time, its amusements are various and
diversified. Three assemblies are held every
week—Monday and Friday for an undress,
and Wednesday for a dress ball. An elegant
card-room, which adjoins the ball-room, is open
every evening; a small commodious theatre is
usually well filled by a genteel audience, three
evenings a week; and for the diversion of gentlemen, a pack of good harriers are kept by
subscription:—in short, to the admirer of mixed societies, such a place as Buxton cannot fail
of being agreeable; and it possesses many more
comforts, than a number of the fashionable
bathing and marine resorts can boast of.

Prayers are read, during the season, in the
assembly-room, the chapel at Buxton being
too small, and in too ruinous a state, for the
company. The allowance for the minister is

---

ling; breakfast and supper, one shilling and six-pence each.
A single bedded room is half-a-guinea per week; a double,
fourteen shillings; and a sitting room, according to its
quality, &c: from twelve to sixteen shillings. The subscription to the ball and card room, is one guinea; but if
a family, the two first only pay a guinea each, the others
half-a-guinea; six shillings for a single night. The subscription to the news-room, six shillings for the season.—
The different billiard-rooms, as in other places.

defrayed by subscription. But, for the better accommodation of visitors, the Duke of Devonshire is erecting an elegant new church, at a little distance to the North of the town, on the bank of the brook which divides the parishes of Bakewell and Tideswell, and separates the diocese of Lichfield and Coventry from that of York.

In front of the Crescent is a fine rising lawn, planted with trees, upon which is an eminence called *Stain-Cliffs*, or *Hans-Cliff*, over the top of which a pleasant walk has been made.— Here is a low or barrow, of different shape to any other that has been discovered in Derbyshire. It is long, narrow at top, and slants off at the sides and ends: the length at the bottom is about fifteen, the breadth six, and its height about two, yards. This barrow is encompassed by a ditch, and has a cavity at each end, near the south-west, and north-west corners. Some remains of an ancient settlement, supposed to be Roman, were visible about thirty years ago, on this piece of ground.

The number of houses in Buxton is about 100, which are built chiefly of stone: that of resident inhabitants, about 400. The number of visitors, who sojourn here during the season, is uncertain; but, as the public and private lodg-

ing-houses contain accommodations for about
700, it may be concluded, that a greater number than that, are annually entertained; particularly as of late years, many of the company
have been obliged to seek residences in the
neighbouring villages. The principal, if not
the only, dependance of the inhabitants, is on
the expenditure of the crowds who assemble
here.

About a mile to the westward of Buxton is
POOLE's HOLE, a vast cavern formed by Nature
in the limestone rock, and which was, according to tradition, the residence of an 'outlaw
named *Poole.* The entrance into this cavity
is low and contracted, and the passage at first
so very narrow, that it is impossible to go
forward without stooping; but after having
proceeded in this posture for about twenty-five
yards, the passage widens into a lofty and spacious cavern, " from whose roof depends a
quantity of *stalactite,* produced by the droppings of water laden with calcareous matter.—
Part of this substance adheres to the roof, and
forms gradually those pendent spiral masses
called *water-icles* or stalactites; another portion
drops with the water to the ground, and at-
taching itself to the floor is here deposited,

and becomes the *stalagmite*, a lumpy mass of
the same matter. One of the former, of immense size, called the *flitch of bacon*, occurs
about the middle of the cavern, which here becomes very narrow, but after a short passage,
spreads again to a greater width, and continues
large and lofty, till we reach another surpri-
singly large mass of *stalactite*, to which the
name of *Mary Queen of Scots' Pillar* is attached, from the tradition of that Queen having
paid a visit to the cavern, and proceeded thus
far into its recesses,"* at the time she visited
Buxton. As this pillar cannot be passed without some difficulty, few people venture beyond
it ; nor does it seem desirable, for by proceeding
thus far, a pretty complete idea of the cavern
may be formed. The path hitherto is along the
side, and at some height from the bottom of
the cavern ; but to visit and examine the interior extremity, it becomes necessary to descend a
few yards by very slippery and ill-formed steps :
the path at the bottom is tolerably even and
level for eighteen or twenty yards, when an almost perpendicular ascent commences, which
leads to the extremity of the fissure, through
the *Eye of St. Anthony's Needle*, a narrow

---

* Warner's Northern Tour, Vol. I. p. 161.

strait, beyond which, the steepness of the way
is only to be surmounted by clambering over
irregular masses of rock. The cavern terminates at about ninety-five yards beyond the
Queen of Scots' pillar: near the end is an ap-
perture through a projecting rock, behind
which a candle is generally placed, when any
person has arrived at the extremity; this, when
seen at that distance, appears like a dim star.
The way by which the visitor returns, lies along
the bottom of the cavern, underneath a considerable portion of the road by which he entered; and by thus changing the path, an opportunity is furnished of better ascertaining the
height and width of the cavern in every part,
and of viewing other accumulations of watery
icle, some of which are of a prodigious size and
extraordinary form. In one part of this passage, is a fine spring of transparent water;
and a small stream, which becomes more considerable in rainy seasons, runs through the
whole length of the cave, and makes the way
a little disagreeable. The various masses of
stalactitic matter that are met with in this excavation, are distinguished by different names,
according to the objects they are fancied to resemble. *Poole's Saddle*, his *Turtle*, and his
Woolsack, the *Lion*, the *Ladies' Toilet*, *Pil-*

lion, and *Curtain*, the *Tripe*, the *Bee-Hive*, the *Organ Pipes;* and a variety of other appellations, bestowed from a real or supposed likeness to the things themselves, are all pointed out by the guides, who having the names by rote, attend very little to the resemblance, which is continually varied by the depositions left by the water which percolates through the roof, and sides of the rock. The whole length of this subterraneous passage, is about 769 yards: it belongs to the Duke of Devonshire, and is granted by him to nine old women, who act as guides, and receive the money given by the visitants.

Above Poole's-Hole, on the side of the hill, are the kilns and limestone quarries before noticed, as pointing out the spot near which Buxton is situated. The limestone in this neighbourhood is of several kinds; and more than a hundred families have been occupied from father to son, in working the quarries and converting it into lime. The workmen and their families, live like the Troglodytes of old, in caverns of the earth; and though exposed to the variations of the seasons, and the ragings of the storm, they exhibit a longevity unknown to the population of the more civilized parts of the kingdom. The name by which this series of mole-hills is distinguished is the *Ass-Hillocks.**

A little to the South of Buxton, is the romantic Dale and Rock called LOVER's LEAP.

---

* " I looked in vain," says a Traveller who visited these quarries, " for the habitations of so many labourers and their numerous families, without being able to see so much as one cottage, when I at length discerned that the whole tribe, like so many moles, had formed their residence under ground. This comparison is strictly just; not one individual of them lodged in a house, or even the hollow of a rock. Their dwellings were in the midst of heaps of cinders, and refuse of lime, which formed so many mounts or mole-hills.

" These materials, which the workmen have hollowed into subterranean habitations, have been consolidated by rain, into a compact cement, which is now impenetrable to the water. As the excavation is not very difficult, these families have taken sufficient precaution against cold and wet, by fixing their abode immediately contiguous to the lime-kilns, which communicate to them a comfortable degree of warmth.

" The greater part of these habitations have three or four rooms, almost all of a round form, for the purpose of greater solidity. They are lighted by the side, when the position is such as to admit it; or merely by the chimney, which is nothing else than a round hole pierced through the middle of the roof to allow the smoke to escape. Appertures are also made by the door of the place to admit a little light. Such is the effect of the whole, that when the workmen descend into their caves, at the hours of repast, and a stranger sees so many small columns of smoke issuing out of the earth, he imagines himself in the midst of a village in Lapland."—St. Fond's Travels, Vol. II. page 282.

Each side of this beautiful dell is bounded by
elevated rocks, so near together, that for a considerable space, there is hardly more room than
for the passage of the bubbling current of the
Wye: some of them are perpendicular, and
completely bare of vegetation; others are covered with ivy, yew, and ash-wood, but have
a craggy steep occasionally starting through the
verdure. The name of *Lover's Leap* is given
to the Dale, from a vast precipice that forms
one side of a narrow chasm, which breaks from
the main rift nearly at right angles; and from
the summit of which, a love-lorn female is said
to have flung herself into the rocky gulph below. A circular road, extending in circumference about three miles, passes in view of the
most romantic part of this Dale, and forms a
most pleasant walk or ride from Buxton. At
the southern extremity, the scenery assumes a
milder character; and the hollow takes the appellation of *Mill-Dale*, from a mill which is
turned by the stream; and, in conjunction
with a rude bridge, a mountain path, and other
accompaniments, composes a very picturesque
view. Another fine scene is formed by a lofty
rock, called *Swallow-Tor*, which soars over a
mass of wood, and has the river roaring at its
base over broken masses of limestone.

" The *Marvel Stones*, a natural curiosity, to
which probably Dr. Stukely alluded, when he
mentions having heard of what appeared to
him a Druidical work near Hope, is situated
about three miles from Buxton, and two from
Chapel-in-le-Frith, in a pasture on the right of
the road. It is a rock of about 280 feet long,
and 80 broad at the widest part; but does not
any where rise more than three feet above the
surface of the ground... The face of it is deeply
indented with innumerable channels or gutters,
of various length, breadth, shape, and depth;
from nine inches to thirty feet long; from five
inches to five feet wide. There are also a
great number of holes; some round, some of
an irregular shape, from the size of a large
basin to that of a large kettle. The channels
or gutters, generally run north and south; but
none of them go quite across the stone: there is
always some seam or ridge in the rock, terminating the channel; and in a few instances another channel commences, which is also crossed by
another seam or ridge. These seams or ridges,
are from four inches to four feet broad; but
there can hardly be found four feet square,
without a hole or channel. The stone is not
jointed, or of a loose kind, but one hard, firm
rock. At the east and west ends, are a great

number of irregular shaped stones, standing a few inches from each other; the interspaces filled with earth: perhaps, if the earth was removed, it would be found that these are parts of the same rock. The whole is certainly the work of nature."[*]

Three miles north-west of Buxton, near the northern extremity of an eminence called *Combe Moss*, are some ancient military works, consisting of two deep trenches, which run parallel to each other to an extent of about 200 yards. That which lies nearest to the edge of the hill, is carried down the declivity by two traverses, and reaches to the distance of a quarter of a mile; it it also much wider than the other.

BEELEY, *Begelie*, is a village, standing in a valley near the banks of the Derwent. It contains about sixty houses, whose inhabitants are chiefly supported by agriculture. The church, which is a chapelry under Bakewell, is dedicated to St. Anne. In the year 1280, the inhabitants of Beeley paid, in one sum annually, five marks to the priest ministering in their chapel.

---

* Bray's Tour into Derbyshire, &c. 2nd Edit. p. 237. Beauties of England, Vol. III. p. 447.

Besides the chapelries which have been mentioned in the parish of Bakewell, there are also a few hamlets, the principal of which are deserving of notice.

UPPER HADDON, contains about forty houses, and GREAT ROWSLEY about thirty; the inhabitants of the former place, rely on the mining business; but those of the latter, derive their support, principally, from agriculture.

The hamlet of HASSOP, formerly belonged to the *Foljambs*, and from them descended to the *Plomtons*, of Plompton in Yorkshire, whose coheirs sold a part of the estate in the reign of Edward the Sixth, and the remainder in the time of Queen Elizabeth, to the family of *Eyre*. It is at present the seat of Francis Eyre, Esq. who is descended from this ancient and respectable family, a branch of which resided at Hassop as early as the reign of Henry the Seventh. The present possessor has a very large collection of exotic plants in his green-houses; and has continued the extensive plantations carried on by his father.

The hamlets of ROWLAND, and CALVER, contain one hundred and ten houses. The village of WARDLOW is also within the parish of Bakewell, and contains, together with its liberty,

about twenty houses. In the year 1759, the
Rev. Mr. Evat of Ashford, examined a barrow
situated near this village, an account of which
was published in the Philosophical Transactions
for that year.

The villages of FLAGG, BLACKWALL, Cow-
DALE, and STADEN, (near which is *Staden-low*,
the ancient work already mentioned) contain
altogether, about fifty houses, and two hundred and forty inhabitants.

, CHATSWORTH, the celebrated and magnificent seat of the Duke of Devonshire, stands
on a gentle acclivity, near the bottom of a high
hill, finely covered with wood, in a narrow
and deep valley, bounded by bleak and elevated tracts of land. " The broad valley
through which the road from Matlock to Chatsworth runs," says a Tourist, " affords some
good flat landscapes, regarded, perhaps, with
greater pleasure, from the contrast produced
by the naked hills that hedge them on every
side; this circumstance gives additional interest
also to the approach of the Duke's seat through
the park; on entering which, a long reach of the
Derwent, (whose banks art has both extended
and adorned) a cascade made by the whole river
throwing itself down a descent of ten or twelve
feet, and a partial view of the house, seated at

the foot of a hill, (a grand mass of wood) surrounded by mountains deformed with crags,
are all unfolded to the eye at once."

Strangers who visit Chatsworth-House, generally leave their equipage, &c. at the Inn at
Edensor, and then walk through the park, at the
entrance of which is a modern built Lodge, with
an elegant arched gate-way. On gaining an easy
eminence, ornamented with fine oaks, a view is
presented of the house, offices, and stables,
with several ornamental buildings in the gardens. The river Derwent winds gracefully
through the park, over which is the approach
to the mansion by an elegant stone bridge of
three arches, erected by Paine, and ornamented with figures sculptured by Cibber. The
road then leads to the northern entrance of this
stately edifice, when the visitor is conducted
through the porter's lodge to view the interior
parts of it.

The estate of Chatsworth, was purchased in
the reign of Elizabeth, of the ancient family
of *Leeche*, by Sir William Cavendish, husband
to Elizabeth, Countess of Shrewsbury, whose
sister married a Francis Leeche of this place.
Through the persuasion of the Countess, Sir
William began to erect a noble mansion-house
here, which, after his death, in the year 1557,

was carried on, and completed under her direction. This building was taken down about
the close of the seventeenth century, when
William, the first Duke of Devonshire, began
on the site of the more ancient fabric, the present extensive residence, which was finished in
the year 1702.

The house, which is built in the Ionic order,
with a flat roof, surrounded by a neat balustrade, may be considered as a noble specimen,
of that highly decorated style of building, im-
ported from Italy, about 130 years ago, and
so much in vogue in this country for about half
a century—magnificent but heavy; expensive
but devoid of taste. Its form is nearly a square
of about 190 feet.

After passing the porter's lodge, the visitor
is conducted through a long court into the
anti-room, and from thence into another court,
round which the apartments are built: on the
two opposite sides is a colonnade—while large
festoons of armour and military trophies, en-
twined with branches of palm, and wreaths of
flowers, carved in stone, adorn the outside of
this interior front; and, in the centre of the
court is a fountain, with a statue of *Orpheus*
in the middle. The principal entrance on the
West, by a noble flight of steps to a terrace,

which extends the length of the whole building, has a fine effect.

The interior, as well as the exterior, of this
edifice is characterized by heaviness and gloom;
and though splendidly ornamented with magnificent walls and ceilings, presents but few of
those captivating productions of the pencil,
which embellish the apartments of many other
mansions in this county. It possesses, however,
some attractions of another kind, which amply
repay the visitant's attention; these are, the
beautiful carved ornaments by Gibbon, of whom
Walpole observed, that he was the first artist,
" who gave to wood the loose and airy lightness
of flowers, and chained together the various
productions of the elements, with a free disorder natural to each species."

The *Entrance-Hall*, 60 feet by 27, is grand
but dark; the ends, ceiling, and one side finely
painted, in 1694, by Verrio and Lewis La Gu-
rere, with a representation of the *Assembly of
the Gods; Julius Cæsar Sacrificing;* and his
Assassination at the foot of Pompey's statue.—
The paintings in this room were some years
ago in a decayed state, but have, since, been
judiciously retouched.

From this room, the approach to the stair-
case is most magnificent—ascending by a dou-

ble flight of steps of root of amethyst, guarded
by a rich guilt balustrade, between two rocks
of varigated alabaster. This part of the house
was thought by *Kent*, sufficiently elegant to
be immitated in the princely seat of *Holkham*
in Norfolk. At the foot of the stair-case are
several figures in chiaro oscuro; particularly
one of *Hercules:*—the ceiling is painted with
the *Triumph of Cybele*. From the stair-case, a
plain unornamented gallery, extending along
one side of the quadrangle, leads to the,

Chapel, a beautiful room wainscotted with
cedar, ornamented with the exquisite carvings
of Gibbon, (who was killed by a fall in the act
of fitting it up); and painted by La Guerre,
whose powers are displayed in the altar-piece—
Christ reproving Thomas's Incredulity. On
each side of the altar, are the statues of *Faith*
and *Hope*, the works of Cibber, the draperies
of which are uncommonly fine. The walls are
covered with painting; and on the ceiling is represented the *Ascension*.

The *Music-Room*, adjoins the gallery of the
chapel, in which the Devonshire family are
seated when divine service is performed. The
organ is placed in this room, and not in the
chapel, and has a fine effect. Over the chimney-piece, in one picture, is a half-length of

the late *Duchess of Devonshire* and her daughter *Lady Georgina*, now *Lady Morpeth*, when a child, in her arms.` This room is hung with white watered tabby, with chairs and sofas to match.

The *Drawing-Room*, 36 feet by 30, is hung with pea-green silk; and over the chimney-piece, is a whole-length portrait of *William Duke of Cumberland*; and has an immense silver chandelier.

The *Dining-Room*, 50 feet by 30, contains a fine whole-length, by Sir G. Kneller, of *William first Duke of Devonshire*; who was distinguished as a wit, a soldier, a scholar, and a gentleman. The inscription he is reported to have left for his monument, which was never erected, is a faithful epitome of his political character:—

WILLIELMUS DUX DEVONIÆ,

BONORUM PRINCIPIUM SUBDITUS FIDELIS

INIMICUS ET INVISUS TYRANNIS.

The *Ball-Room* is about 100 feet long, hung with tapestry, from the story of *Signor Fido*, divided into compartments, by pilasters painted in imitation of verd antique. Over the fireplace, in basso relievo, are *Cupids* in white marble.

The *Billiard-Room*, contains several pic-

tures, and among them, one of *Diana* and *Ac-
teon*; and a view of the former house at *Chatsworth*:—the ceiling is by Thornhill.

. .The *Best Bed Chamber*, contains a bed and
furniture of white satin, painted.

. The *Duchess of Devonshire's Dressing-Room*,
commands a view of the water, and the fine
plantations in the garden. A *Cabinet* has a
good collection of the mineral and fossil productions of Derbyshire, properly marked, and
well arranged;—a few curiosities, such as a large
tooth, supposed to be an elephant's grinder,
found on *Crooks-moor*, near Sheffield,—a ring
with a fine Vesuvian Hyacinth, collected by the
late Duchess, at Vesuvius;—several beautiful
petrefactions, &c.

. The *Duke of Devonshire's Dressing-Room*,
is hung with tapestry, from the story of *Hero*
and *Leander*. In the *Anti-Chamber* is a fine
painting of *Michael* and the *Fallen Angels*, by
Raphael; and *Andromeda and the Sea Mon-
ster*, by Sir James Thornhill,

> " So sweet her frame, so exquisitely fine,
> " She seems a Statue by a hand divine."

The *Back Staircase* ornamented with statues,
and painted with the *Fall of Phaeton*, by Sir
J. Thornhill, leads to the *Painted Anti-Chamber*, which contains the *Rape of the Sabines*, by

Thornhill:—the ceiling represents the Assembly of the Gods.

" Panditur intereà domus omnipotentis Olympi
Consiliumq.y vocat Divum pater atq; hominum rex
Sideram in sedem."

The *Chintz Apartment*, contains paintings
from *Orlando Furioso*, and portraits of the second *Duchess of Devonshire*, her father, *Lord
William Russell*, and four children.

State Apartments;—in the *Dressing-Room*,
is, the *Sleeping Shepherd*, by Salvator Rosa;
and the *Flight into Egypt*, by Gennari, &c. The
Bedchamber is hung with fine tapestry; the bed
and furniture of crimson silk damask. The
Drawing-Room, has its ceiling painted by Varrio, with *Phæton taking charge of the Chariot.*
Here are the following portraits;—*John, first
Duke of Rutland;* obiit 1710, ætat 72. The
*second Earl of Pembroke. William, first Earl
of Devonshire:* This picture is ascribed to Mytens, but considered by Mr. Walpole to be by
Van Somer, though equal to Vandyck, and one
of the finest single figures ever painted on canvas. *Edward Lord Bruce*, father-in-law of the
second Earl of Devonshire. *Colonel Cavendish,* who was killed in the civil wars, near
Newark, in 1643. *James, Duke of Ormond,*

Chancellor of the University of Oxford, father-in-law of the first Earl of Devonshire. *General Russell.* Over the chimney-piece in this room, is a beautiful carving of several Dead Fowl, by Gibbons; and in an adjoining room, a carved delineation, by the same master, of a Pen, so finely executed, that Mr. Walpole characterized it as " not distinguishable from a real feather."

. The *Presence Chamber*, is hung with tapestry from the cartoons of Raphael, and contains the state chairs and footstools, used by their present Majesties at the Coronation, being part of the perquisites belonging to the late Duke of Devonshire, as Lord Chamberlain. The rest of the chairs and seats are covered with crimson velvet. In an oval compartment in the ceiling, is the *Discovery of Mars and Venus.*

The *State Dining Room* is ornamented with five antique marble busts, and has a painted ceiling. The *Anti-chamber* is hung with tapestry; and contains an invaluable work of Holbein, *Henry VII.* and *Henry VIII.* in one picture. It is in black chalk, heightened, and as large as life. Here is also *Our Saviour and Mary Magdalene in the Garden*, by Titian. No grace in the figures, but a sweet expression in the face of Mary. In the *Cut-velvet Bed-*

Chamber, are paintings of *Nessus the Centaur*, and *Deianira*. The *Crimson Bed-chamber*, contains the bed in which George the Second expired, another perquisite of the late Duke.— The *Dressing-Room* adjoining, has a fine head in basso relievo, over the chimney, of a Knight of the Golden Fleece;—perhaps *Philip de Valois*.

The *Bed-chamber of Mary Queen of Scots*, adjoins the last-mentioned suite. The room is so called, from its containing a bed, hung with crimson velvet and gold, and chairs, which were used by that princess, during her confinement in the Old House at Chatsworth: from hence she wrote a letter to Pope Pius, dated Oct. 31, 1570, which was more than a century before the present mansion was erected.

In the Gardens, the principal objects of curiosity and attention, are the Water-Works.— The famous Cascade, one of those grand water-works, which half a century ago, rendered Chatsworth the greatest wonder of Derbyshire, and gave it a celebrity which it has not yet lost, lies to the south-east of the house. It consists of a series or flight of steps, extending nearly two hundred yards from one end to the other, down a steep hill, crowned at the top with a Temple. This fane, (observes Mr. Warner)

should certainly be dedicated to Mercury, the
god of fraud and deceit, as a piece of roguery
is practiced upon the incautious stranger within
its very sanctuary; from the floor of which, a
multitude of little fountains suddenly spout
up, whilst he is admiring the prospect through
the portal, and quickly wet him to the skin.
After this practical joke, the cascade is put in
motion by another screw, and certainly is grand
in its kind; the water rushes in a vast quantity,
and with great force and noise, from the domed
roof of the temple, and from a great variety
of dolphins, dragons, and a number of other
figures that ornament it; and falling into a
basin in front of the building, (which also
throws up several fountains) is thence discharged, and rolls down the long stages of steps
before-described; and having reached the bottom, disappears by sinking into the earth.

There is also in the wood, at a little distance
from the Temple, a Copper Tree, made to represent a decayed willow, the branches of which
produce an artificial shower: and on turning
by the same path and descending the hill, a
large basin presents itself, in the middle of
which, is a fountain, which throws the water
up to the height of sixty feet; and at a small
distance is the grand Canal, three hundred and

twenty yards long, and twenty-five broad; near
the north end of them are two *Sphinxes*, on
large bases, with ornaments in good taste, well
executed by Cibber: in this canal is a fountain
or jet d' eau, which throws the water ninety
feet high; and in a basin near the house, are
four *Sea Horses* and a *Triton*, from whose heads
small streams issue. All these works, are supplied by a large reservoir of water, situated on
the top of the hill, and covering fourteen acres
of land, from whence the water is conveyed by
pipes laid under ground; and the gardener,
who is with the company, gives notice to a person on the hill, which pipe he wishes to be filled. These different water-works are still in
tolerable order; but they are rather curious
than beautiful; and generally fail to interest,
as the improved taste of the present day can
only regard them as formal puerilities.

At the highest point of eminence, eastward
of the gardens, is the *Hunting Tower*, a building supposed to have been erected as a station,
where the female visitants at Chatsworth could
partake in the diversion of stag-hunting, without incurring its dangers; as its height (ninety
feet) enabled them to overlook the surrounding
hills. It is of a square form, having a rounded
tower at each angle. In another part of the

grounds, near the river side, to the north of
the bridge, is another tower, encompassed by
a mote, and called the *Bower of Mary, Queen
of Scots*, from a garden which occupied its
summit, wherein that princess spent many of
the tedious hours of her confinement.

On the north-east side of the house, and at
the distance of two or three hundred yards, on
a more elevated site, are the *Great Stables*,
which are magnificent and well contrived: the
west and north fronts extend about 202 feet.
These were erected about fifty years ago, by
the late Duke. On the side of the valley opposite the house, are several small hills covered
with plantations; beyond which, but more
especially to the north, the mountains of the
Peak rear their lofty heads;—in short, every
object in view, appears with an unusual air of
greatness and sublimity.

Chatsworth Park is very extensive, measuring above nine miles in circumference, and is
beautifully diversified with hill and dale, as
well as various plantations, which range in fine
sweeping masses over the the inequalities of the
ground. The prospects from the adjacent parts,
are exceedingly fine; and one view, looking
back from the south, possesses extraordinary
grandeur. Immediately below the eye, is the

rich vale animated by the meandering current
of the Derwent; more distant, is the house,
with a fine back ground of wood, rearing in
solemn majesty; and far beyond, the blue hills
of Castleton, skirting the horizon.

Chatsworth appears to have been, for more
than two centuries, the property of the noble
family to which it now belongs. Robert de
Gernon, the first ancestor of the family of Cavendish, of whom we have any certain account,
came from Normandy with William the Conqueror, and contributed considerably towards
the success of the expedition. Geoffery de Gernon, one of his descendants, resided at Moor-
Hall in Derbyshire, in the reign of Edward the
First. Roger, his son, married the daughter
and heiress of John Potton, or Potkin, of Cavendish, in Suffolk; and his children, according
to the custom of the age, and in compliment
to their mother, assumed the name of Cavendish. The eldest son, an eminent lawyer, was
appointed Lord Chief Justice in the year 1366;
but was afterwards seized and beheaded, by the
insurgents of Suffolk, in revenge for the death
of Wat Tyler, whom his son was reported to
have slain. John, the second son of the Judge,
received the honor of Knighthood, and an annuity for himself and his heirs for ever, in re-

ward for his services in quelling the insurrections that were then prevalent : he filled some offices under Richard II. and Henry V. and was present at the battle of Agincourt. Thomas Cavendish, his great grandson, studied the law, and in the reign of Henry VIII. was Clerk of the Pipe in the Exchequer. He had four sons ; William, the second, was patronized by Wolsey, and, after the fall of the Cardinal, was knighted by Henry, in the thirty-eighth year of his reign. He was married three times ; and by his last wife, the famous Countess of Shrewsbury, had three sons ; the second of which, William, was raised to the dignity of a Peer, by the title of Baron Cavendish of Hardwick, in the county of Derby. He died in 1625, and was succeeded by his son William, the second Earl of Devonshire, who was educated under the famous Hobbes. He died in 1628, and was succeeded in his title and estates by his son William, who at the death of his father was only eleven years old. His education also was superintended by Mr. Hobbes ; and owing to his attachment to the Royal cause during the Civil Wars, he was obliged to go abroad, and had his estate confiscated ; but on the Restoration, he was reinstated in his title and possessions.— He died at Roehampton in the year 1684, and

was succeeded by his eldest son, William, the
fourth Earl of Devonshire, who, in several striking qualities and accomplishments equalled, and
in others greatly surpassed all his ancestors.

His name occurs in early life, as Lord Cavendish, member for the county of Derby; when
his political conduct evinced those true patriotic
principles, which he afterwards so eminently displayed in assisting to bring about the glorious
Revolution, and persuading the gentry of Derbyshire and Nottinghamshire, to transfer to
king William, that allegiance and affection to
which James had forfeited all claims. He was
the inseparable friend of the amiable Lord Russel, and offered to change clothes with him in
prison, and thus contrive his escape; an attempt so desperate must have proved fatal to
one, if not to both, these noble characters; and
was therefore declined by Lord Russel. On the
accession of William, he was admitted to the
Privy Council, and appointed Lord-Steward
of the Household; and very soon after, constituted Lord Lieutenant of Derbyshire, and a
Knight of the Garter. He attended William
to the famous Congress in Holland; and on his
return, was created, in May 1694, Marquis of
Hartington, and Duke of Devonshire. The

same ardent love of liberty as marked the early
period of this nobleman's life, distinguished
the latter part of it. He departed this life in
the year 1707. His Grace, the present noble
Duke, is the fifth in descent from this illustrious ancestor; and to the honor of the fifth
Duke of Devonshire, and his immediate predecessors, be it said,—neither he, nor any of
them, have deserted those principles which
have secured to his memory, the reverence and
esteem of his countrymen.

EDENSOR, *Ednesoure*, is a small village near
Chatsworth, containing together with its liberty, about ninety houses. The living is a vicarage, the church is dedicated to St. Peter, and
the Duke of Devonshire is the patron. This
church was in former times, given by Fulcher,
the son of Fulcher, to the monastery of Roces-
ter, in Staffordshire. The church contains the
tomb of the first Earl of Devonshire, with a
long Latin epitaph, expressive of his virtues
and offices; a large and costly monument to
the memory of Henry Cavendish, the eldest son
of Sir William, who was famed for his gallant-
ries: here is also a long Latin epitaph, to the
memory of one of the domestics of the Queen
of Scots, who died, while in her service, at
Chatsworth.

PILSLEY is a hamlet in the parish of Edensor, and contains about thirty-five houses.

EYAM, a small village and parish, contains
about one hundred and ten houses, and nine
hundred and thirty inhabitants. The living is a
rectory, and the church is dedicated to St. Helen.

This parish includes the hamlets, of *Fowlow*,
Grindlow, and *Grindelford*, containing, together with the *Woodlands*, about 112 houses.

About one hundred and and forty years ago,
Eyam was greatly depopulated by the plague:
it appears from the register, that between the
seventh of September 1665, and the beginning
of November 1666, there were two hundred
and sixty burials.*

---

* The following is an account of this dreadful scourge,
extracted from a letter of the late Miss Seward:—

" Eyam was one of the last places in England visited by
the plague. The summer after its ravages in London, it was
conveyed to that village in patterns of taylor's cloth.—
Raging with great violence, it swept away four-fifths of the
inhabitants. Mr. Mompesson was at that time Rector of
Eyam, and in the vigour of his youth. He had married a
beautiful young lady, by whom he had a girl and boy, of
three and four years old.

" On the commencement of the contagion, Mrs. Mompesson threw herself with her babes at the feet of her husband, to supplicate his flight from that devoted place; but
not even the entreaties and tears of a beloved wife could induce him to desert his flock, in those hours of danger and
dismay. Equally fruitless were his solicitations that she

In the lead mines at *Eyam Edge*, the per-
cussions of the earthquake which destroyed
Lisbon, on the first of November, 1756, were
very distinctly felt; the soil fell from the joints,
or fissures of the rocks, and violent explosions,
as if of cannon, were heard by the workmen.*
In a *drift* about 120 yards deep, and above 50
yards from one end to the other, several shocks
were felt by the miners; and after each, a loud
rumbling was heard in the bowels of the earth.
The interval between the shocks was about four
or five minutes: the second was so violent, as
to cause the rocks to grind one upon another.†

TIDESWELL, is a small market town, situated in a bottom, which is surrounded on all

should retire with her infants; The result of this pathetic
contest was a resolve to send their children away, and to
abide together the fury of the pestilence.

" Mr. Mompesson, constantly visiting and praying by
the sick,

" Drew, like Marseilles' good bishop, purer breath,
" When nature sicken'd and each gale was death."

From a rational belief, that assembling in the crowded
church for public worship during the summer heats, must
spread and increase the contagion, he agreed with his afflicted parishioners, that he would read prayers twice a
week, and deliver his two customary sermons on the sab-
bath, from one of the perforated arches in the rocks of a

* Whitehurst's Theory, p. 189.
† Philosophical Transactions, Vol. XLIX.

sides by barren and desolate moors. It is supposed to have received its name, from an ebbing and flowing well, situated in a field near
the town, but which has now ceased to flow for
more than a century. The manor anciently
belonged to William Peverel, and being after-

---

deep dingle near the village. By his advice they ranged
themselves on its grassy steep in a level direction to the
rocky pulpit; and the dell being so narrow, a speaker, as
my father often proved to us, might be distinctly heard
from that arch. Do you not see this dauntless minister of
God, stretching forth his hands from the rock, instructing
and consoling his distressed flock in that little wilderness?
How solemn, how affecting must have been the pious ex-
hortations of those terrible hours.

"The church-yard soon ceased to afford room for the
dead. They were afterwards buried in a heathy hill above
the village. Curious travellers take pleasure in visiting,
to this day, the mountain tumulus, and in examining its
yet distinct remains; also in ascending, from the upper
part of Eyam, those cliffs and fields which brow the dingle,
and from whence the descent into the consecrated rock is
easy. It is called Lucklet church by the villagers.

"Mr. Mompesson remained in health during the whole
ravage of the pestilence; but Providence saw fit to call
his fortitude to a severer trial, than if he had seen the
plague spot indurated upon his own body.

"Amongst other precautions against the disease, Mrs.
Mompesson prevailed upon her husband to suffer an inci-
sion to be made in his leg, and kept open. One day she
observed appearances in the wound, which induced her belief, that the contagion had found a vent that way; and,
therefore, that its danger was over as to him. Instead of
being shocked that the pestilence had entered her house,
and that her weakness (for she was not in health) must next

wards vested in king John, was given by him
to his esquire, whose female descendant, in
Richard the Second's time, being married to a
Stafford, obtained a grant of a weekly market,
and a yearly fair to be held here. The estate
afterwards came to the *Meurills* or *Meverills*,

---

endure its fury, she expressed the most rapturous joy for
the apprehended deliverance of her beloved husband.—His
letters, though he seems to think her conviction concerning his having taken the distemper groundless, make pathetic and grateful mention of that disinterested joy. But
Mrs. Mompesson soon after sickened of the plague, and
expired in her husband's arms, in the 27th year of her age.
Her monument is now in Eyam church-yard, protected by
iron rails, its inscription distinct.

" When first the plague broke out in Eyam, Mr. Mompesson wrote to the then Earl of Devonshire, residing at
Chatsworth, some few miles from Eyam, stating that he
thought he could prevail upon his parishioners to confine
themselves within the limits of the village, if the surrounding country would supply them with necessaries, leaving
such provisions as should be requested in appointed places,
and at appointed hours, upon the encircling hills. The
proposal was punctually complied with; and it is most remarkable, that when the pestilence became, beyond all
conception, terrible, not a single inhabitant attempted to
pass the deathful boundaries of the village, though a regiment of soldiers could not, in that rocky and open country, have detained them against their will; much less could
any watch, which might have been set by the neighbourhood, have effected that infinitely important purpose.

" By the influence of this exemplary man, obtained by
his pious and affectionate virtues, the rest of the county of
Derby escaped the plague; not one of the very nearly
neighbouring hamlets, or even a single house, being in-

of Throwley, in Staffordshire; and was conveyed, by the marriage of an heiress, to Lord
Cromwell, of Oakham in Rutlandshire, one of
whose descendants sold it, between the death of
Charles the First and the period of the Restoration, to the *Eyres* of Highlow. Since the
death of John Archer, Esq. of Welford, in
Berkshire, the male heir of this family, the
manor has been sold, under the authority of
the Court of Chancery, to the Duke of Devonshire.

At the compilation of Domesday, there were
a church and a priest at *Tidesuuelle;* and king
John in the year 1215, gave the chapel at Tideswell, as well as the church at Hope, to the
canons of Lichfield, for their common provision of bread and beer. The present church
was erected in the fourteenth century, as appears from an inscription on a flat stone in the
chancel, to the memory of John, son of Thomas
Foljambe, who died in 1358; and is said to

fected beyond the limits of Eyam village, though the distemper remained there near seven months.

" In the summer of 1757, five cottagers were digging on
the heathy mountain above Eyam, which was the place of
graves after the church-yard had become too narrow a repository. Those men came to something which had the
appearance of having once been linen. Conscious of their
situation, they instantly buried it again. In a few days,

have contributed much towards the building of the edifice. The church is a handsome building of the conventual form, with a neat tower at the west end, terminated by eight pinnacles; those at the angles rising from octagonal bases, and being much higher than the intermediate ones. The living is a vicarage, the church is dedicated to St. John the Baptist, and the Dean and Chapter of Lichfield are the patrons.

In the church is a raised tomb to the memory of *Sampson Meurill*, who was born in 1388, and died in 1462. It appears from the inscription, that, in the space of two years, he was in eleven battles in France, where he served under the command of the great Duke of Bedford, who knighted him at St. Luce, and made him Knight Constable of England, &c. On his tomb, bread is given away every Sunday, to some of the indigent parishioners. Another monument records the memory of a native of

_____

they all sickened of a putrid fever, and three of the five died. The disorder was contagious, and proved mortal to numbers of the inhabitants. My father, who was then Canon of Lichfield, resided in that city with his family, at the period when the subtle, unextinguished, though much-abated power of the most dreadful of all disease awakened from the dust, in which it had slumbered ninety-one years."

Tideswelle, named *Robert Pursglove,* described
as Prior of Gisburn Abbey, Prebend of Rotherham, and Bishop of Hull, who died in the
year 1579. Henry the Eighth allowed him a
pension, in reward for his ready compliance,
with his wishes; his conduct, as Dugdale records, being so very obsequious, that, after he
had surrendered his own house, he was employed as a commissioner to persuade others to do
the like. At the beginning of Queen Mary's
reign, he was made Archdeacon of Nottingham, Suffragan Bishop of Hull, &c. but re-
fusing to take the oath of supremacy to Queen
Elizabeth, he was deprived of his Archdeaconry,
and other spiritualities, in the year 1560. He
afterwards retired to this town, and founded
a Grammar-School, which adjoins the church-
yard; and a Hospital for twelve poor people.
In the south transept is a tomb, with whole-
length figures of a man and a woman, of whom
nothing is with certainty known; but tradition
represents them as the effigies of Thurstan de
Bower and his wife, who are said to have built
the transept.

The town of Tideswell consists of two rows
of low houses, built of rough gray stones, on
the opposite sides of a clear rivulet. The
weekly market is held on Wednesday, but is

not much attended. The place consists of about 250 houses, and 1100 inhabitants, who are supported chiefly by the mining business.

LITTON, *Litton*, is a hamlet in the parish of Tideswell, containing about 74 houses, and 348 inhabitants.

WORMHILL, *Wruenelle*, is another hamlet in this parish, and contains about 30 houses: its chapel is dedicated to St. Margaret. Near this little village, is a most romantic and deep hollow, where the river Wye flows beneath a stupendous mass of rock, called *Chee Tor*,—a vast perpendicular mass of limestone, rising more than 360 feet above the level of the river which meanders at its base. The channel of the river is here confined between huge rocks of limestone, which seem, from their general correspondence of situation and form, to have been once united. In some parts, they are partially covered with brushwood, nut-trees, and mountain-ash; in others, they are totally naked, precipitous, and impending. The chasm runs in a direction so nearly circular, that the sublime Chee Tor, and its dependant masses of rock, are almost insulated by the river which rolls at their feet. Its length, as far at least as it possesses any considerable beauty, is, between five and six hundred yards; a distance which presents se-

veral picturesque, and interesting views. Some
plantations on the neighbouring heights increase the general effect of the scenery. Near
the bottom of a steep descent that leads to this
spot from the village, is a strong spring, from
which a great quantity of water flows into the
river. About midway up the acclivity, the
limestone stratum gives way to a mass of toadstone of considerable extent, above which another stratum of limestone occurs.* From a particular station in this romantic scene, the four
vallies of Wye Dale, Chee Dale, Flag Dale,
and Water Dale, may be all seen, together
with the Tor and river:—these dales will afford
the Botanist many curious plants.

A small hamlet in the liberty of Wormhill, had the honor of giving birth to that
extraordinary genius, the late Mr. Brindley,
so celebrated for planning navigable Canals.
We shall copy the interesting memoir of him,
given by Dr. Aikin, in his History of the Country round Manchester.*

" JAMES BRINDLEY was born at Tunsted in
the parish (liberty) of Wormhill, Derbyshire,
in 1716. His father was a small freeholder,
who dissipated his property in company and

---

* Which see page 139.

field-amusements, and neglected his family.
In consequence, young Brindley was left destitute of even the common rudiments of education, and till the age of seventeen, was casual-
ly employed in rustic labors. At that period
he bound himself apprentice to one Bennet, a
mill-wright, at Macclesfield, in Cheshire, where
his mechanical genius presently developed itself. The master being frequently absent, the
apprentice was often left for weeks together to
finish pieces of work, concerning which he had
received no instruction; and Bennet on his return, was often greatly astonished to see improvements in various parts of mechanism of
which he had no previous conception. It was
not long before the millers discovered Brindley's merits, and preferred him in the execution of their orders to the master, or any other
workman. At the expiration of his servitude,
Bennet being grown into years, he took the
management of the business upon himself; and
by his skill and industry, contributed to support his old master and his family, in a comfortable manner.

" In process of time, Brindley set up as a
mill-wright on his own account, and by a number of new and ingenious contrivances, greatly
improved that branch of mechanics, and ac-

quired a high reputation in the neighbourhood.
His fame, extending to a wider circle, he was
employed in 1752 to erect a water engine at
Clifton, in Lancashire, for the purpose of
draining some coal mines. Here he gave an
essay of his abilities in a kind of work for
which he was afterwards so much distinguished,—driving a tunnel under ground, through a
rock nearly 600 yards in length, by which water was brought out of the Irwell, for the purpose of turning a wheel fixed thirty feet below
the surface of the earth. In 1755 he was employed to execute the larger wheels for a silk
mill at Congleton; and another person, who
was engaged to make the other parts of the
the machinery, and to superintend the whole,
proving incapable of completing the work, the
business was entirely committed to Brindley;
who not only executed the original plan, in a
masterly manner, but made the addition of
many curious and valuable improvements, as
well in the construction of the engine itself, as
in the method of making the wheels and pini-
ons belonging to it. About this time too, the
mills for grinding flints in the Staffordshire
Potteries received several improvements from
his ingenuity.

, " In the year 1756 he undertook to erect a

steam-engine upon a new plan, at Newcastle-
under-Line; and was for a time very intent
upon a variety of contrivances for improving
this useful piece of mechanism. But from these
designs, he was, happily for the public, called
away, to take the lead, in what the event has
proved to be a national concern of high importance—the projecting of the system of Canal Navigation. The Duke of Bridgewater
*(to whose patronage the subsequent success of
this system is incontestibly owing)* had formed a
design of carrying a canal from his coal works
at Worsley to Manchester, and was induced by
the reputation of Mr. Brindley to consult him
as to the most judicious mode of executing it;
and having the sagacity to conceive, and strength
of mind to confide in the original and commanding abilities of this self-taught genius, he
committed to him the management of the ar-
duous undertaking.

" In the progress of this enterprize, which
was attended with complete success, Mr. Brindley projected and adopted those leading principles for the execution of these kind of works
which he ever afterwards adhered to, and in
which he has been imitated by all succeeding
artists. To preserve as much as possible the
level of his canals, and to avoid the mixture

and interference of all natural streams, were objects at which he constantly aimed. To accomplish these neither labour nor expence were spared; his genius seemed to delight in overcoming all obstacles by the discovery of new and extraordinary contrivances.

" The most experienced engineers upon former systems were amazed and confounded at his project of aqueduct bridges over navigable rivers, mounds across deep vallies, and subterraneous tunnels; nor could they believe in the practicability of some of these schemes till they saw them effected. In the execution, the ideas he followed were all his own; and the minutest as well as the greatest expedients he employed bore the stamp of originality.

" Every man of genius is an enthusiast: Mr. Brindley was an enthusiast in favor of the superiority of canal navigations above those of rivers; and this triumph of art over nature led him to view, with a sort of contempt, the winding stream, in which the lover of rural beauty so much delights. This sentiment he is said to have expressed in a striking manner at an examination before a committee of the House of Commons, when on being asked, after he had made some contemptuous remarks relative to

rivers, what he conceived they were created
for:—he answered, *To feed navigable canals.*
" After the successful execution of the Duke
of Bridgewater's canal to the Mersey, Mr.
Brindley was employed in the revived design
of carrying a canal from that river to the Trent,
through the counties of Chester and Stafford.
This undertaking was commenced in the year
1766; and from the great ideas it opened in
the mind of its conductor of a scheme of inland navigation, which should connect all the
internal parts of England with each other, and
with the principal sea-ports by means of *branches*
from this main stem, he gave it the emphatical
name of the *Grand Trunk.* In executing this,
he was called upon to employ all the resources
of his invention, on account of the unequality,
and various nature of the ground to be cut
through ; in particular the hill of Hare Castle,
which was only to be passed by a tunnel of
great length, bored through strata of different
consistency, and some of them mere quicksand,
proved to be a most difficult and expensive obstacle, which, however, he completely surmounted. While this was carrying on, a branch from
the Grand Trunk, to join the Severn near
Bewdley, was committed to his management,

and finished in 1772. He was also concerned in the projection and execution of several others; and indeed there was scarcely any design of canal navigation set on foot in this kingdom during the latter years of his life, in which he was not consulted, and the plan of which he did not entirely form, or revise and improve.

" The attention and application which all his various and complicated employments required probably shortened his days; as the number of his undertakings, in some degree, impaired his usefulness. He fell into a kind of chronic fever, which after continuing some years, with but little intermission, at length wore out his frame, and put a period to his life, on September the 27th, 1772, in the 56th year of his age. He died at Turnhurst, in Staffordshire, and was buried at New Chapel, in the same county.

" In appearance and manners, as well as acquirements, Mr. Brindley was a mere peasant. Unlettered, and rude in speech, it was easier for him to devise means for executing a design, than to communicate his ideas concerning it to others. Formed by nature for the profession he assumed, it was there alone that he was in his proper element: and so occupied was his

21 Q 4

mind with his business, that he was incapable of
relaxing in any of the common amusements of
life. As he had not the ideas of other men to assist
him, whenever a point of difficulty in contrivance
occurred, it was his custom to retire to his bed,
where in perfect solitude, he would lie one, two,
or three days, pondering the subject in his
mind, till the requisite expedient had presented
itself. This is that true *inspiration* which poets
have almost exclusively arrogated to themselves,
but which men of original genius, in every walk,
are actuated by, when, from the operation of
the mind, acting upon itself, without the intru-
sion of foreign notions, they create and invent.
A remarkable retentive memory was one of the
essential qualities which Mr. Brindley brought
to his mental operations. This enabled him to
execute all the parts of the most complex machine in due order, without any help of models
or drawings, provided he had once settled the
whole plan in his mind. In his calculations of
the powers of machines, he followed a plan peculiar to himself; but indeed the only one he
could follow without instruction in the rules of
art. He would work the question some time
in his head, and then set down the result in
figures: then taking it up in this stage, he
would proceed by a mental operation to another

result, and thus he would go on till the whole
was finished; and making use of figures only
to mark the several results of his operations.—
But, though by the wonderful powers of native
genius, he was thus enabled to get over his
want of artificial method to a certain degree,
yet there is no doubt that when his concerns
became extremely complicated, with accounts
of various kinds to keep, and calculations of all
kinds to form, he could not avoid that perplex-
ity and embarrassment which a readiness in
the processes carried on by pen and paper can
alone obviate. His estimates of expence have
generally proved wide of reality; and he seems
to have been better qualified to have been the
contriver than the manager of a great design.
His moral qualities were highly respectable.
He was far above envy and jealousy, and freely
communicated his improvements to persons capable of receiving and executing them; taking
a liberal satisfaction in forming a new generation of engineers, able to proceed with the great
plans in the success of which he was so deeply
interested. His integrity, and regard to the
advantage of his employers, were unimpeach-
able. In fine, the name of *Brindley*, will
ever keep a place among that small number of
mortals who form *eras* in the art or science to

which they devote themselves, by a large and
durable extension of its limits." ,

HATHERSAGE, *Hereseige*, a small village situated at the foot of a very lofty and extensive
hill, cóntains about 100 houses.   In the direction of the streets there is no regularity, but
the houses are scattered over an extensive piece
of ground.   The church stands on an eminence
at the north end of the village: it is a neat,
clean, light building, with a spire and six bells.
In the chancel are several monuments of ancient date, belonging to the family of *Eyres*,
who came from *Highlow* in the parish of Hope.
Lying against the north wall, is a tomb-stone,
with brass figures of a man and a woman, and
several children, indented in the stone ; and
also a brass tablet, bearing the following Latin
inscription, in Old English characters:—*Hic
jacet Robertus Eyre, armiger: qui obiit xxi.
hic Mensis Maye, anno Millimmo CCCCLIX:
et Joahne uxor ejus, qui obiit ix die mensis Maye.
Millimmo CCCCLXIV.*   There is also another
brass tablet to the memory of *Rudulphus Eyre*,
of Offerton in the county of Derby, Esq. and
Elizabeth his wife, who died in the year 1493.
The living is a vicarage, the church is dedicated to St. Michael, and the Duke of Devonshire is the patron.

It is handed down by tradition, that *Little John*, the companion and coadjutor of Robin Hood, lies buried in this church-yard. His grave is shewn to the traveller. Two grey stones, one at the foot and the other at the head, mark the spot, where this hero lies. The distance from one stone to another, is, nearly, four yards—a space, whatever might have been Little John's ambition while alive, it is unreasonable to suppose he could occupy when dead: however the person that was buried in the spot, whether Little John or not, was a man of great stature, as the grave was opened some years ago, and a thigh bone found, which measured two feet and a half.

In the church-yard, there is also, the remains of a stone cross, around which it was customary in Popish times, (and it has been done in the memory of some of the present inhabitants) to take the corpse of the deceased before its interment, in order to its more speedy release from Purgatory. There are several Roman Catholics in the village and neighbourhood, who assemble at a very neat chapel at the western extremity of the village. This place of worship was erected about 150 years ago, but since that time, it has often been the object of popular fury, and the inside completely destroyed by the overheated zeal of Protestant bigots. The congregation consists of about 70 individuals, and a priest, who lives in a large and handsome house adjoining the chapel.— The eastern gable-end of the chapel, is ornamented with a cross of blackish stone, worked in among, and projecting above, the free-stones which compose the building, and which may be seen at a great distance.

. " The earth here seems to possess some very peculiar properties, as will appear from the following extraordinary relation, chiefly extracted from a letter written by a Clerk of Hathersage, but corroborated by enquiries made among other persons who were acquainted with the fact.

" On opening a grave in Hathersage churchyard for the interment of a female, on the 31st. of May, 1781, the body of Mr. Benjamin Ashton, who was buried on the 29th. of December 1725, was taken up, ' congealed and hard as flint. His breast, belly, and face, and all the parts that lay under, were nearly the same colour as when put into the coffin.' The coffin was of oak boards, inch and a half thick, and as sound as when first deposited in the grave, which was so extremely wet, that men were employed to lade out the water, that the coffin might be kept from floating, till the body was returned to it. The face was partly decayed; conveying the idea, that the putrifactive process had commenced previously to that which had hardened the flesh into stone. The head was broke off in removing the body from the coffin, but was placed in its first position when again interred. Mr. Ashten was a corpulent man, and died in the forty-second year of his age.

" Above the church, at a place called *Camp Green*, is a circular area, 144 feet in diameter, encompassed with a high and pretty large mound of earth, round which is a deep ditch. A road has been carried across the area from west to east; and an outlet and path have also been formed on the south side. In the eighth volume of the Archæologia, is an account by Mr. Hayman Rooke, of some ancient remains on Hathersage Moor, particularly of a *Rocking-stone*, twenty-nine feet in circumference; and near it, a large stone, with a rock-basin, and many tumuli, in which urns, beads, and rings, have been found. At a little distance he mentions observing another remarkable stone, thirteen feet six inches, in length, which appeared to have been placed by art on the brow of a precipice, and supported by two small stones.

On the top is a large rock-basin, four feet three
inches in diameter; and close to this, on the
south side, a hollow, cut like a chair, with a
step to rest the feet upon. This, in the traditions of the country, is called *Cair's Chair.*
Not far from this spot are also some rocking-
stones, and of such a kind, as seems plainly
to indicate, that the first idea of forming Rocking-stones at all, was the appearance of certain stupendous masses, left by natural causes
in such a singular situation, to be even. prepared, as it were, by the hand of nature, to exhibit such a curious kind of equipoise."*

DERWENT, is a chapelry belonging to Hathersage; and the liberty contains about thirty houses.

STONEY-MIDDLETON, is a small hamlet, situated among grey rocks, surrounded by a
wild, dreary, and desolate country. The church,
which is dedicated to St. Martin, is of an octagonal form, and was built some years ago by
subscription, the greater part of which was
furnished by the Duke of Devonshire.

Middleton Dale, a narrow, winding, and
deep chasm, is, in grandeur and beauty, inferior to most of the other dales in Derbyshire:

---

* Munimenta Antiqua, Vol. I.

yet the rocks in it are of so peculiar a shape,
that they never fail to make a striking impression upon the minds of those who visit the place.
On the north side, they bear a strong resemblance to the round towers and buttresses of a
ruined castle; in other parts, there is such an
appearance of mouldings, that one can scarcely help thinking, that the chissel has been employed in their formation. The rocks, more
especially on the north side, are perpendicular, and rise to the height of three or four hundred feet; but every where naked and un-
adorned, excepting near the entrance in *Eyam
Dale*. Thus deprived of every verdant covering, the picturesque is excluded; whilst their
clumsy, heavy, round forms preclude the idea
of grandeur. It has the appearance, as if the
rocks which form this chasm had been rent
asunder by some convulsion of nature; and the
turnings of the Dale are so sharp, as, occasionally to give the idea of all further progress being prevented by the opposition of an insur-
mountable barrier of precipitous rock. Its
character, therefore, is rather singularity, than
magnificence or loveliness. The road from
Chesterfield to Tideswell, passes through it,
accompanied by a streamlet, which runs beside

it, a great part of the way. Here are some remarkable caverns; one of which is called *Bos-
sen Hole;* but the chief is *Bamforth Hole* in
Charleswork, of great extent, and beautifully
ornamented with stalactitious petrifactions.

On the north side of Stoney Middleton is
St. Martin's Bath, enclosed by four walls, but
open at the top. These tepid waters very much
resemble, in their chemical properties, and medicinal virtues, those of Matlock, and have
been found efficacious by those who have been
afflicted with rheumatism. The thermometer
stands at 63 degrees in the bath; and, perhaps,
if the spring were covered in, and a convenient
room built adjoining it, the place would be
more resorted to then it is at present; though
its want of charming scenery would prevent
its becoming so eminently distinguished, or so
attractive, as Matlock. Several other warm
springs rise in the environs, and also a chalybeate one.

PEAK FOREST, is another chapelry belonging
to Hathersage. The church is said to have
been built by the Countess of Shrewsbury, and
is now under the patronage of the Duke of
Devonshire. William Ferrers, Earl of Derby,
gave to the Monks of Lenton, in Nottinghamshire, the tithe of all his essarts in the forest of
High Peak.

The village is but small, containing together with the whole liberty 100 houses. The name (Peak Forest) is not applicable to the village only, but to an extensive tract of land, formerly covered with trees, but now naked, forlorn, and apparently unprofitable. The forest was anciently called *De alto Pecco*, and included the parishes of Castleton, Hope, Chapel, or.Boden, and Glossop, in this county; and Mottram in Longdendale, in the county of Chester. It was stocked with red deer, which, by tradition are reported to have traversed the country so low as Ashford. Most of the deer perished in a deep snow, about the time of Elizabeth, or the beginning of the reign of James the First. Many petrified horns have been found in the limestone tracts. •

The *Limestone Quarries* on the Peak Forest, occupy an extent of nearly half a mile in length, and two or three hundred yards in breadth. Here many workmen are continually employed in boring the rocks, and shattering them into pieces by the explosions of gun-powder. A *Rail-way* extends from the quarries to Chapel-en-le-Frith, where an inclined plane has been formed on the side of a mountain, to convey the limestone to the Manchester canal. The velocity with which the loaded carts descend is regulated by mechanical principles.

Eldon Hole, is situated on the side of a gentle hill about a mile to the north-west of the village of Peak Forest. It is a deep chasm in the ground, surrounded by a wall of uncemented stones, to prevent accidents. Many exaggerated descriptions, and marvellous reports, have been propagated concerning this fissure: it has, at one time, been represented as perfectly unfathomable; at others, as teeming, at a certain depth, with such impure air, that no animal could respire it without immediate destruction. Cotton affirmed more than a century ago, that he endeavoured to plumb the cavity with a line 884 yards long, but could not find the bottom; and that upon examining the lower end of the line, he found that 80 yards had sunk through water.* And a gentleman, whose account was quoted in Catcott's Treatise on the Deluge, from the second number of the Philosophical Transactions, has asserted, that he let down a line 922 yards, without meeting with a bottom. But these descriptions of its depth are, for some reason or other, certainly erroneous: as several persons have, at different periods, descended into it, and affirmed, that the depth of the first landing below the surface, was not above seventy yards.

---

* Wonders of the Peak, published in 1681.

About fifty years ago, a Mr. Loyd, descended into it; and communicated an account of
his descent, through the sixty-first volume of
the Philosophical Transactions.* He says, that
for the first twenty yards, he descended somewhat obliquely, and that the passage then became difficult from projecting crags. At the
depth of ten yards more, the inflexion of his
rope varied at least six yards from the perpendicular. From hence, the breadth of the chink
was about three yards and the length six; the
sides irregular, moss-grown, and wet. Within
fourteen yards of the bottom, the rock opened
on the east, and he swung till he reached the
floor of a cave, sixty-two yards only from the
mouth, the light from which, was sufficiently
strong to permit the reading of any print. The
interior of the chasm, he describes as consisting of two parts; one like an oven; the other,
like the dome of a glass-house, communicating
with each other by a small arched passage. On
the south side of the second cavern, was a
smaller opening, about four yards long, and
two high, lined throughout with a kind of
sparkling stalactite, of a fine deep yellow colour, with some stalactitical drops hanging from

---

* Page 250.

the roof. Facing the entrance he found a noble column, above ninety feet high, of the same
kind of incrustation. As he proceeded to the
north, he came to a large stone which was covered with the same substance; and under it he
found a hole, two yards deep, uniformly lined
with it. From the edge of this hole sprung up
a rocky ascent, sloping like a buttress against
the side of the cavern, and consisting of vast,
solid, round masses of the same substance and
colour. Having climbed this ascent to the
height of about sixty feet, he obtained some
fine pieces of stalactite, which hung from the
craggy sides of the cavern. Descending with
some difficulty and danger, he proceeded in
the same direction, and soon came to another
pile of incrustations of a brown colour; above
which he found a small cavern, opening into
the side of the vault, which he entered. Here
he saw vast masses of stalactite, hanging like
ice-icles from every part of the roof; some of
these being four and five feet long, and as thick
as a man's body. The sides of the largest
cavern were mostly lined with incrustations of
three kinds;—the first was a deep yellow stalactite; the second a thin coating, which re-
sembled a light stone-coloured varnish, and reflected the light of the candle with great splen-

dour; and the third a rough efflorescence, the
shoot of which had the similitude of a kind of
rose-flower. These are the principal facts communicated respecting Elden Hole by Mr. Loyd,
the only scientific person who visited it, and
whose account is the only one on which any re-
liance can be placed—this it may be observed,
furnishes no arguments of immeasurable depth.

" We shall now," say the editors of the Beauties of England and Wales, " state our own observations, and also the result of enquiries
made in the neighbourhood. The mouth of
this chasm opens longitudinally, in a direction
from north to south. Its shape is nearly that
of an irregular ellipsis; about thirty yards in
length, and nine broad in the widest part. The
northern end is fringed with small trees; and
moss and underwood grow out of the crevices
on each side to the depth of forty or fifty feet.
As the fissure recedes from the surface, it gradually contracts; and at the depth of twenty
or twenty-five yards, hades (inclines) considerably to the west; so that the eye can no longer
trace its course. The bushes and projecting
masses of stone, are, excepting at a point on
the west side, extremely unfavourable to plumb-
ing it with accuracy. From this point, a weight
was carefully let down, and, in the opinion of

several persons by whom the line was repeatedly felt, was adjudged to have reached the bottom. The line had been previously measured;
and the depth to which the weight descended,
was found to be no more than *sixty-seven yards
and one foot!* That this is the *real depth of
the chasm,* or as near it as can be ascertained,
the assertion of three miners,* questioned separately, who have been let down into it, at different periods, within the last thirty-four or
thirty-six years, abundantly corroborates:

"Two of them imagined its depth to be
about sixty-eight, or seventy yards: but as
many years had elapsed since the time of their

---

* The last of these was, unfortunately, dead, when the
author of the present History visited Elden Hole, last summer. The occasion of their descent, was the discovery,
sometime in the year 1767, of the two horses of a gentleman and a lady without their riders near the abyss. The
country people immediately imagined (and perhaps with
reason) that the latter had been robbed, murdered, and
thrown into Elden Hole; and let down some miners into it
in order to search for the bodies, but nothing was discovered to justify the report of the murder. About the year
1800, a similar circumstance of a man's horse without its
master being discovered near Elden Hole, induced a body
of miners to undertake a like expedition, but with as little
success as their predecessors, and without making any additional discoveries. It is said, that some years ago, a cruel
wretch confessed at the gallows, that he had robbed a traveller, and afterwards thrown him into this chasm.

subterraneous expedition, they would not speak to a fathom or two. The third, whose descent into the chasm had been more recent, affirmed, that the length of the rope which enabled him to reach the bottom, was *thirty-three fathoms*, and a *trifle more*. So nearly do these different relations correspond, that we can hardly suppose the depth of Elden Hole will again be made a question. It should be remarked, that the rise of the hill in the vicinity of the chasm, is about one foot in six; and consequently, that the variation of a few yards, in divers admeasurements, may at once be reconciled, by supposing the stations to have been different."

HOPE, is a small village, on the road between Hathersage and Castleton, situated on the banks of the Derwent, which is here but an inconsiderable stream. Hope is mentioned in Domesday-book as having a priest and a church, in the time of Edward the Confessor. The living is a vicarage, the church is dedicated to St. Peter, and the Dean and Chapter of Litchfield are the patrons.

It has been asserted, that William Peverel had a mansion at Burgh in this parish, and that in the reign of Edward the First, John, Earl of Warren and Surry, was made governor

22   s 4

of it. In some manuscript papers of the late
Mr. John Mander, of Bakewell, Hope has been
described as an ancient market-town; but
the advantage of this privilege it no longer
enjoys.

"The moors of Hope parish afford an extraordinary instance of the preservation of human
bodies interred in them. One Barber, a gra-
zier, and his maid servant, going to Ireland in
the year 1674, were lost in the snow, and remained covered with it from January to May,
when they were so offensive, that the Coroner
ordered them to be buried on the spot. About
twenty-nine years afterwards, some countrymen, probably having observed the extraordinary properties of this soil in preserving dead
bodies, had the curiosity to open the ground,
and found them in no way altered; the colour
of the skin being fair and natural, and their
flesh as soft as that of persons newly dead.—
They were exposed for a sight, during the
course of twenty years following, though they
were much changed in that time by being so
often uncovered. In 1716, Mr. Henry Brown,
M. B. of Chesterfield, saw the man perfect, his
beard strong, and about a quarter of an inch
long: the hair of his head short; his skin hard,
and of a tanned leather colour, pretty much

the same as the liquor and earth they lay in: he had on a broad cloth coat, of which the doctor in vain tried to tear off a skirt. The woman was more decayed, having been taken out of the ground, and rudely handled; her flesh particularly decayed, her hair long and spongy, like that of a living person. Mr. Barber of Rotherham, the man's grandson, had both bodies buried in Hope church, and, upon looking into the graves sometime afterwards, it was found, they were entirely consumed. Mr. Wermald, the minister of Hope, was present at their removal: he observed that they lay about a yard deep, in moist soil, or moss, but no water stood in the place. He saw their stockings drawn off, and the man's legs, which had not been uncovered before, were quite fair: the flesh, when pressed by his finger, pitted a little; and the joints played freely, and without the least stiffness: the other parts were much decayed. What was left of their clothes not cut off for curiosity,' was firm and good; and the woman had a piece of new serge, which seemed never the worse."*

BROUGH, a small hamlet in the parish and

* Gough's Additions to the Britannia, as detailed from the Philosophical Transactions.

neighbourhood of Hope, is supposed to have
been a place of some importance in the time of
the Romans. Mr. Pegge, who visited the spot
in 1761, was of opinion, that it was once a
Roman station; and in proof, mentions, a rude
bust of Apollo, and of another deity, which
had been found in the fields. He likewise remarked the vestiges of an oblong square building, where a coarse pavement, composed of
pieces of tiles and cement, was discovered; and
in searching among the rubbish, he met with
the fragment of a tile, on which a part of the
word *Cohors*, was impressed. At Brough-mill
a gold coin of Vespasian had been found in good
preservation.

Mr. Bray, who visited and examined this
place at a later period, says, that the Roman
camp was at the place called the *Castle*, near the
junction of two small streams, named Noo or
Noa, and the Bradwell water. The inclosed area
was of a square form, measuring 310 feet from
south to north, 270 feet from east to west.
Many of the old buildings lying on every side of
this spot, have been turned up by the plough;
between the castle and the river, bricks have
been taken up; and on the other side of the
water, urns have been found. On some of the
bricks, Roman letters were impressed: and on

the rim of an urn, was this inscription in three
lines:—VIR .. VIV .. TR the two last letters being smaller than the others. Pieces of swords,
spears, bridle-bits, and coins have also been
found here: and a few years ago, a half-length
figure of a woman, with her arms folded across
her breast, cut in rough grit-stone, was turned
up by the plough; and afterwards sold to a
gentleman at Bakewell. Not many years ago,
a double row of pillars crossed the point of
land at the conflux of the two streams: they
were of grit-stone, and three persons could walk
a-breast between them.

On the road between Hope 'and Castleton,
rises the lofty eminences called, *Win-hill*, and
Loose-hill, from the event of a battle, which,
according to tradition, was fought near them,
between two armies who had previously encamped on these eminences. On the summit
of the former of these points, is a mound composed of stones, covered with heath and moss,
in the middle of which is a rude seat of stones,
called *Robin Hood's Chair*. Under a large heap
of stones, a little to the eastward of *Win-hill-
pike*, about the year 1779, an urn was discovered, made of clay, badly baked, and of very
rude workmanship.

BRADWELL, *Brudewelle*, is a large village in

the same parish. The whole liberty contains nearly 100 houses, whose inhabitants are chiefly supported by the mining business.

A natural excavation has been recently discovered in the neighbourhood of Bradwell, called the *Crystallized Cavern:* it is situated within 200 yards of the village, and is thus described by a late Tourist:

On entering, " there is no grandeur in its first appearance, it is rather terrific than otherwise, and is as much like going down into a deep dungeon, as any thing I can compare it with. After descending about three hundred steps, very abruptly, you then walk, or more properly creep, on an inclined way, for near quarter of a mile, the opening being so low, that it is impossible, at times, to get forward without going on all fours. The different crystallizations which now attract the attention on every side, and above and below the passage, cause you to forget the irksomeness of the road, and to drive away every idea of fatigue. New objects of curiosity begin to crowd one upon another; here, there is the appearance of the pipes of an organ, in a place called the music chamber. In other places, the stalactites are formed into elegant small colonnades, with as exact a symmetry as if they had been

chiselled by the greatest artist. Candles judiciously disposed in the inside of them, give an
idea of the palaces of fairies, or of sylphs and
genii, who have chosen this magnificent abode.
In a recess, on the left, there appears the resemblance of a set of crystallized surgical instruments.

" But still you have seen nothing in comparison with what you are to expect; for, in the
course of one hundred yards further, creeping
at times, and passing down rugged places, you
enter the *Grotto of Paradise*. This heavenly
spot, for it cannot be compared with any thing
terrestrial, is, of itself, a beautiful Crystallized
Cavern, about twelve feet high, and twenty feet
long, pointed at the top, similar to a Gothic
arch, with a countless number of large stalactites, hanging from its roof. Candles placed
amongst them, give some idea of its being
lighted up with elegant glass chandeliers,
while the sides are entirely incrusted, and
brilliant in the extreme:—The floor is chequer-
ed with black and white spar; and altogether
it has the most novel and elegant appearance
of any cavern I ever beheld. This paradisiacal
apartment would be left with a kind of regret,
should you not expect to see it again on returning.

"Still continuing a similar road to what has
been passed, and entertained at various times
with the curiosities of the place, and the gentle droppings of the water, which scarcely
break the solemn silence of the scene, at length
you arrive at the *Grotto of Calypso*, and the
extremity of the Cavern, above 2000 feet from
the first entrance. In order to see this to advantage, it is necessary to rise into a recess,
about two yards high. There, indeed, from
the beautiful appearances of the different crystallizations, some of them of an azure cast,
from the echoes reverberating from side to side,
you fancy yourself to be arrived at the secluded retreat of some fabled deity. The water
also running near this Cavern, brings a cool refreshing air, which from the exertion used, and
the closeness of the place, is very acceptable.
The size of this Grotto is nearly equal to
that of the last, and, indeed, it is difficult to
determine, which is the most interesting.

"After returning by the same path for a considerable distance, there is another Cavern to
be investigated, which branches in a south-
western direction from the one already explor-
ed. The roads here, are still more difficult of
access, but certainly the stalactites are most
beautiful. Great many of them are pendent

from the roof more than a yard long, and almost as small as the smallest reed. The top
and sides of this second Cavern in many places
are remarkably smooth, particularly the part
called the amphitheatre. In general, this place
is of a very dark stone, to which the transparent appearances before mentioned,. with each
a drop of water hanging at the bottom, form a
fine contrast; and indeed, this cavern is, in
some degree, a contrast to the one before examined.

"Returning back, we still admire the curiosities before noticed, and with regret, leave
this beautiful Crystallized Cavern; its representation, in idea, still continuing before the
mind's eye; where it will remain so long as
memory holds her seat."*

FAIRFIELD, is also a chapelry in the parish
of Hope, though situated near Buxton. The
church is dedicated to St. Peter, and is a tolerably good edifice. The village is straggling
and small; containing no more then sixty-three
houses, and about 280 inhabitants.

CASTLETON is situated in a valley, which,
owing to the strong contrast it forms, with the
bleak and elevated tracts that environ it, is the

* Hutchinson's Tour through the High Peak, p. 20.

most striking in the High Peak, or perhaps in
any other part of the county. The immediate
approach to the town, by a road across the
mountains from Chapel-in-the-Frith, is, " by
a steep descent called the *Winnats*, or Wind-
gates, from the stream of air that always sweeps
through the chasm. This road is a mile in
length, and carried on in a winding direction,
in order to render the natural declivity of the
ground passable by carriages. Happy was the
imagination that first suggested its name—*the
gates or portals of the winds;* since, wild as
these sons of the tempest are, the massive rocks
which nature here presents, seem to promise a
barrier sufficiently strong to oppose their mad-
dest fury. Precipices one thousand feet in
height, dark, rugged, and perpendicular, heave
their unweildly forms on each side of the road,
(which makes several inflections in its descent)
and frequently presenting themselves in front,
threaten opposition to all farther progress. At
one of these sudden turns to the left, a most
beautiful view of Castleton vale is unexpectedly
thrown upon the eye; refreshing it with a rich
picture of beauty, fertility, and variety, after
the tedious uniformity of rude and hideous
scenery to which it has been so long confined."*

* Warner's Northern Tour, Vol. I. p. 166.

The breadth of the vale, is in many parts two miles, its length between five and six, and its depth, below the level of the surrounding country nearly 1000 feet. Several rivulets flow through it, and to the north and south form lesser dales, opening in different directions.— The villages of Hope, Castleton, and Brough, are situated in its bosom ; and the former, with its spire and church, forms a very agreeable feature in the scenery, when viewed from this part of the descent.

As the road winds along the declivity, a view is presented of Castleton, which appears clustered near the bottom of the steep eminence at whose feet, the famous cavern discloses itself, and whose summit is occupied by the ruins of the ancient Castle that gave name to the place. Near the entrance of the village, a bridge has been thrown across the stream which issues from the cavern. The number of houses in Castleton and its liberty, is, about 200, and are built, chiefly, of stone. The support of the inhabitants is derived from the mining business, and from the expenditure of those, who are induced to visit the remarkable places in the neighbourhood. The town was once fortified, as a ditch and a vallum, which formerly extended in a semi-circular course round it, from the mountain on which the castle stands, may yet be traced in particular directions. The living is a vicarage, and the church is dedicated to St. Edmund: the Bishop of Chester is impropriator and patron.

The remains of the Castle are still visible: its situation is very elevated, and the almost perpendicular chasms, that nearly insulate the eminence it occupies, must, prior to the invention of gun-powder, have rendered it almost impregnable. The east and south sides are bounded by a narrow ravine, called the Cave, which ranges between two vast limestone rocks, and on the east is nearly 200 feet in depth. On the west it is skirted by the high precipice which hangs over the great cavern, and rises to the height of 260 feet. The north side is the most accessible; yet, even here, the path has been carried in a winding direction, in order to make the ascent more practicable.

The Castle-yard is spacious, and would contain a small army: and the wall by which it was enclosed, still remains in several places, measuring twenty feet in height on the outside. On the north side were two small towers, now destroyed. The entrance was at the north-east corner, as appears by a part of an arch-way yet remaining. Near the north-west angle is

the *Keep*, the walls of which, on the south and
west are still pretty entire, and, at the north-
west corner, are fifty-five feet high; but the
north and east sides are much shattered. On
the outside it forms a square of thirty-eight feet
two inches; but on the inside, it is not equal,
being from north to south, twenty-one feet four
inches; from east to west, nineteen feet three
inches. This difference arises from the various
thickness of the walls, which are composed of
broken masses of limestone, and mortar of such
excellent temper, that it binds the whole together like a rock: the facings of both outside and
inside, are of hewn grit-stone. In the wall within is a little *herring-bone* ornament.

This building, in its present state, has neither roof nor second floor; but anciently consisted of two rooms—one on the ground floor,
and one above; over which the roof was raised
with a gable-end to the north and south, but
not of equal height with the outer walls. The
ground floor was about fourteen feet high, the
upper room about sixteen: the entrance to the
former, appears to have been through a door-
way on the south side of the upper room, by a
flight of steps, now wholly destroyed, but said
to have existed within the memory of some of
the oldest inhabitants of the place. The pre-

dent entrance is through an opening made in
the wall. At the south-east corner, is a narrow
winding stair-case, communicating with the
roof, but in a ruinous condition.*

This Castle is a place of considerable antiquity; and is supposed, by Mr. King,† to have
been a fortress and place of royal residence, in
the Saxon times; but other antiquarians are of
opinion, that it is of Norman origin, and erected by William Peverel, natural son of the Conqueror—to him it is also ascribed by the traditions of the neighbourhood; and its ancient
appellation, of *Peverel's Place in the Peke*,
countenances this opinion. Whatever is the
truth, it is certain that Peverel possessed it, at
the time of the Domesday Survey, by the
name of *Castelli in Pechesers*, (Castle in the
Peak), with the honor and forest of *Peke*, and
thirteen other Lordships in this county. About
this time, a tournament is said to have been
held here, occasioned, according to Mr. Pilkington, by the following circumstance:—

" William, a valiant knight, and sister's son
to Pain Peverel, Lord of Whittington, in the
county of Salop, had two daughters, one of
whom, Mellet, was no less distinguished by a

martial spirit, than her father. This appeared from the declaration she made respecting the choice of a husband. She firmly resolved to marry none but a knight of great prowess; and her father, to confirm her purpose, and to procure and encourage a number of visitors, invited all noble young men, who were inclined to enter the lists, to meet at Peveral's Place in the Peke, and there decide their pretensions by the use of arms; declaring, at the same time, that, whoever vanquished his competitors, should receive his daughter, with his castle at Whittington, as a reward for his skill and valour. Guarine de Meez, a branch of the house of Lorraine, and an ancestor of the Lords Fitz-Warrine, hearing this report, repaired to the place above-mentioned; and there engaged with a son of the king of Scotland, and also with a Baron of Burgoyne, and vanquishing them both, obtained the prize for which he fought."

But the Castle in the Peak, did not remain many years after this, in the possession of the Peverels: for William Peverel, grandson of the first possessor of this name, having poisoned Ranulph, Earl of Chester, was obliged to secure his safety by flight; and his castles and other possessions, were left at the king's dis-

posal. This monarch, (Henry the Second)
granted them to his son John, Earl of Mor-
taigne, who afterwards succeeded to the crown.
In the sixth year of the reign of king John,
Hugh de Neville was made Governor of the
Peak Castle; but within ten years afterwards,
it is said to have been possessed by the rebellious Barons, from whom it was taken for the
king by William Ferrers, the seventh Earl of
Derby; who, in recompence for this service,
was appointed its governor. In the fourth of
Edward the Second, John, Earl of Warren,
obtained a grant of the Castle and honor of
Peke, in Derbyshire, with the whole forest of
High Peke, in as ample a manner as it was
anciently enjoyed by the Peverels. In the for-
ty-ninth year of Edward the Third, the Castle
was granted to John of Gaunt, and from that
time, it has descended in the same manner as
the Duchy of Lancaster. The present Constable of the Castle is, the Duke of Devonshire.

It has been observed by Mr. Bray, that this
fortress was not well calculated for defence, except against any sudden assault, as it was neither large nor furnished with a well. The re-
mark concerning the supply of water, is correct—there is no reservoir within the walls; but
it has been supposed that the spring, which is

situated in the upper part of the Cave Valley, and at no great distance from the Keep, might formerly, by some contrivance, have supplied the garrison with this necessary article. At present, its waters sink between the clefts of the limestone, and fall in continued drops from the roof of the great cavern at the place called, *Roger Rain's House.*

About half way up the Cave Valley, is a stratum of *Basalt*, which appears at the surface; and in one part, assumes the form of an hexagonal column, and is similar in texture and hardness, to those of Staffa, in the Hebrides, and of the Giant's Causeway, in Ireland.— Some crystallized quartz is incorporated in it, approaching in appearance to chalcedony.— This column is a part of a vast basaltic mass of great thickness and considerable dip, which ranges north and south for fifty or sixty yards, and is covered with a thick stratum of a substance resembling scoria, or half-baked clay. In its immediate neighbourhood is a stratum of toadstone, some of which is decomposed, and appears like indurated clay, full of holes, and varigated with green spots, and calcareous spar: other specimens are extremely hard, with zeolite, and jasper occasionally occurring in them.

PEAK CAVERN, which is also sometimes called the *Devil's Cave*, is one of those magnificent, sublime and extraordinary operations of nature, which at all times excite the admiration and wonder of their beholders. And the description of the Mantuan Bard, when introducing his hero into a similar excavation, may with propriety be applied to it,—

"Spelunca alta fuit, vastoque immanis hiatu."

Virg. Æn.

This cave has, at all times, been regarded as one of the principal wonders of Derbyshire, and celebrated by several poets. It is situated at the distance of about 100 yards from the Inn at Castleton, and is approached by a path along the side of a clear rivulet, crossed by a small bridge, which conducts to the fissure, or separation of the rock, at the end of which is the cavern. It would be difficult to imagine a scene more august, than that which presents itself to the visitor, at the first appearance of the mouth of the cavern. On each side, the huge grey rocks, rise almost perpendicularly, to the height of nearly three hundred feet; and meeting each other at right angles, form a deep and gloomy recess. In front, the mouth of the cave, overhung by a vast canopy of un-pillared rock, assuming the appearance of a de-

...arch, strikes the mind as solemnly grand. This natural arch is regular in structure, and extends, in width, one hundred and twenty feet—in height, forty-two—and proceeding depth about ninety. In this entrance, or first cavern, a singular combination is produced—human habitations and manufacturing machines (the appendages of some twine ..., here, who have fixed their residence within this cavern) blending with the sublime features of the natural scenery. After penetrating about thirty yards into the cave, the roof becomes lower, and a gentle descent conducts, by a detached rock, to the interior entrance of this tremendous hollow. Here, the light of day, which gradually softens, wholly disappears; and candles are put into the hands of the inspector, to illuminate his farther progress through the stygian darkness of the cavern.

After passing through a wicket-gate, which the proprietor unlocks, the way becomes low and confined, and the visitor is obliged to proceed in a stooping posture, twenty or thirty yards, when he arrives at a spacious opening, which from its form is called the *Bell House*. From here, the path conducts to the margin of a small lake, locally termed the *First Water*:— it is, about fourteen yards in length, but not

more than two or three feet in depth. A small
boat; or rather a tub, provided by the guide,
is ready to convey the passenger to the interior
parts of the cavern, beneath a massive vault of
rock, which in some parts descends to within
eighteen or twenty inches of the water. Owing
to the lowness of the vault, the visitor is obliged to stretch himself at full length in the
boat; and the guide entering the lake, and
bending his head, almost to the surface of the
water, pushes forward the skiff with one hand;
while he carries his light in the other. " We
stood some time," says M. St. Fond, " on the
brink, and the light of our dismal torches,
which emitted a black smoke, reflecting our
pale images from the bottom of the lake, we
almost conceived that we saw a troop of shades
starting from an abyss to present themselves
before us. The illusion was extremely striking." This place, indeed, is very favorable to
the wanderings of the imagination; and the
man versed in classic lore, is immediately re-
minded of the passage of the Styx in the fabled
bark of Charon.

Landed again on the rock, the stranger pursues his course, like Æneas and his guide,

" Obscuri solâ sub nocte per umbram,
Perque domos Ditis vacuas et inania regna ;"

and enters a spacious vacuity, 220 feet in length,
200 feet broad, and in some parts, 120 feet
high, opening in the bosom of the rocks; but
from the want of light, neither the distant
sides, nor the roof of this abyss, can be seen.
In a passage at the inner extremity of this vast
cave, the stream which flows through the whole
length of the cavern, spreads into what is called the *Second Water*, which is generally passed
on foot, but sometimes requiring the assistance
of the guide. Near the termination of this
passage, is a projecting pile of rocks, distinguished by the appellation of *Roger Rain's
House;* from the circumstance of water inces-
santly falling in large drops through the crevices of the roof. A little beyond this is an
extensive hollow, called the *Chancel*, where
there are many detached pieces of rock; the
roof rent and broken, and large masses of stalactite incrust the sides, and glitter with the
lights. The chancel is not an inappropriate
name to this cave, and the illusion is still rendered stronger, when the ears are suddenly sup-
prised by the sound of vocal harmony. The
strains produced can not be said to be such as
" take the imprisoned soul, and lap it in Ely-
sium ;" but being unexpected—issuing from a
quarter where no object can be seen—in a place

where all is still as death—and every thing
around calculated to awaken attention, and
powerfully impress the imagination with aw-
some ideas, can seldom be heard without that
mingled emotion of fear and pleasure, astonishment and delight. After being entertained
awhile by this invisible choir, the persons become visible—eight or ten women and children,
each holding a lighted taper in her hand, ranged along a natural gallery of the rock, about
fifty feet above the floor; a situation they obtain, by clambering up a steep ascent, which
commences in the first opening on this side the
lake.

Quitting the chancel, the path conducts to
the *Devil's Cellar*, and *Half-way House*; and
after passing these, the way proceeds beneath
three natural regular arches, to another vast
concavity, called the *Great Tom of Lincoln*,
from its uniform bell-like appearance. This
part, when illuminated by a strong light, has
an extremely pleasing effect—the according position of the rocks, the stream flowing at their
feet, and the spiracles in the roof, make a very
interesting picture. The distance from this
point to the termination of the cavern, is
not more than twenty-five yards: the vault
gradually descends, the passage contracts, and

at length nearly closes, leaving no more room
than is sufficient for the passage of the water,
which flows through a subterraneous channel
of some miles, as the *ratchall*, or small stones,
brought into the cavern after great rains, from
the distant mines of the Peak Forest, evidently
prove.

The intire length of this wonderful cavern,
from its entrance to its termination, is about
2250 feet; and its depth, from the surface of
the mountain, above 621 feet. From different
parts of the cavern, some communications open
with other fissures; but none of them equal it,
either in extent or grandeur. In extremely
wet weather, the interior cannot be visited, as
the water fills up a great portion of the cavern,
and rises to a considerable height even near the
entrance: at other times, the access is not very
difficult, and quite safe. On the visitor's return, the eye, having had time to accommodate
itself to the darkness around, embraces several
objects, which had escaped it before; and the
gradual illumination of rocks, which become
brighter, as the entrance is approached, and
the clustered blaze of day, that " shorn of its
beams," arrays the distant objects in morning
serenity, is, perhaps, one of the most beautiful
scenes, that the pencil could be employed to
exhibit.

· MAM TOR, or the SHIVERING MOUNTAIN, another of the wonders of the Peak, is situated about two miles to the west of Castleton. The name of *Mam Tor*, is said to be an ancient British appellation; but its modern title, the *Shivering Mountain*, seems to have been given it, because of the crumbling of the shale, which decomposing under the action of the atmosphere, the fragments are perpetually gliding down its face into the valley below. The vulgar error, that the mountain has suffered no diminution in bulk, though the shale and grit have been shivering from its face for ages, is confuted by the appearance of the valley beneath, which is overwhelmed with its ruins to the extent of half a mile. At some distance to the north-west, is another break in the mountain, called *Little Mam Tor*, from which the shale and grit frequently shiver, but not in so great a degree as at the former: for after long frosts, heavy gales of wind, rain, &c. such large quantities decompose and fall from the Mam Tor, that the rushing noise it makes in its descent, is sometimes so loud, as to be heard at Castleton.

On the summit of Mam Tor, are the remains of an ancient Roman encampment. The camp was surrounded by a double trench, which is

still in good preservation; except on the side
facing Castleton, where it has been destroyed
by the frequent shivering of the earth. It extended from north-east to south-west, along
the ridge of the eminence, and occupied somewhat more than fourteen acres of ground, the
circumference being above 1000 yards. The
principal entrance was from the west. At the
north-east corner is a perennial spring; and
near the south-west side are two barrows, one
of which was opened a few years' ago, and a
bras celt, and some fragments of an unbaked
urn, discovered in it. Mam Tor rises to the
height of 1300 feet above the level of the valley, and on every side is very steep.

At the foot of Mam Tor, on the south, is a
very ancient mine, called the *Odin*, supposed
to have been worked by the Saxons, who gave
it the name of one of the Scandinavian deities.
It still furnishes employment for many men,
women, and children: it consists of two levels
running horizontally under the mountain; the
upper a *cart-gate*, by which the ore is brought
from the mine; the lower one a *water-level*, to
drain the works, which have been carried above
a mile from the entrance: they are ventilated by
shafts sunk into them from above, at the distance

of every thirty yards. At the mouth, the level is
not more than a fathom and a quarter from
the surface of the earth; but at the further extremity, above one hundred and fifty. It belongs to several proprietors, and sometimes has
made great returns. The quality of the ore
differs in different parts of the mine: but yielding about three ounces of silver to the ton weight '
of lead. The elastic bitumen, described in page
106, is obtained in this mine; and also blende,
barytes, manganese, fluor spar, sulphuret of
iron, and various other substances. At the two
mines called the *Tre-cliff*, and the *Water-Hull*,
that singularly beautiful substance the *Blue
John* is found. These subterraneous excavations, will well repay the trouble of exploring them, and furnish some extraordinary instances of nature's scenery.

The only remaining object worthy of inspection in the neighbourhood of Castleton, is the
Speedwell Level, or *Navigation Mine*, which is
situated at the foot of the Winnets, in the
mountainous range called the Long Cliff.—
This level was originally driven in search of
lead ore, by a company of speculators from
Staffordshire, who commenced their undertaking about five and thirty years ago, but with
such little success, that after expending £14,000

and eleven years ceaseless and unavailing labor, were obliged to relinquish it. Being provided with lights, the guide leads the visitor
beneath an arched vault, by a flight of 106
steps, to the sough or level, where a boat is
ready for his reception, and which is put in
motion, by pushing against some pegs driven
into the wall for that purpose. The depth of
the water is about three feet; the channel
through which it proceeds was blasted through
the heart of the hardest.rock. As the boat proceeds, several veins of lead ore may be observed in the rock, but not thick enough to defray
the expence of working them.

After proceeding about 600 yards, through
various caverns, " the level bursts into a tremendous gulph, whose roof and bottom are
completely invisible; but across which the navigation has been carried, by flinging a strong
arch over a part of the fissure where the rocks
are least separated. Here, leaving the boat,
and ascending a stage erected above the level,
the attention of the visitor is directed to the
dark recess of the abyss beneath his feet; and
firm indeed, must be his resolution, if he can
contemplate its depth unmoved, or hear them
described, without an involuntary shudder. To
the depth of ninety feet, all is vacuity and

gloom; but beyond that, commences a pool of
stygian waters, not unaptly named the *Bottom-
less Pit;* whose prodigious range may in some
measure be conceived, from the circumstance
of its having swallowed up, more than 40,000
tons of rubbish made in blasting the rock, without any apparent diminution either in its depth
or extent. The guide indeed, informs you, that
the former has not been ascertained; yet we
have reason to believe that this is incorrect, and
that its actual depth in standing water is about
320 feet. There cannot, however, be a doubt,
but that this abyss has communications with
others, still more deeply situated in the bowels
of the mountain, and into which the precipitated rubbish has found a passage. The super-
fluous water of the level, falls through a water-
gate into this profound cauldron, with a noise
like a rushing torrent.

"This fissure is calculated at being nearly
280 yards below the surface of the mountain;
and so great is its reach upwards, that rockets
of sufficient strength to ascend 450 feet, have
been fired without rendering the roof visible.
The effect of a Bengal light discharged in this
stupendous cavity, is extremely magnificent
and interesting. Beyond the fissure, the level
has been driven to a similar length to that part

which precedes it; but in this division of its course, little occurs to excite admiration."

EDALE, *Aidele*, is a chapelry under Castleton: it is dedicated to the Holy Trinity; and the hamlet and liberty contain about 70 houses.

Mr. Bray, in his Tour mentions, that about a mile north-east of *Nether-booth*, in Edale, there was a pile of unhewn masses of stone, which he thought was a *Druid's Altar;* but which have now, for several years been destroyed, for the sake of the stone. The altar was circular; about sixty-six feet in diameter, composed of rough stones of various sizes, rudely piled together, without mortar or cement, in form of a haycock, about eighteen feet perpendicular height. The top was hollow, in the form of a basin, about four feet deep and six feet in diameter: the stone on the inside of this basin was black, and much burned, as if large fires had been often made in it.

A few years before the last-mentioned Tourist visited this part, a large stone, lying on the side of the hill near the village of Edale, was removed; and under it were found fifteen or sixteen beads, about two inches in diameter, and about the thickness of the stem of a large tobacco-pipe. One was of amber, the rest of different coloured glass. He supposes, that they were amulets used by the Druids.

710 HISTORICAL AND DESCRIPTIVE

"Among the sequestered vallies in this quarter of the county is the pleasant *Edale*, where,
secluded in the bosom of the mountains from
the bustle of the world, the inhabitants appear
to enjoy all the quiet and security which per-
vaded the Happy Valley of Rasselas. The
Dale is wide and fertile, and better cultivated
than most others in the regions of the Peak: the
bottom is enlivened by a little rivulet, which
flows near the village of Edale, and aids, by
its motion, the operations of a cotton factory,
established at a little distance. Various other
dales branch off from this to an extensive tract
called the *Woodlands of Derbyshire*, the upper
parts of which display some fine oak, fir, and
larch trees. The ground of the Woodlands
mostly belongs to the Duke of Devonshire, by
whose direction the plough has been introduced, and many acres brought into cultivation."

CHAPEL-IN-THE-FRITH.

CHAPEL-IN-THE-FRITH, or CHAPEL-EN-LE-
FRITH, is a small, but neat town, pleasantly
situated on the declivity of a convex hill, rising
in a valley, surrounded by lofty mountains. It

is a free borough, and a market-town; and its market, which has been on the decline, is now represented as being more fully attended. The church was erected, at the commencement of the fourteenth century, by virtue of a commission *ad quod damnum*, upon the king's soil, by the inhabitants there dwelling, in the time of king Henry the Third; and consecrated by Alexander de Savensby, Bishop of Lichfield and Coventry. The chancel is said to have been built by one of the Bodens, a wealthy family, who lived at Boden-Hall, in this parish, now in ruins: the other part of the church and tower, were afterwards erected by the parishioners. The east-end was lengthened, some years ago, at the expence of Mrs. Bower, whose daughter bequeathed her harpsichord to the church, with a salary of about twenty pounds yearly, for a person to play, and find coals to air it. The living is a donative curacy, and the church is dedicated to St. Thomas Becket.

The High Peak Courts, for the recovery of debts and damages under five pounds, are regularly held at Chapel every three weeks. The Market-house, which is a tolerably good building, was erected in the year 1700, by John Shalcross, of Shalcross, Esq. The inhabitants, who amount to nearly 500 families, are chiefly supported by the manufacture of cotton.

In this parish is *Bradshaw-Hall*, which was once the seat and residence of Lord President Bradshaw, Chief Justice of Chester, who made so conspicuous a figure in the Civil Wars, and who was one of the judges at the trial of Charles the First, at which he presided. He was born in the year 1586, at Wibbersley-Hall, in Cheshire, and died before the Restoration, and was buried with great pomp at Westminster Abbey; but, to the disgrace of humanity, at that time, his body was dragged from the grave, and putrid as it was, exposed upon a gibbet, with those of Cromwell and Ireton. His female descendants are still in possession of the estate, near Chapel-in-the-Frith; and several other branches of the same family, live in the greatest respectability in the county.

THE EBBING AND FLOWING WELL, the last of the Wonders of the Peak,* is about a mile and half from Chapel-en-le-Frith, on the road to Tideswell. It is situated in Barmoor Clough, close to the south-side of the turnpike road, and immediately under a steep hill, which rises to the height of more than one hundred feet.—This well, is merely a small pool, of an irregu-

---

* The following are generally called the Seven Wonders of the Peak ;—Poole's Hole, St. Ann's Well, Chatsworth, Elden Hole, Peak's Hole, Mam Tor, and the Ebbing and Flowing Well.

lar form, but nearly approaching to a square, from two to three feet deep, and about six or seven yards in width. Its ebbings and flowings are far from being regular, depending upon the quantity of rain which falls in the different seasons of the year. In very dry seasons, it has sometimes ceased to flow, for two, three, and four weeks together; sometimes it flows once in twelves hours; at others, once in every hour; and in very wet weather, perhaps, twice or thrice within that time. When it first begins to rise, the current can only be perceived by the slow movement of the blades of grass, or other light bodies, that float upon the surface; yet before the expiration of a minute, the water issues in considerable quantity, with a guggling noise, from several small appertures on the south and west sides. The interval of time between the ebbing and flowing is not always the same; and, of course, the quantity of water it discharges at different periods, must also vary. In the space of five minutes flowing, sometimes the water rises to the height of six inches; and after remaining a few seconds stationary, begins to run back: in three minutes, the well assumes its former quiescent state.

The cause of the intermittent flowing of this well, may be satisfactorily explained, on the principles on which the syphon acts; and that a natural one communicates with a cavity in the hill, where the water accumulates:—but for the phenomenon of its ebbing, no satisfactory reason has been given. The opinion of a second syphon, as ingeniously advanced by a modern Tourist,* which begins to act when the water rises, is inconsistent with the appearance of the well, and therefore not well founded.

GLOSSOP, is a parish which comprehends a large tract of country in the north-west extremity of the High Peak. The village is small, and situated on a rising bank, surrounded by a deep valley. The inhabitants are principally employed in spinning and weaving cotton; several factories being established in the adjacent parts. The church, which is an ancient building, is dedicated to All-Saints, and the Duke of Norfolk is the patron. It was given by Henry the Second to the Abbey of Basingwark, in the county of Flint. Within it is a neat marble tablet, with an inscription to the memory of Joseph Hague, Esq. of Park-Hall, near Hayfield, who acquired considerable property by

---

* See Mavor's British Tourist, Vol. I. p. 227.

persevering industry; and bequeathed the annual interest of £1000. for ever, towards clothing twenty-four poor men and women, out of eight townships of Glossop-Dale: above the tablet is a fine marble bust of Mr. Hague, executed by Bacon.

, HAYFIELD, *Hetfelt*, is a long straggling village, in the parish of Glossop: it is situated on the road to Chapel-in-the-Frith and Glossop, and is divided into two parts by a fine stream of water. The inhabitants are, chiefly, clothiers; but several are supported by the manufacture of cotton.

MELLOR is a chapelry under Glossop; the chapel here is dedicated to St. Thomas.

CHARLESWORTH, is another village, of considerable extent in Glossop, with a chapel dedicated to St. Mary Magdalene. The houses are built on the acclivity of *Charlesworth-Nick;* a name given to a range of the highest hills in this part of Derbyshire. Both the size and population of this place have been much increased of late years, owing to the establishment of cotton manufactories in the neighbourhood. At the distance of one or two miles southward, are the collieries, which furnish the surrounding villages with fuel.

At *Gamesbey*, a small hamlet north of Charlesworth, are some vestiges of an ancient station, called *Melandra Castle*, which from its appearance, and an inscription found there, is supposed to have been Roman. The late Rev. Mr. Watson, of Stockport, has given the following description of it:—

" It is situated, like many Roman stations, on moderately elevated ground, within the confluence of two rivers, and was well supplied with good water. Very fortunately, the plough has not defaced it, so that the form cannot be mistaken: the ramparts, which have considerable quantities of hewn stones in them, seem to be about three yards broad. On two of the sides were ditches, of which part remains; the rest is filled up: on the other sides, there are such declivities, that there was no occasion for this kind of defence. On the north-east side, between the station and the water, great numbers of stones lie promiscuously, both above and under ground: there is also a subterraneous stream of water here, and a large bank of earth, which runs from the station to the river. It seems very plain, that on this and the north-west side have been many buildings; and these are the only places where they could safely stand, because of the declivity between them and the two rivers. The extent of this station is about, 122 yards by 112. The four gates or openings, into it, are very visible; as is also the foundation of a building withing the area, about twenty-five yards square, which in all probability, was the *Prætorium.*"*

The parish of Glossop is the most northern in the county of Derby, and its description, completes the plan of the present work.

---

* Archæologia, Vol. III. p. 237.

THE END.

INDEX.

INDEX.

INDEX.

INDEX.

INDEX.

INDEX.

luwbold.

INDEX.

INDEX.

Queen of Scots, confined at South-Wingfield, 509; at Hardwick, 531; at Chatsworth, 643; tried, condemned, and beheaded, (note) 526.

Radbourn, 283.
Rake-work, in mining, described, 81.
Raunston, 362.
Red Lead, how made, 89.
Repington, description of the deanery, 359.
Repton, 382; its ancient names, 383; monastery, 384; free-school, 388; ancient crypt; antiquities, 390.
Revolution, of 1688, first planned at Whittington, 559.
Ripley, 329.
Risley, 319.
Romans come to Britain, 6; Roman road in Derbyshire, 18; Roman pig of lead, 74.
Rosliston, 365.
Rousseau, Jean Jacques, resides at Wooton-Hall, near Ashbourn, 440.
Rotten Stone, 116.
Rother, the river, 30.
Rowter, rocking stones, 574.

Sandiacre, 322.
Sawley, and its chapelries, 318.
Saxons come to Britain, 12; their uncivilized state, 14.
Scarsdale, Lord, some account of the family, 285.
Scarcliff, the parish of, 541.
Scots and Picts, 10.
Scrapton, 313.
Sessions, the Derbyshire, where held, 124.
Sheep, different breeds of the county, 52.
Shipley, the seat of E. M. Mundy, Esq. 325.
Shirley, 414.
Shirland, 521.
Shivering Mountain, near Castleton, described, 704.
Shottle, its sulphureous spring, 358.
Shrewsbury, the Countess of, her monument, 146.
Situation of Derbyshire, 17.
Slate, or schistus tegularis, 117.
Smalley, 326.
Smithesby, or Smisby, 455.
Snitterton-Hall, an ancient house near Darley, 571.

23   A 5

INDEX.

.INDEX.

INDEX.

DIRECTIONS TO THE BINDER.

Printed by S. Mason, Belper.